Praise for *Cloud Native Data Security with OAuth*

This book is a fantastic guide and resource to anyone looking to implement OAuth within their Cloud Native architecture. The authors have done an excellent job covering the basics but also tackling the more complex and advanced areas. They make the topic accessible and relevant to readers wanting to understand the topic in depth, and I'd highly recommend it.

—*Matthew Auburn, coauthor of* Mastering API Architecture

This book offers a comprehensive and practical guide to securing APIs in cloud-native environments. It strikes an excellent balance between theory and practice, providing clear explanations and code examples. I highly recommend this book to anyone involved in building, deploying, or securing APIs in a cloud-native context, as it equips you with the knowledge and tools needed to safeguard your applications and data in today's dynamic and distributed systems.

—*Narang Dixita Sohanlal, software engineer, Google*

This book is a must read for anyone looking to adopt OAuth standards. The authors are subject matter experts on the topic and have provided an excellent overview combined with practical advice and examples.

—*Veena Rajarathna, product manager*
focused on API security, Kong Inc.

Cloud Native Data Security
with OAuth
A Scalable Zero Trust Architecture

Gary Archer, Judith Kahrer,
and Michał Trojanowski

Cloud Native Data Security with OAuth

by Gary Archer, Judith Kahrer, and Michał Trojanowski

Published by O'Reilly Media, Inc., 1005 Gravenstein Highway North, Sebastopol, CA 95472.

O'Reilly books may be purchased for educational, business, or sales promotional use. Online editions are also available for most titles (*http://oreilly.com*). For more information, contact our corporate/institutional sales department: 800-998-9938 or *corporate@oreilly.com*.

Acquisitions Editor: Simina Calin	**Indexer:** Judith McConville
Development Editor: Virginia Wilson	**Interior Designer:** David Futato
Production Editor: Clare Laylock	**Cover Designer:** Karen Montgomery
Copyeditor: Krsta Technology Solutions	**Illustrator:** Kate Dullea
Proofreader: Vanessa Moore	

March 2025:   First Edition

Revision History for the First Edition

2025-03-06:   First Release

See *http://oreilly.com/catalog/errata.csp?isbn=9781098164881* for release details.

978-1-098-16488-1

[LSI]

Table of Contents

Part I. Introducing Cloud Native OAuth

Part II.   Securing APIs with Tokens

Foreword

Our team successfully coded an advanced OAuth and OpenID Connect server that supported the complex security standards covered in this book. In doing so, we gained deep insights into these standards and productive ways to use them. Despite our years of hard work, we quickly realized that it would be for naught if we were unable to help others understand where our product fit in the confluence of digital identity and API security.

As organizations digitalize their services, they inevitably need to expose data as web services. These APIs are consumed by mobile apps, single-page applications, and traditional websites. In effect, this makes those APIs platforms for new digital processes, business models, and experiences. This metamorphosis to digital natives requires organizations to authenticate users and authorize access to data APIs. These are difficult problems that the OAuth and OpenID Connect specifications were designed to help solve. It is paramount that those seeking to adopt digital business also embrace and deploy these standards.

To explain how to do so, we needed to add to our team people that had not only mastered these technologies but also had an ability to teach them to others. Those people had to be skilled communicators, engaging instructors, and fluent writers. We found these qualities in Gary, Judith, and Michał and were immediately fond of their desires to uplift the industry through knowledge sharing. All three of them have a passion to teach complex topics and articulate the value behind them in ways that normal software teams can understand.

As we worked together, the new team frequently used cloud native technologies to demonstrate OAuth standards and back up the theory. We realized that there was another convergence of technologies that needed to be taught. The team's learning resources explained how digital identity and APIs were coupled while also showing how these technologies could be used in cloud computing as native components. By protecting data exposed in meshes of microservices, repeatable patterns emerged from their work that spanned use cases and industries. As we learned new techniques from them, we understood that this critical knowledge also needed to be disseminated.

When the authors proposed writing a book on these topics as a part of their day jobs, we agreed without hesitation because Curity's mission is to play a part in making the internet safer by, among other things, spreading knowledge on identity topics. Because of our roles at Curity, we had the unique opportunity to read each chapter as the authors wrote them. With each, we appreciated their advocation of design patterns, adherence to best practices, and clear communication of protocols devoid of product-related promotions.

With the knowledge they captured in the chapters you're about to read, the authors not only explain how digital identity and API security intersect but also how to deploy solutions to such problems in cloud-native environments. If you haven't performed such deployments before, this book should help you to understand the approach and how to deal with multiple components and endpoints, to help you ensure that your installations are secure, modern, and easy to operate.

The book uses both OAuth and cloud native in a technology-neutral and vendor-neutral manner. The tools and techniques remain relevant even if you do not operate in a cloud native environment. Ultimately, it is about serving APIs in the best ways, which in turn serves your business and users. In many organizations, you need to consider regulatory restrictions, multicloud strategies and migrations from legacy identity infrastructure to enable OAuth. Cloud native can help you with these goals. As the authors will show you, integrating OAuth and cloud native is not as hard as you may think and comes with many benefits.

With this said, we recommend this book to you, and leave you now in the hands of the authors.

— Travis Spencer and Jacob Ideskog,
Cofounders of Curity

Preface

When you build digital solutions, your users run applications that access data over the internet. These applications can run on browsers, mobile devices, servers, or any other platform. They have one thing in common, though: they are API clients, and that means they call APIs to access data. APIs must enable secure data access because the data they serve may include intellectual property, personal data belonging to citizens or users, or information belonging to business partners. To protect data and access to it, you must secure both APIs and the application fetching the data. Such security requirements can originate from compliance and regulatory initiatives. One example is the European Union's General Data Protection Regulation (GDPR), which governs user privacy and consent.

Managing data security and privacy in APIs and API clients is a difficult problem that requires an architectural solution. Your APIs must process user identities correctly so that each user gains access to only the correct API resources. To achieve that, you must apply business authorization in APIs. The exact authorization rules depend, of course, on your business use cases. Ideally, you ensure that every API request from a client includes an unforgeable and least-privilege API message credential. This credential conveys business permissions. You first verify such a credential in the API before you enforce your particular rules. When you protect every API request in this manner, for both external and internal requests, you get a zero trust API architecture.

When implementing API security, we assume you want certain architectural qualities, including reliability, scalability, and a productive developer experience. Your architecture should enable you to meet all of these nonfunctional requirements in addition to security. We show you how to achieve such an architecture using solid design choices. We demonstrate a separation of concerns approach to externalize difficult areas from your application code. For example, you can host security components on a cloud native platform with modern clustering and elasticity features to meet your high-availability requirements. Similarly, you can manage cryptography and other security plumbing using specialist endpoints and libraries. Your choices should enable a future-proof setup and scale to many applications, APIs, and teams.

Why We Wrote This Book

We (the authors) all work at Curity, a company specialized in identity and access management for APIs. In our day-to-day jobs, we teach OAuth and related technologies to a wide audience. We base some of our online material on the Curity Identity Server, yet the majority of our content is not product-specific and explains a standards-based architecture. Our work involves presentations, videos, online articles, and code examples as well as investigations and explorations in the space of secure authentication and API access. Although cloud native is the state of the art when it comes to deploying APIs, we noticed that resources on cloud native security mainly focus on the infrastructure. We acknowledge that infrastructure security, such as encryption, is important to secure data, and so are processes, policies, and governance. Authorization is the piece of the puzzle that we happen to be experts in.

We wrote this book because we believe that OAuth has major architectural benefits for applications and APIs, yet it is widely misunderstood. This prevents organizations from making the right choices and fully realizing the benefits. In particular, we believe that access tokens are often used suboptimally. When you design access tokens correctly, they enable you to set security boundaries and control authorization to your secured business resources in a way that benefits all kinds of organizations— from small to very large. By combining a centralized token issuer with smart authorization techniques, you can monitor, audit, and govern resource access at any scale.

We explain the main security requirements for APIs and API clients with regard to authorization and show how OAuth helps you to meet them. Part II is the core of the book and we recommend that you take special care when reading it. We think that if we can help you to understand how identity and business components work together, you will be able to make the right choices and fully benefit from OAuth for a secure and scalable solution. We explain a sequential journey from the viewpoint of developers and organizations building digital solutions. We provide theoretical content along with practical content to back up the theory.

Who This Book Is For

The content is aimed at any developer, architect, or site reliability engineer interested in API security. You may work with APIs that already have some basic security but want to learn how to update to a zero trust architecture. Preferably, you have an intermediate-level knowledge of APIs and API security.

We use Docker and Kubernetes to provide examples that implement our security designs. Thus, if you are familiar with containers, you will get a more hands-on experience from the book. However, you can apply the concepts we describe to any cloud native platform.

The book is detailed in places, so you should be prepared to absorb a considerable amount of content on identity topics. Above all, you should be willing to adopt a separation-of-concerns approach to software engineering.

What You Will Learn

You will learn how to secure APIs and clients using the OAuth 2.0 authorization framework. We will present designs, patterns, and best practices that help you to enforce business permissions in APIs. You will learn how to perform the following tasks:

- Design least-privilege access tokens.
- Operate an authorization server.
- Issue access tokens to API clients, then send them to APIs.
- Validate access tokens in APIs, then authorize access to business data.
- Implement a code flow in clients, to enable many ways to authenticate.
- Manage token confidentiality for internet clients.
- Follow best practices for browser-based applications, to limit damage if there is a cross-site scripting (XSS) exploit.
- Implement OAuth 2.0 for platform-specific applications, to secure both desktop and mobile applications.
- Manage client-specific security differences in an API gateway.
- Combine OAuth 2.0 with infrastructure security.
- Keep application code portable and standards-based.
- Deal with error conditions and ensure reliable end-to-end flows.

Cloud Native Environments

We decided to set this book in a cloud native environment because we believe that such an environment provides the optimal features for managing secured APIs.

> Cloud native technologies empower organizations to build and run scalable applications in modern, dynamic environments such as public, private, and hybrid clouds. Containers, service meshes, microservices, immutable infrastructure, and declarative APIs exemplify this approach.
>
> —CNCF Cloud Native Definition v1.0

In the context of this book, the relevant technologies for the security architecture, as well as the code examples, are containers, services meshes, and microservices. We do not make any assumptions about whether you run a public, private, or hybrid cloud.

You will be able to apply the concepts that we present in this book no matter the type of cloud.

We like the choice, portability, and future-proofing that cloud native platforms provide. We think you should utilize these features not only for your APIs but also for supporting (security) components. Security components are critical, so they must be highly available. Therefore we explain some operational behaviors in addition to security.

What is really great about cloud native is the fact that it provides rich options for us to demonstrate end-to-end security on a standalone computer. Ultimately, though, you can apply the design patterns that we describe to other types of environments. When possible, we base solutions on published standards and best practices. Therefore you should be able to benefit from the content we provide, regardless of the hosting platform you use or your technology preferences.

What This Book Is Not

This book is not a complete guide to cloud native security. We won't teach you cloud native and Kubernetes from the ground up, but we will show you how to configure cloud native security components on a development computer, within a Kubernetes cluster. For the best understanding, you should have some existing knowledge about running applications in Kubernetes.

We also do not provide a comprehensive reference that covers all aspects of OAuth 2.0. We will introduce you to OAuth 2.0 and you do not need prior experience with the protocol. We want to focus, however, on practical aspects of designing a security solution based on OAuth 2.0, instead of explaining every flow step by step or describing every specification from the OAuth 2.0 family.

We will skip in-depth examinations of low-level security. For example, we will inform you about the current recommended algorithms for signing tokens, but we will not explain these algorithms or their robust cryptography. We also do not cover how to secure operating systems, containers, databases, or other infrastructure.

Using Code Examples

We supplement the book's theory with code examples that you can download from the book's GitHub repository (*https://oreil.ly/CNDS-supp*). Using code examples is entirely optional but may be useful if you want a working implementation to compare against. The examples meet some difficult security requirements using standards-based code that externalizes difficult security from applications. Some code examples are fairly complex, since they use a highly distributed architecture, and you may need to take time to study the code and *README* documents.

Each code example provides an end-to-end solution that you can run without restrictions on a Windows, macOS, or Linux development workstation. When applicable, you can also deploy examples to a local Kubernetes cluster. Once you understand the local deployment, you can use the same techniques to deploy the examples to a remote cloud native environment, such as the Kubernetes platform provided by your cloud provider.

We want you to be able to get up and running quickly, so we use the free version of the Curity Identity Server as the default authorization server. We also use various other cloud native security components and respected security libraries. When needed, you can replace security components with alternative ones, as long as they support the required standards and extensibility. Because of variations in implementations of standards, we cannot guarantee that code examples will immediately work with every replacement product.

Example APIs and clients follow current best practices at the time of writing. Most code examples and code snippets use TypeScript, as a simple yet expressive language. On mobile platforms we use languages specific to the platform, namely Kotlin and Swift. You can implement the same patterns in alternative technology stacks.

If you have a technical question or a problem using the code examples, please email *support@oreilly.com*.

This book is here to help you get your job done. In general, if example code is offered with this book, you may use it in your programs and documentation. You do not need to contact us for permission unless you're reproducing a significant portion of the code. For example, writing a program that uses several chunks of code from this book does not require permission. Selling or distributing examples from O'Reilly books does require permission. Answering a question by citing this book and quoting example code does not require permission. Incorporating a significant amount of example code from this book into your product's documentation does require permission.

We appreciate, but generally do not require, attribution. An attribution usually includes the title, author, publisher, and ISBN. For example: "*Cloud Native Data Security with OAuth* by Gary Archer, Judith Kahrer, and Michał Trojanowski (O'Reilly). Copyright 2025 Curity AB, 978-1-098-16488-1."

If you feel your use of code examples falls outside fair use or the permission given above, feel free to contact us at *permissions@oreilly.com*.

Terminology

We use the term *OAuth* to represent the modern OAuth 2.0 authorization framework, first defined in RFC 6749. OAuth 2.0 has strong technology support in all current API, web, and mobile technology stacks. OAuth 2.0 supersedes the OAuth 1.0 protocol from RFC 5849, which was a more limited solution with fewer architecture benefits. Consequently, we do not cover OAuth 1.0 but always mean OAuth 2.0 when we refer to *OAuth*.

API is an overloaded term in the IT world. In the book, we will mainly use the term *API* to represent Web APIs that expose data to various types of clients, and we use the terms *APIs* and *microservices* interchangeably. We use the term *endpoint* to represent an entry point to a concrete function in your APIs or a security component. We use the terms *clients* and *applications* to represent API clients. APIs can also act as clients to other APIs. Our primary focus is to apply the OAuth 2.0 framework in a way that best serves APIs and clients.

If you work with Kubernetes, you might see the term *API* used in conjunction with the Kubernetes configuration or control plane. When we use Kubernetes terms that conflict with the normal world of APIs and clients, we clearly explain the context.

This Book's Structure

Many OAuth books start with user logins, which are often the most visible part of OAuth. However, it is common for newcomers to OAuth to get logins working and then run into deeper problems with APIs later. To prevent this type of outcome, we follow an API-first approach. Part I begins with an introduction that explains the business rationale behind OAuth 2.0 and cloud native in Chapter 1, "Why Do You Need OAuth?". Next, Chapter 2, "OAuth 2.0 Distilled", provides an overview of how OAuth works. Chapter 3, "Security Architecture", then explains the building blocks for integrating with OAuth. Finally, Chapter 4, "OAuth Data Design", shows how to approach data design so that your data supports integrating with OAuth.

Part II dives deep into access tokens and APIs. This shows you how to design access tokens, how to write code to secure access to data in APIs, and how to avoid common security pitfalls when working with tokens. You will also learn how to use API gateway design patterns in a Kubernetes setup.

Part III explores OAuth and its components in a cloud native environment, how you can combine features of OAuth and the cloud native platform, and how you operate cloud native OAuth components. It also shows how to get workload identities and other advanced setups running on a developer workstation.

Finally, Part IV covers clients and user authentication. It includes web and mobile code examples that follow current OAuth security best practices. Chapter 14, "User Authentication" covers user authentication. The chapter explains a few topics that comprise modern authentication, including secure user registration and cryptography-backed user logins that also provide a friendly login user experience. We also cover migration of users from an older to a newer authentication method while keeping the user identity the same for APIs.

Some chapters are heavy on theory and others are code-centric. You should feel free to switch between chapters when you want to run some code. For example, after reading Chapter 2, you may want to get a code flow working. To do so, you could jump ahead to Chapter 12, "OAuth for Native Applications", on platform-specific applications and run the simplest type of OAuth client, a console application. For the most complete understanding, though, we recommend then continuing by reading all chapters in sequence.

Conventions Used in This Book

The following typographical conventions are used in this book:

Italic
> Indicates new terms, URLs, email addresses, filenames, and file extensions.

`Constant width`
> Used for program listings, as well as within paragraphs to refer to program elements such as variable or function names, databases, data types, environment variables, statements, and keywords.

`Constant width italic`
> Shows text that should be replaced with user-supplied values or by values determined by context.

> This element signifies a tip or suggestion.

> This element signifies a general note.

This element indicates a warning or caution.

O'Reilly Online Learning

 For more than 40 years, *O'Reilly Media* has provided technology and business training, knowledge, and insight to help companies succeed.

Our unique network of experts and innovators share their knowledge and expertise through books, articles, and our online learning platform. O'Reilly's online learning platform gives you on-demand access to live training courses, in-depth learning paths, interactive coding environments, and a vast collection of text and video from O'Reilly and 200+ other publishers. For more information, visit *https://oreilly.com*.

How to Contact Us

Please address comments and questions concerning this book to the publisher:

O'Reilly Media, Inc.
1005 Gravenstein Highway North
Sebastopol, CA 95472
800-889-8969 (in the United States or Canada)
707-827-7019 (international or local)
707-829-0104 (fax)
support@oreilly.com
https://oreilly.com/about/contact.html

We have a web page for this book, where we list errata, examples, and any additional information. You can access this page at *https://oreil.ly/cloud-native-data-oauth*.

For news and information about our books and courses, visit *https://oreilly.com*.

Find us on LinkedIn: *https://linkedin.com/company/oreilly-media*.

Watch us on YouTube: *https://youtube.com/oreillymedia*.

Acknowledgments

This book was a cooperative project. Not only did it include three authors but many people in the background that got us to where we are. Some people helped before we even got properly started. One of them was James "Jim" Gough who helped us establish the contacts with O'Reilly at the very beginning. The world may have missed out on a good book if it wasn't for you, Jim! Another person who was involved early was Sunny Wear who, once submitted, reviewed our proposal for O'Reilly. Thank you, Sunny, for believing in our idea and recommending it to O'Reilly so that we could publish the book.

We also want to thank our employer Curity for backing the book from the very first idea to the final chapters and beyond. Special thanks to Jacob Ideskog and Travis Spencer for their foreword and continuous feedback during the process. It meant a lot for us to get that support from our employer!

We also want to thank all the technical reviewers, in alphabetical order, Matthew Auburn, Anders Eknert, Narang Dixita Sohanlal, Aaron Parecki, Veena Rajarathna, and Mukund Sarama for their valuable input to further shape the content. Thank you all for critically reflecting on our statements with regard to your expertise, correcting our mistakes, amending missing pieces, and improving wording. Your feedback, questions, and suggestions helped us to reflect upon and improve our message. The book wouldn't be what it is without you! Many thanks also to our editor, Virginia Wilson, for guiding us through the process, making sure we stayed on track and got the feedback we needed.

Last but not least, thank you to all the people who help to promote the book and spread the word so that readers find it. We feel very grateful to be surrounded by such a great community. Thank you all so very much!

PART I

Introducing Cloud Native OAuth

CHAPTER 1

Why Do You Need OAuth?

Around 2010, if you were part of a team developing digital solutions, you would probably have built a website that exposed data to a single client, the browser. In those days, users authenticated with a username and password, after which the website issued an authentication cookie. This cookie secured calls to the backend and included the user identity and an expiry timestamp. The backend then enforced security rules using the cookie user identity, such as preventing user A from accessing user B's data.

To meet today's business needs, you use a more modular system. A backend platform typically consists of multiple APIs, which serve data to web, mobile, and business-to-business (B2B) clients. As with websites, you need a way to authenticate and authorize requests to and between APIs. While cookies still qualify for authenticating requests in certain scenarios, you need a solution that works for a variety of clients. In addition, many organizations operate a large number of APIs and clients, so you also need a solution that scales. This is where OAuth comes into play.

OAuth provides the protocols and tools to implement consistent, scalable access controls in APIs. At its core lies the access token that conveys permissions to access APIs and consequently (business) data. APIs are now business products, whose exposed data generates the business value. Hardened API access is not a technical but a key business concern. OAuth allows you to customize API authorization to meet business requirements.

In this chapter, you will first learn the main steps we recommend for enabling modern API-first security, with a primary focus on correct authorization. We explain how OAuth 2.0 enables this authorization and we recommend applying it to every API request. We call this zero trust API security. To enable the right security, you need components that support your APIs and applications. You also need to operate both APIs and supporting components. We explain how cloud native platforms provide some leading operational capabilities, including advanced infrastructure security. You will see how your technical choices play an important role in determining whether you achieve the best business outcomes.

API-First Security

Security for a digital business is a multifaceted topic with many best practices, including the following:

- Follow a secure development lifecycle to protect against threats like SQL injection.
- Secure the software supply chain using techniques such as vulnerability scanning.
- Run backend components on secure operating systems using a low-privilege service account.
- Expose data to the internet using Transport Layer Security (TLS).
- Apply network protection using proxies or firewalls.

Yet these strategies alone are insufficient to secure business data. For that, you need a security architecture that focuses on your applications, APIs, and users. A key behavior of such an architecture is the principle of least privilege. You should grant applications only the API permissions that they strictly need, and each API must enforce those permissions. At the same time, you should use hardened security for user authentication but also provide a modern and friendly user experience. What is more, the security behaviors should scale to many APIs and clients without a linear increase in complexity. To achieve that, use the OAuth 2.0 authorization framework.

What Is OAuth 2.0?

We explore the details of the OAuth 2.0 protocol in Chapter 2, but first we want to provide a high-level overview of its primary behaviors. As the name suggests, OAuth is centered on authorization. At its core, it uses an API message credential, the access token, based on which APIs can enforce authorization. The framework was designed to meet the security needs of any type of API client, including browser-based applications and mobile applications, and to work in any technology stack. User privacy and consent are a core part of the design, and users can also authenticate in many possible ways.

There are a number of benefits when leveraging OAuth. First, you avoid homegrown security solutions because you can build upon best practices that many experts have vetted. You can write simpler code and reduce the risk of security flaws. Second, an OAuth architecture is highly extensible and scalable. For example, you can reconfigure user logins in many possible ways, without needing to change any code in clients or APIs. Finally, since OAuth is a well-established standard, there are many security libraries that implement the protocol, which helps to cut the time to market for your secure solution.

OAuth 2.0 was introduced in the RFC 6749 specification (*https://oreil.ly/8wZDS*), published in 2012. It introduces a component called the authorization server. This component externalizes most low-level security from clients and APIs. Before calling APIs, the client must get an API message credential, the access token. As part of that process, the authorization server authenticates the user (if applicable) before it returns an access token to the client. The client then sends the access token to APIs, typically through an API gateway. APIs only accept requests if they include a valid access token. Figure 1-1 shows an end-to-end flow where the user authenticates before the client receives an access token that it forwards to APIs.

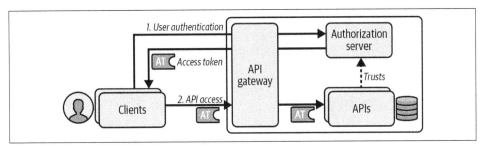

Figure 1-1. OAuth interaction between clients, the authorization server, and APIs

The user login is often the most visible part of OAuth, yet the heart of OAuth is the access token. The access token can provide the user identity and other secure values to APIs in a cryptographically verifiable and auditable manner. You design access tokens in terms of business privileges to APIs. You should customize the access token for each client to only give them least-privilege API access. Since every business is different, there is no fixed way to design access tokens. Similarly, you can choose from many forms of user authentication provided by your authorization server. We explain your choices for access token design in Chapter 6 and your choices for authentication in Chapter 14.

Business authorization is part of your domain logic. Therefore, you usually implement it in the API code alongside other domain logic. On every request to APIs and microservices, the API must validate the access token and authorize access using the received token data. With the access token, you can forward the user identity and other secure values between microservices while keeping the user identity verifiable and auditable so that upstream microservices can also implement security correctly.

There are various other application security frameworks, though most of them provide only user authentication. If you use an authentication framework, you eventually need to invent an API message credential to implement authorization. This results in homegrown solutions that are hard to maintain because of their complexity and reduced interoperability. OAuth 2.0 focuses on API authorization. With OAuth, you can use interoperable security standards for end-to-end flows and base your solution on the work of security experts. This work includes API, client, and user behaviors. Finally, OAuth lets you implement security that scales to many clients and APIs.

OAuth is a framework rather than an out-of-the-box solution. How you apply the framework varies depending on your business requirements for authorization, user authentication, and other security areas. More generally, OAuth is a family of specifications, each mapping to use cases for software organizations. Implemented correctly, OAuth not only improves your security architecture but also simplifies it by externalizing security complexity from APIs and clients.

For all of these reasons, adopt OAuth as your security design if you have an API architecture with user-facing clients. We see it as a security strategy that can work for any organization. We also recommend a particular implementation approach to API security called the zero trust architecture, where we define zero trust in terms of business permissions to access your APIs.

Zero Trust Security

Traditionally, security controls focused on the perimeter of the infrastructure. In that model, a strong border divides the infrastructure into external and internal parts. It assumes that internal parts are trustworthy and thus focuses only on external security threats. Cloud computing blurs the border, as organizations commonly use cloud services for internal functions. Consequently, the perimeter approach is insufficient for securing a digital business nowadays. Modern API security must therefore address both internal and external threats.

A zero trust approach does not assume any implicit trust, for example, based on infrastructure rules such as internal network addresses. Zero trust means that you should use explicit trust and not assume that requests come from a certain client or user. With regard to API security, this implies that APIs must always verify the caller. To understand the problems with implicit trust, let's start by examining the threats inherent in perimeter security.

APIs with Perimeter Security

When organizations first built web APIs, it was common to adopt a perimeter security approach, where the perimeter represents entry points into the backend cluster called by internet clients. Figure 1-2 shows an example where the website implements strong security by requiring browser clients to send a secure encrypted cookie containing a user ID.

During the processing of web requests, the website calls internal APIs that are not exposed to the internet. The website uses weak security for internal connections. In the example, the website uses an API key for the API message credential and forwards the user identity to APIs in a plain HTTP header.

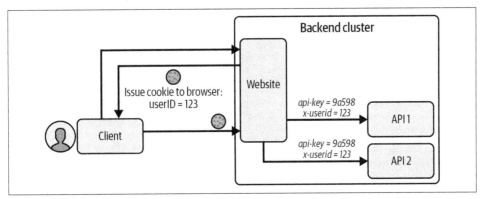

Figure 1-2. Internal APIs with weak security

There are several problems with this design. First, a malicious party inside the network might be able to steal and reuse the API key. Second, you might only rarely renew API keys, in which case an attack could continue against the APIs for a long time. Finally, the user ID is a sensitive value that you need to protect. A malicious party should never be able to bypass security by injecting their own user ID, to get data for another user. With this security design, target APIs cannot know whether sensitive values that they received are correct.

A first attempt to improve the internal API security might rely on infrastructure. Let's examine this type of solution next so that you understand the problems infrastructure cannot solve.

APIs with Infrastructure Security

You can improve API security by securing internal connections with the help of infrastructure security, such as the mutual TLS (mTLS) that cloud native service mesh solutions provide. Figure 1-3 shows an updated example where the entry point website continues to implement strong security by requiring a secure cookie. The website then interacts internally with microservices using a client certificate credential.

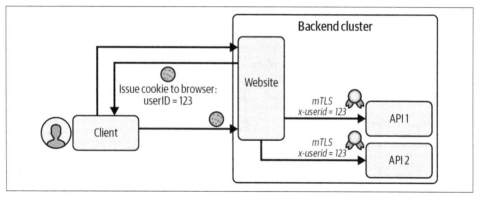

Figure 1-3. Internal APIs with infrastructure security

Adding infrastructure security to protect calls between microservices is certainly an improvement over perimeter security since it is now more difficult for a malicious party to call internal APIs. The stronger connection does not deal correctly with authorization, though. Instead it is an authentication-only solution between backend components. Sensitive values, such as user IDs, continue to be sent in HTTP headers. The API cannot verify that it receives a correct user identity. A malicious or misbehaving API client in the environment could call the API with incorrect HTTP headers and access unauthorized data. To avoid that, we recommend a zero trust OAuth implementation using token-based security. Let's look at that next and explain its benefits.

APIs with Token-Based Security

You can easily enforce explicit trust with OAuth. For that, require that every call to every API endpoint contains an access token with cryptographically verifiable information about the caller. Every API needs to validate the access token to verify its integrity and to ensure that the access token meets that particular API's security requirements. If a token is altered or is not valid for other reasons, the API must reject the request. This means that the API accepts requests only if they contain a valid access token. The trust is explicit because all internal APIs validate the token on every request.

Access tokens are your API credentials. Design them in a way that enables APIs to enforce least-privilege access. First, you can design access tokens to restrict access by business area. Next, you can include values in the access token that your APIs use for authorization. These can be user attributes or runtime values such as the authentication strength. This provides the most powerful ways for your APIs to authorize requests. Finally, assign access tokens a short lifetime to limit the impact of any potential misuse.

When an API validates access tokens, it must reject any requests containing altered or expired tokens. Otherwise, the API trusts the identity attributes in the access token and uses them for business authorization. When implemented correctly this approach provides zero trust in terms of your business. The access token payload in Example 1-1 shows some example attributes.

Example 1-1. Access token payload

```
{
    "sub": "556c8ae33f8c0ffdd94a57b7eab37e9833445143cf6847357c65fcb8570413c4",
    "customer_id": "16771",
    "iss": "https://login.example.com",
    "aud": ["api.example.com"],
    "scope": "products",
    "membership_level": "1",
    "level_of_assurance": 3,
    "exp": 1721980485
}
```

In Chapter 5 we explain the meaning of the standard fields of an access token, such as the iss, aud, sub, and scope fields shown in Example 1-1. We also show how you can write API code to correctly validate access tokens. For now, you should understand that you have full flexibility in how you design the access token and lock down API access, to meet your business needs.

There is also a more subtle point about APIs only allowing requests that include valid access tokens. Figure 1-4 shows how each API downloads a cryptographic public key from the authorization server and uses it to verify access tokens. You should configure each API with a trusted URL to the authorization server that expresses a trust relationship. APIs do not trust each other. Instead, they only trust the authorization server.

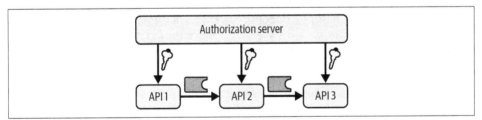

Figure 1-4. API trust

OAuth and infrastructure security solve different problems in your security architecture. Infrastructure security provides data confidentiality and can require an immediate backend caller to authenticate with your API using a strong credential. OAuth enables clients to send restricted access tokens to APIs, which then authorize requests based on the attributes in the access token. You can use OAuth to scale security to many APIs. If you design access tokens effectively, this can be done in a simple and maintainable way. We explain our recommendations for designing and scaling the use of access tokens in Chapter 6.

So far, we have described how to protect against internal API threats. Next, you need to think more about clients and users, since they are located outside the backend cluster and subject to external threats. You need to prevent a malicious party from impersonating the real client and user by calling your APIs. To prevent such attacks, let's briefly summarize what zero trust means for clients and users.

Zero Trust for Clients

Since clients receive access tokens, you must ensure that a malicious party cannot steal access tokens from the client environment and use them against your APIs. Most commonly these clients are web applications, mobile applications, or backend APIs from your business partners. In Chapter 7 we explain how you can harden the use of access tokens differently for each type of client. When designing zero trust for clients, you must first consider their execution environment and what threats exist there. You must then follow best practices for protecting against those threats.

Web applications typically run in the browser and use JavaScript to enable a fast interactive user experience. The Single Page Application style is popular, due to its use of modern and productive web frameworks. At the same time, the browser is a hostile environment for executing code since many attack vectors exist there. We dive deep into using browser security with OAuth in Chapter 13. You will learn that following current best security practices requires backend components that help to secure the front end.

A general threat for any type of client is that of impersonation, where a malicious application tricks the user into initiating a login flow. This could lead to the malicious application receiving valid access tokens with which to call your APIs. Keeping up to date with standards and best practices provides the best protection. Impersonation is a particular concern for platform-specific applications. Chapter 12 explains the OAuth current best practices for both desktop and mobile applications.

Even if both APIs and clients have great security, you still need to involve the user in security. The most visible place where security involves users is during authentication. These days, your security solutions should always consider user privacy. Let's provide a brief overview of zero trust for users next.

Zero Trust for Users

Often, the caller of APIs is a user. Consequently, the user must authenticate before calling APIs. Users do not interact directly with APIs and instead use a client application as their delegate. When possible, authenticate both the user and the client application before issuing the client an access token. Also, consider user privacy as part of your base setup when integrating OAuth. We say more about user privacy in Chapter 4.

You should design authentication processes according to your particular requirements and preferences. Traditionally, users have authenticated with passwords, yet these have many weaknesses. Since users often use the same password across multiple applications, there is considerable scope for password abuse. A malicious site could use a phishing attack to trick users into revealing passwords. Even worse, server breaches could potentially reveal the passwords of many users. Your authorization server should provide up-to-date authentication methods, to give you choices that enable user authentication with both strong security and modern usability.

These days, the trend is to move away from passwords and use more secure options such as WebAuthn, passkeys, and digital credentials. We believe that cryptography-backed authentication methods will become the norm. These methods use standardized capabilities built into operating systems, browsers, or wallet applications. The result is that users generate a key pair using those capabilities. When authenticating, the user produces a cryptographic signature with the private key of the key pair. This signature serves as a user credential that the user sends to the authorization server. The authorization server knows the public key of the user's key pair with which it can verify the signature to authenticate the user. We say more about modern forms of user authentication in Chapter 14.

OAuth allows you to apply a zero trust architecture that supports modern, secure, and user-friendly authentication methods via the authorization server. The authorization server is not the only security component, though. You also need to run other components alongside your APIs, which perform both security and operational tasks. Next, let's take a closer look at what we mean by supporting components.

API Supporting Components

You can host APIs and their data in multiple ways in the cloud. One option is to spin up and manage a virtual private cloud (VPC) with an isolated network running virtual machines. Another strategy is platform-as-a-service (PaaS) hosting, where a cloud provider manages the infrastructure behind the scenes. Both of these options may require investing in vendor-specific technology, complicating future backend migrations. Some hosting options may also impose restrictions on the API code that you write, the data storage options, or the supporting components you can use. Ideally, you should instead be able to make technology choices without limitations.

Your APIs use supporting components such as a message broker and a log aggregation system. The authorization server is a supporting security component, but other security components also play an important role. In Chapter 3 we explain how best to separate security responsibilities across components to simplify code and provide the best future extensibility. Aim to host such supporting components right next to your APIs, as we illustrate in Figure 1-5. This provides optimal performance and also enables you to reduce the OAuth endpoints you expose to the internet.

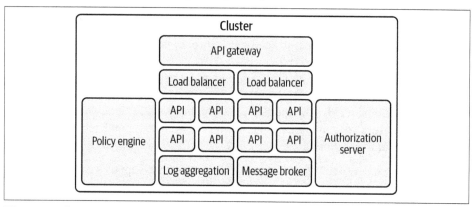

Figure 1-5. Supporting components surround APIs

The platform on which APIs run must support a heterogeneous landscape and provide its own advanced behaviors. These include elasticity, service discoverability, and observability. Ideally, once all components are working together, the entire platform should be portable so that you can deploy it wherever best meets your needs.

You may make suboptimal choices when you select supporting components and hosting platforms, which can work against your goals. For example, though OAuth enables a certain degree of interoperability, it leaves room for vendor-specific implementations. You need to make sure that your authorization server supports not only the authentication methods you need but also a suitable interpretation of standards required for your integrations.

Ensure that you identify important business requirements. Various stakeholders have different requirements:

- Business owners care about technical costs, time to market, and future expansion that may lead to hosting APIs in additional regions.
- The user experience (UX) team needs to blend login security with a simple UX.
- Software architects want the best tools and technologies for future software designs and to keep solutions portable.
- Developers are most productive when they have powerful development options on their local workstations.
- DevOps teams need the best observability and management features for reliable operation and fast problem resolution.
- Compliance teams care about data privacy and require visibility into security-related events.

Take some time to think through your future requirements when choosing technical foundations. At first sight, choices related to security and backend hosting may seem like technical topics relevant only to engineers. In the end, however, they also have a considerable business impact. A modern approach to hosting APIs uses cloud native platforms and design patterns. Consequently, your API security solution needs to fit into such an environment. OAuth is a distributed architecture that you need to operate. The features of cloud native platforms provide operational benefits which we explain in Chapter 11.

Cloud Native Platforms

Cloud native is a technology approach for operating services and infrastructure in a vendor-neutral way. Combining OAuth with cloud native allows us to describe and focus on a security solution that works for the majority of modern deployments. When you design your security architecture, we recommend that you start with OAuth to enable an end-to-end security solution that includes users, clients, APIs, and business data. Ensure that you secure access to all your APIs with access tokens so that you properly restrict access to business data. Add cloud native infrastructure security to harden your security posture further.

As APIs communicate with each other, access tokens flow through your cloud native environment, and join it to the outside world. We illustrate the cloud native deployment with OAuth in Figure 1-6.

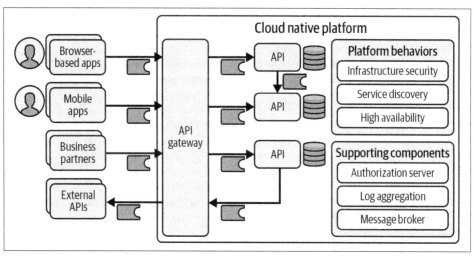

Figure 1-6. OAuth in a cloud native platform

The most mainstream way to apply cloud native is to use a platform like Kubernetes. We use Kubernetes and cloud native design patterns, practices, and tools from the Cloud Native Computing Foundation (CNCF) (*https://www.cncf.io*) to show how to utilize cloud native infrastructure security for OAuth.

One CNCF project of particular interest to API security is the Secure Production Identity Framework For Everyone (SPIFFE) (*https://spiffe.io*), which is a standard for infrastructure security to enable trusted and encrypted connections between workloads. A workload consists of the running instances of your software.[1] A workload can span multiple instances; for example, you can deploy an API workload as a Kubernetes Deployment containing a ReplicaSet with four instances.

You can integrate the SPIFFE Runtime Environment (SPIRE) with a service mesh in a Kubernetes cluster. When workloads call each other, SPIRE transparently upgrades HTTP connections to mTLS to ensure the confidentiality and integrity of requests inside the cluster. SPIRE generates short-lived X.509 client certificates and keys that serve as workload identities. The platform takes care of credential management and automatically renews workload identities. These technologies are a valuable addition to your OAuth security toolbox. We demonstrate the use of SPIFFE and SPIRE in Chapter 10.

---

1 Definition of workload, "Conventions and Definitions" (*https://oreil.ly/2Z6e8*), Section 2 of "Workload Identity in a Multi System Environment (WIMSE) Architecture" (IETF draft).

The result of a cloud native deployment is a modular architecture where you divide responsibilities. To implement the overall technical behavior, you need to orchestrate multiple components. This separation enables reuse as you add new components, such as additional APIs, to your architecture.

Summary

We believe that the optimal way to implement OAuth security is within a modern cloud native platform. This enables you to choose the best-of-breed components to support your APIs. The cloud native platform also provides built-in capabilities, which both your APIs and their supporting components use. Solid technical choices then help to ensure the right business outcomes. We explain more about the security architecture and the setup of security components in Chapter 3.

You should apply a zero trust approach to address external as well as internal risks. In terms of API security, it means that you should authenticate and authorize every caller of a request. OAuth 2.0 enables a zero trust approach for API authorization and access to business data. In our experience, OAuth 2.0 combined with some cloud native patterns provides the most complete architectural solution for a scalable security architecture. It allows you to externalize much security code from APIs (and clients). Let's have a closer look at OAuth and various flows in Chapter 2.

OAuth 2.0 Distilled

In this chapter, we explain the main design principles behind OAuth 2.0. Remember that we use OAuth and OAuth 2.0 interchangeably, which means that we always refer to the OAuth 2.0 authorization framework as released in RFC 6749 (*https://oreil.ly/ hvfiV*). We provide an overview of the main behaviors for applications on how to get, refresh, and revoke unforgeable API message credentials—access tokens. These tokens are the key to access protected data in APIs.

It can be hard to get started with OAuth because there is a lot to digest. Hence, if you are new to OAuth, read on to learn the most important basics. Feel free to skip this chapter if you are familiar with the framework. We provide practical guides in other chapters that show you how to work with OAuth in your APIs and in frontend applications.

The core of OAuth's design is a mechanism for obtaining the access token. To implement the framework, you need a component, called the authorization server—a specialized piece of software that, among other things, issues those access tokens. The authorization server is one of four roles in OAuth.

Roles

The framework defines four main roles involved in any flow:

Resource owner
    The entity granting access to resources, typically a user

Resource server
    The entity hosting the protected resources, typically a backend API

Client
   The application calling an API with an access token

Authorization server
   The entity that authenticates the resource owner and issues access tokens to the client

Informal terminology

In this book, we use the term *user* when we mean the resource owner and *API* when we talk about the resource server. We find those terms less formal and easier to understand for the common reader.

Resource owners (users) interact with a client (application) to access protected resources at a resource server (API). Those applications need to obtain access tokens from the authorization server that allow them to access APIs on behalf of a user. Each access token has a scope that limits its purpose, that is, which API functionalities a client can access. The specifics of how to obtain such access tokens vary but the main message types are the same across the different flows. We outline them in the following section. Let's have a look at the abstract flow to get an understanding of the basic messages of OAuth before we dive into the particulars.

The Abstract Flow

OAuth defines an abstraction of three main steps to get an access token:

1. First, the client initiates an authorization request in which it signals the authorization server the scope of the requested access (message 1 in Figure 2-1). The user then grants the client explicitly or implicitly the requested access (message 2 in Figure 2-1).

2. Next, the client uses the grant to get an access token (message 3 in Figure 2-1). The authorization server issues an access token to the client that reflects the access that the user granted (message 4 in Figure 2-1).

3. Finally, the client can send the access token to resource servers, and work with secured data on behalf of the user (messages 5 and 6 in Figure 2-1). The resource server uses the access token to perform user-level access control and returns appropriate data.

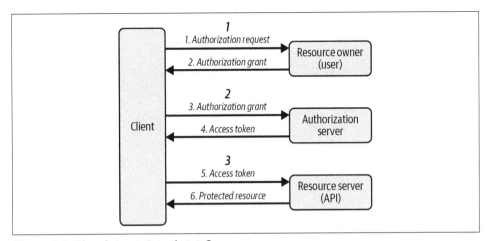

Figure 2-1. The abstract OAuth 2.0 flow

You can implement various use cases or *flows* with OAuth. In some cases, you do not have a user present (skipping step 1). In others, users are present and you need to authenticate them. Regardless of the use case, in the end OAuth access tokens control the behavior of the resource server, the API.

The Access Token

The access token is an unforgeable API message credential with a short lifetime. Unforgeable means that an attacker cannot (easily) predict a valid access token or change an existing access token without detection.

There are two types of access tokens: opaque and structured tokens. Opaque tokens are random strings with a (relatively) high entropy. The authorization server associates such a token internally with attributes called claims. An API always needs to call the authorization server to check whether an opaque token is valid and to retrieve the associated claims. It is unfeasible for an attacker to guess a valid, opaque token. Structured tokens, on the other hand, have a format that is self-contained. An API can parse a structured token to retrieve the claims without having to call the authorization server. The authorization server always includes a digital signature in structured tokens to protect their integrity. The most mainstream example is the JSON Web Token (JWT) format.

An access token has a limited scope. The scope restricts which resources a client may access with the access token. For example, a client may only use an access token with the scope purchases to list purchases but not to put orders. You can express this rule through different scope values. Depending on the implementation, users may be able to influence the power of an access token by granting or denying some access that the client requested.

Claims add information to the access token (e.g., about the user). The access token contains claims associated with its scope. That is, not all access tokens contain the same data but (ideally) only a bare minimum depending on the context (e.g., the client). APIs read claims and judge whether they permit a request or not, as well as determine what data they should return.

The client sends the access token to APIs to access business data. The access token is most commonly a bearer token like the one in Example 2-1. A bearer token implies that anyone who can gain access to the token can send it and access protected resources. The request in Example 2-1 carries the bearer token in the HTTP Authorization header. Do not add access tokens to URLs, because URLs, in contrast to the authorization header, may end up in logs and other places.

Example 2-1. An API request with the access token

```
GET https://api.example.com/protected HTTP/1.1
Authorization: Bearer _0XBPWQQ_4a75d8de-6659-4eb9-8c54-edb5a04b3e3d
```

Since the access token is an API message credential, clients should treat it as an opaque value independently of its type. Clients should not try to parse a structured access token and use its data. If clients actively implement logic based on the access token and its data, you leak data to them—potentially sensitive data that is intended for the API. In addition, clients may start malfunctioning or break if the authorization server changes the access token and its content. You don't want that. Therefore, we emphasize using opaque values for access tokens that enable clients to operate with least privilege on business resources. In your APIs, you must verify that access tokens relate to those privileges by checking scope and claim values. Access tokens are the deepest part of OAuth. We cover them in depth in Part II.

The principle of least privilege

The principle of least privilege is a concept in information security that aims to grant entities only the bare minimum of permissions that their function or a specific task requires for a legitimate purpose. We talk about it in more detail in Chapter 9.

Client Capabilities

OAuth defines several ways for clients on how to obtain an access token. For a client to be able to integrate with an authorization server, it needs to communicate its capabilities (e.g., which flows it supports or what credentials it uses). Authorization servers should issue tokens only to clients they trust. Independently of the means of how you establish the trust, whether you register a client using static configuration or via the Dynamic Client Registration (DCR) protocol, or whether you trust it implicitly, the authorization server must know the client capabilities. The client, as well as the authorization server, can describe their capabilities and configuration via metadata formats.[1] The authorization server associates a set of client capabilities with a client ID. The client uses this client ID to identify itself at the authorization server, and its client credentials to authenticate (when applicable). Whether or not a client can authenticate depends on whether it is a public or confidential client.

Public and Confidential Clients

There are two main types of clients, called public clients and confidential clients. Public clients cannot securely keep a secret that they could use to authenticate at the authorization server. This means that neither the authorization server nor APIs can verify the identity of a public client, and consequently they are less secure. We talk more about such clients in Chapters 12 and 13.

Whenever possible, implement confidential clients. As you will learn in Chapter 13, you can even turn a browser-based application into a confidential client using a backend-for-frontend approach. A confidential client can use different types of credentials—for example, a client secret (which is just a string password), or a more advanced one that proves ownership of a private key, like a client certificate.

The Code Flow

The most widely used flow is the authorization code flow, often referred to as simply the *code flow*. It is the main flow that you should focus on when learning how OAuth works. It is particularly interesting because it supports a common use case, user authentication. Therefore, use the code flow as the standard solution when implementing OAuth in user-facing applications, including web, desktop, mobile, and even console clients.

A multistep approach

The code flow consists of multiple steps. In the first step, the client (application) initiates the flow on behalf of the resource owner (user). In the next step, the authorization server returns a so-called authorization code that represents the user's grant. In the end, the client receives a set of tokens, including an access token that it can send to a resource server (API). Figure 2-2 outlines these steps.

---

1 See "OAuth 2.0 Dynamic Client Registration Protocol" (RFC 7591) (*https://oreil.ly/lymMc*) and "OAuth 2.0 Authorization Server Metadata" (RFC 8414) (*https://oreil.ly/cdNzm*).

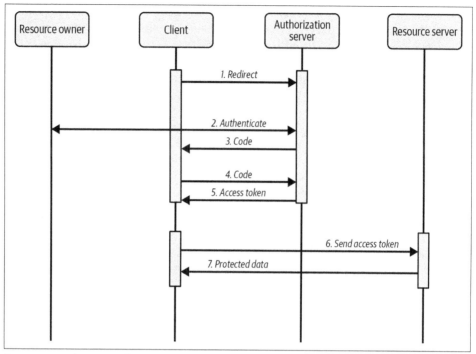

Figure 2-2. The steps of an OAuth 2.0 code flow

The flow starts with an authorization request. The client creates this request to initiate an authorization flow at the authorization server. However, the client does not send the authorization request itself but creates an HTTP redirect that triggers the browser to open the URL and send the request to the authorization endpoint at the authorization server as shown in step 1 in Figure 2-2.

Involving the browser actively has a very important effect: users can interact with the authorization server directly (see step 2 in Figure 2-2). This means that the authorization server can communicate with users like any other website. Typically, the authorization server presents one or more login screens. Users can then decide how to log in and approve any actions if required. At some point, users present their credentials (e.g., by entering a password). The important aspect here is that users share credentials with the authorization server and not the client (the application). This fundamental premise of the OAuth framework is especially important when dealing with third-party clients. If users share credentials with clients, a malicious client might steal and misuse the credentials.

Terminology

The term *third-party clients* describes clients created by entities not affiliated with the entity that provides the API. For example, if you build an application that will call Google's Calendar API, you are building a third-party client from Google's perspective. We call clients created by the same entity that provides the API *first-party clients*.

OAuth does not define how authentication works. You can authenticate users in many possible ways with the code flow depending on your needs and security requirements. For example, you can choose to authenticate customer users via branded login screens and support both passwords and passwordless authentication. Meanwhile, you may offer employee users a corporate login method. In cases where the client is a third party that requests access to data that users own, you should prompt users with a consent screen after they authenticate. The consent screen allows users to control the (API) permissions that they grant a client. When you do not support user consent, the grant is at the discretion of the authorization server but typically contains the scopes that the client requested.

Use HTTPS with OAuth

HTTPS and the underlying transport protocol TLS are important to keep secrets safe over the wire—even or especially in OAuth. Therefore, use HTTPS to secure all endpoints including internal API endpoints within your backend cluster.

Once the user has completed authentication and consent steps, the client receives an authorization code (step 3 in Figure 2-2). The authorization server redirects the browser to send the authorization code to the client—most commonly in a URL query parameter. The authorization code is a short-lived, one-time-use value (it is usually valid only for about a minute). The client sends the authorization code in a request, the token request, to the token endpoint at the authorization server (step 4 in Figure 2-2). A successful response contains a set of tokens. Finally, the client sends the access token to one or more resource servers to access the protected, precious data.

Terminology

Requests that pass data through browser redirects are referred to as *front-channel requests*. An OAuth request that does not involve browser redirects is called a *back-channel request*. You may come across these terms when consuming various resources related to OAuth.

A two-step approach for getting tokens is more secure than returning tokens directly in the browser response (i.e., via the URL). If you return tokens to the browser, you can unintentionally leak them to the browser history, or to web server logs. The back-channel request mitigates this risk. The authorization code may still end up in the user's browser history or web server logs, but contrary to tokens, the authorization code is a one-time code. The authorization server is able to detect if someone—within the short validity period—replays the authorization code. This is not the case for bearer tokens.

It is still important that the authorization server forwards the authorization code to the correct client and not to anybody else that may exchange it for (comparably long-lived) tokens. Therefore you need to specify a URI, the so-called redirect URI, when registering the client with the authorization server. This is the URI to an endpoint of your client where you expect to receive the authorization code. The authorization server forwards the authorization code only to known, trusted redirect URIs.

When you implement an OAuth client, you must prevent open redirects at the redirect URI. Attackers can misuse open redirects to get hold of authorization codes or access tokens. In addition, always protect endpoints with HTTPS. You learn more about client implementations in Part IV.

Code flow HTTP messages

To better understand the code flow, it can be useful to gain an understanding of the basic shape of its HTTP messages. As mentioned previously, the flow starts with an authorization request that the client creates and that the browser sends. The authorization request is an HTTP GET request. It includes, among others, the parameter response_type=code, which informs the authorization server to return the authorization code to the redirect URI of the client. The request also includes the client_id, the identifier of the client, so that the authorization server can process the request accordingly (e.g., check the redirect URI and scopes).

You should specify the redirect URI explicitly to make sure the authorization code ends up where you expect it to. The authorization server must validate the redirect URI. It returns the authorization code only if it trusts the redirect URI. Traditionally, this means that the authorization server compares the string against the list of registered redirect URIs for the client. If the authorization server finds an exact match, it considers the redirect URI trustworthy for the given client.

Example 2-2 shows an authorization request for the code flow that includes the recommended parameters.

Example 2-2. An authorization request using the OAuth 2.0 authorization code grant

```
GET https://login.example.com/oauth/v2/authorize
    ?client_id=web-client
    &redirect_uri=https%3A%2F%2Fwww.example.com%2Fcallback ❶
    &response_type=code
    &scope=purchases
    &state=1599045135410-jFe
    &code_challenge=C7xnOuphJek_30j_cHAAhwKZvzQC3bLdSNirEHrGLAs
    &code_challenge_method=S256 HTTP/1.1
```

❶ *https://www.example.com/callback* (URL-encoded)

The values for the `client_id`, `redirect_uri`, and `scope` parameters are pre-configured for each client. While you can define the redirect URI for your client, you cannot choose the scope values. Those are values that the authorization server provides. Traditionally, the authorization server also generates a client ID as part of registering the client.

You should add the `state` parameter in the authorization request. It holds a random unguessable value that is unique for every authorization request. Once the authentication server has authenticated the user and completed the authentication flow, it returns an authorization response with the authorization code and the same state to the redirect URI of the client. Example 2-3 shows the client receiving an authorization response as an HTTP `GET` request with the authorization code and state in query parameters.

Example 2-3. An authorization response with an authorization code

```
GET https://www.example.com/callback
    ?code=DY9jAYHPuHSiW2OpWUaNRW4otei
    &state=1599045135410-jFe HTTP/1.1
```

The `state` parameter helps the client to connect requests and responses. The client can use the `state` parameter to mitigate certain attacks. For example, a client may receive a crafted authorization response from a malicious party in a cross-site request forgery attack. If the client cannot validate that the authorization response belongs to the user whose browser forwarded the response, a malicious party could connect a user's session with tokens from another user. To mitigate this attack, the client should generate an unguessable, random value that it binds to the user's session (e.g., via a session cookie) and that it includes in the `state` parameter of the authorization request. When the client receives an authorization response, it checks whether the state in the response matches the current user's session. If this is not the case, the client must reject the response. A malicious party cannot guess a valid state value for a given user session, which prevents cross-site request forgery attacks.

If the authorization response is valid, the client posts the authorization code to the authorization server's token endpoint. This request is an authorization code grant request, aka the *token request*. The client specifies `grant_type=authorization_code` and adds the value of the authorization code in the `code` parameter. If applicable, the client must authenticate; it must include its credentials (e.g., the `client_id` and `client_secret`) in the HTTP `Authorization` header. Example 2-4 shows a token request where the client sends the authorization code to the authorization server.

Example 2-4. A token request with the authorization code grant

```
POST https://login.example.com/oauth/v2/token HTTP/1.1
Content-Type: application/x-www-form-urlencoded
Accept: application/json
Authorization: Basic d2ViLWNsaWVudDpVMlU5RW5TS3gzMWZVbnZnRwo=

code=DY9jAYHPuHSiW2OpWUaNRW4otei
&grant_type=authorization_code
&redirect_uri=https%3A%2F%2Fwww.example.com%2Fcallback
&code_verifier=6ETzSa6UcIgE0FWroDJFYQ3vDE3KLZqYxISt6rWWTNJkWDOTy4sew1rOJSNmCt7T
```

Client authentication example

The `Authorization` header in Example 2-4 provides encoded client credentials in the form `client_id:client_secret` according to "The 'Basic' HTTP Authentication Scheme" (RFC 7617) (*https://oreil.ly/EatKz*).

The successful response to the token request contains an access token, optionally a refresh token and/or an ID token depending on the flow, the policy of the authorization server, and whether the client requested an ID token or not. Example 2-5 shows a token response. The client takes the access token from such a response and sends it to the resource server (API) to gain access.

Example 2-5. A token response with an access token

```
{
    "token_type": "Bearer",
    "access_token": "_0XBPWQQ_277ba7b8-9efe-48d9-b0d0-ec1d85c33ee2",
    "expires_in": 900
}
```

Proof Key for Code Exchange

While the state parameter allows a client to associate an authorization request with the current user's session, the Proof Key for Code Exchange (PKCE) extension (RFC 7636) (*https://oreil.ly/ZN4au*) allows the authorization server to correlate an authorization request and a token request. Without PKCE (pronounced *pixie*), a malicious party may intercept an authorization code and send it to the authorization server to fetch tokens. This attack is called an *authorization code interception*. For public clients, where the attacker does not need to provide any client credential when redeeming the code, authorization code interception enables an attacker to easily retrieve tokens.

If an attacker manages to trick a client to exchange a stolen code, the attack is called *authorization code injection*. Authorization code injections are impersonation attacks that allow an attacker to exchange a stolen authorization code for tokens via a legitimate client—including any confidential client. Authorization code interception and injection are possible when the authorization server does not or cannot verify that an authorization code belongs to the current session. PKCE solves this problem.

PKCE introduces a mechanism that allows the authorization server to verify that an authorization request and token request are part of the same flow by binding the authorization code to a challenge. PKCE requires the client to generate a random runtime secret called a code_verifier that it binds to the current session. The client calculates a hash over the code verifier, the code_challenge. It adds the code_challenge and the hash method in the authorization request. Example 2-6 illustrates an authorization request with PKCE that includes both a hash in the code_challenge and the hash method in code_challenge_method.

Example 2-6. An authorization request with the authorization code grant using PKCE

```
GET https://login.example.com/oauth/v2/authorize
    ?client_id=web-client
    &redirect_uri=https%3A%2F%2Fwww.example.com%2Fcallback
    &response_type=code
    &scope=purchases
    &state=1599045135410-jFe
    &code_challenge=C7xnOuphJek_30j_cHAAhwKZvzQC3bLdSNirEHrGLAs
    &code_challenge_method=S256 HTTP/1.1
```

The authorization server binds the authorization code to the code_challenge and records the hash method. Later, the client adds the code verifier from the session to the token request along with the authorization code. Example 2-7 shows an example of such a request. Now, the authorization server can calculate the hash of the code verifier and check if it matches the code challenge that it bound the authorization code to. Only the party that initiated the flow is able to send a correct code verifier in the token request. In this way, PKCE ensures that the party that began the OAuth flow is the party ending it. As a rule of thumb, always use PKCE with the code flow for public as well as for confidential clients.

Example 2-7. A token request with the code flow using PKCE

```
POST https://login.example.com/oauth/v2/token HTTP/1.1
Content-Type: application/x-www-form-urlencoded
Accept: application/json
Authorization: Basic d2ViLWNsaWVudDpVMlU5RW5TS3gzMWZVbnZnRwo=

code=CF6AA2DFIZO5rPeIFTzbJrwZM8RVnjf2
&grant_type=authorization_code
&redirect_uri=https%3A%2F%2Fwww.example.com%2Fcallback
&code_verifier=6ETzSa6UcIgE0FWroDJFYQ3vDE3KLZqYxISt6rWWTNJkWDOTy4sew1rOJSNmCt7T
```

The Device Flow

Some devices like TVs, media consoles, and other Internet of Things (IoT) devices or console interfaces have limited capabilities for capturing user input. In such cases it may not be possible to run the code flow (because there is no browser), or it may be impractical for the user to authenticate at the device where the client is running (because of input constraints). The *device flow*, formally called "OAuth 2.0 Device Authorization Grant" (RFC 8628) (*https://oreil.ly/oeb9M*), is an extension to OAuth that addresses such constraints. It is a flow that allows the user to start the flow at one device and authenticate on a different one, as we illustrate in Figure 2-3.

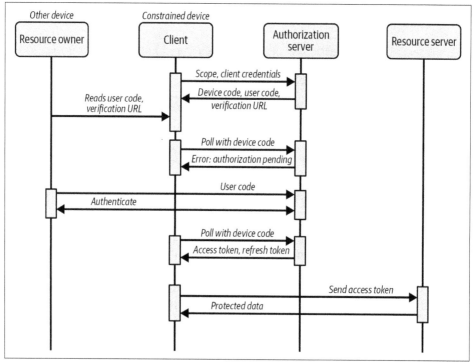

Figure 2-3. OAuth 2.0 device flow

The flow starts with the device authorization request from the client to the authorization server's device authorization endpoint. The request includes the client ID and requested scopes. When possible, the authorization server should authenticate the client. The authorization server then responds with a device code, a user code, and an authentication URL. The client can encode these details and present them as a QR code. We give a demonstration of such a response in Example 2-8.

Example 2-8. A device authorization request

```
{
    "device_code": "4464ca05-b71e-4b27-adfb-4acf4f1e11f9",
    "user_code": "X55E-O6LG",
    "verification_uri": "https://login.example.com/authn",
    "expires_in": 300
}
```

The user opens the URL on a different device, enters the user code, and authenticates at the authorization server. In the meantime, the client on the constrained device polls for the tokens in the background using the device code that it received from the authorization server. Example 2-9 shows a poll request.

Example 2-9. A poll request with a device code (URL-encoding omitted for readability)

```
POST https://login.example.com/oauth/v2/token HTTP/1.1
Content-Type: application/x-www-form-urlencoded
Accept: application/json
Authorization: Basic am9iLWNsaWVudDpVMlU5RW5TS3gzMWZVbnZnRwo=

grant_type=urn:ietf:params:oauth:grant-type:device_code
&device_code=4464ca05-b71e-4b27-adfb-4acf4f1e11f9
```

Both the OAuth code flow and device flow require that a user is present who can start the authorization flow and authenticate at the authorization server. There are other use cases where no user is present and you do not need a user identity in the access token. You then use the client credentials flow.

The Client Credentials Flow

The *client credentials flow* is a flow that does not support user authentication. You can use it when the client is a backend component, like an API calling an external API from a business partner. In this case there is no need to authenticate an end user, as you can see in Figure 2-4.

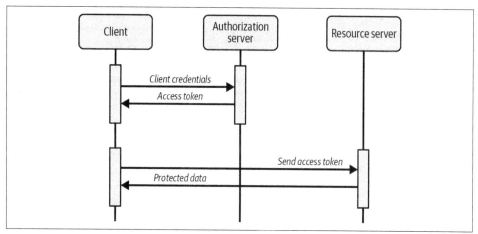

Figure 2-4. OAuth 2.0 client credentials flow

The flow consists only of a single request to the authorization server's token end-point. The client simply authenticates with any supported client authentication method to get tokens. Example 2-10 shows such a request where the client uses a client ID and client secret with the HTTP `Basic` authentication scheme.

Example 2-10. A token request with the client credential grant

```
POST https://login.example.com/oauth/v2/token HTTP/1.1
Content-Type: application/x-www-form-urlencoded
Accept: application/json
Authorization: Basic am9iLWNsaWVudDpVMlU5RW5TS3gzMWZVbnZnRwo=

grant_type=client_credentials
&scope=purchases
```

You should use the client credentials flow only in calls that do not involve an end user. Access tokens from the client credentials flow do not contain any user data. Therefore, you should not apply the flow to scenarios where users are present. For example, if users log in to a client that calls an API which calls another API, the first API should share a user-level access token with the second API instead of retrieving a new token with the client credentials flow. If you send user-level access tokens between APIs, the user identity and other attributes remain verifiable and auditable throughout the call chain. You can read about API to API flows in detail in Chapter 6.

The Refresh Token Flow

When a client uses an expired access token in a call to an API, the API returns an error with a 401 HTTP status code. In this case, the client needs to get a new access token. When a client gets an access token, the authorization server can return a refresh token together with the access token. The refresh token is an opaque token that the client can use to renew an expired access token without the user having to re-authenticate. The client simply posts the refresh token to the token endpoint in a refresh token grant message. We outline the flow in Figure 2-5.

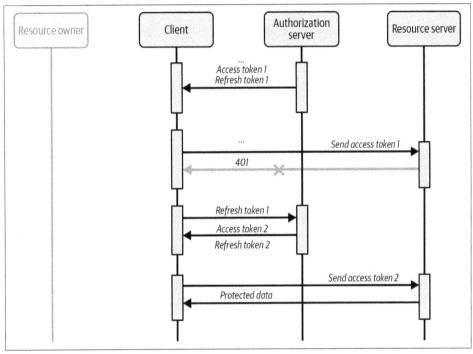

Figure 2-5. OAuth 2.0 refresh token flow

You can see an example of a token refresh request in Example 2-11.

Example 2-11. A refresh request

```
POST https://login.example.com/oauth/v2/token HTTP/1.1
Content-Type: application/x-www-form-urlencoded
Accept: application/json
Authorization: Basic d2ViLWNsaWVudDpVMlU5RW5TS3gzMWZVbnZnRwo=

grant_type=refresh_token
&refresh_token=_0XBPWQQ_669d0021-7286-4b69-b689-adbc81ea0c69
```

The response to a refresh request returns a new access token and, optionally, also a new refresh token. Example 2-12 shows a token response that contains both a new access token and a new refresh token. Refresh tokens are commonly long-lived credentials and clients must store them securely. We discuss access token expiry and token refresh in more detail in Chapter 5.

Example 2-12. A token response with an access token and refresh token

```
{
    "token_type": "Bearer",
    "access_token": "_0XBPWQQ_e78566d6-45bf-479b-8837-06c02205d890",
    "refresh_token": "_1XBPWQQ_680bd9fb-4d0a-4510-8583-f137ba7b1dd5",
    "expires_in": 900
}
```

Outdated Flows

The authorization code flow is *the* flow that you should implement when you need to authenticate users. However, the original RFC 6749 specification describes several other flows for authenticating users, namely the resource owner password credentials flow and the implicit flow. You should understand the historical perspective of those flows. The resource owner password credentials flow was designed as a bridging solution for password-based logins (we simply call it *the password flow*; it's shorter and concise). It did not require many changes to existing applications. Back in the day, it was therefore a useful tool to speed adoption and migrate applications to using the OAuth protocol. The implicit flow addressed the need to overcome former browser limitations that are not relevant anymore. You should not use either of those two flows and instead stick to the authorization code flow. We list the password flow and implicit flow here because we want you to understand their security weaknesses.

Password flow

In the resource owner password credentials flow, the client itself captures the user's password. It posts a single token request with the user's password to the authorization server's token endpoint and gets a token response in return. Example 2-13 shows a token request using the password flow. It contains the username and password in form parameters.

Example 2-13. A token request with resource owner password credentials flow

```
POST https://login.example.com/oauth/v2/token HTTP/1.1
Content-Type: application/x-www-form-urlencoded
Accept: application/json

client_id=legacy-client
&client_secret=legacyClientsSecret
```

```
&grant_type=password
&scope=purchases
&username=mytestuser
&password=myPassword
```

The password flow is problematic from both a security and architectural viewpoint. It enables the client to gain access to the user's password, which goes against the principle of OAuth. Since the password flow only supports authentication with username and password, you cannot implement or enforce any other authentication methods or authentication factors. All in all, the password flow limits the security capabilities of an application. Do not use it.

Known threats of the password credentials flow

OAuth made a trade-off for the resource owner password credentials flow. The specification urges to minimize the use of this flow. See also Section 4.4.3 of "OAuth 2.0 Threat Model and Security Considerations" (RFC 6819) (*https://oreil.ly/obWdV*).

The implicit flow

The implicit flow was designed to work around browser limitations that prevented cross-origin requests to the authorization server's endpoints. Historically, those limitations prevented browser-based applications from implementing the code flow and they had to fall back to the implicit flow. As with the code flow, the implicit flow also starts with an authorization request. It includes the parameter response_type=token, as shown in Example 2-14.

Example 2-14. An authorization request using the implicit flow

```
GET https://login.example.com/oauth/v2/authorize
    ?client_id=browser-client
    &redirect_uri=https%3A%2F%2Fwww.example.com%2Fcallback
    &response_type=token
    &scope=purchases
    &state=CVZU3iBS7guJi9j8TgkIujj2nfBAjtRQ6jJUrYhLbeNZvnkCCnvPLPK5jErAQEs HTTP/1.1
```

Do not use the implicit flow

Web technologies have evolved since the release of OAuth and all modern browsers now support cross-origin requests. You do not need the implicit flow anymore. Instead you should implement the code flow, which is a more secure alternative.

With the implicit flow, the authorization server returns tokens directly in a fragment of the redirect URI. This means the token is visible in the URL, as you can see in Example 2-15. The implicit flow therefore does not include a separate token request like in the code flow.

Example 2-15. An authorization response with the access token in the URI fragment

```
GET https://www.example.com/callback/
    #access_token=_0XBPWQQ_277ba7b8-9efe-48d9-b0d0-ec1d85c33ee2
    &token_type=bearer
    &state=CVZU3iBS7guJi9j8TgkIujj2nfBAjtRQ6jJUrYhLbeNZvnkCCnvPLPK5jErAQEs HTTP/1.1
```

The implicit flow has a number of security weaknesses. Since tokens are part of the URL, they may leak via the browser history via server logs or due to flaws like invalid redirect URI validation or browser bugs.[2] An attacker may replay stolen access tokens to gain access to protected resources. Therefore, you should not use this flow. In particular, you should avoid any flow that returns access tokens in authorization responses (i.e., URLs) according to the security best current practices.[3] Use the code flow instead.

OpenID Connect

OpenID Connect (OIDC) (*https://oreil.ly/WH4_R*) is an authentication protocol on top of OAuth that allows applications to verify the user's identity based on the actions that the authorization server performed. It provides, among others, some predefined scopes to access user account information. For example, you can use the scope profile to gain access to default information about the user's profile like the user's full name, nickname, website, or picture. For that, OpenID Connect defines a new token, the ID token that the client can parse to get information about the authentication event—in contrast to the access token that is opaque to clients. OpenID Connect also defines a set of standard claims—that is, information about a user or authentication event that the authorization server returns in the ID token. The client includes the static scope openid to signal the authorization server that it uses an OpenID Connect flow and that it expects the authorization server to issue an ID token.

OpenID Connect also enables the client to take some control over how and when users need to authenticate, by adding parameters to the authorization request. For example, you can add a prompt parameter to avoid single sign-on (SSO) and instruct the authorization server to prompt the user to log in. With the acr_values

---

2 See "OAuth 2.0 Threat Model and Security Considerations," RFC 6819 (*https://oreil.ly/obWdV*).

3 See "Best Current Practice for OAuth 2.0 Security," RFC 9700/BCP 240 (*https://oreil.ly/k9-PE*).

parameter, you can further send a list of preferred authentication methods that you want the authorization server to apply when authenticating the user. The authorization server should include the acr claim in the ID token so that you can verify whether the authorization server fulfilled your request concerning the authentication method.

Different terminologies

OpenID Connect has its own terminology. An authorization server that supports OpenID Connect is called the *OpenID Provider*, and the OAuth 2.0 client is called the *relying party* (RP). We decided to keep it simple and stick with the terms *authorization server* and *client*, respectively.

Besides authentication features, OpenID Connect also provides extra security mechanisms. It defines a nonce request parameter that the authorization server copies to the ID token. In this way, the client can bind an ID token to the current session. Such binding prevents ID token injection; that is, it allows a client to detect whether the ID token belongs to the current session or not (similar to what PKCE provides for the authorization server). Further, OpenID Connect enables the authorization server to bind the authorization code, access token, or state parameter to an ID token as well, which mitigates other injection attacks.

The Hybrid Flow

These days, clients usually implement a code flow using OAuth 2.0 and OpenID Connect together to get the best application security features. Actually, you can also use a different flow, the hybrid flow, where the authorization server returns the ID token immediately in the fragment of the redirect URI next to the authorization code. The hybrid flow uses the parameter response_type=code id_token, as you can study in Example 2-16.

Do not use insecure variants of the hybrid flow

The OpenID Connect standard also allows you to get the access token immediately in an authorization response, by using response_type=code token or response_type=code id_token token. However, you should not use these options due to the problems we described with the implicit flow. We strongly advise you to keep away from these versions of the hybrid flow.

Example 2-16. An authorization request with the hybrid flow

```
GET https://login.example.com/oauth/v2/authorize
    ?client_id=web-client
    &response_type=code%20id_token
    &redirect_uri=https%3A%2F%2Fwww.example.com%2Fcallback
    &state=1599045202487-sVG
    &scope=openid%20purchases
    &code_challenge=y2upJc5ieYeoQaU0c25iG87qxEXXC7h_0LvIYgQ6ufk
    &code_challenge_method=S256
    &nonce=1707135330806-za6 HTTP/1.1
```

In the hybrid flow, the authorization server returns the ID token and authorization code in the URI fragment of the redirect URI. You can see an example of an authorization response using the hybrid flow (`response_type=code id_token`) in Example 2-17 (we truncated the value of the ID token for readability). The client gets the ID token immediately but needs to send a token request with the authorization code to get the access token.

Example 2-17. An authorization response with the ID token in the URI fragment

```
https://oauth.tools/callback/hybrid
#id_token=eyJraWQiOiItMTQ5NzQxMDcwMSIsIng1dCI6...SvzBXSg436g6tX0ZSAI7QA
&code=qVVBui7wGhpRmxTaFSLUpde9hZylvO4d
&state=1599045202487-sVG
```

You should think of the hybrid flow as an optimization. When a client receives an ID token on the front channel, there are more threats to consider. We therefore recommend to use the code flow rather than the hybrid flow. In the code flow, the authorization server sends all tokens, including the ID token, on the back channel. OpenID also provides standardized ways for clients to get additional information about authenticated users.

User Info

OpenID Connect gives the client two sources of information about the user that performed an OAuth flow: the ID token and a userinfo endpoint of the authorization server.

The ID token asserts an authentication event. It is always a JWT. Clients can read the ID token to obtain information about who authenticated, how, and when. For example, the token always includes a unique identifier of the user in the sub claim. It may also contain the acr or amr claims that reveal how the user authenticated, and with which factors. If you want to make sure that the user authenticated fairly recently, you should check the value of the auth_time claim that holds the time of the user's latest authentication. An ID token can also contain proprietary, custom claims.

Example 2-18 shows an ID token with predefined and required claims such as iss, sub, and aud, as well as custom claims like purpose or delegation_id. The ID token can contain information about the user such as name, email, or gender as well.

Do not forward ID tokens

The ID token is for the client and should never leave it. You must not use it as an API message credential.

Example 2-18. Example of an ID token

```
{
    "exp": 1697020984,
    "nbf": 1697017384,
    "jti": "71e61b52-63a0-4cfd-8141-9fef48c928de",
    "iss": "https://login.example.com",
    "aud": "web-client",
    "sub": "danademo",
    "auth_time": 1697017380,
    "iat": 1697017384,
    "purpose": "id",
    "acr": "urn:authentication:username-password",
    "delegation_id": "e3c04dee-8b8a-4db7-a1c7-43d250cbfeb5",
    "s_hash": "JBH6uR2Hh5dJmvq8lli0Cw",
    "azp": "web-client",
    "amr": "urn:authentication:username-password",
    "sid": "kN04uyCD32qmRsMo"
}
```

Clients should verify the ID token before accepting a token response. It is a good practice that helps to identify errors and misconfigurations. The client should validate the JWT signature of the ID token, ensure that the time in the exp claim has not yet passed, and also ensure that iss (issuer) and aud (audience) claims have the expected values. The audience for an ID token should always contain the client ID of the client. We say more about JWT validation in Chapter 5.

As an alternative to getting user info from the ID token, clients can retrieve information about the currently authenticated user from the userinfo endpoint of the authorization server (and so can APIs). The request is a simple API request that includes the access token, as illustrated in Example 2-19.

Example 2-19. A userinfo request

```
GET https://login.example.com/oauth/v2/userinfo HTTP/1.1
Authorization: Bearer _0XBPWQQ_277ba7b8-9efe-48d9-b0d0-ec1d85c33ee2
```

The OpenID Connect Core specification defines a set of scopes for the access token and which data (claims) the userinfo endpoint should return for them. For example, if the client requests a `profile` scope, and the user grants the client access to their profile, then the client can receive, among others, the `given_name` and `family_name` values. The client can add further OpenID Connect scopes, such as `email`, `phone`, and `address`, to request additional user information. The authorization server can also issue those claims to access tokens. In this way, it can provide user information directly to APIs. Example 2-20 contains a userinfo response.

Example 2-20. Example userinfo response

```
{
    "sub": "danademo",
    "family_name": "Demo",
    "given_name": "Dana",
    "updated_at": 1697017359
}
```

OAuth Evolution

OAuth 2.0 and OpenID Connect are not static and their best practices evolve (*https://oreil.ly/BbCvQ*). The draft specification called OAuth 2.1 (*https://oreil.ly/-dziQ*) collects important updates since 2012 and thus consolidates much of the knowledge. We expect OAuth 2.1, for example, to remove deprecated flows and require PKCE for the code flow. So, in OAuth 2.1 you will not find the implicit flow or password flow. We believe that OAuth 2.1 will improve the understanding and security of OAuth implementations. We follow its current recommendations to a great extent throughout this book.

The OpenID Foundation (*https://oreil.ly/Nivyo*) as well as the OAuth working group at IETF (*https://oreil.ly/DenBy*) design many security standards. They enable you to work with other security use cases. OAuth and OpenID profiles, for example, specify how to utilize the protocols in a certain context, such as for protecting high-worth data and meeting high security standards. A couple of examples are the Financial-grade API Security Profile (FAPI), the Health Relationship Trust Profile (HEART), and various open banking profiles.

One emerging technology that has garnered much attention in the OpenID community at the time of writing is Digital Credentials Protocols (DCP) (*https://oreil.ly/a4lyV*). Digital credentials enable users to manage their own identity attributes in digital wallets. You can combine OAuth with digital credentials and have users authenticate using their wallet. An authorization server that supports emerging and modern standards enables you to stay up-to-date with authentication methods while continuing to protect your data using access tokens.

Sessions and Lifecycle

After login, the user has a session with the authorization server. This includes HTTP-only cookies to enable SSO. When users navigate with the same user agent (browser) to another client that uses the same authorization server, they can sign in without having to reauthenticate. When you do not want SSO, you can use the OpenID Connect `prompt=login` parameter to enforce a fresh login.

The Revoke Flow

Clients can request the authorization server to invalidate an access token by revoking it. You can use the revoke flow for that purpose.[4] The revoke flow is a simple request to the revocation endpoint of the authorization server. The client sends its credentials as well as the token it wants to revoke in a POST request to the authorization server. You can see such a request in Example 2-21.

Example 2-21. A revoke request

```
POST https://login.example.com/oauth/v2/revoke HTTP/1.1
Content-Type: application/x-www-form-urlencoded
Accept: application/json
Authorization: Basic d2ViLWNsaWVudDpVMlU5RW5TTS3gzMWZVbnZnRwo=

token=_1XBPWQQ_680bd9fb-4d0a-4510-8583-f137ba7b1dd5
```

Clients can use the revocation endpoint to also revoke refresh tokens. When a client revokes a refresh token, the authorization server should also revoke any related access tokens. Token revocation is not always straightforward because it has some caveats. We dive deeper into the subject in Chapter 7.

Terminating SSO

Clients can also notify the authorization server to log the user out and thus end its SSO session. This feature is called RP-initiated logout (*https://oreil.ly/BI7bS*). The authorization server can further inform other clients to perform a (local) logout, which triggers a chain of logouts—a single logout. The idea is that users can terminate their SSO session with the authorization server and their sessions with other, related applications at once. Some of the single logout protocols in OpenID, however, depend on iframes for sending the SSO cookies of the authorization server. Many browsers do not support third-party cookies anymore, which breaks those single logout solutions. When implementing single logout, make sure your users are aware of

---

4 See "OAuth 2.0 Token Revocation," RFC 7009 (*https://oreil.ly/GLanG*).

the behavior as they otherwise may get frustrated when they are unexpectedly logged out from applications. You can learn more about OAuth sessions in Part IV.

Summary

This chapter provided a distilled overview of the main OAuth behaviors. It discussed various flows that clients may run to obtain, refresh, and revoke access tokens. We discussed the code flow that user-facing applications should use to retrieve tokens. With the code flow you can authenticate users in many ways, with minimal code. Ensure that you use PKCE to secure the code flow and mitigate common attacks.

There are three tokens in OAuth and OpenID Connect: the ID token, the access token, and the refresh token. The access token has scopes and claims that control the client's level of access to protected data. Clients can get tokens only when the authorization server trusts them. The policy of the authorization server then controls the user authentication flow and authorization.

To be able to fully utilize the access token for authorization decisions, you need to understand your user identity data and how APIs use (or can use) it to perform business decisions. We get into the details in Chapter 4. In Chapter 3, we introduce the components that you need in your IT architecture to protect your cloud native APIs with OAuth so that you understand their roles in an end-to-end flow.

Security Architecture

A good approach for an API security architecture combines the principle of separation of concerns with open standards. This way, the security architecture can scale and mature over time and you can extend it with additional functions or services when needed.

This chapter introduces a cloud native security architecture for APIs that combines identity management, API management, and entitlement management with the help of the OAuth 2.0 protocol. It provides a conceptual overview of the components involved and what you need to consider when implementing API security in a cloud native environment.

What Is an API Security Architecture?

An API security architecture describes the techniques that protect APIs. In a nutshell, an API security architecture defines how to secure access to APIs and the data they expose. As with buildings, you need a good foundation for building an architecture. You need to continuously maintain the architecture throughout the API lifecycle, from design, development, and testing to deployment and retirement. Even if it may not be your primary focus, you need to consider things like secure software development and deployment processes, network and transport security, or server security for your overall API security. We assume that you take care of such aspects when implementing an API security architecture.

Securing access to APIs means that you ensure that only the callers that are entitled to access APIs (data) are allowed to do so when they need to. Consequently, you need to be able to determine who is requesting access when securing APIs. This process is called *authentication*. You also need to check the entitlements and allow or deny access. This concept is called *authorization*. Authorization is the process of ensuring that users and applications access the right data. Obviously, to answer if someone or something is authorized to access some data, you need to know who that entity is. Consequently, authentication and authorization are tightly coupled.

Authorization uses the result of an authentication process—that is, the (user) attributes—to make a decision of whether or not to grant access (see also Chapter 9). Thus, the output of an authorization process is often a simple yes, access allowed, or no, access denied. Authentication and authorization are central parts of a zero trust architecture. To implement a zero trust architecture for your cloud native APIs you need certain security functions in your organization.

Functions in the API Security Architecture

Security functions are the pillars of a security architecture that enable, drive, and own a security implementation. The following three functions are of relevance to your API security architecture:

- Identity management
- API management
- Entitlement management

All three management functions play their role in protecting APIs. The OAuth authorization framework enables them to work together. Let's have a closer look at the behaviors of each function.

Identity Management

Identity management, also known as identity and access management (IAM), is a security function responsible for handling identities and their level of access. IAM systems support protocols and techniques such as the Lightweight Directory Access Protocol (LDAP), the Security Assertion Markup Language (SAML), the System for Cross-domain Identity Management (SCIM), OpenID Connect, and OAuth 2.0. We recommend using OAuth as your main protocol in IAM for protecting your APIs, because it is a lightweight and extensible protocol. You can combine OAuth with other protocols like LDAP for accessing data sources, SAML to implement federated logins, or SCIM to manage user accounts.

In an API security architecture, the IAM system is responsible for authenticating users and providing information about them. The first security control is knowing who you are dealing with, which makes IAM essential for the security architecture. There are many methods to prove that you are who you claim to be. Which method you choose for your security architecture depends on the context. In some cases, you can justify a simple username and password, whereas in others you need more secure methods that are harder to compromise like passkeys or certificates. Choose an authentication method that meets your requirements. That is true for both humans (users) and machines (applications, APIs).

The result of an authentication is attributes that describe a subject (i.e., the user or application). Those attributes often include some metadata about the authentication process itself like a timestamp or the method. At a minimum, the attributes include an identifier that allows you to distinguish different subjects. With OAuth you put identity attributes in the access token to communicate them to APIs.

The key security component in OAuth is the authorization server, which—as you've learned in Chapter 2—authenticates users. This implies that the authorization server maintains identity-related (user-related) data and thus is part of the identity management system. We dive deeper into modeling identity data in Chapter 4.

API Management

An API management system creates an extra layer in front of APIs that provides a number of important behaviors: it can enable API aggregation, provide developer access in some use cases, or simplify API security. Cloud providers commonly include products for this function in their portfolio. From an API security viewpoint, the API gateway is of particular interest. Avoid exposing APIs directly to the internet and instead expose only the API gateway. If an attacker somehow gains access to the gateway environment, they should not be able to connect to your data sources.

As you place the API gateway in front of your APIs, all requests originating from outside your infrastructure pass through the API gateway. Therefore, it lends itself well to the role of a central point that enforces a consistent basic level of security for your APIs. The API gateway can protect your APIs from common attacks. We say more about the API gateway in Chapter 8.

When it comes to authorization, the API gateway can act as a gatekeeper and perform coarse-grained access control. It ensures that all incoming requests conform to a minimal set of policies. For example, it can reject any obviously malformed or unauthenticated requests. What is more, it compensates for any client-specific differences so that the requests it forwards to APIs are uniform. In this way, APIs can apply the same authorization logic to all requests. That is, independently of how the authorization server issues tokens to applications or how applications communicate tokens with the API gateway, APIs always receive an access token in the same way and format.

Entitlement Management

An entitlement management system enables centralized security policies that you can maintain independently from the API code. It complements the authorization logic in APIs with dynamic processing of rules that live outside of the code base. For example, you can have a security team that is responsible for certain important rules that it needs APIs to enforce and that it wants to audit. Consequently, an entitlement management system can provide greater agility and centralized auditing.

The access token here serves as an input for your policies. When you use an entitlement management system, you still need to implement authorization in APIs, but you use the results from a policy engine like the Open Policy Agent (*https://oreil.ly/aSZHk*) to enforce authorization decisions. In this way, you can implement one and the same policy across many APIs, control the versions of policies, and upgrade rules consistently. We discuss the entitlement management system and the policy engine in more detail in Chapter 9.

The Role of the Client

The client is an application such as a web application, mobile application, or service from a business partner that works on data that APIs expose to provide business value to users. The client needs to comply with the rules that the API security architecture dictates. Using OAuth, the authorization server provides a level of access to applications in the form of the access token. This means that the client needs to obtain an access token from the authorization server, as discussed in Chapter 2, and send it in all API requests. The access token enables the client to (or not to) perform certain actions, which in turn impacts the user experience.

The client must handle the access token with care. An API security architecture is only as strong as its weakest link. When the access token becomes central to the API security architecture, the ability or inability of a client to securely obtain, store, and transport the access token (or refresh token) impacts the overall security state of an API architecture. It is also a client responsibility to ensure a good login user experience. Though we refer to the client as a single party in this chapter, it has different prerequisites and capabilities depending on its technical platform. As a result, we devote several chapters in Part IV to highlight best practices for handling access tokens in various types of OAuth clients.

The Role of the Access Token

There are different types of tokens in OAuth and the most important one in the context of API security is the access token. The access token allows applications to access data, and APIs to enforce access rules. For that, the access token conveys enough information for the API to perform an informed authorization decision. This assumes that the access token delivers identity data in a cryptographically verifiable and auditable manner to APIs (i.e., in the form of JWTs). As a consequence, the design of the access token becomes fundamental for securing APIs and protecting data. In fact, we believe this is so important that we devoted two whole chapters to the access token—Chapters 6 and 7.

Once you have OAuth in place to secure APIs, you can start to unfold the power of the access token and build a token-based security architecture. The idea of a token-based security architecture is to utilize the access token for (basically) all security decisions concerning, but not limited to, data access. It means, for example, that the API management and entitlement management systems can also process access tokens for their decisions. If you use JWTs for access tokens, you can design self-contained access tokens that a resource server can validate locally. In this case, resource servers only need to get the keys to validate the digital signatures. We explain the details in Chapter 5.

The OAuth authorization server is the component that connects the dots and establishes trust between clients, APIs, and other components. These components need to be able to connect to the authorization server endpoints before granting access to users or applications.

What Security Components Do You Need?

To implement the three main security functions, namely identity management, API management, and entitlement management, you need security components that fit into your current architecture. These security components are:

- The authorization server (part of the identity management system)
- The API gateway (part of the API management system)
- The policy engine (part of the entitlement management system)

The security components work with a typical IT architecture. The typical IT architecture includes a frontend application that users interact with and a backend system with APIs that the application calls to retrieve data. The APIs are part of the backend platform that you host in a Kubernetes cluster. They can consist of many microservices, data stores, and third-party components. Commonly, you deploy a microservice on a pod, and group pods into a service for load balancing and service discovery. Then, you use an API gateway to consolidate your services to an external API that the frontend application interacts with. The API gateway commonly terminates the TLS connection, then validates and transforms requests before routing them to a service. The particulars may of course vary. In Figure 3-1 we illustrate how the security components fit into such an IT architecture.

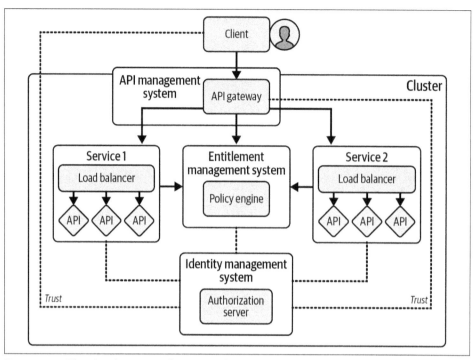

Figure 3-1. The cloud native reference architecture with security components

A cloud native API security architecture should build upon open standards. In that way, you can replace security components later or move them to other platforms to avoid vendor lock-in. Open standards promise you a flexibility to change your mind in the future or act upon events (think of, e.g., discontinued products) without having to invest in rebuilding your security architecture from scratch. When you switch vendors, however, you may have to adapt to some differences. Even though open standards provide interoperability, they also leave room for vendor-specific implementations. Adjusting to these irregularities should not affect your general architecture or which standards you use.

The security architecture in Figure 3-1 assumes you use OAuth as a standards-based approach for protecting your cloud native APIs where access tokens travel from the frontend application—the OAuth client—through the API gateway to APIs. Optionally, the access tokens may also pass a policy engine for more dynamic and fine-grained access decisions. The authorization server is the central component that issues and manages the access tokens. This token-based approach enables a scalable, vendor-independent security architecture. In that way, you are able to keep using the same security architecture for your APIs even when parts of your architecture change.

You can adapt the security architecture from Figure 3-1 to your particular requirements. The only assumption is that the client, the API gateway, the APIs, and the policy engine trust the authorization server—that is, they must be able to retrieve the keys, or connect to endpoints to get, refresh, or validate access tokens. At a minimum you need to add just one specialist security component to your current environment—the cloud native authorization server—to satisfy the reference architecture. At a later stage, you may consider adding a policy engine as well.

We encourage you to utilize the API gateway when implementing token-based access control. When you use Kubernetes, you get an API gateway with minimal effort. You can use the API gateway to implement coarse-grained authorization to ensure that access tokens meet basic requirements and reject invalid requests early. You can also perform routing decisions based on the data in access tokens and make sure that requests end up at the right location.

The security components enable you to implement an API security architecture using a token-based approach. You need to orchestrate the security components with your existing components, your frontend applications (OAuth clients), and APIs, as we have illustrated in Figure 3-1. Let's study each of the components to understand their role in the API security architecture. We start with the most important one—the authorization server.

The Role of the Authorization Server

The authorization server is the component that orchestrates authentication and issues access tokens. This component is built by security specialists who are well-versed in specifications and implementing security standards. Therefore you should plug in an authorization server rather than develop your own.

The authorization server has two main functions:

- The authentication service
- The token service

The authentication service is responsible for authenticating users. It can offer many authentication methods and factors. Typically, the authorization server can use external identity providers (IDPs) and cloud-managed services to authenticate users. The token service integrates with the authentication service and issues access tokens in accordance with OAuth 2.0. Technically, users interact with the authentication service to prove their identity but APIs and applications only integrate with the token service.

The token service ensures that access tokens contain the appropriate data so that APIs can make the correct access decisions. Though there is a contract between the

API and the token service regarding the structure of the access token, it is at the discretion of the authorization server to decide which scope and data it issues in an access token depending on its policies. In particular, this means that an authorization server may decide to narrow the scope of an access token and limit the actions a client can perform even after it received an initial access token. For example, when refreshing an access token using a refresh token as described in "The Refresh Token Flow" on page 31, the authorization server may—based on its internal policies— return a new access token with a narrower scope than the original one. In this way, you can dynamically apply the principle of least privilege. Therefore, the capabilities of the token service are instrumental in the implementation of your API security architecture.

The authorization server serves different types of consumers: external ones (i.e., the applications) and internal ones (i.e., the API gateway and APIs). Consequently, you should design external and internal interfaces for your authorization server as shown in Figure 3-2.

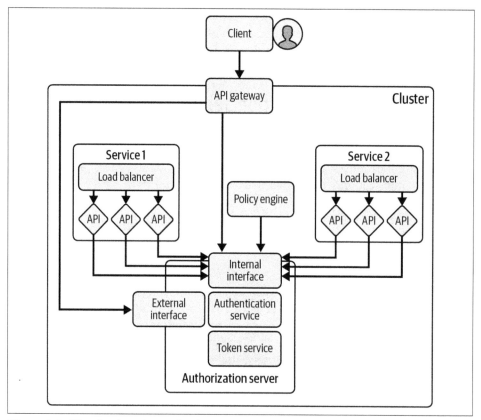

Figure 3-2. The cloud native authorization server

As with your business APIs, you can use the API gateway to expose the public URLs of the authorization server to the internet. As a best practice, you should limit the public interface of your authorization server to what your (external) applications need (e.g., user authentication and token issuance endpoints). Connections between the authorization server, the API gateway, the policy engine, and business APIs can use internal URLs. Such a setup reduces the attack vectors, improves privacy, and provides the best performance.

When you use a cloud native backend—which we assume you do—the optimal place to host an authorization server is beside the APIs it protects. A cloud native authorization server can use the features of the platform to provide the best elasticity and observability. Like other services in your cluster, the authentication and token services of the authorization server can consist of many instances. In other words, you can deploy a cloud native authorization server just like any other API in the platform. You can port it to different cloud provider or host it on-premise, as required.

An alternative option is to use an external authorization server located outside of your cluster, using a PaaS approach. This can provide some convenience but you still need to operate it and manage its security settings over time. The main point is that the authorization server should support your business and provide you with the security standards and behaviors you need. Whatever platform you use, host your APIs behind an API gateway. The API gateway has some interesting capabilities that you can utilize for your security architecture.

The Role of the API Gateway

Use an API gateway to expose API endpoints to the internet via one or more routes. The API gateway manages external access for all APIs and provides entry points for clients. It adds features like routing, versioning, and monetization to the interface. What is more, the API gateway lends itself very well to security.

An API gateway is the first entry point in the cluster, as shown in Figure 3-3. It typically performs security-related tasks like TLS termination, monitoring, request throttling, and authorization. For example, it can enforce the presence of an access token in the request headers. Furthermore, it can integrate with the authorization server and validate access tokens to ensure only valid tokens pass. It can ask the authorization server to exchange a token from one format to another and cache any results to improve performance.

A complete OAuth solution requires more than simply validating access tokens in APIs. As mentioned, there are various types of applications, such as browser-based applications, mobile apps, and connections from business partners, each with unique security best practices. The API gateway can handle these differences and address concerns like HTTP-only cookies or cross-origin resource sharing (CORS). In this way, you can simplify APIs and, more importantly, their security implementation as they can apply the same security code to all requests.

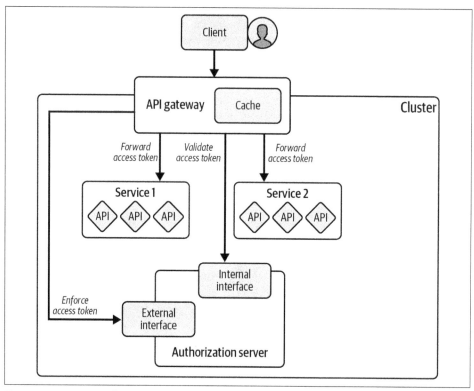

Figure 3-3. Access tokens at the perimeter

In the context of this book, the API gateway is a role rather than a dedicated product. You do not have to depend on a specialist API management system to get an API gateway. Components such as a Kubernetes Ingress or a reverse proxy often have sufficient features or extensibility to enforce and validate access tokens at the entry point. As long as all incoming requests pass the component and as long as it can integrate with the authorization server to validate or translate access tokens, it is suitable for the API gateway role. We discuss the role of the API gateway in detail in Chapter 8.

With the authorization server and the API gateway you already have a working foundation for your security architecture. Those two components allow you to externalize authentication from application code and simplify API authorization code. You can further advance your security architecture with the policy engine to outsource policy enforcement from APIs.

The Role of the Policy Engine

The policy engine is the heart of the entitlement management system. The idea of an entitlement management system is to have security policies that you can enforce throughout the entire architecture. It is the job of the policy engine to parse and process policies. You define those policies once and manage them separately from the infrastructure and application code.

You can apply the policies when you need to make a security-related decision (e.g., when accessing APIs). The role that makes the decision is the policy decision point (PDP). The point where you enforce those decisions is called the policy enforcement point (PEP). Though you can have many policy decision and enforcement points, the policy is central. Central, documented policies simplify security audits and can be a handy tool when proving compliance with regulations.

With OAuth, you can take the access token into account when making policy decisions. You can design policies to work with identity attributes. Even when you have a policy engine, an API remains responsible for authorization. This means that an API implements the policy enforcement point where it consults the policy engine for a decision, with the policy engine being the policy decision point. The API can add the access token to its inquiry for the policy engine. The access token serves as the policy information point (PIP). This means it enriches the request with additional information that the policy engine uses when processing a policy. In other words, the policy engine can then use the data in the access token to make an access decision that it communicates back to the API.

Components may use the policy engine for both coarse-grained and fine-grained access decisions, as shown in Figure 3-4. For example, an API gateway may coordinate with the entitlement management system for coarse-grained authorization and send it the access token. Then the API gateway also contains a policy enforcement point. APIs, on the other hand, may rely on the policy engine for fine-grained decisions based on the identity data of the access token.

Figure 3-4 illustrates the policy engine as a single service to emphasize the role of a central policy. The policy engine is not necessarily a single point of failure. For example, the Open Policy Agent is a cloud native policy engine that you can deploy in sidecars to each service. You can learn more about how to utilize the entitlement management system in a cloud native environment in Chapter 9.

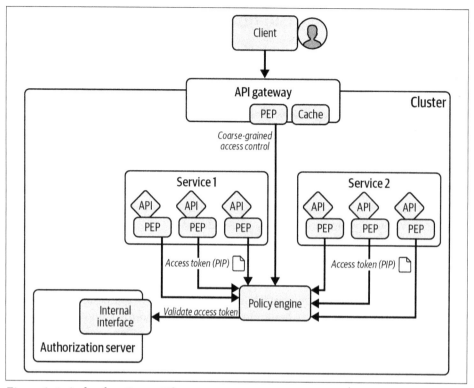

Figure 3-4. A cloud native entitlement management system

API Responsibilities

APIs are the components that provide business value. They have access to protected resources (i.e., data and information of users, customers, business partners, intellectual property, and other assets). APIs serve data to clients for visualization and user interaction. Since APIs are a substantial part of an organization's digital solutions, protecting them and any data they expose over the whole lifecycle is crucial. Protecting data means securing access to it.

Before OAuth 2.0, APIs had to implement security in multiple ways. One such method that we still see in action today is API keys. However, API keys do not authenticate the user and typically never expire. Kerberos tickets and X.509 certificates can potentially provide user information, but they introduce a dependency on complex infrastructure. Not all clients may support that complexity and you may have to treat various clients differently. OAuth leads to simpler APIs by using access tokens for all clients.

APIs need to validate access tokens not only in terms of the expiration date and signature but also in terms of the scope of access. An access token represents the scope of access that the end user directly or indirectly granted the client. API endpoints must specify a required scope they expect access tokens to include and reject any access token with insufficient scopes. APIs use the data (claims) of valid access tokens when processing access rules. In the end, APIs return authorized data to the client.

Service-level agreements

Take the service-level agreement (SLA) of the authorization server into account when setting up SLAs for APIs. Since APIs depend on the authorization server, any unintended changes that affect token issuance could result in business interruptions and thus impact the SLA of your APIs.

Client Responsibilities

Clients in the context of this book are typically applications that offer an interface for end users. They call APIs to retrieve data for their logic and visualization. For the APIs to return accurate data, clients must provide information about the user or itself and the requested access. When you use OAuth, the client does not authenticate users directly. Instead, the client requests an access token from the authorization server, which the client later sends to APIs.

Access tokens provide access to data. If an access token gets into the wrong hands, you will have a data leak. The client must make sure to protect the access token in transit and at rest from unauthorized access. This means, for example, that clients must:

- Communicate with the authorization server using only HTTPS.
- Validate the HTTPS certificates of the authorization server and APIs.
- Send access tokens using only HTTPS.
- Discard and revoke access tokens when they are done with them (e.g., user logged out).
- Choose a secure flow (e.g., use the code flow).
- Protect redirect URI (e.g., with HTTPS).
- Not send access tokens in URLs.
- Store access tokens securely.

Sometimes the nature of the client's implementation and deployment restricts the client's capabilities. For example, it is impossible to keep secrets safe in browser-based applications. Such applications are, therefore, considered public clients and thus have different security properties than a confidential backend client. The security architecture, and the authorization server, in particular, need to consider client capabilities.

For many applications, you can get basic OAuth 2.0 and OpenID Connect functionality working pretty quickly. It is straightforward to produce OAuth messages in basically any technology stack. Typically, you use standards-based security libraries for the job. Note that any OAuth message, whether on the front or back channel, can result in an OAuth error response. A resilient client must handle errors correctly for every OAuth message that it sends. This also includes automatically security renewing access tokens when they expire. We outline client best practices in Part IV.

When you build an API security architecture, you should choose security components that support open standards and integrate them with your clients and APIs. Writing code to integrate clients and APIs is, however, just part of the story. We believe that, when you build a security architecture for cloud native applications, you should also operate the security components in a cloud native manner. Cloud native operational best practices are a major topic that we do not explain in detail. Nevertheless we highlight some basic characteristics that you should aim for because reliable operation has an impact on the security architecture (e.g., on the ability and means to upgrade, monitor, audit, and troubleshoot).

Operating Security Components

Security components that support your APIs should work with paradigms like infrastructure as code (IaC) and continuous integration and continuous delivery (CI/CD). These are the same approaches that you already use for other components in your architecture. Look for security components that support techniques like file-based configuration and environment variables for adjustments that enable cloud native best practices. Using cloud native paradigms for security components makes it easy to audit, verify, and roll back (security) deployments.

Security components are critical components and as such should expose their health status in a way that integrates with liveness and readiness probes of the platform. Kubernetes uses those probes to determine that a pod is healthy and only routes requests to pods in a ready state. With the help of liveness probes, it can detect unhealthy pods and restart them to restore a working state. This behavior is commonly referred to as an auto-healing or self-healing capability. Both liveness and readiness probes are important tools for functional, healthy security components in Kubernetes.

Another trait for a cloud native component is the ability to operate clustered instances. This characteristic is important for the ability to dynamically scale horizontally—that is, the ability to adapt the number of instances depending on a configured desired state. Therefore, you should be able to cluster critical security components like the authorization server in the same way that you cluster your API instances. We illustrate an example in Figure 3-5, where the authorization server consists of several instances. The security behavior for your clients, APIs, the API gateway, and (if you use one) the policy engine must remain consistent as you scale up or down a security component.

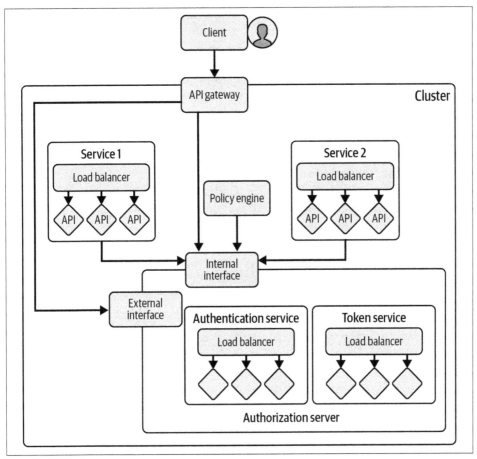

Figure 3-5. A cloud native authorization server

Security components like the authorization server must provide metrics such as CPU, memory usage, and an average request time. The metrics should follow standardized formats so that existing monitoring tools can make sense of them. The Kubernetes platform can then use Kubernetes API resources to define conditions for horizontal scaling (adjusting number of pods) or vertical scaling (adjusting available resources for each pod).

Monitoring is of particular importance for the authorization server because it handles many important security events. It must publish useful metrics related not only to reliability but also to security insights. Such metrics concern HTTP requests, authentication and SSO events, tokens, and credentials. You can then define (security) alarms for the authorization server based on its metrics. For example, an increased number of failed authentication attempts can indicate ongoing malicious activity.

You will need detailed logs when investigating and collecting information about activities in the system. Log aggregation systems can centralize logs and, in that way, help you to significantly reduce the time it takes to analyze log data. Any component in the security architecture should integrate with your existing logging system. For this, they should put structured logs at the standard output or error stream, where Kubernetes can pick them up and save them to files. Log shippers and other agents can then monitor folders and forward data to the log aggregation system. We talk more about operating an authorization server in a cloud native environment in Chapter 11.

When you operate OAuth, your options should not limit you. Instead, you should be able to take finer control over behaviors so that you can meet your exact requirements. To do so you are likely to need to implement customizations. Thankfully, OAuth is a framework, which means it allows you to extend behaviors in different areas, whenever there is such a need.

Extending OAuth

When getting started with OAuth think of the authorization server as a component that you simply plug in. Once you do it your frontend applications can authenticate users and receive access tokens with which to call APIs. While an authorization server does indeed provide an out-of-the-box solution, the details may not match your exact requirements. For example, your digital services may need to satisfy some real-world use cases:

- Integrate with existing data stores for user accounts and user credentials.
- Transform an access token as it flows between APIs.
- Implement impersonation where one user acts on behalf of another.
- Authenticate users at an external system that uses a vendor-specific implementation.

Your authorization server can meet some of your requirements using its support for security standards. Specifications, however, are not meant to account for all of your practical needs. There are areas of OAuth specifications where the authors did not fix some details and left freedom to the authorization server implementers. The most visible place where behavior is open-ended is user authentication. There are also some less visible aspects of OAuth, like the OAuth token exchange, or access token design, where the specifications merely define the boundary decisions. To fulfill these requirements, your authorization server should allow you to design tokens, their format, scopes and claims, signature, and encryption algorithms. It should allow you to transform tokens, change any of its technical characteristics or the associated claims at runtime, and allow you to define conditions for such a transformation.

The authorization server is a toolbox for implementing and evolving security solutions. This toolbox should enable you to implement your security customizations (e.g., via plug-ins or scripts) while continuing to operate within the OAuth framework. Ideally, your customizations become composable units of your authorization server that you can reuse for multiple clients and APIs. They help to prevent blocking security issues, and to avoid the need to implement complex workarounds at the application level. We show techniques that leverage this in further chapters.

Summary

A modern security architecture uses a token-based approach. Its security components work together to provide an ecosystem. This enables you to externalize difficult responsibilities from applications and APIs, which instead perform their security work by using respected standards-based security libraries. With these components in place, the architecture enables a separation of concerns that allows you to evolve your security in future, to keep it up-to-date.

You now understand the big picture and have learned which security components you need to build a cloud native API security architecture. The coming chapters of the book focus on the design of APIs and tokens. We start with a closer look at the identity data that the authorization server needs to both authenticate a user and build a robust access credential.

CHAPTER 4

OAuth Data Design

OAuth is a distributed architecture, and the authorization server has its own data sources. When you get started with OAuth, an early consideration should be to enable a future-proof data setup. You should be able to deploy the authorization server and its data in a straightforward manner. User attributes from the authorization server should flow to your APIs in a way that enables APIs to correctly authorize access to the user's business resources.

In this chapter, we explain how an authorization server manages data. We then explain the design choices you have for operating this data. In particular, we discuss user accounts and user attributes. We also discuss manageability so that you get the right level of dependency between your APIs and your authorization server. We then cover some wider topics related to multitenancy and multiregion so that you can take your OAuth data with you as your business data grows. Finally, we show how to use the authorization server's user management APIs to populate user accounts. First, let's understand the types of data your authorization server uses.

Authorization Server Data

Your authorization server stores several types of identity data, which you manage separately from your business data. The types can be broadly categorized as configuration data, operational data, and user identity data. Figure 4-1 illustrates some example authorization server data.

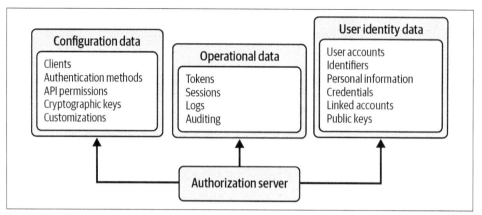

Figure 4-1. Data managed by the authorization server

Your configuration data includes client settings. You typically must register clients at the authorization server before they can receive tokens. For each client, you need to define policies, such as supported authentication methods. When users log in via a client, the authorization server selects the appropriate authentication methods depending on its configured policy.

Configuration also controls the API permissions included in access tokens for each client, and the cryptographic keys that the authorization server uses to digitally sign access tokens. As secret and key management is a common challenge, many cloud providers offer services, like a vault, to store secure values. You can also, for example, use a hardware security module to generate and store key material. In this way, the authorization server does not have to store any sensitive key material.

Your authorization server writes operational data due to user activity. This includes token and session-related information, as well as various types of logs. You keep this operational data only as long as you need it. You use technical logs for support purposes, and audit logs for insights into security events, such as the frequency of failed login attempts.

Your user identity data requires the most design consideration. It is usual to create user accounts in the authorization server so that you can store attributes against users. The authorization server also stores other security-related data against user accounts, such as hashed passwords, or public keys used to verify more advanced types of login credentials. In many use cases, user creation is the result of activity in clients that run OAuth flows where users can sign up. In other use cases, administrator actions or migration processes create users. Users may sometimes authenticate at an external identity system, in which case the authorization server can create a linked account associated with the main user account.

Your authorization server can connect to various data sources. When operating in a cloud native environment, you may connect your authorization server to cloud native SQL or NoSQL databases. You may also be able to use cloud-managed database storage. Many authorization servers can use LDAP to interact with existing directory services containing user accounts and user credentials.

When getting started with OAuth, you can use the default data sources that the authorization server provides. First, focus on configuring a working integration between your clients and APIs that allows users to authenticate and clients to retrieve access tokens that they can send to APIs. So, let us explain the basic OAuth configuration that you need.

OAuth Configuration Settings

When getting started, manage configuration using the authorization server's administrative user interface, where the meaning of settings is visually clearest. In the admin UI, you first configure a user authentication method. You also register a client. You then assign a user authentication method to the client. Example 4-1 shows a JSON object with the settings for an OAuth client, which include a client ID, client credentials (the client secret), and a list of scopes that the authorization server allows the client to request.

Example 4-1. Basic client configuration

```
{
    "client_id": "web-client",
    "client_secret": "drLChAwreS6&teh7Va?1",
    "redirect_uri": "https://www.example.com/callback",
    "post_logout_redirect_uri": "https://www.example.com/loggedout",
    "scope": "openid profile purchases",
    "authentication_methods": ["username_password"]
}
```

Once you configure a client in the authorization server, and the client runs an OAuth flow, the client can get tokens. Clients that implement the code flow can also trigger user authentication, as Chapter 2 explains. When sending the protocol messages, the client uses a copy of the configuration settings. The client in Example 4-1 can use OpenID Connect because it supports the openid scope. The client can therefore receive an ID token with information about the authentication event. The client could decide to use only a subset of its allowed scopes, such as omitting openid to use only OAuth, without OpenID Connect.

You can, optionally, configure the authorization server to require user consent before it issues an access token to a client. Enable this for use cases where the user must approve API permissions that the authorization server grants to a client. Doing so causes the authorization server to present a consent screen to the user once authentication completes. You can configure scopes in the authorization server to be required or optional for a client. For any optional scopes, the user can deselect values in the consent screen. When consent is active, the authorization server only issues scopes that the user approves to access tokens.

You also design identity attributes to issue to access tokens. These access token values are called claims and you configure them in the authorization server alongside scopes. You associate each claim with one or more scopes. When the authorization server issues a scope to an access token, it also issues the claims associated with the scope. The authorization server evaluates each claim at runtime. For clients that implement the code flow, claims include user attributes. For the example client in Example 4-1, you might decide to associate the purchases scope with a roles claim and a department claim. At runtime, the values of the roles and department claims issued will vary depending on the user interacting with the client. In Chapter 6 we dive deeper into using scopes and claims.

The authorization server stores many more configuration settings. These include token formats, lifetimes, and signing algorithms. APIs should receive cryptographically verifiable access tokens. Therefore, in the authorization server, you also need to configure a key store for token signing. The authorization server typically provides a default key, which you can replace. When required, you can also configure key stores and trust stores used for TLS. This cryptographic material should be different for each stage of your deployment pipeline. Figure 4-2 shows that configuration data consists of multiple areas.

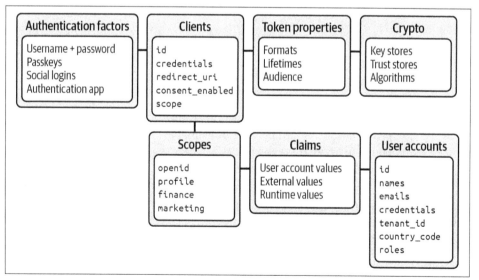

Figure 4-2. OAuth configuration settings

Configuration settings are often easiest to manage in plain text storage formats, such as JSON, XML, or YAML. This enables you to version control the configuration using an IaC approach. You can then store the nonsecret settings in source control, and the secret settings in a secure vault. You then deploy the same configuration, with minor differences, down a pipeline, with stages like test, staging, and production. You manage the minor differences as environment variables and encrypted secrets. In later chapters, we provide Kubernetes deployment examples that demonstrate these techniques.

With the basic configuration and a working integration in place, you can start to think more about user accounts and user attributes. Therefore, let's explain the storage of user data in the authorization server.

Designing User Accounts

In most use cases, you need to create user accounts in the authorization server. A user account can contain informational fields and also more advanced information. For example, if a user authenticates using an external IDP, the authorization server can create a linked account that stores the external user ID. Similarly, if a user authenticates with newer cryptography-backed authentication methods, the authorization server can store public keys against the user account. We explain more about these forms of user authentication in Chapter 14.

Personal Data

Authorization servers provide ways to store user account records and assign attributes to users. You start with built-in fields and then add any custom user attributes that you need. Table 4-1 shows a default schema that contains built-in fields that your authorization server might use during authentication operations. For example, a forgot password process may send an email to the user and use the given_name value in the email content.

Table 4-1. Example user attributes

Field	Description
account_id	A generated database identifier for the user
subject	An immutable user identifier supplied in access tokens
given_name	The forename(s) of the user
family_name	The surname(s) of the user
emails	One or more emails associated with the user

Authorization servers usually provide built-in fields based on OpenID Connect claims, to enable issuing those claims to tokens. Some authorization servers model their user attributes on the "System for Cross-domain Identity Management (SCIM) Core Schema" (RFC 7643) (*https://oreil.ly/wAcg9*). SCIM is an interoperable set of specifications for managing user identity data.

As a best practice, you should aim to make the authorization server the source of truth for all personal data. Store only personal data that you need, and store it only for as long as you need to. Ideally, applications and APIs should not store any personal data and should instead receive it from the authorization server in tokens or by calling the userinfo endpoint. The authorization server enables you to protect and audit personal data in a single place. Table 4-2 extends the default user attributes with custom fields to manage address, Social Security, and legal terms.

Table 4-2. Personal data user attributes

Field	Description
account_id	A generated database identifier for the user
subject	An immutable user identifier supplied in access tokens
given_name	The forename(s) of the user
family_name	The surname(s) of the user
emails	One or more emails associated with the user
address	The user's address fields
social_security_number	A government-issued identifier for the user
terms_accepted	Whether the user has accepted legal terms for your organization
terms_accepted_date	When the user last accepted legal terms for your organization

Table 4-2 shows a cleaner data design than storing personal data in multiple places. Centralizing personal data usually makes it easier to meet user privacy regulations, such as the General Data Protection Regulation (GDPR) (*https://oreil.ly/HWV6C*) in the European Union. If you need to leave some personal fields in the business data, make these fields read-only.

The authorization server uses other privacy-related behaviors. For example, you might decide to show a postauthentication screen to ask the user to accept your organization's legal terms, then record the date when accepted. You can use the consent features of the authorization server when users need to grant your application access to their personal data. Ideally, you can configure the authorization server to show these screens only once rather than on every user login. If the conditions change, you can update the authorization server to force the user to reconsent on the next login.

Protect personal data

Store personal data in your authorization server and encrypt it at rest. Use the features of the authorization server to help manage privacy and consent before sharing personal data with clients.

Personal data is not the only type of user data. Most digital solutions also store business-related user attributes. You might classify some of these to be part of a user's core identity and others to be specific to a particular product or area. Let's explore this further.

Business User Attributes

When getting started with OAuth, it is common for business data to store existing user attributes for both personal data and business settings. Table 4-3 shows the user attributes for a standalone website that models users as customers. Each customer record contains a `customer_id` to uniquely identify the user, along with other business-related fields. If the user makes an online purchase, the website creates a business resource, such as a purchase record, and associates it with the customer ID.

Table 4-3. User attributes in business data

Field	Description
`customer_id`	The user's business identifier
`tenant_id`	The user's organization
`name`	The user's name
`email`	The user's email address
`membership_level`	Business privileges may depend on the user's membership level
`roles`	Business privileges may depend on the user's roles

When updating to an OAuth architecture, you usually migrate some existing user attributes to the authorization server's user accounts. In a simple use case, such as a standalone website, the easiest way to do this is to run a migration process that moves all user attributes to the authorization server. We provide a worked example for user migration later in the chapter.

If you work at a large organization, you might have multiple product lines, each with its own user stores and business attributes. Migrating all user attributes across all products to the authorization server is likely to be very disruptive. You may change or remodel some business user attributes often. Fields such as `roles` or `address` may even have different meanings or data shapes in different contexts. Without care, this could lead to productivity problems where user data has to be frequently updated in the authorization server.

Therefore, in larger setups, think carefully about which attributes to store in the authorization server and which to leave in the business data. Aim to use the authorization server as a toolbox that operates on stable user attributes. In your organization, an identity team who are security specialists might operate the authorization server. The best people to manage volatile business settings are likely to be your API teams.

For your organization's digital solutions, you may consider some business fields to be central to the user's identity. When these are the same for all products, managing them centrally is usually a better option than duplicating them across products. Multiple APIs and applications can then receive the same values from the authorization server. The fields from Table 4-4 are often good choices to manage in the authorization server. In use cases where values vary considerably across products, leave them in the business data.

Table 4-4. Shared business settings

Field	Description
customer_id	The user's business identifier
tenant_id	The user's organization
country_code	The user's country of residence
roles	The user's classification to determine allowed access

You should be free to design where to store user attributes based on your own requirements. For example, instead of storing a business user identifier in the identity data, you might prefer to store the subject claim within the business data. Even if you prefer to store some user attributes in your business data, your authorization server should still be able to access them. To understand how, let's explain API user identities.

API User Identities

When designing user accounts, do some early thinking about how your APIs will identify users and authorize requests on their behalf. When the authorization server issues access tokens to a client, it includes a subject claim in the token, to identify the user account. The subject is typically a stable technical value such as a Universally Unique Identifier (UUID). It remains the same even if the user's name changes. When the client sends the access token to the API, the API needs to identify the user in business terms. The subject claim may not be the best value to enable this.

In Figure 4-3 the `customer_id` field represents an existing business user identifier that the API understands. For example, customers may generate business data after events such as an online purchase. APIs then store purchase database records mapped to the customer ID. Including identifying fields in your authorization server's user account records makes it easy to issue them as claims in access tokens. APIs that receive access tokens can then easily locate the user's business resources.

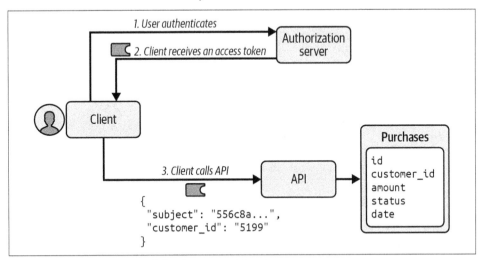

Figure 4-3. API request with business user identity

Field names for user identifier

The SCIM core schema provides an `external_id` field that you can use to store a business user identifier, or you can use a custom field if you prefer.

When designing API identities, also be aware of the risk of unintended user tracking. You do not have to always send the same user identity to every API. It is possible to define distinct user identifiers for each client (or group of clients). Use pairwise pseudonymous identifiers (PPIDs) from the OpenID Connect core specification for that purpose. One use case where you might use PPIDs is when issuing tokens to a less trusted subdivision of a large organization. Figure 4-4 shows an authorization server issuing access tokens with distinct subject claims for the same user account to different sets of clients.

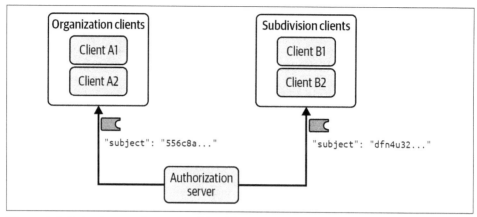

Figure 4-4. Pairwise pseudonymous identifiers

Once your APIs receive useful user identifiers for existing users, you should also understand how the authorization server can interact with your APIs.

Identity Operations

During security-related operations, such as user registration, user authentication, or token issuance, the authorization server should have access to any user attributes it needs. For example, the authorization server should be able to verify the correctness of a business user attribute that the user enters in a custom authentication screen. Similarly, the authorization server should be able to retrieve a business user attribute and issue it as an access token claim. To do so, the authorization server makes an external call, such as to a utility API endpoint that you provide. Figure 4-5 shows a request that sends authorization server user attributes and receives external attributes in the response.

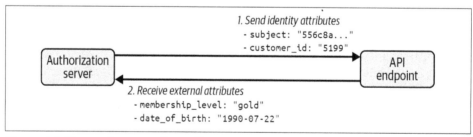

Figure 4-5. External user attributes flow

If you store user attributes in multiple data sources, your user account design should also account for future user onboarding. Aim for a solution that allows your APIs to receive the same claims in access tokens for both new and existing users. The example in Figure 4-6 shows a self-signup operation that could run during a code flow.

The user fills in a registration form. The authorization server then sends some of the form fields in an external API request, to create a customer record in the business data. The external API response returns a `customer_id`. The authorization server creates its own user account with the remainder of the form fields and the customer ID. The business user identity for the new user account is thus available in access tokens that APIs receive.

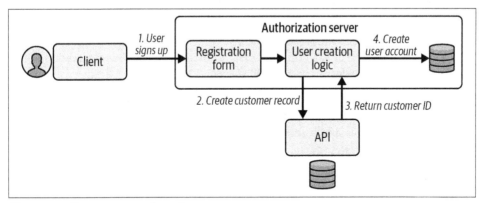

Figure 4-6. Future user registration

Shared user identifier

If you split user attributes between the authorization server and your business data, ensure that there is a shared user identifier that you can use to match data records together.

After designing user accounts, implement the design with a user migration process that calls the authorization server's user management APIs.

User Management APIs

The user accounts that you store in your authorization server belong to you and you should be in control of the data so that you can design your preferred schema. You also need API access to user accounts in a way that meets your usage requirements. The authorization server's user management APIs should enable you to operate on built-in user attributes and also any custom user attributes you need. Therefore, user management APIs should provide similar behaviors to your business-focused APIs.

Access to user management APIs requires a message credential. Typically, the authorization server will require an access token. You may be able to configure a particular scope such as `accounts`, and also associate claims to that scope, to control access. This enables you to design access tokens that restrict clients to a particular user account or a subset of user accounts. Field-level rules are also common. For example, an administrator may be able to set an initial temporary password for a user but should not be able to read passwords.

You usually first call user management APIs when you migrate existing user accounts in the authorization server. You can also call user management APIs for several other use cases, like creating, updating, deleting, or deactivating users from an administrator application. User management APIs should also allow you to build a self-service portal where users can update their profile from within a frontend application.

Some authorization servers follow standards for user management APIs, such as the SCIM protocol from RFC 7644 (*https://oreil.ly/DYit5*). Authorization servers that follow this standard provide you with a well-designed JSON-based API that you can call from any application or API, regardless of technology stack.

When migrating users to the authorization server you typically develop a small program such as a console application. This program iterates over users in an existing data source, then creates or updates user accounts in the authorization server. Example 4-2 shows a request payload to create a new user account.

Example 4-2. Example SCIM request

```
{
    "schemas": [
        "urn:ietf:params:scim:schemas:core:2.0:User"
    ],
    "userName": "danademo",
    "emails": [
        {
            "value": "dana.demo@example.com",
            "primary": true
        }
    ],
    "customer_id": "345",
    "active": true
}
```

A successful create operation returns the new user. Example 4-3 shows an example response that includes a generated user identifier in the id field. You can invoke various other operations, such as updating a user via a PUT request, partially updating the user via a PATCH request, or removing the user with a DELETE request.

Example 4-3. Example SCIM response

```
{
    "schemas": [
        "urn:ietf:params:scim:schemas:core:2.0:User"
    ],
    "userName": "danademo",
    "emails": [
        {
            "value": "dana.demo@example.com",
            "primary": true
        }
    ],
    "customer_id": "345",
    "active": true,
    "id": "VVNFUjo2ZmZiZTNjMi1kYWM5LTExZWQtYjIxMi0xNjk3MTNlZGRjNDk"
}
```

You now understand that you can flexibly store user accounts and user attributes and also have API access to that data. In some use cases though, your APIs may have more advanced data requirements. These can include hosting APIs in multiple global locations or providing API access to users from multiple organizations. Let's briefly summarize how the authorization server fits into these deployments.

Multiregion

In global setups, when using APIs across multiple regions with different legal requirements, you may need to meet data sovereignty regulations.[1] This can result in you needing to store each user's business transactions and personal data in the user's home region.

In a zero trust architecture, you should not rely on the infrastructure to enforce the correct regional access. For example, a basic multiregion deployment might store data in the location that receives the API request, or use data replication to save all transactions to all regions. Global load balancing may occasionally route users to the wrong location, perhaps one that the user is physically closest to but that is not their home region. Figure 4-7 shows an example where the infrastructure initially routes the user to the incorrect region. The API gateway inspects the access token and reads a region or country claim from the access token. When required, the API gateway then re-routes the user to the correct region.

---

1 Christian Banse, "Data Sovereignty in the Cloud—Wishful Thinking or Reality?" (*https://oreil.ly/CaYKS*) in *Proceedings of the 2021 on Cloud Computing Security Workshop (CCSW '21)* (2021): 153–154.

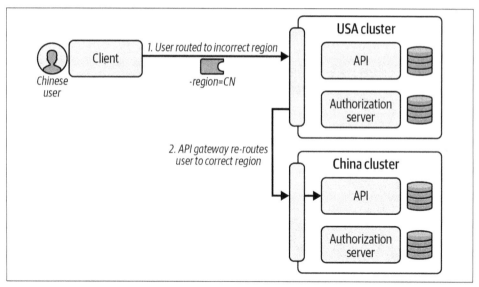

Figure 4-7. Dynamic user routing

In a multiregion deployment, you should use independent deployments of the same authorization server. All regions usually share the same configuration settings, but you should avoid replicating operational data or user data. Instead, aim to store a user's personal data only within the user's home region. You can follow an equivalent approach for any sensitive transactions in the business data.

You may also need to provide API access to multiple companies, where each company has its own users. Let's explain the options your authorization server provides to enable isolation between tenants.

Multitenancy

In some use cases, you may need to supply APIs and clients to business partners, in a B2B2C model, where each organization has its own user base. It is then essential in clients and APIs that each user can never access data that belongs to other organizations. You can meet this requirement in multiple ways. At one end of the spectrum, you could provide each business partner a separate copy of all identity and business components, to ensure full isolation. In some deployments this may not be the most cost-effective design.

Therefore, you could instead design data and components that are multitenant aware. You could assign each business partner a tenant ID that you use to partition resources in both the identity data and business data. You would then issue the tenant ID to access tokens, and use it during API authorization, to only allow users to access information for their tenant. Doing so may give you additional deployment options. For example, a default deployment could store data for multiple smaller tenants, while larger tenants pay extra for an isolated deployment.

You can configure your authorization server to be multitenant aware by including a tenant ID user attribute in the identity data. You then need to design how to populate this value when you onboard users. Alternatively, your authorization server can provide high isolation per tenant, using a mechanism such as a `profile` or `realm`. This can result in isolated copies of data sources, configuration, credentials, and OAuth endpoints. You then give each tenant a distinct base URL to the authorization server, as we show in Figure 4-8.

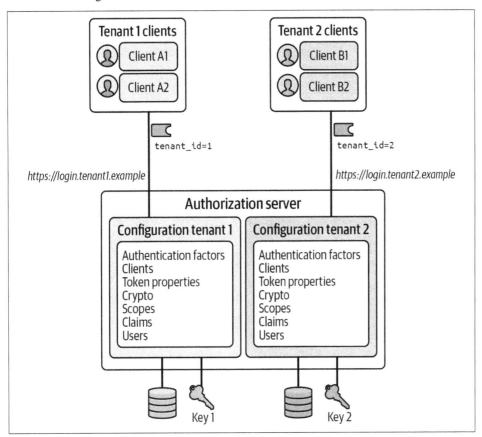

Figure 4-8. Multitenancy using isolated profiles and data sources

By now you should understand that there are a number of design considerations for user attributes. We finish with some practical content, to show how to connect to an authorization server's user management APIs and migrate user accounts.

User Migration Code Example

The GitHub repository for this book (*https://oreil.ly/CNDS-supp*) provides a user migration code example that demonstrates a user migration. You can find it in the *chapter-04-scim-user-migration* directory. The code example is a simple console application that acts as a SCIM client and calls the authorization server's SCIM endpoints to create user accounts. You can follow the *README* instructions to first deploy a cloud native authorization server, then run an example program that iterates over users. Figure 4-9 shows that, originally, each customer record consists of both business and identity attributes, where business resources link to customer IDs.

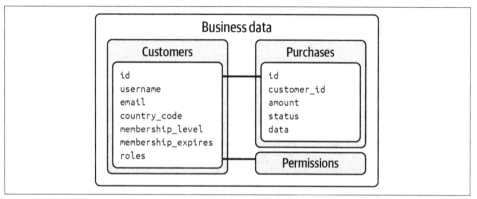

Figure 4-9. Original user attributes

In this example, the migration will store personal data in the authorization server, along with a business user identity and role information. Membership details remain in the business data, along with fine-grained permissions. After the migration, user attributes exist in both the authorization server's user accounts and the business data, with personal data removed from the business data. Figure 4-10 shows that the customer ID links the two data sources together.

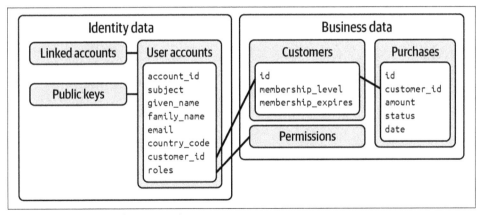

Figure 4-10. Migrated user attributes

Example 4-4 shows a JSON structure for the original business data.

Example 4-4. Original customer record

```
[
    {
        "id": 2099,
        "username": "dana",
        "email": "dana.demo@example.com",
        "country": "US",
        "membershipLevel": "gold",
        "membershipExpires": "2024-10",
        "roles": [
            "customer"
        ]
    }
]
```

Example 4-5 shows a JSON configuration file that the migration program uses. The configuration settings include the URL of a token endpoint from which the program retrieves an access token with the accounts scope. In the example setup, access tokens issued with this scope have full access to administer all user accounts. The program sends a client credentials grant request to get such an access token, then sends the access token in multiple requests to the SCIM endpoint, each of which creates a user account in the authorization server.

Example 4-5. SCIM client configuration settings

```json
{
    "clientId": "scim-client",
    "clientSecret": "?rlfRiVoPrLp8v$St0Ph",
    "scope": "accounts",
    "tokenEndpoint": "http://localhost:8443/oauth/v2/oauth-token",
    "scimEndpoint": "http://localhost:8443/scim/Users"
}
```

As the program migrates each user, it removes personal information from the customer record. Example 4-6 shows the user attributes that remain in the business data after the migration.

Example 4-6. Migrated customer record

```json
[
    {
        "id": 2099,
        "membershipLevel": "gold",
        "membershipExpires": "2024-10"
    }
]
```

Once the program completes you can list all user accounts created in the authorization server. Example 4-7 shows an example user account containing personal data, a business user identity, and roles.

Example 4-7. User account in the authorization server

```json
[
    {
        "id": "VVNFUjplYmYwZjQyYy0wYTY2LTQxOWItYjA0Yy0yZDkzMmY0NzgxMGU",
        "userName": "dana.demo@example.com",
        "schemas": [
            "urn:ietf:params:scim:schemas:core:2.0:User"
        ],
        "active": true,
        "name": {
            "givenName": "Dana",
            "familyName": "Demo"
        },
        "emails": [
            {
                "value": "dana.demo@example.com",
                "primary": true
            }
        ],
        "addresses": [
            {
```

```
                "country": "US"
            }
        ],
        "roles": [
            {
                "value": "customer",
                "primary": true
            }
        ],
        "customerId": "2099"
    }
]
```

Although OAuth migrations require some design thinking, the code example shows you that an implementation should be straightforward in any technology stack. The example migration improves the data architecture and you can run the migration multiple times without creating duplicate accounts. User migrations should have minimal impact on the existing business data.

When you implement user migrations, also consider future user migrations. For example, if you ever want to upgrade to a different authorization server, you could update the code example to read user accounts from the old authorization server's user management APIs and import them using the new authorization server's user management APIs.

Summary

Authorization servers use three main types of data, for configuration, operational data, and user identities. Configuration data is largely the same for all stages of your deployment pipeline, unlike the operational and user data. A key area of identity data is the storage of user accounts. You should be able to design your user attribute storage in a way that best meets your business needs. Aim to store core user identity fields in the authorization server, including personal data and any business user identities.

The best way to manage identities in an OAuth architecture requires up-front design thinking. Once complete, you have powerful options for managing difficult security requirements. These can include management of personal data, dealing with user consent and legal terms, and implementing multitenant and multiregion behaviors.

Once user accounts exist in the authorization server, you can return user attributes to applications in OAuth tokens or expose them from the authorization server's userinfo endpoint. This enables you to share the user data stored in the authorization server across many applications. The fields returned to APIs in access tokens are called claims and are fully explained in Chapter 6. In particular, use of claims enables your APIs to receive a business user identity and other values needed for authorization.

The first part of the book focused on explaining some ground concepts that we use in practice further in the book. We showed all the components that a security architecture uses and explained the most important parts of OAuth and how to properly design data that your security system uses. In the next part, we make a deep dive into access tokens and how you use them in a cloud native environment to build robust API security. We start with Chapter 5 where we explain how APIs use access tokens. You will learn how to receive access tokens, validate them, and use their claims to implement authorization. We also demonstrate a technique for writing integration tests so that you can test API security as early as possible in your deployment pipeline, on a development computer.

PART II

Securing APIs with Tokens

Secure API Development

In this chapter, we focus on secure API development by showing how to implement zero trust authorization in OAuth-secured APIs. We first explain how to enable unified API security with JWT access tokens. You then learn how to validate JWT access tokens and how to utilize the token data to implement API authorization logic. We then discuss how to handle access token expiration to ensure end-to-end API reliability. As you have to test your APIs, we also show a productive method for testing zero trust APIs. Finally, we demonstrate the theory with an API code example.

Let's get started by showing how JWT access tokens can enable you to use the same API security code for all types of clients.

Unified API Security with JWT Access Tokens

Different types of client applications have their own best practices for sending access tokens. You should understand that your API code does not need to deal with all of these variations. The API should only ever need to deal with a single unified type of message credential. An API gateway can manage any client-specific security differences so that APIs receive an access token in a format that enables the best API security. That format is a JSON Web Token (JWT). Figure 5-1 illustrates the architecture.

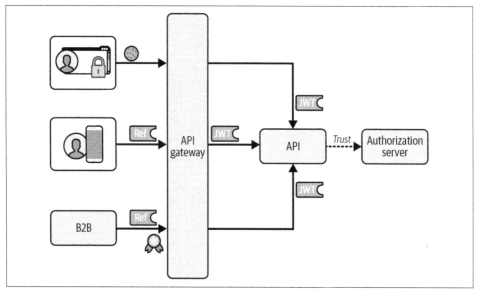

Figure 5-1. End-to-end access token flow

JWTs have a standardized format defined in the JWT specification (RFC 7519) (*https://oreil.ly/cXeS8*). A JWT is a self-contained, URL-safe, and verifiable format for communicating data. APIs should always receive JWT access tokens in the HTTP `Authorization` header. In this way, you can minimize the likelihood of unintentionally leaking access tokens to server logs or the browser history.[1] Example 5-1 shows an HTTP `Authorization` header that carries a JWT bearer access token (with line breaks for display purposes). When you use JWTs with OAuth, as we show in this book, we recommend you follow recommendation from RFC 9068 (*https://oreil.ly/DHpFq*), which is an interoperability profile for OAuth JWT access tokens.

Example 5-1. The HTTP `Authorization` header with a JWT access token

```
Authorization: Bearer eyJraWQiOiI3NzkxIiwiYWxnIjoiRVMyNTYifQ.eyJpc3MiOiJodHRwczovL2x
vZ2luLmV4YW1wbGUuY29tIiwiYXVkIjoiYXBpLmV4YW1wbGUuY29tIiwic2NvcGUiOiJvcGVuaWQgcmV0YWl
sL29yZGVycyIsInN1YiI6ImMyYWRmYjc1LWQ3M2UtNDAxMi05ZmYxLTBkZDBhNWFhOWMwMyIsImlhdCI6MTY
5MDU2NDk4MTY1NywiZXhwIjoxNjkwNTY1OTQxNjU3LCJjdXN0b21lcl9pZCI6Ijc3OTEiLCJyb2xlcyI6WyJ
jdXN0b21lciJdLCJyZWdpb24iOiJVU0EiLCJtZW1iZXJzaGlwX2xldmVsIjoiZ29sZCIsImxldmVsX29mX2F
zc3VyYW5jZSI6Mn0.BBNlyLQVkZEA7r4APWQoNePcsMkbNU-4ojaSbza7c_HPZmxEUWsjQh3BDjxv8mJRfWS
T9wdf_nUElS5jiWBPhA
```

---

1 "Authorization Headers" (*https://oreil.ly/KuYet*), Section 5.4.1 of "OAuth 2.0 Threat Model and Security Considerations" (RFC 6819).

In this chapter, we focus on the most popular way of using JWTs as access tokens—signed JWTs that you send in the HTTP authorization header. There are different solutions and techniques to use JWTs. For example, you can encrypt the tokens using "JSON Web Encryption (JWE)" (RFC 7516) (*https://oreil.ly/5bSoG*), or send the token in the body of a request. You can study RFC 7519 on JWT and RFC 6750 on bearer token usage (*https://oreil.ly/SZxvP*) if you want to learn more about these variations. In most cases, we believe you shouldn't need them.

Signed JWTs consist of three dot-separated Base64URL-encoded parts, representing a header, a payload, and a digital signature. This representation is called the JSON Web Signature Compact Serialization (JWS compact serialization).[2] Both the header and payload are JSON objects. The header of a JWT contains cryptography-related information (e.g., the signature algorithm and verification key) while the payload contains the main data. Example 5-2 shows the decoded header and decoded payload of the JWT access token from Example 5-1.

Example 5-2. Decoded JWT access token

```
{
    "alg": "ES256",
    "kid": "7791"
}
{
    "iss": "https://login.example.com",
    "aud": "api.example.com",
    "scope": "openid retail/orders",
    "sub": "c2adfb75-d73e-4012-9ff1-0dd0a5aa9c03",
    "iat": 1690564981657,
    "exp": 1690565941657,
    "customer_id": "7791",
    "roles": ["customer"],
    "region": "USA",
    "membership_level": "gold",
    "level_of_assurance": 2
}
```

Digital signatures are a cryptographic mechanism that allows a recipient to verify the integrity and authenticity of a message. If a malicious party alters the data, the signature verification fails. When an authorization server issues a JWT access token, it uses its asymmetric private key to sign the data in the JWT header and payload, which protects their integrity. APIs must therefore validate the digital signature before allowing an API request.

---

2 "JWS Compact Serialization" (*https://oreil.ly/-WD5T*), Section 7.1 of "JSON Web Signature (JWS)" (RFC 7515).

Use HTTPS

While digital signatures provide integrity and authenticity, they do not provide data confidentiality. JWTs are commonly unencrypted. Therefore, although intermediate parties cannot manipulate token data, they may still be able to decode and read tokens, which can lead to data leaks. To securely transmit JWT access tokens, you need to protect the communication using TLS. Therefore, always secure both the endpoints of the authorization server and your API endpoints with HTTPS. In this way, you mitigate the risk of leaking information from tokens.

As with any technology solution, you can sometimes hear about the drawbacks of using JWTs. For example, the string representation of the token can get quite large, especially when you decide to use some older but still popular signing algorithms. This means that you might need to transport an increased load between your services. You can also hear about key management or token validation adding complexity to your code and infrastructure. There are no perfect solutions; nevertheless, we believe that JWTs give the best security options for your APIs.

JWTs give you a convenient and secure way of delivering credentials to your APIs. One of their assets is the ability to verify the token offline so that your APIs don't need to keep an open connection to your authorization server. We describe how to achieve this in the next section.

Validating JWT Access Tokens

Once your APIs receive an access token they must validate the JWT's digital signature. For that APIs need to determine the algorithm of the signature from the JWT and load the correct signature verification key. The verification key should always be a public key that the authorization server shares in some fashion. This is where JSON Web Keys (JWKs) usually come into play.

JSON Web Keys

During the base setup of your authorization server, you choose an algorithm and generate an asymmetric key pair for token signatures. The authorization server makes its public keys available to applications in the "JSON Web Key (JWK)" format (RFC 7517) (*https://oreil.ly/57IMO*). Each public key is a JWK object contained in a JSON Web Key Set (JWKS). An endpoint that hosts the JWKS is called the JWKS URI. Example 5-3 shows a JWKS that contains a single public key.

Example 5-3. JSON Web Key Set

```
{
    "keys": [
        {
            "kty": "EC",
            "x": "EnhRQEJDziDD19UKkbwJum8jSlACmiwLFicOX4uaTWg",
            "y": "wy3S2TWVR9jq1SrD3f-HxEH0UlCVFLffjM0wwchgHnc",
            "crv": "P-256",
            "kid": "7791",
            "alg": "ES256"
        }
    ]
}
```

The exact contents of a JWK depend on the asymmetric algorithm you choose. Example 5-3 uses an algorithm called ES256 (ECDSA with SHA-256). This algorithm uses elliptic curve cryptography, where public keys consist of x and y coordinates on a curve (e.g., P-256). When your API first receives an access token with a particular key identifier (kid) in its JWT header, your API should download the JWKS from the JWKS URI and cache the response. Some security libraries do this for you.

Registered signature algorithms and key parameters

The Internet Assigned Number Authority, IANA, maintains the list of registered identifiers for JSON Web Signature algorithms and JSON Web Key parameters at the IANA registry for JSON Object Signing and Encryption (JOSE) (*https://oreil.ly/naofn*).

Fetching public keys from a JWKS URI is the most mainstream and easiest-to-manage option for your APIs since it externalizes all key management responsibilities. In order to fetch the keys from a JWKS, your API needs to know the URI and there are different options to achieve that. Usually, you configure a JWKS URI for the API at deployment time to express a trust relationship with the authorization server. This way, you make sure that no malicious party can override that trust by sending tokens with a malicious key. Another option is for the API to get the JWKS URI value directly from the token—the token header's jku claim. However, reading keys from a JWKS URI is not the only way to get them. The "JSON Web Signature (JWS)" specification (RFC 7515) (*https://oreil.ly/iy-XS*) explains some alternative ways of doing that. For example, a JWT can carry the key needed for signature verification directly in its header in the jwk claim. You can study the specification to understand caveats of the different solutions, should you need to work with them.

Your API should maintain an allow list of issuers, then use this list to make sure that it only uses public keys from an expected source. Otherwise, a malicious party could forge a token that will make the API use the attacker's public key for signature verification. You should ensure such validation in your API regardless of how the API gets the public key—whether it reads from a JWKS URI endpoint, receives the key directly in the token, etc.

Do not use symmetric algorithms for signing tokens

Some online tutorials use symmetric algorithms such as HS256 to sign JWTs. You should never do this for your JWT access tokens. We discuss choosing the right signature algorithm in "Choose a JWT Signature Algorithm" on page 145.

Rotating Token Signing Keys

As a good practice with any passwords or certificates, you should periodically generate new signing keys that your authorization server uses. Once you create a new signing key, you add its public key to the authorization server's JWKS with a new kid value. The server will sign any new tokens with the new private key and put the new kid value in the token's header. You should make sure, however, that APIs can still properly validate tokens the authorization server issued to clients before the key rotation. To achieve that, you keep the old public key in the server's JWKS. For a short period, the JWKS endpoint will return both public keys—the new and the old one. You should keep serving both public keys from the JWKS endpoint for as long as you expect to receive tokens signed with previous keys. For example, if you issue access tokens with a 15-minute expiration time, then you will need to keep the old keys for about 15 minutes. After that time any tokens signed with old keys will have expired anyway.

Your APIs use the kid entry from the access token's header to identify which key from JWKS they should use to verify the signature. Whenever the API encounters a kid value that it does not recognize, it should first call the JWKS endpoint to check whether the server offers any new keys. As the JWKS endpoint now returns both keys, the API will be able to properly verify signatures of both new and old tokens. This way, key rotation becomes seamless for your APIs and clients, and you won't impact your users with the technical event of rotating signing keys.

After your APIs have confirmed the integrity of incoming JWT access tokens, there are a number of built-in claims that they should always validate. We describe them in the next section.

JWT Standard Claims

The JWT specification introduces a list of standard claims. The specification reserves their claim names, so you can use them only in the way the specification describes. This enables interoperability between OAuth-protected systems that use JWT access tokens. Most security libraries implement default verification of the standard claims. Here is the list of the JWT standard claims:

- `iss`—the token issuer. It identifies the authorization server that issued the token.
- `sub`—the token subject. Most times this will identify a user, but it can also identify a client.
- `aud`—the intended token audience. See "The Audience Claim" on page 114 of Chapter 6.
- `jti`—a unique identifier of the token. You can use it to mitigate replay attacks.
- Time-based claims that you can use to check the expiration status of the token. All the following claims have the format of Unix time:
  - `iat`—issued at. The time when the token was issued.
  - `exp`—expires at. The time when the token expires.
  - `nbf`—not valid before. The time before which receivers should deem the token as invalid.

Even though very often you will use reputable security libraries to validate JWTs, it is important that you understand the best practices for JWT validation. Let's see what these practices are.

JWT Validation Best Practices

Follow these best practices when validating JWTs:

- Always configure an asymmetric token signing algorithm in your authorization server.
- Use a strong cryptographic algorithm, as we explain in Chapter 7.
- Use a mainstream and respected security library for your API technology stack.
- Perform JWT cryptographic verification on every API request, for all APIs.
- Supply your API's expected algorithm(s) to your security library.
- Always verify the issuer to ensure that the JWT comes from the expected authorization server.
- Always verify the audience(s) to ensure that the API accepts access tokens intended only for it.

- Always apply time-based checks to ensure that the JWT is valid for use at the current time.
- Ensure that your API correctly rejects invalid access tokens.

Have a look also at RFC 8725 that describes current best practices for handling JWTs (*https://oreil.ly/EwQLH*).

Rely on a mainstream and respected security library for cryptographic operations. Such libraries are typically used by many other organizations and have mature support for JWT validation best practices. Make sure you validate JWTs on every request. There are a few technical behaviors you need to understand about digital signatures and JWT access tokens, but when you work with a JWT validation library the code impact should be minor. In the next section, we provide some example code.

JWT Validation Code

You should implement JWT validation in an OAuth filter class or module that runs before any business logic on every API request. First, the OAuth filter extracts the JWT string value from the HTTP Authorization header. If the API request does not contain an access token, you should immediately reject the request. Then, validate the JWT. In the pseudocode in Example 5-4, a hypothetical respected security library provides a JwtSecurityHandler that validates the JWT.

Example 5-4. JWT validation code

```
class OAuthFilter {

    private readonly options = {
        jwksUri: 'https://login.example.com/oauth/v2/jwks', ❶
        expectedIssuer: 'https://login.example.com', ❷
        expectedAudience: 'api.example.com', ❷
        expectedJwtAlgorithm: 'ES256',❷
    };

    function validateJwt(accessToken: string): ClaimsPrincipal {

        try {

            const handler = new JwtSecurityHandler();
            const claims = handler.validateJwt(accessToken, options);
            return claims;

        } catch (e: JwtValidationException) {

            throw ErrorFactory.unauthorizedError(e);
        }
```

```
        }
}
```

❶ Link to the public keys of the authorization server

❷ Expected values for claims in the access token

In Example 5-4, the JWT validation function of the hypothetical security library takes the access token as input. It also accepts some additional input options to enable you to follow JWT validation best practices:

- The JWKS URI is the endpoint of your authorization server from which the API downloads public keys. Your API configures this URL as a trusted location and does not use public keys from other sources.
- The expected identifier of the token issuer, which is usually the base URL of your authorization server.
- The expected audience(s), which is a resource identifier representing one or more APIs that this token is intended for.
- The JWT algorithm(s), which you expect the authorization server to use when signing access tokens. Your API should reject any tokens with unexpected algorithms.

In Example 5-4, the security library's handler object would run a series of steps to verify the JWT's digital signature and validate the JWT:

- Decode the access token.
- Download public keys from the JWKS URI of the authorization server.
- Parse the JWT header to read the kid (key identifier) and alg (signing algorithm) fields.
- Verify whether the alg value matches an expected value.
- Locate the public key matching the kid value.
- Run the cryptographic algorithm for the alg value, to validate the JWT's digital signature.
- Perform the semantic checks by comparing the values of the JWT against expected values:
  — issuer
  — audience
- Check expiration status.

Signature verification fails if an attacker tampers with any bytes of the JWT or sends a JWT with a signature that does not match the verification keys from the authorization server. Attackers can, however, try to circumvent signature validation. There is an algorithm called none that indicates an unsecured JWT (i.e., a JWT with no digital signature). Attackers may try to tamper with JWTs and edit the alg value in the JWT header, perhaps using a case-sensitive variant of the algorithm, such as noNe, to trigger APIs to skip signature validation. You must ensure that this type of attack cannot succeed as it would eliminate any security characteristics of your JWT access tokens. Therefore, do not accept any arbitrary algorithm but instead configure your APIs with a list of expected values. Supply this list to your security library when validating JWTs.

As part of the JWT validation, and in addition to signature verification, you must ensure that your API or the security library you use implements the following checks:

- The received iss claim must match the expected issuer value.

- The received aud claim must match the expected audience value.

- The current UTC time must be within the range of the received nbf (not before) and exp (expires) values.

In Example 5-4, the library returns success or error objects. After successful validation, it returns an object to the API's code that corresponds to the payload of the access token. We call this the "Claims Principal" since that is a common term used in API technology stacks. On failure, the hypothetical security library throws a JwtValidationException error object. Real security libraries implement similar behavior to signal an error.

There are many API resource server libraries and frameworks that you can use to perform JWT validation. The exact security inputs, outputs, and behaviors may vary. Your library may require you to provide a public key object as input rather than a JWKS URI. In some cases, you may also need to validate the iss, aud, nbf, and exp claims manually in your API code. Some libraries may return an error response rather than throwing an exception. We recommend always taking some time to read your library documentation. Run some API integration tests with invalid JWTs so that you can be sure your JWT validation logic covers best practices and your API behaves as expected.

If the access token is missing, invalid, or expired, your API should return a response with an HTTP 401 status code to the caller. The "OAuth 2.0 Authorization Framework: Bearer Token Usage" specification (RFC 6750) (*https://oreil.ly/plC9g*) provides further details on standard error responses in a WWW-Authenticate header, to convey an error code and description to clients. Example 5-5 shows a 401 error response simply indicating that the token is invalid (with line breaks for display purposes).

Example 5-5. Unauthorized API response

```
HTTP/1.1 401 Unauthorized
WWW-Authenticate: Bearer realm="example", error="invalid_token",
error_description="The access token is invalid."
```

We have now highlighted that each API needs only a small OAuth filter class that sets up your API's authorization logic with a claims principal. Your authorization logic is where you implement your API's main security logic and where you enforce the business rules to ensure that clients and users access the correct data.

API Authorization Logic

Once JWT validation succeeds, your API should receive a claims principal object that preserves the types of values in the access token payload. Your security library may provide you with such an object or you may need to create your own. Example 5-6 shows how you might express a claims principal in TypeScript.

Example 5-6. Example claims principal

```
export class ClaimsPrincipal
{
    public sub: string;
    public scope: string;
    public customerId: number;
    public roles: string[];
    public region: string;
    public levelOfAssurance: number;
}
```

Your exact API authorization logic depends on your business requirements. You can implement any possible business authorization using the claims principal and two main techniques:

- The first technique is to apply coarse-grained checks using scopes, to detect the wrong type of access token.
- The second technique is to apply fine-grained authorization checks using claims.

Let's start by explaining OAuth scopes.

Use Scopes for Coarse-Grained Authorization

The scopes in an access token typically represent an area of business data for which a client can request access. You may design different scopes across different API endpoints, or a single scope for your entire API. We say much more about how you can design scopes in Chapter 6.

In the end, every API has a list of required scopes. Your API should enforce its scopes right after it validates the JWT. This means that an API must accept only those access tokens with matching scopes. In Example 5-7, we illustrate how the API can check if the scopes string of an access token contains the required scope name.

Example 5-7. Checking required scopes

```
function enforceRequiredScope(requiredScope: string) {

    const scopes = this.scope.split(' ');
    if (scopes.indexOf(requiredScope) === -1) {
        throw ErrorFactory.forbiddenError();
    }
}
```

If an API endpoint receives an access token that does not include the required scope, the client usage is invalid since the client sends an access token to an endpoint outside of its remit. The API must reject the access token. As stated in the "OAuth 2.0 Bearer Token Usage" specification (*https://oreil.ly/plC9g*), the API should deny the request by returning a `Forbidden` response with an HTTP 403 status code and an `insufficient_scope` error code. Example 5-8 shows an HTTP error response when an access token lacks the required scope (with line breaks for display purposes).

Example 5-8. Forbidden API response

```
HTTP/1.1 403 Forbidden
WWW-Authenticate: Bearer realm="example", error="insufficient_scope",
error_description="The access token cannot be used against this API endpoint"
```

Scopes can set security boundaries but they do not provide a complete authorization solution. Whenever you need dynamic authorization, with different values per user, you should use claims instead. Next, let's explain how an API can use claims for fine-grained authorization.

Use Claims for Fine-Grained Authorization

In addition to JWT standard claims such as `iss`, `aud`, and `exp`, you can issue any custom claims you need to access tokens. An access token should contain the main values that an API needs for its authorization. As your APIs implement rules that are specific to your business, with your unique data design, you will need custom claims in your claims principal for your authorization logic. Therefore, the claims principal from Example 5-6 includes a number of custom claims:

- The customer ID as a business identity for the user
- The user's roles for authorization

- The user's region in your API logic
- The level of assurance that represents the strength with which the user authenticated

When your API populates the claims principal, you should check that it contains all required custom claims. If any claims are missing that your API depends upon, the cause is likely a configuration problem in the authorization server that you need to correct. We explain more about how you should design the token contents and how the authorization server populates it in Chapter 6. When your API does not receive required claims, it should return a 403 Forbidden response similar to that in Example 5-8.

Once you have a correct claims principal, inject it into your business logic and use the claims to implement your API's main authorization. The claims principal should enable your API code to easily operate on user-specific resources, such as a user's order history, and keep that data private to each user. You can implement authorization according to your coding preferences. One popular option is to implement authorization in unit-testable methods within service logic classes.

In Example 5-9, the listOrders method applies authorization to filter a collection of resources. In this example, if a client sends an API request with an access token for a customer, the API returns only the orders that belong to that customer. The API does not allow a customer to access any orders of other customers. Meanwhile, administrators can access all orders of any customer in their region, but only if they authenticate using a strong authentication method. The API receives a levelOfAssurance claim that informs it of the strength with which the administrator authenticated. It filters at the data access level using a repository object and the claims from the token.

Example 5-9. Claims-based authorization on collections

```
public listOrders(claims: ClaimsPrincipal) : OrderSummary[] {

    if (claims.hasCustomerRole()) {
        return this.repository.getOrdersForCustomer(claims.customerId);
    }

    if (claims.hasAdminRole() && claims.levelOfAssurance >= 2) {
        return this.repository.getAllOrdersForRegion(claims.region);
    }

    return [];
}
```

In Example 5-10, the example getOrderDetails method applies the same authorization rules to an individual order resource. If authorization fails, the API returns a null result from its service logic. The API's REST logic could then return an error response with an HTTP 403 status when access is forbidden.

When dealing with collections, you should prevent a malicious client from being able to use their access token to test which items exist based on the HTTP status code. We recommend returning an error response with an HTTP 404 status for authorization errors and nonexisting resources to indicate that the API did not find the resource for the current user. In this way, a client cannot distinguish whether the resource did indeed not exist or an authorization error occurred.

Example 5-10. Claims-based authorization on individual resources

```
public getOrderDetails(orderId: string, claims: ClaimsPrincipal)
    : OrderDetails | null {

    const order = this.repository.getOrder(orderId);

    if (claims.hasCustomerRole()) {
        if (order.summary.customerId === claims.customerId) {
            return order;
        }
    }

    if (claims.hasAdminRole() && claims.levelOfAssurance >= 2) {
        if (claims.region === order.summary.region) {
            return order;
        }
    }

    return null;
}
```

The example authorization code uses multiple authorization techniques. It uses role-based access control (RBAC) to determine the type of user and to apply the permissions it associates with the user's roles. The example also applies attribute-based access control (ABAC). For example, it uses data from the access token, to validate the runtime authentication strength. Further, it compares claims from the access token with properties of the order resource to make sure customers can access only their own resources and administrators can operate only on orders in a certain region.

When implementing authorization rules, follow the principle of least privilege when applying authorization logic. Do so for both queries that return data and commands that update data. By default, APIs should deny access. Once the API logic identifies that claims allow access, you can process the request, but ensure that clients only gain access to API operations and data that they need. Keep in mind that authorization is not static. In many business systems the rules can change often over time. You should account for flexibility when designing your API code so that you can more easily evolve your authorization logic.

Design for Flexibility

Your authorization logic should be flexible enough to accommodate future changes to business rules and also remain easy to test. Therefore, when you implement authorization in your APIs, consider using dedicated classes whose only responsibilities are to receive claims as input and return an authorization result as output. The authorization result can include a Boolean value to allow or deny access. When required, the result can also return conditions to provide further detail on what is allowed.

Example 5-11 shows some updated service logic that authorizes access to a collection of resources. The main service logic no longer works directly with claims and instead asks an authorizer object for decisions. The authorizer returns a result along with an output value that the service logic can pass down to its data access. The data access methods are therefore able to filter using either the customer ID or the region from the authorization result.

Example 5-11. API logic to request authorization decisions

```
public listOrders(authorizer: Authorizer) : OrderSummary[] {

    let result = authorizer.canListOwnedOrders();
    if (result.allowed) {
        return this.repository.getOrdersForCustomer(result.condition.customerId);
    }

    result = authorizer.canListOrdersForRegionalUsers();
    if (result.allowed) {
        return this.repository.getAllOrdersForRegion(result.condition.region);
    }

    return [];
}
```

With this kind of code you place your authorization rules in one place, the authorizer. The authorizer object is responsible for implementing your access policies. In Chapter 9 we say more about the various authorization approaches your APIs can use and also show how you can decouple authorization rules from application code with policy-based authorization.

Once you have completed your API authorization and can adapt to future changes, your API security implementation is almost complete. Now, you should ensure that your APIs also use access tokens reliably. You should account for access token expiration and APIs that call each other. Each API client must receive useful error responses to enable recovery. So next let's discuss ways to manage expiration and retrying of API requests so that users receive a reliable experience.

Handling Token Expiry in APIs

We recommend that you design token expiry in an end-to-end manner so that you enable your APIs and clients to operate predictably and avoid any user experience problems. Access tokens should have a short lifespan (we explain why in Chapter 7); thus they live shorter than your users' sessions.

This means that when the client sends its access token to APIs it expects to eventually receive 401 Unauthorized responses due to access token expiration. To ensure the correct client behavior, APIs must return 401s only when the access token is missing, invalid, or expired. APIs should also return an invalid_token error with the response (e.g., in the WWW-Authenticate HTTP response header) as RFC 6750 recommends. Returning a 401 with invalid_token error from APIs triggers access token refresh or user reauthentication in clients. Therefore, an API should not return 401s for other types of failures. For requests with a valid token that fail business authorization, return a 403 or 404 status code.

When multiple microservices call each other, as part of an end-to-end API workflow, you need to handle various failure conditions to ensure a resilient solution. This includes temporary network failures after one microservice has completed its work. When using zero trust API development, another such failure condition is JWT access token expiration. Figure 5-2 shows an example flow, where the first API completes its work but the access token is expired when the second API receives it. We talk more about best practices of sharing access tokens between services in "Designing Token Sharing" on page 125.

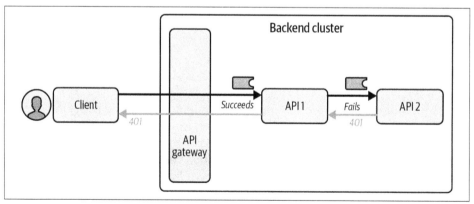

Figure 5-2. Access token expiration during request processing

As an optimization, the client may use the `expires_in` field to refresh the access token before its expiration time. APIs can return 401s for reasons other than expiration, such as when the token got revoked. Therefore, we recommend that API clients use resilient logic to retry API requests with fresh access tokens so that users do not experience problems. The original API client should attempt a token refresh using a generic routine. Figure 5-3 shows what the flow looks like, while Example 5-12 presents how you could implement it in code. This code handles 401s and attempts a token refresh. If the token refresh succeeds, the client can retry the API request. Otherwise, the session has expired and the client must redirect the user to re-authenticate.

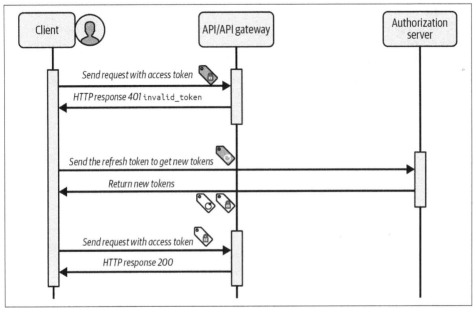

Figure 5-3. Access token refresh flow

Example 5-12. Access token expiration logic in API clients

```
function async callApi(options: ApiRequestOptions): Promise<any> {

    let apiResponse = await callApiWithToken(options);
    if (apiResponse.statusCode === 401) {

        const refreshResponse = await synchronize(() => refreshToken()));
        if (refreshResponse.statusCode != 200) {
            throw ErrorFactory.loginRequired();
        }

        apiResponse = await callApiWithToken(options);
    }
```

```
    if !apiResponse.isSuccessStatusCode()) {
        throw ErrorFactory.apiException(apiResponse);
    }

    return apiResponse.data;
}
```

When API clients are user-facing applications they often render a tree of multiple views. When these views execute they may trigger multiple concurrent API requests. In Example 5-12, the code synchronizes token refresh to avoid sending the request for every view. The synchronize method could queue up a collection of promises, but only send the token refresh request for the first view, then resolve all promises with the same token refresh result. We recommend refresh token synchronization to avoid the possibility of some views sending an invalid refresh token that the authorization server would reject, leading to usability problems in applications. You should therefore be aware of client usage of access tokens so that clients get a good experience when they call your APIs.

An API may sometimes need to act as an OAuth client and call other APIs. You can then use similar retrying techniques in your API code. The most productive way to ensure that you handle expiration conditions resiliently is to rehearse them during development, using automated tests. As an API developer, it can therefore be useful to know how to mock difficult infrastructure when testing OAuth-secured APIs.

Testing Zero Trust APIs

There are many ways to test your API's authorization logic. For example, you should be able to easily unit-test service logic classes productively by just passing in a claims principal object. For each test, you can specify a particular user identity and other claims.

Sometimes you want to test your API's security from outside, by making HTTP requests with access tokens. Real-world OAuth setups can involve complex infrastructure. For example, to get a user-level access token, a client may need to use a browser to trigger an OAuth authorization code flow and a user may need to sign in using multifactor authentication. When you want to focus only on testing your API security logic this is not the most productive way to get an access token.

For a more automated solution you can mock the OAuth infrastructure. One way to do so during development is to again use a security library and implement the following steps:

- Create an asymmetric key pair.
- Use an HTTP server to host a mock JWKS endpoint containing the public key of the asymmetric key pair.
- Configure the API to use the mock JWKS endpoint.
- Use the private key to programmatically issue mock access tokens during each integration test.
- For each integration test, take full control over the access token data and send it to an API endpoint.

Example 5-13 shows some pseudocode to host a JWKS endpoint over HTTP. You can start the HTTP server as part of your test setup before you run a suite of tests and stop the HTTP server as part of your test teardown after all tests finish executing.

Example 5-13. Mock JSON Web Key Set

```
function hostJwks(): string {

    const kid = 1;
    const alg = 'ES256';
    const keypair = new KeypairGenerator().generate(alg);
    keypair.kid = kid;
    keypair.alg = alg;

    httpServer.start(3001);
    httpServer.get('/jwks', keypair.toJwks());
}
```

Once you have a mock setup, each integration test can create mock access tokens with claims needed for that test. This enables you to easily test your API's OAuth logic for different users. The test in Example 5-14 first gets an access token for a customer with which to call an API and then creates an order record. Next, the test gets an access token for a different customer and attempts to get the order record of the original customer. Both access tokens pass JWT validation, but the business authorization for the second API request fails, as expected.

Example 5-14. Example integration test

```
it ('Requesting an item owned by another customer returns not found for user',
async () => {

    const apiClient = new ApiClient(apiBaseUrl);

    const tokenOptions1 = new TokenProperties();
    tokenOptions1.customer_id = '2099';
    tokenOptions1.roles = ['customer'];
```

```
    tokenOptions1.region = 'USA';
    const accessToken1 = await issueMockAccessToken(tokenOptions1);
    const orderId = await apiClient.createOrderForCustomer(
        accessToken1
    );
    assert.equals(statusCode, 201);

    const tokenOptions2 = new TokenProperties();
    tokenOptions2.customer_id = '2817';
    tokenOptions2.roles = ['customer'];
    tokenOptions2.region = 'USA';
    const accessToken2 = await issueMockAccessToken(tokenOptions2);
    const [statusCode, data] = await apiClient.getOrderDetails(
        orderId, accessToken2
    );
    assert.equals(statusCode, 404);
});
```

This technique enables API developers to frequently run a suite of integration tests that verify all of the API's security behavior locally, as part of a secure development lifecycle. When using mock access tokens, do not change any of the API's security code. Ensure that the values in the JWT header and JWT payload have an identical structure to the real tokens your authorization server issues. The only difference should be that a different key pair cryptographically signs the JWT access tokens. Also, combine this developer testing with end-to-end tests that use real access tokens from your authorization server. To end this chapter, let's summarize the behavior of a code example we provide that uses the OAuth behaviors we have explained.

API Code Example

The GitHub repository for this book (*https://oreil.ly/CNDS-supp*) provides a secure API development code example. You can find the example in the folder called *chapter-05-secure-api-development*. Follow the *README* instructions to run and test the API in a standalone manner on a development computer. The API uses Node.js and TypeScript although you could follow the same approach in any other programming language.

Example 5-15 shows the environment variables that serve as configuration settings for the API. These settings include, as we highlight in "Validating JWT Access Tokens" on page 84, the JWKS URI of the authorization server and the values the API expects for algorithm, issuer, audience, and scope when it validates JWT access tokens.

Example 5-15. Configuration settings to cover best practices

```
PORT=3000
JWKS_URI='http://localhost:3001/jwks'
REQUIRED_JWT_ALGORITHM='ES256'
REQUIRED_ISSUER='https://login.example.com'
REQUIRED_AUDIENCE='api.example.com'
REQUIRED_SCOPE='retail/orders'
```

The code example layout separates concerns into several small classes. You can study the code to understand how the techniques we explained might work in a real API:

- The `OrdersController` implements the API's REST logic.
- The `OrdersService` implements the API's main service logic.
- The `OrdersRepository` implements the API's data access logic.
- The `OAuthFilter` implements JWT validation, builds a claims principal, and enforces the API's required scopes.
- The `ClaimsPrincipal` contains the access token claims once validation succeeds.
- The `CodeAuthorizer` uses claims to make attribute-based authorization decisions.
- The `RolePermissions` applies some additional permissions that are not part of the access tokens.

The example demonstrates that you do not have to include every business permission in access tokens. Instead, the example API receives a `roles` claim in access tokens and then looks up finer-grained role permissions from its own data. Although you should include the main identity values in access tokens, you should usually exclude volatile business permissions. We say more about this topic when we explain claims and manageability in Chapter 6.

When you run the code example, also study the tests so that you understand how each test controls the claims within its access token, to cover many success and failure scenarios. The test setup provides a productive way for API developers to frequently test their security. Example 5-16 shows the type of security conditions that can be verified by API developers. You could even publish this type of test report to your stakeholders to ensure that your API security tests cover all important business rules.

Example 5-16. Example test results

✓ A malformed access token results in a 401 status.
✓ An access token with an invalid issuer results in a 401 status.
✓ An access token with an invalid audience results in a 401 status.
✓ An expired access token results in a 401 status.
✓ An access token with an invalid signature results in a 401 status.
✓ An access token with an invalid scope results in a 403 status.
✓ An access token with missing required claims results in a 403 status.
✓ Customers get a filtered list of orders with only their data.
✓ Customers can access details for one of their own orders.
✓ Customers get a 404 status for non-existent order details.
✓ Customers get a 404 status for order details of other customers.
✓ Administrators get a filtered list of orders for their region.
✓ Administrators can get order details for customers in their region.
✓ Administrators cannot get order details for customers in other regions.

Summary

We have explained how the code in OAuth-secured APIs should only ever need to work with JWT access tokens and claims, to enable a productive object-based way of implementing API security. On every request, your APIs need to verify the API message credential and apply authorization logic. Use the following steps for both internal APIs and APIs exposed to the internet so that all of your APIs follow a zero trust approach:

- Validate the JWT access token.
- Enforce required scopes.
- Apply claims-based authorization.

You can scale the coding approach for OAuth-secured APIs to many APIs, yet you also need to scale your scopes and claims design. In Chapter 6 we provide recommendations for designing access tokens, as well as their scopes and claims, so that your OAuth-secured APIs can grow without pain points.

Access Token Design

We can't emphasize enough the importance of the access token. That is why we focus on it for two consecutive chapters. In this chapter, we talk about the token itself, and how to design access tokens to best serve your APIs. In Chapter 7, we cover exposing access tokens to the outside world. We divided the content into two chapters so that you can reference it and get back to it more easily, but we think that you should study both chapters to understand the different aspects of the access token and how they impact your API security.

The access token delivers a set of claims that your APIs use to make authorization decisions. The token can contain the claims as a payload or it can serve as a reference to them. In either case, it is important that you understand what information you will eventually associate with the access token and how your authorization server will retrieve that information during token issuance.

In this chapter, we focus on that design so that your access tokens allow your APIs to authorize requests correctly. We first explain how you use scopes to set security boundaries. We then focus on claims, the fundamental building block that enables fine-grained authorization. We briefly discuss the role of user consent when releasing claims in tokens. We then explain how to scale your access token design to many services with good manageability. Finally, we examine how sharing access tokens between APIs in a microservices architecture influences the token design. By the end of the chapter, you will have a set of techniques for managing zero trust.

Before we dive into the token design itself and talk about scopes and claims, we want you to understand that you should treat the content of the access token as a contract. It is an agreement between architects, identity teams, security teams, API developers, and client developers. This also includes any external integrators that create clients which consume your APIs.

The Access Token Contract

The access token must provide APIs with sufficient identity data to perform detailed authorization decisions. Your APIs enforce authorization decisions and the access token provides the API with data and context that it will use to make those decisions. It is thus the access token's content that can cause the API to allow either overprivileged or underprivileged access. You should design an access token with the least privilege needed to perform a set of related actions in a given context. For example, you might have a mobile app that you want to call your APIs and only read data, not modify it. Therefore, you should ensure that this app gets tokens that allow only read operations on your API, even if the user operating the app could otherwise modify the data. This means that you must design the token with just enough data to satisfy the least-privilege requirement.

Various stakeholders may take an interest in the access token contract:

- API developers must know what information they can get from the access token. They must be able to receive the data that they need to correctly implement business authorization.

- Frontend developers and third-party integrators must know how the token's content relates to the features offered by the API. In other words, API consumers must know how to request tokens that contain enough scope for the application to perform its tasks. For example, if a third-party application must modify user resources, it needs to be able to request an access token that authorizes that action.

- Security teams may be interested in permissions an access token conveys so that they can help to govern access to secure resources.

Developers should be able to read the contract information so that they can reliably work with APIs and tokens.

Publish the Contract

A useful approach is to document the access token contract for all of your APIs, to promote a wider understanding of the API permissions used:

- The scope values that the API requires
- The claims the authorization server adds to the access token when a client requests a given scope
- The data sources for the claims

You might publish a document with these details on your internal developer portal, or allow stakeholders read access to your authorization server's configuration where you defined these values and relations. The important point is to share the information within your organization.

For external integrators, who consume your APIs, there should be a simpler process. These developers need access only to the scope values configured in your system and to the relations between scopes and your API functionality. Tools like the OpenAPI Specification (*https://www.openapis.org*) provide features to document these relations.

Version the Contract

You should be very careful when making changes to the access token contract. If you remove any token claims without informing your stakeholders, it may cause API requests to fail. If you make any changes to the available scopes, it can break both backend and frontend applications and integrations. Even purely technical changes can cause unexpected interruptions. For example, if you change the token format and make the token string considerably larger, it can break clients even if they treat the access token as opaque. If the client stores the access token for later use in a database, for example, changing the token size considerably can overflow the database field.

The contract describing the token's content should by no means be immutable, as this will hinder your potential to enhance your APIs. When you add new APIs or extend existing ones with new features, you may have to update the access token. For example, you may decide to include additional user attributes. You should have procedures in place that allow you to change the access token contract.

Always make changes in a controlled manner and with appropriate governance in place so that you keep any negative impact to a minimum. You will not want to introduce any breaking changes to the access token contract that disrupts your APIs and their clients. Note that while you can assign versions to any documents you use to describe the access token contents, it is not possible to version the access token itself in a standardized way.

The design of the access token contract defines the token content. To implement the token contract, you use two main mechanisms: scopes and claims. We first explain the concept of scopes.

Understanding Token Scope

The token scope, in simple terms, defines which APIs the token bearer will have access to. As we shall see, scopes do not provide a full authorization solution. Instead, scopes set business boundaries for your APIs and clients.

Scopes are an abstract concept that you can implement and enforce in different ways. Very often, people associate it with OAuth's `scope` request parameter but the scope can also result from "Rich Authorization Requests (RAR)" (RFC 9396) (*https:// oreil.ly/xVEKR*). An access token should always have a limited scope; that is, it should always limit what the client can do with a given token. Usually, this will mean limiting which API endpoints or API operations the client can call with the given token. Often, scopes represent business areas. Although it is technically possible to issue access tokens with an unlimited scope, doing so violates the principle of least privilege. Always design tokens with a limited scope.

Always limit the token scope

We can't stress enough how important it is to always limit the scope of an access token. You should never deal with omnipotent tokens, even if you keep them only within your infrastructure. If someone manages to steal such a token, they may be able to do everything they want with your API. Your APIs should always reject tokens that have unlimited scope.

When a client uses OAuth to get tokens, it can use the `scope` request parameter to signal to the authorization server that it wants an access token with particular permissions. How APIs later enforce that scope is not part of the standard and is up to implementers. A common approach is to use scopes to represent business areas to set boundaries on the API endpoints where the client can use the scoped access token. In addition, the authorization server associates the scope of an access token with a set of claims, as we explain in "Understanding Token Claims" on page 110. You use both scopes and their associated claims for your API authorization.

Scopes allow clients to easily request tokens with limited privileges. With OAuth, clients communicate the desired scopes of an access token in the authorization request's `scope` parameter as a space-separated list of values. Client developers need to know only the scope values they can use in their applications and to which functions of an API these values grant access. In other words, the developers will know that requesting a given scope value results in an access token that allows them to call a given set of endpoints. For example, a `retail/inventory` scope might only allow read access to inventory-related endpoints using the GET HTTP method while `internal/ inventory` may allow POST requests from internal clients. We show an example of an authorization request that includes the `scope` parameter in Example 6-1.

Example 6-1. An OAuth authorization request to get an access token limited to inventory and sales information

```
GET https://login.example.com/oauth/v2/authorize
    ?client_id=web-client
    &redirect_uri=https://www.example.com/callback ❶
    &response_type=code
    &scope=retail/inventory retail/sales ❶
    &state=CVZU3iBS7guJi9j8TgkIujj2nfBAjtRQ6jJUrYhLbeNZvnkCCnvPLPK5jErAQEs
    &code_challenge=enhsNFoEQhUy_ZeIQwWgGuBE2fFwRHGXWDCHy5Ln1Wg
    &code_challenge_method=S256 HTTP/1.1
```

❶ Note that normally you would URL-encode query parameters, but we left them unencoded for better readability.

Scopes provide a simplified way for client developers to deliver the correct claims to API endpoints. Client developers do not need to know what claims the authorization server issues to the access token—this information is usually relevant only to API developers. This simple model means that you can change the contents of an access token while the scope value remains unchanged. Client developers do not have to adapt their applications when there are minor changes to the access token contract.

When designing scopes, you need to consider both security and manageability as your APIs grow. We recommend the following best practices:

- Consider designing scopes based on business areas, not technical areas.
- Consider using hierarchical scopes to grant partial access to large business areas.
- Start small and keep your list of scopes short, but do some thinking ahead on how you will grow scopes in the future.

Scopes are strings and you can structure them to make them descriptive (e.g., by adding a separator like / as we show in Figure 6-1). The right-hand side in the example shows technical scopes that represent APIs not business areas. Avoid naming scopes directly after particular services. If you design scopes in too technical a manner, it can result in an unnecessarily large number of scopes. We call this scope explosion and it can result in manageability problems. We say more about this topic in "Managing Access Tokens at Scale" on page 120.

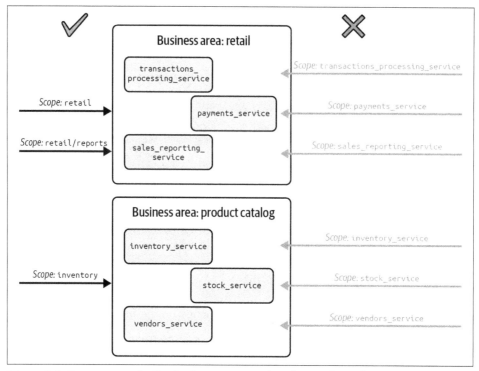

Figure 6-1. Scopes named after business areas rather than technical areas

You should not change the list of available scope values frequently. Add new scope values only when new endpoints do not fit any of the existing scopes. You should never add new scopes for purely technical reasons (e.g., when splitting a large code base into smaller services). It is best to avoid removing scope values or changing the endpoints associated with a given scope value, as this can break existing integrations.

We recommend always using scopes and performing boundary checks to avoid clients being able to call APIs that they obviously should not have access to. This means that you should always issue access tokens with the scope claim, even though the OAuth standard does not mandate it. When designing your scopes, you can use the OpenID Connect specification as a source of inspiration. Let's take a look at the standard user information scopes that OpenID Connect provides.

OpenID Connect Scopes

Clients can request identity data using the OpenID Connect (OIDC) identity protocol (*https://oreil.ly/u0C4M*) that builds upon OAuth 2.0. For that, clients use scopes defined by the specification. The client can request OIDC standard scopes like openid, profile, and email to access the user's ID, name, and email details, respectively. When the client requests scopes, it gains access to the underlying standard claims. For example, the `profile` scope can contain the `given_name` and `family_ name` claims. When the client has sufficient scope, it can retrieve this information in two ways, as we show in Figure 6-2.

- The client can receive user attributes as ID token claims.
- The client can use the access token to get user attributes from the userinfo endpoint.

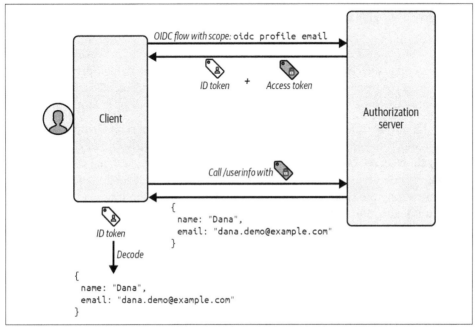

Figure 6-2. Client uses OpenID Connect scopes to access areas of user information

You can use the OIDC approach as an example when designing your scopes. It shows how to manage access based on resource areas, which we highly recommend. You should also be aware that clients can vary the scopes they use, depending on the level of security they need. Let's briefly summarize a couple of ways in which you can manage high privilege scopes.

High Privilege Scopes

In simple cases, a client requests access to all of its scopes and can use the same access token at all API endpoints that the client calls. However, it is common in many front-end applications to ask a user to reauthenticate to confirm a high privilege operation. In OAuth, a client can run with normal privilege scopes by default but request high privilege scopes only when needed. This allows you to design the following types of flows:

- A client runs an initial code flow to trigger user authentication with only normal privilege scopes.
- If the client sends this token to a high privilege API endpoint, the API can return an `insufficient_scope` error.
- The API response can also indicate the required scope, like `retail/orders/payments`.
- The client can then run a second code flow that includes the high privilege scope, to get an elevated access token.
- The client can then successfully call the high privilege API endpoint.

In this example, the client's normal access token does not allow high privilege access. This reduces the impact if such an access token is ever intercepted, since a malicious party cannot use the stolen access token to perform high privilege operations.

This technique is called step up authentication and another reason to use it is to achieve the best balance between security and usability. For the initial code flow, the authorization server might inspect scopes and allow a convenient login method. For the second code flow, the authorization server might inspect scopes and apply logic to require strong multifactor authentication. We say more about how to dynamically change authentication behavior in "Step-Up Authentication" on page 337.

When you design scopes, you should divide your APIs into logical areas. You then need to enforce your business authorization rules for those areas. However, scope values are static and fixed at design time. You will find that they have limited value for business authorization. Claims are much better suited for this purpose since the authorization server populates their values dynamically per user at runtime. Let's explain claims next.

Understanding Token Claims

Claims are access token attributes that carry sufficient information so that your APIs can perform fine-grained authorization. They have the form of a key-value pair, where the key is the claim name. The claim value can have practically any format—it can be a string, a number, a date, an array, an object (map), etc. If the format of the token allows it, a claim could even contain binary data.

An important trait of a claim is the authorization server's assertion of the claim value. Assertion means that given the access token is valid, APIs can trust the claim value to the extent they trust the token issuer. The APIs trust that the authorization server issues correct claims values. APIs do not have to additionally validate the data that they receive in claims. Using the validation techniques that we explain in Chapter 5,

APIs know that claims are asserted by the authorization server and that no one has tampered with the claim values.

Most claims contain information about the token subject, which is usually the user, but there are also claims that describe the token itself. The standard claims come from RFC 7519, the JWT specification (*https://oreil.ly/OybFb*), and RFC 9068, the JWT profile for access tokens (*https://oreil.ly/V8qz7*). We describe the claims in "JWT Standard Claims" on page 87. When you use JWT access tokens in a standardized way, you combine built-in and custom claims.

Claims describing the subject enable APIs to identify users in business terms and perform specific authorization. They enable your APIs to perform dynamic authorization on a per-user basis. Unlike scopes, whose values are static, claims can take any value that the authorization server assigns at runtime. For example, claims about a user can contain a simple value like a user's ID or an array of countries for which you authorize the user to access data. The authorization server can take into consideration, for example, which markets are open at the time of token issuance and adjust the list of countries accordingly.

Claims allow APIs to easily perform fine-grained authorization decisions. For example, a `customer_id` might be a value that you store against order records. When your API receives this claim in an access token, it is straightforward to restrict access to allow the customer access to only the order records that they own. The API can combine the `customer_id` with other claims to enforce its business rules.

With claims, you can lock down the token in practically limitless ways. Claims-based authorization makes it straightforward for APIs to enforce zero trust access and for authorization servers to issue least-privilege tokens with a limited lifetime. In some use cases, this enables you to restrict access to a subset of the user's full permissions or to limit the token's usability to a single API request. For example, you might create an access token as a result of a user's consent to a transaction. The access token would contain claims for the transaction details like a specific transaction ID and the money amount the user has consented to transfer. The client would send the access token to an API, whose authorization could restrict access to that specific transaction. OAuth therefore provides you with a mechanism to give APIs dynamic authorization values that APIs cannot calculate on their own.

Another use case that you can implement using the combination of claim values and short token lifetimes is just-in-time access management. Using this approach you can grant your users access to systems and components only for the time when they actually need it. For example, instead of giving an administrator a database password, which they can easily lose, you might be able to enable access to the database using short-lived access tokens.

As claim values are dynamic, the authorization server needs a means of getting the correct value for a claim. The value does not have to originate from the authorization server's own database. Instead, the authorization server can retrieve it from another trusted source. Through the access token, the authorization server further propagates that trust to other services. We say more about sources for claim values in "Data Sources for Claims" on page 115.

We explained what claims are and how your APIs use them. However, this does not mean you should issue every possible authorization value that your APIs need to access tokens. Instead, it is important to understand what types of values are a good fit for access token claims.

What Constitutes a Good Claim?

Even though claims can have any value, you should take care when you decide which values to issue to tokens. You should remember the access token's purpose—APIs use claims to enable their authorization decisions. This means that you should only add data to a token when it is useful from the authorization point of view. Start with main identity values that provide you with useful information for authorization, such as the following claims:

- `customer_id`
- `tenant_id`
- `roles`
- `country` or `region`

For example, with the customer ID and tenant ID you might quickly verify whether the given user can access specific transactions. On the other hand, consider the following examples that are less likely to be useful as access token claims. Also, since they contain personal information, you should avoid sharing such data with all of your services.

User's home address
> It's unlikely that you will need a user's address to perform authorization. Even if a particular API requires this data, there is usually no need for all services that use the access token to receive this information.

User's email address
> Unless you use the user's email as a system-wide unique identifier then it has limited usability for authorization. It is most likely that only an email-sending service will need email details.

Another aspect that you should consider is the claim value volatility. APIs will trust a claim for as long as the access token itself is valid. This means that values that change often are usually not a good candidate for a claim unless used in a single-purpose token. For example, you should not use a user's account balance or a product's stock level as access token claims since they change far too often. Instead, aim to issue immutable claims to access tokens whose values remain constant for the lifetime of the token.

If you use access tokens with a long lifetime, then even a value that is not especially volatile might not be a good fit for a claim. When you decide to add a claim to the access token, you have to consider what happens when the claim value becomes stale. Remember that claim values are effectively a snapshot from the moment when the authorization server issues the token. You can't change values in the token after the authorization server issues it. Another reason to keep access tokens short lived is to enable your APIs to promptly receive updates to claim values.

Now that you understand how to use both scopes and claims, let's summarize how they relate to each other.

Relation of Claims to Scopes

You can consider each scope to contain a set of claims. Scopes are essentially a short-hand for the client to request a concrete set of claims. For example, when a client requests a `transactions` scope value, it might get an access token with `customer_id` and `subscription_level` claims. When the user calls a service to create transactions, the service can verify whether the user has the required subscription level to create a particular type of transaction. A client requests a token that has a given scope but leaves the final authorization implementation to the service receiving the token. If required, you can issue a claim to multiple scopes. For example, you will usually do this for identifiers such as customer IDs.

The scope itself is a claim issued to an access token. OAuth does not require the access token to explicitly contain the scope values that the client requested. However, RFC 9068 recommends that you add the `scope` claim to your access tokens if the client used the `scope` request parameter when initiating the authorization flow. We recommend that you always add the `scope` claim to your access tokens. Scopes enable your APIs to easily enforce coarse-grained authorization and deny access if they ever receive the wrong type of access token.

APIs should use claims for their main authorization, since an API cannot usually authorize requests correctly using only scope values. When a client requests scopes, it triggers the issuance of an access token with claims, to enable the correct, and least-privilege API access for the client. The meaning of a claim does not usually change, since a `subscription_level` claim always asserts the same property. This is not the case with scopes. For example, over time you may add extra claims to a `retail/transactions` scope, to enable further API access.

Another standardized claim with particular behavior that RFC 9068 mandates is the audience. Let's explain how to use that claim next.

The Audience Claim

An important claim that developers sometimes overlook is the audience claim (aud). The audience claim identifies the intended recipient of the access token. Other parties might be bearers of the token, or handle it in transit, but only the party identified by the audience claim should consume the access token for its intended purpose—request authorization. The audience claim of an access token should identify the API (the resource server) that you call with the token. Very often, the audience value is an API name or base URL. In service-to-service communication it can be common to restrict the audience claim to the identifier of the target service.

APIs should always configure their audience value and reject requests whose access tokens have a different audience. This is especially important if the token is otherwise perfectly valid. The token can have the correct signature, have the expected issuer value, and can even contain all the required claim values that the service needs to authorize the request. However, an unexpected value of the audience claim can mean that:

- When the user consented to issuing the given token, they expected that the client would use it in a different context. The usage of the token in a different context violates the user's consent.

- A malicious actor might be trying to get unauthorized access to resources.

- A client uses a token against its intended purpose. For example, an ID token might happen to contain the right claims that a service needs to authorize a request. Still, an ID token's audience is the client, not the API, and services should never authorize requests secured with ID tokens.

Enforcing audience restriction is an essential behavior for a zero trust API. The API should correctly validate the standard access token claims, even if some might seem irrelevant at first sight. For example, there have been incidents where broken audience claim validation resulted in data breaches for large companies.[1]

Choosing the right value for the audience claim is an important security decision. For a large API, it might be reasonable to create separate audience values for parts of the API that form a cohesive security boundary. If there is a need to give the token a broader scope of access, the audience claim can contain an array of values, as you can see in Example 6-2.

---

1 Aviad Carmel, "Oh-Auth—Abusing OAuth to Take over Millions of Accounts" (*https://oreil.ly/Dv8dU*), *Salt Labs* (blog), Salt Security, October 24, 2023.

Example 6-2. The audience claim can contain a single value or an array of values

```
aud: "https://profile-api.example.com"
aud: ["https://transactions-api.example.com", "https://products-api.example.com"]
```

We recommend using the audience claim to define logical access rather than using the concrete ID of a particular service. Think of it as a set of one or more related APIs that comprise a business area. Using the same audience across multiple related APIs can help to enable token sharing, which we describe in "Designing Token Sharing" on page 125.

In the case of an ID token, which conveys identity information to the client, the audience claim contains the ID of the client. ID tokens are not a good fit for performing authorization, since they do not contain scopes and usually do not contain the correct claims. They also do not have the correct lifetime, their content is not usually confidential, and you cannot refresh ID tokens. If an API ever receives an ID token as the request credential, it must immediately reject the request as part of its audience restriction checks.

Never send an ID token from the client

The ID token delivers verifiable information about the authentication event to the client. Only the client should use its ID token and you should never send the ID token as an API request credential.

We looked at what claims are and how they relate to scopes, but we also mentioned that, unlike scopes, claims get their values dynamically at runtime. This means that you need to retrieve claim values, so let's see where they come from.

Data Sources for Claims

The authorization server assigns claim values to the access token dynamically at runtime. Whenever it issues a token, the authorization server must gather relevant information about the subject to put it in the token's claims. The authorization server should be able to get claim values from various data sources. Examples of possible claims data sources include:

The authorization server's database
    The authorization server usually manages its own database of identity data and stores user accounts containing user attributes, as we explain in Chapter 4. An identity team often owns this data.

An API request

Sometimes it is more convenient to store some user attributes in a separate database and expose it via an API that a different team owns. The authorization server can call an API endpoint, sending its own attributes in the request and receiving external values in the response.

An external identity provider (IDP)

The authorization server can authenticate the user using an external authentication system like an OpenID Connect Provider, and get information about the subject. For example, your authorization server might get the groups or roles for an employee user from an IDP.

Derived from other values

The authorization server can perform transformation procedures on the subject attributes to create new claim values. For example, you can calculate an is_adult claim from the subject's birthdate.

Obtained from the authentication flow

The authorization server can run custom actions during authentication that gather additional data from the authenticated user. For example, the authorization server can ask the user to accept terms and conditions, then use the answer as a claim in the access token.

Figure 6-3 shows how an authorization server can call an API endpoint that returns extra user information. In a cloud native environment, you can keep such an API endpoint internal and additionally protect the connection with infrastructure-level security. For example, you can use workload identities that we explain in Chapter 10 so that the API endpoint accepts only those requests from the authorization server.

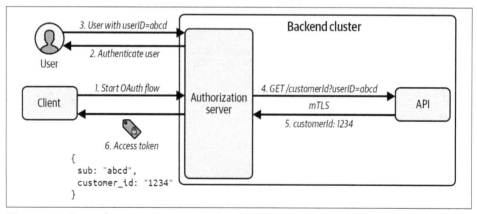

Figure 6-3. An authorization server might obtain some claim values from an external service

Whatever a claim's source, it is the authorization server's responsibility to verify its integrity. The authorization server asserts claim values, so it must trust the source and communicate with it securely. Once a value ends up in an access token, APIs will trust the value and use it to make authorization decisions. APIs should not be concerned with checking the correctness of a claim value—they trust the authorization server on that matter.

You should be able to choose how to manage your claims values, and use whatever data sources work best for you. Maybe you are still migrating to a new solution that uses a centralized authorization server and users' data are in a legacy database, or perhaps you have a regulatory requirement to keep some data in a separate service. The authorization server could manage only minimal information about the user's credentials (like the username and password) to perform authentication and then read additional user data from an external source. It is not uncommon for the authorization server to manage no user data of its own. The authorization server might use an external IDP to authenticate the user and receive all (or most of) the relevant user information. The authorization server's role is then that of a centralized token issuer.

An interesting use case that shows how claim values can originate from authentication is an "act as" scenario. Imagine a customer service operative that needs to act as a customer to investigate technical issues in a frontend application. To enable this, the authorization server could run a custom action after the operative authenticates. The action could prompt for a customer email address, to enable the operative to impersonate the user. The authorization server could then issue an access token with a sub claim that contains the operative's identity and an act_as claim that contains the customer's identity. APIs that receive tokens with such claims can show the customer's data but also change the allowed operations, for example, to allow only read access.

Theoretically, there are no limits as to where claim values could come from. However, you should not overuse external claims data sources. If you need to read a claim from an external source but subsequently only a small number of rarely called services use it, it might be beneficial to let these services get the information themselves. You should take additional care if you plan to get claim values from external APIs that you must reach through a public network. Such calls might impact the latency and throughput of the authorization server's token issuance. They could also create additional points of failure and open new attack vectors. Note that the service-level agreement (SLA) of all the services from which you read data will directly impact the SLA of your token issuance. You should understand the risks and benefits of using external claims data sources.

Whatever claim sources you decide to use, eventually you operate on user information. In some use cases, the client accesses data that belongs to your users. You will want to keep your users informed about how the client uses their personal data. So let's describe how you should ask the user for explicit consent when issuing access tokens.

Obtaining the User's Consent

Very often you (and your organization) will be the same party that supplies both APIs and the clients that call those APIs. In this case, when the authorization server issues access tokens to first-party clients, it does not need to ask the user for explicit consent, which might also confuse the user. Instead, the user enters into an agreement with you when they register an account and accept your terms of use and privacy policies. In a first-party scenario, access tokens only use resources that you or your organization manages.

The situation is different when you issue tokens to third-party clients that operate on API resources that the user owns. In such cases, the authorization server should ask the user to consent to the sharing of areas of data to the third-party client. When you activate user consent, part of your access token design should be to ensure that the consent process is as understandable and simple to the user as possible. Cluttering the consent screen with too much information will probably mean users consent to everything, without giving much thought to what the client requests or needs.

Instead, present a consent screen that provides the user with accurate information about the client and the resources it requests access to. Scope and claim values, though important for API authorization, do not provide a user-friendly description of the access being requested. For example, asking the user if the client can get a token with the `retail/orders` scope is not very helpful. Instead, the authorization server should provide the user with a meaningful description of what the client will be able to do with the resulting token; for example, "Client X will be able to place orders in your name and read your historical orders."

Figure 6-4 shows a well-designed consent screen that GitHub uses. The screen clearly explains what the client will be able to do with the access token and presents additional information about the client that can help the user to decide whether to authorize the client.

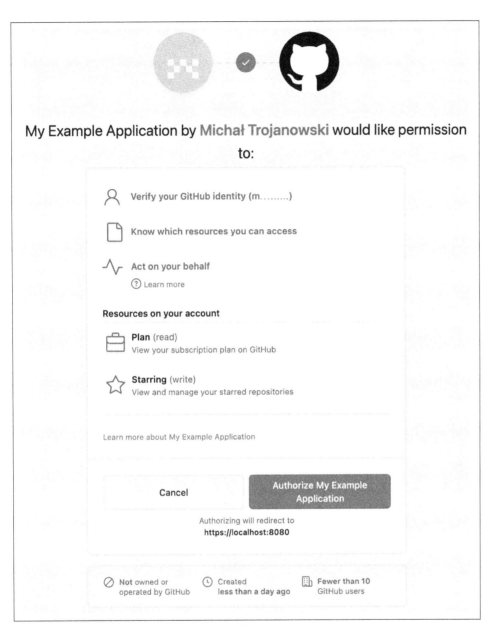

Figure 6-4. Example consent screen from GitHub

Clients usually use refresh tokens to ensure good usability so that users do not have to reauthenticate often. For third-party clients, however, it also means that the client will be able to access the user's resources even after the user stops using the app—for as long as the refresh token is valid. We recommend that applications that need a user's consent also explicitly ask the authorization server for a refresh token (e.g., by asking for an offline_access scope). This way, the authorization server can inform the user on the consent screen that the client will be able to refresh access on its own. The authorization server can also inform the user about the validity period of the refresh token (e.g., inform the user that the application will be able to access their resources for eight hours).

When the client uses an OIDC flow it will get information about the user, either in an ID token or from the userinfo endpoint. In this case, the scope values that the client requests and the claim values that the authorization server issues are personal data returned to the client. The authorization server should clearly inform the user about that fact when collecting consent; for example, "Client X will use your name, e-mail address, and birthdate."

An authorization server can request the user's consent only the first time it issues an access token for the given user and client, and then store it. We sometimes call such a perpetual consent a delegation. The authorization server stores the delegation to record information about the user's consent, such as the scopes and claims that were consented to, for which client, and when the consent took place. In such cases, you should allow your users to manage and remove delegations that they issued to third-party clients. Your authorization server might also provide screens to enable users to revoke their consents. Consider issuing delegations only to confidential clients. Public clients have greater impersonation risks, so it is usually better to ask the user to consent every time a public client initiates a new authorization flow.

Now that we have explained scopes, claims, and user consent we can dive into some additional topics. Let's start by explaining ways to keep scopes and claims manageable as your APIs grow.

Managing Access Tokens at Scale

Designing scopes and claims at scale is not a trivial task. Your APIs may need more and more data to properly authorize requests. This type of complexity can increase as you grow your APIs. Without care, it can put a strain on various stakeholders:

- Architects have to grasp the full picture of all scopes and claims that your system uses.

- The identity team gets swamped with requests to add, change, or remove scopes and claims.

- Both API and client developers may need to wait for an identity team to implement the requested changes.

- Both API and client developers may have to implement versioning logic and testing, to cover both old and new access tokens.

A solid approach to designing scopes and claims is therefore essential for you to achieve both the correct authorization and good manageability. You can run into problems with OAuth if you design scopes that do not scale. Therefore, let us explain how to scale scopes.

Scaling Scopes

When designing scopes in your system, start with a short list of scopes that you should map to business areas. We recommend using hierarchical formatting for scope values. In this book we use the forward slash (/) as a separator, though you might prefer to use a colon (:) character. You can also use Uniform Resource Names (URNs) (*https://oreil.ly/MGXFU*) (e.g., `urn:myorganization:finance:reporting`) or a URI with an HTTPS scheme (e.g., `https://scopes.myorganization.example/finance/reporting`—note that this does not have to be a URL). You can choose any format you like, but be consistent so that scopes remain understandable and easy to use across all APIs and clients.

Divide your APIs into blocks that span functional areas and assign each block scope values. Once you have the initial list, you can team up with architects and security specialists to explore ways in which you might grow scopes in the future. For example, you might work at an organization that sells products or services to both public and commercial customers. You might have different APIs that you target at these two groups of customers. You could start with a simple list of high-level scopes that use a basic hierarchical structure to separate your API functionally such as the following:

- `retail/sales`
- `commercial/sales`
- `commercial/legal`

You might then decide that some endpoints need more fine-grained access control. You might add some analytics endpoints that only your internal clients should consume. You could then further expand the hierarchical structure of your scopes. The overall scopes should be visible to stakeholders and enable governance of the level of resource access. After modifications, your list might look like this:

- `retail/sales`
- `retail/sales/pricing`

- `retail/sales/analytics`
- `commercial/sales`
- `commercial/sales/support`
- `commercial/legal`
- `commercial/legal/policies`

It is possible to use verbs so that scopes represent both an area of data and permissions on that data. For example, you might use `retail/sales/read`, `retail/sales/write`. In some use cases, a read scope can help to ensure that a user can only ever perform safe operations. In many business systems, however, there can be many fine-grained rules within a single business area that determine the precise values a user can view or edit. In such cases, read and write scopes are not a good fit.

One particular problem to avoid is what we call scope explosion—a situation where you end up with so many scopes in your system that it's hard to manage and utilize them. This can add unnecessary complexity for both client and API developers. Figure 6-5 shows an example of scope explosion when there is insufficient design and governance. In this particular example, the cause of scope explosion is the use of verbs in scope names.

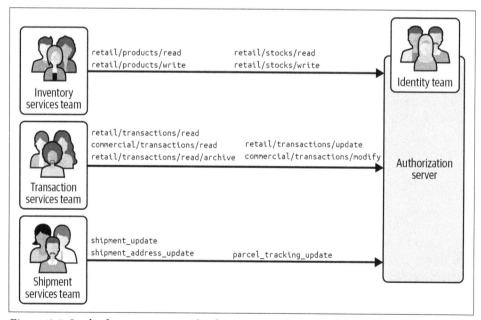

Figure 6-5. Lack of governance can lead to scope explosion and inconsistencies in scope formats

Another cause of scope explosion is when you use scopes where you should use claims. For example, a developer new to OAuth might initially create scopes based on runtime values, such as a region, to produce `transactions/usa` and `transactions/europe`. This type of approach is usually a sign of an incorrect scope design. A correct design would be to issue a `transactions` scope that contains a `region` claim. If your scopes look similar to those in the following list, it is usually a sign of a suboptimal scope design:

- `transactions/usa`, `transactions/europe`
- `transactions/archive`, `transactions/future`
- `transactions/shipments/packages/read`, `transactions/shipments/packages/write`
- `admin`, `customer`
- `customer_transactions_service`, `transactions_search_service`

A solid scope design should not feel complex. Instead it should be businesslike and understandable to stakeholders. The scope design should also prevent confusion for client developers, who might request too broad a scope if they do not understand the meaning of scopes. Therefore, keep the list of available scope values reasonably short at first, based on the slices of your hierarchical business data that a client needs access to. If you have very large APIs that use multiple scopes, create tools that help developers to easily find scope values and understand their usage.

Scope values change over time and one option is to use an additive approach. For example, you might start with a `retail/sales` scope used by a customer-facing application, where that scope represents the main customer privileges. Later, you may need to add an internal client that your customer support team uses. You might assign it a `retail/sales/support` scope and require that scope at new API endpoints used for technical support purposes. You might then assign new claims to the new scope, and update API authorization at the new endpoints. You might optionally decide to change the original scope in the customer application. However you evolve scopes, the outcome should be that both customers and support staff operate with least API privilege.

Once you understand how to scale scopes and also keep them manageable, you should aim for the same qualities for claims. Let's explain some considerations when you scale claims.

Scaling Claims

As you grow your scopes, you will also add new claims to enable new types of authorization decisions and assign the new claims to scopes. When doing so you should continue to keep the client's access token privileges restricted and also enforce the correct authorization rules on every API request. The access token helps to enable authorization but scaling claims is also a balancing act. Without care, as the number of claims grows it can become difficult to maintain all of them in the authorization server. When you design claims, you should therefore avoid claims explosion—where the authorization server becomes overly coupled to volatile business data.

When designing claims, remember what we said in "What Constitutes a Good Claim?" on page 112. Claims that are a core part of the user identity, stable, and used by multiple APIs for authorization are a good choice to issue to access tokens. If only one API uses a particular claim for authorization, then looking up its value in the API can be a more manageable option than receiving the claim in the access token. This is especially true if the authorization server does not store the claim's value and would have to read it from a remote source.

Some types of claims are derivable from values in the access token. For example, you might receive a role in an access token. That role might have many fine-grained permissions. The following list shows some example fine-grained permissions that you might associate to a role:

- can_update_delivery_comments
- can_order_courier1_shipment
- can_read_special_products
- can_update_related_transactions

You should not usually issue all of those values to the access token, since you are likely to frequently change or redesign such permissions. If you design a claim name with can_ it should raise a red flag. It is not the authorization server's responsibility to keep track of every fine-grained business permission. If you configure those in the authorization server, you may need to frequently update the authorization server when those values change, leading to unwelcome deployment dependencies between API and identity teams. Instead, use claims that represent user attributes or runtime context and manage volatile business permissions in your APIs.

Use authorization values only from trusted sources

In simple systems, claims in the access token may be sufficient for an API to implement its complete authorization. In more complex systems, with many fine-grained business permissions, you might need additional information, other than the token claims, to make authorization decisions. For example, you could read some extra data from the service's own database, or you could call another service to get that data. Whenever you do so, make sure that you always trust the source of that additional data and never elevate the token's privileges. Never accept authorization values as input, such as in headers or query string parameters.

In a microservices architecture, you also need to design how to use scopes and claims when APIs call each other. In such an environment, a single request from a client can result in multiple service calls that must all perform authorization. In the next section, we describe some techniques that you can use to share tokens and continue to operate with least privilege.

Designing Token Sharing

To adhere to the zero trust principle, whenever multiple services handle one client request, you must propagate the user's identity and other claims to each service. The easiest solution is to just forward the original access token that the client sends. You can design the access token with sufficient data for each service to authorize the request. The user identity and other claims remain verifiable as APIs call each other.

However, scaling this approach can become difficult when your APIs comprise many services. When you forward the original access token, it means that every service that receives the token can perform all of the operations that the client can perform. Without care, this can lead to services receiving overprivileged access tokens, even when they don't have a need for such a token.

A malicious actor who manages to intercept an access token in just one of those services may be able to successfully call many API endpoints. The risk may be greater when the request crosses departmental boundaries and less trusted APIs use the access token. To alleviate this concern, let's take a look at how OAuth enables you to reduce an access token's privileges before calling an upstream API.

Token Exchange

When you need to call an upstream service, you can use "OAuth 2.0 Token Exchange" (RFC 8693) (*https://oreil.ly/T2coC*) to obtain a new access token with a reduced scope. Doing so maintains the user's identity and other claims, so that they remain verifiable, while also reducing the access token's privileges. The new token can contain reduced scopes and claims, with only those needed by upstream APIs. Figure 6-6 demonstrates the technique.

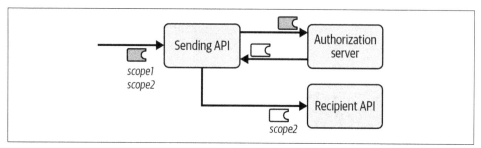

Figure 6-6. You can use token exchange to dynamically transform access tokens and reduce privileges

When you use token exchange, you design how an access token changes in an end-to-end flow that starts with the original client. Usually, you will want the new token to have the same or a narrower scope than the original token. You should ensure that services cannot use the new access token to call your external API endpoints directly. For example, the authorization server might issue a different value for the audience claim for internal tokens.

There are scenarios where you might want to broaden the access token scope during token exchange. For example, you might have a reporting service that you don't want your clients to be aware of. Your services can perform a token exchange to get an access token for the same user with a scope that allows you to call the reporting service, as we show in Figure 6-7. This results in a new access token with greater permissions.

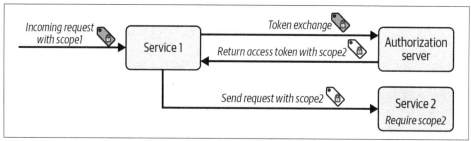

Figure 6-7. Elevating token privileges during token exchange

You should avoid this approach when you activate user consent and the upstream API operates on user resources, since you would then operate outside of the user's consent. You should always be extra cautious if you use token exchange to get a new access token with a broader scope, to ensure that you do not introduce security vulnerabilities. An alternative option, which may perform better, is to use an embedded tokens approach.

Embedding Tokens in Tokens

You use embedded tokens when you issue a child access token as a custom claim within a parent access token. In some cases, multiple services might then use the same embedded access token. The embedded token approach helps you to save resources, as services no longer need to call the authorization server to perform token exchange.

Consider a scenario where you have multiple services that call a third-party logging service and all of your services need the same access token to call that service. In such a case, your authorization server may enable you to run custom logic to get the third-party access token when it issues the main access token. In Example 6-3, you can see an example embedded token. The `logging_service_token` claim contains another access token (truncated for display purposes) that each service can extract and send to the third-party service. The embedded token can have any format—it can be an opaque token or a JWT.

Example 6-3. Example of a JWT payload with an embedded access token

```
{
    "scope": "retail/transactions",
    "aud": "https://api.myorganization.example",
    "sub": "37ddb753-ef9c-4f9b-9029-375a2f74440d",
    "iat": "1727792520",
    "exp": "1727792820",
    "logging_service_token": "eyJhbGciOiJFUzI1NiJ9.eyJhdWQ...yNTIwfQ.S1WDc...B2pG_Q"
}
```

Once you understand token sharing concepts, you may sometimes need to deal with use cases where your APIs call another organization's APIs or vice versa. Let's summarize how that works in an OAuth architecture.

API Integrations

It is common to need to design API integrations that sometimes involve more than one identity system. We want to provide you with an OAuth thought process to briefly explain the main categories of solution and the design principles that you can use when you face such a requirement.

Consider a common B2B use case where a client organization needs to get data from your APIs to show in its frontend applications. To enable this, the client organization must get an access token from your authorization server. There are two main types of OAuth flow that the client organization could use:

- In some cases, the access token does not need a user identity, so you should enable the client organization's APIs to use the client credentials flow to call your authorization server. You might configure your authorization server to issue an access token that contains a `tenant_id` claim. The customer's APIs then make remote requests to your APIs and its frontend clients should have no awareness that its APIs use external access tokens.

- In other use cases, you might implement a B2B2C model, where your APIs have a direct relationship with users from external organizations. Typically, your APIs store user-specific resources that you partition per tenant. In such cases, to get a user-level access token, you should enable the client organization's clients to run a code flow against your authorization server. You might configure your authorization server to issue an access token that contains a `tenant_id` claim and a `sub` claim.

Other API integrations that involve multiple access tokens can take place within a single organization. For example, you might replace an old identity system with a new authorization server. If you have a large number of clients and APIs, you could decide to implement a phased migration and use a bridging solution where clients that use one identity system can call APIs secured by the other identity system. In such a case you should be aware of authorization grants called *user assertions*, which may enable you to swap an existing access token to get a new access token suitable for the target API. Read more about this flow in the "JSON Web Token (JWT) Profile for OAuth 2.0 Client Authentication and Authorization Grants" specification (RFC 7523) (*https://oreil.ly/arCWh*).

We summarized how OAuth can scale across organizations. You can read more about techniques in the "OAuth Identity and Authorization Chaining Across Domains" draft specification (*https://oreil.ly/5q088*). To finish up our content on access token design, let's consider business authorization when an API uses asynchronous communication to notify upstream services.

Tokens for Asynchronous Communication

Most commonly, microservices call each other synchronously where you send a request and wait for the response. Yet sometimes you may use other messaging patterns to call upstream APIs. Operations can be "fire-and-forget" where the sender does not receive a result. The result can also be returned asynchronously, at a later time. For asynchronous communication, it is common for an API to use a message broker (e.g., Kafka, Hermes, or RabbitMQ) and publish events to the broker. The broker then forwards a response to one or more recipients, who subscribe to particular types of events.

In some cases, event messages may introduce additional threats. For example, an attacker might be able to publish a malicious event message that triggers updates to an unauthorized area of your business data. Subscribers might process event messages without authorization to enable the exploit to succeed. In a zero trust architecture you should be able to send access tokens in event messages to protect against this type of threat in the same way as for synchronous communication. Recipients could then verify the integrity and provenance of received identity data and apply business authorization before processing event messages.

However, if you forward an access token using asynchronous communication, the broker might publish events with a delay so that the access token expires by the time the recipient processes the request. Unlike with synchronous requests, the original client is no longer present to retry and recover the operation. Unfortunately, there are no OAuth standards for asynchronous service-to-service communication, but you can utilize known techniques to create bespoke solutions.

One solution that we recommend for secure asynchronous communication is to use the token exchange standard.[2] The publishing API can ask the authorization server to exchange the original short-lived access token for a long-lived access token that has a very limited scope. During the token exchange, you could issue extra claims to the new access token to bind the token to a specific event message or transaction. Figure 6-8 shows an example flow.

---

[2] You can read a more detailed explanation of our asynchronous service-to-service approach in our article "Zero Trust API Events" (*https://oreil.ly/vdL3T*).

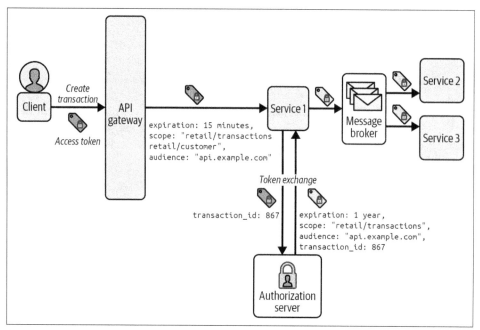

Figure 6-8. You can use token exchange to secure asynchronous communication in APIs

This type of solution may be difficult to manage if you design scopes in too technical a manner, such as a different scope per API. If you follow our recommendations of designing scopes per business area, you should find it easier to flow tokens between asynchronous microservices. Your APIs should only process long-lived (reduced privilege) access tokens at messaging endpoints, and short-lived (full privilege) access tokens at HTTP endpoints. One technique you can use to manage the different types of tokens is to change the audience during the token exchange.

There are a number of other aspects to consider when designing a zero trust solution for asynchronous communication. You should secure the message store so that no one can inspect messages, extract access tokens, and replay them against APIs. Also, if your message broker replays event messages at a much later time, there may be new token signing keys that prevent recipients from validating access tokens. The extra call to perform token exchange will also affect the throughput of your event messages. A complete solution to authorize asynchronous communications may therefore be nontrivial.

We recommend that you do some design thinking about unauthorized access when your APIs process asynchronous messages that operate on business data. You could design bespoke solutions, which might vary depending on the security impact of each message type. Access tokens and token exchange are building blocks that you should consider.

Summary

By now you should understand that access token design requires care. Authorization is the most crucial part of your API security. Well-designed access tokens with useful claims enable APIs to correctly enforce your authorization policies with straightforward code. You should also be able to set security boundaries between APIs and keep the overall use of access tokens manageable and understandable.

To design access tokens for your use cases, start with scopes. Keep the list small but do some thinking ahead on how you will scale them across multiple APIs in the future. Next, consider the most important claims your APIs need to receive in access tokens that the authorization server issues. Also, consider which fine-grained business permissions you will look up in your APIs. Finally, do some thinking on how you will share access tokens between APIs. Once you have these foundations, you can scale your use of access tokens to many future use cases.

This chapter underlines the importance of a centralized token issuer. The authorization server collects and asserts the data issued to access tokens, to grant clients access to your business resources. It is vital that you handle these business permissions in a manageable, observable, and governable way. Issuing your access tokens from a single trusted source helps to enable this.

We have now explained the key thought processes you should use when designing access tokens. Our deep dive into access tokens continues in Chapter 7, where we focus on access token usage patterns and how the client environment impacts the security of access tokens.

Secure Access Tokens

Access tokens are essentially text strings that serve as message credentials. In some ways, access tokens are similar to API keys but access tokens are much more versatile, offering features such as expiration, limited scope of access, or revocation. They enable an end-to-end security solution that meets the main security requirements of both APIs and clients.

In our experience, developers and architects do not often fully understand the best practices for using access tokens securely. Therefore, in this chapter, we provide an end-to-end set of security requirements for your access tokens that considers both APIs and clients. We explain the different token formats you can use so that clients receive access tokens that do not reveal sensitive data, while APIs receive access tokens that enable them to authorize requests correctly. We then describe how to deliver access tokens from clients to APIs and translate between token formats. Finally, we explain the options you have for increasing the security strength of access tokens and reducing the impact of any token breaches. We show that, with the right separation, you can use the most secure options without adversely affecting either APIs or clients.

Let's get started by providing a list of the main requirements for secure access tokens.

Secure Access Token Requirements

Access tokens play a vital role in the security of your APIs. The main role of access tokens is to provide your APIs with the data they need to authenticate and authorize requests as we explain in Chapter 6. Used correctly, this helps you to prevent the vulnerabilities listed in the OWASP API Security Top 10 (*https://oreil.ly/Wtktr*). Broken authorization is a top concern on the OWASP list.

Securing APIs with access tokens is not just about the token's content or proper validation rules. You must also account for how each type of client protects access tokens. Without care, access tokens, like any other message credential, can become a vulnerability. Access tokens are often bearer tokens, so if an attacker intercepts a token they can impersonate a user and call your APIs to steal data. Access tokens can also unintentionally reveal sensitive data, such as user information or technical data that an attacker could abuse. To correctly handle both API and client concerns, you should meet the following main security requirements:

- APIs accept access tokens only from a trusted token issuer.
- APIs are able to verify the integrity of access tokens.
- APIs receive access tokens containing the claims they need for business authorization.
- Clients receive access tokens in a format that makes it impossible to read the tokens' claims.
- Clients transport access tokens using security best practices for their environment.
- The authorization server uses established security standards to issue access tokens.
- The authorization server issues least-privilege access tokens to limit the impact of exploits.
- The authorization server issues access tokens with a short lifetime to limit the impact of exploits.
- You are able to prevent the use of compromised tokens when there is an exploit.

To meet all the requirements you need to consider more than just the API's view of access tokens. Let's start by explaining the access token formats you can use.

Access Token Formats

The authorization server should be able to issue tokens to clients in either a by-value or by-reference format. By-value tokens such as JSON and CBOR Web Tokens[1] are self-contained so that a recipient can decode them and read their claims. They allow the API to validate the token without contacting the authorization server. By-reference tokens serve as a reference to the token's data that the authorization server keeps securely. This means that APIs need to resolve such tokens by calling the

---

1 "CBOR Web Token (CWT)" (RFC 8392) (*https://oreil.ly/V2O18*).

authorization server to get the token claims. Authorization servers can issue both access and refresh tokens in a reference token format, to keep them confidential.

Token format names

In literature, you will find many names for the two token formats we describe here. For example, for reference tokens authors can use names like "handle tokens," "by-reference tokens," "opaque tokens," "artifact," etc. For by-value tokens, you will find names such as "self-contained tokens" or "assertions." All these names describe the same two formats. In the case of token formats, it is important to convey the characteristics of the format (whether the token contains data or references it) regardless of the actual word you use.

There are multiple formats for by-value and by-reference tokens, so let's inspect the most common ones, starting with the most common type of by-value token—JWTs.

JWT Access Tokens

"JSON Web Token (JWT) Profile for OAuth 2.0 Access Tokens" (RFC 9068) (*https:// oreil.ly/UdJQ1*) standardizes how to utilize the JSON Web Token (JWT) format for OAuth access tokens. JWTs enable multiple security features that API developers and testers can use productively, to verify their API security frequently. Consequently, JWTs became the mainstream format for by-value tokens.

A JWT access token can provide sensitive information that enables an API to perform its authorization. For example, an access token might contain the current user's age information, insurance policy number, marital status, or credit rating. JWTs are also integrity-protected by a digital signature that you can validate in almost any API technology.

Technical Limitations

Some technologies might have limitations as to which cryptographic algorithms you can use. Sometimes you will not have an implementation for a newer algorithm in a programming language or environment. Usually, this will not be a concern, but you may have to adapt. For example, you may have to use an older cryptographic algorithm instead of changing the whole technology stack.

JWTs come with an inherent security issue. Unless encrypted, the content of a JWT is readable to anyone in possession of the token. This means that clients, or even users who trace HTTP requests, might also be able to read the claims intended for APIs. The lack of confidentiality in JWTs leads to two main problems. Firstly, it can result in information disclosure and privacy violations when unauthorized parties parse the content. Users and operators may not be aware of this disclosure. Secondly, if a client relies on the content of the JWT, the token becomes an interface between the authorization server and the client application. Changing anything in the API's access token can then lead to unexpected behavior in its clients.

To solve these problems you must ensure that you keep the contents of access tokens confidential. A first attempt might be to encrypt the JWT access token, so let's see how that would work.

Encrypted JWT Access Tokens

One way to prevent clients from reading JWT access tokens is to encrypt them to form another type of by-value token. "JSON Web Encryption (JWE)" (RFC 7516) (*https://oreil.ly/gFIgI*) is a standard that describes how to encrypt JWTs. When you encrypt tokens your authorization server ensures that only the final recipient can read its content, but not any clients or endpoints that might handle the token in transit. Encrypting the token protects its content by making it unreadable to any bearers and intermediaries. Although this solves the confidentiality problem for clients, JWT encryption also introduces problems for APIs.

To encrypt JWTs, you must manage additional keys. You need to deploy the encryption key to your authorization server so that it can encrypt the JWTs that it issues. You also need to deploy the corresponding decryption key to your APIs so that they can decrypt received JWT access tokens. In addition, as a security best practice you must rotate encryption keys, which adds additional burden of key management. When you use encrypted JWTs, it adds complexity for developers and testers since they also need to use extra keys. The encryption techniques are less well supported in API technology stacks and online documentation. The JWE cryptography is also more complex at a code level and could lead to developers making security mistakes.

So although encrypted JWT access tokens meet the client requirement, they add undue overhead to the API side of your architecture. We believe you should use JWT encryption only in specific scenarios, such as when there is no other way to protect the content of access tokens, when regulations require it, or when it is crucial to verify tokens without having to call the authorization server. Still, we think that opaque tokens provide a simpler solution.

Opaque Access Tokens

An opaque token is the most common type of by-reference tokens. The token has a form of a random alphanumeric string. Such a token does not carry any sensitive information and instead acts as a pointer to data that the authorization server securely stores. No party that receives such a token can read its claims directly from the token. Figure 7-1 illustrates how an opaque (by-reference) token provides optimal token confidentiality for clients compared to JWT (by-value) access tokens.

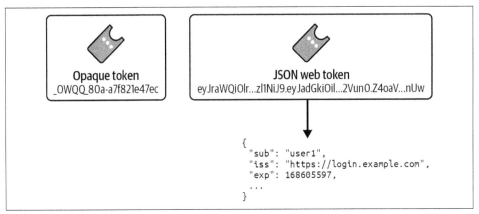

Figure 7-1. Opaque versus JWT tokens

Since an opaque token is just a random string, your authorization server must ensure that it creates the token with sufficient entropy so that a brute-force attack cannot guess a valid access token. When a client sends an opaque access token to your APIs, the API must then send it to the authorization server to read the underlying claims. If the token is valid, the authorization server returns the claims which the API can use for its business authorization.

Sufficient Opaque Token Entropy

At the time of writing, the best practice in order to get secure opaque tokens is to generate them with at least 128 bits of entropy using cryptographically safe random string generators.[2] However, things can change quickly in the cryptography space, so you should always check the current recommendations.

Using opaque access tokens introduces scalability problems to your API architecture. To conform with zero trust principles for securing APIs, every API in the request chain must independently authorize the request; thus, it must validate the token it receives. This means that potentially many services will call the authorization server to verify the same token. We explain how to overcome this challenge shortly. First, let's finish up the discussion on token formats with wrapped opaque tokens.

---

2 "Threat: Guessing Access Tokens" (*https://oreil.ly/-Q3bF*), Section 4.6.3 of "OAuth 2.0 Threat Model and Security Considerations" (RFC 6819).

Wrapped Opaque Access Tokens

Wrapped opaque tokens are by-reference tokens issued in the JWT format, with a payload that contains only some of the token metadata. The minimal JWT allows you to keep sensitive data private but retain some advantages of a JWT. Figure 7-2 shows a wrapped opaque token that contains a minimal JWT payload.

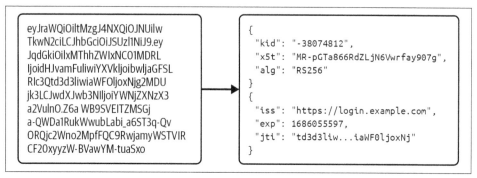

Figure 7-2. Wrapped opaque token example; the token payload contains minimum information required to further process the request

When an API receives a wrapped opaque token, it can first verify the signature and the metadata claims. For example, it can check whether the token is expired or if it comes from an expected issuer. When the initial validation passes, the API sends the whole JWT to the authorization server to get the underlying claims. One use case where wrapped opaque tokens are valuable is when an API accepts tokens from different authorization servers. This might be common in particular industries, such as the health sector. Since the wrapped token identifies the issuer, the API knows which authorization server to call to get the token's claims.

Another use case for wrapped opaque tokens is for middlewares that route requests to APIs. For example, with wrapped opaque tokens you can meet data sovereignty requirements, where you must store user transactions in a particular region for legal reasons. To enable this, you might issue a region claim to a wrapped opaque access token. An API gateway might validate the JWT and then trust its region claim. The gateway could then apply some logic to ensure that it sends the API request to the correct region for a user. Figure 7-3 illustrates the flow. In a similar manner, you can use a wrapped opaque token when you have a multitenant API. With the help of the metadata the token contains, you can direct the request to a concrete tenant's API.

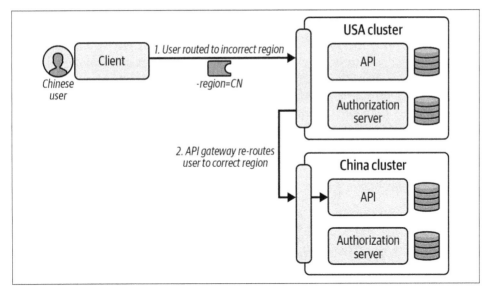

Figure 7-3. Dynamic user routing

When you decide to use wrapped opaque tokens, you should only ever put token metadata in the JWT payload so that the token does not carry any personal information about the user. However, the token will still contain some information. That means you must remain cautious when you design the token's content. Make sure not to reveal any information about the infrastructure that may become useful to a potential attacker.

Wrapped opaque tokens have the same scalability problem as ordinary opaque tokens. In a zero trust architecture, any API that uses the token must ask the authorization server for the underlying claims data. If multiple services process the request, every one of them has to ask the authorization server for that data. We have identified that opaque tokens work well for clients but not for APIs. To solve this problem and provide the most useful tokens for zero trust APIs you need to properly design access token delivery. We focus on that topic next.

Access Token Delivery

Now that you understand token formats, you can use them to meet the secure access token requirements of both APIs and clients. Ideally, you should issue opaque access tokens to clients but deliver JWT access tokens to APIs. To enable this, your APIs must be able to translate from one token format to another. By default, APIs process opaque tokens using OAuth 2.0 introspection.

Introspection

"OAuth 2.0 Token Introspection" (RFC 7662) (*https://oreil.ly/AE_2Y*) describes a standard for exchanging opaque tokens into their underlying claims. Since this is one of the standards from the OAuth canon, many authorization servers support this protocol. The specification describes an endpoint exposed by the authorization server and the request and response format for the exchange. To use introspection, an API would send an HTTP POST to the introspection endpoint of the authorization server. Example 7-1 illustrates this.

Example 7-1. Introspection request

```
POST https://login.example.com/oauth/v2/introspect HTTP/1.1
Content-Type: application/x-www-form-urlencoded
Accept: application/json
Authorization: Basic am9iLWNsaWVudDpVMlU5RW5TS3gzMWZZVbnZnRwo=

token=_0XBPWQQ_f68d15de-637d-47a3-acfd-cab2410cd2e6
```

The introspection response is a JSON document that contains the claims associated with the opaque token. This is usually the same data that a JWT payload contains. The receiving API can trust this data since it comes directly from the authorization server through a trusted backend connection that uses TLS. An API can create a claims principal from the introspection response and then proceed with its business authorization, as we explain in Chapter 5.

To reduce load, an API that uses introspection should combine it with result caching. The authorization server is a critical component, so you should avoid calling it on every API request. For example, when introspection succeeds, your API can add a cache entry for the access token, with a hash of the token as a cache key and the claims as the cache value. You then assign the cache entry a time-to-live, and it is best to ensure that this time does not exceed the token's expiry—the exp claim value from the introspection response. On subsequent API requests with the same access token, you can look up the introspection response from the cache and avoid calling the authorization server.

Only the API that received the introspection response directly from the authorization server can trust the response claims. In a zero trust architecture, you cannot use the JSON response as a credential when microservices call each other. No other API should trust claims from a JSON because it cannot verify the document integrity without a cryptographic signature from the authorization server. Thus, a misbehaving API could alter or make up the JSON before forwarding it to another API. Therefore, every service should receive the opaque token and perform introspection to align with zero trust best practices. Figure 7-4 shows an example with multiple introspection requests for the same access token.

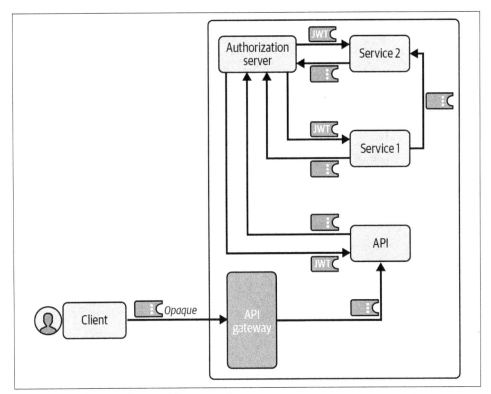

Figure 7-4. Microservices and introspection

Using introspection directly in APIs is not optimal because you need to register each API as an OAuth client with introspection permissions. You should therefore aim to avoid writing code to introspect access tokens in your APIs and have APIs validate JWTs. Next, we provide a couple of security design patterns you can use to issue clients with opaque access tokens, then deliver JWT access tokens to each of your APIs.

The Phantom Token Pattern

The phantom token pattern is an approach that enables you to combine the best features of both opaque tokens and JWTs. In this pattern, the authorization server always issues an opaque token to the client. When the client calls APIs, an API gateway runs a dedicated plug-in that performs token introspection. Instead of returning the introspection response in a JSON payload, the authorization server returns a signed JWT containing the claims for the opaque token.

The API gateway then updates the request's Authorization header to replace the opaque access token with a JWT, before routing the request to the API. The gateway also caches the introspection results to avoid calling the authorization server for every API request. From the client's viewpoint, the token used has no security information and is only a *phantom* of the claims received by the API. We illustrate the flow in Figure 7-5.

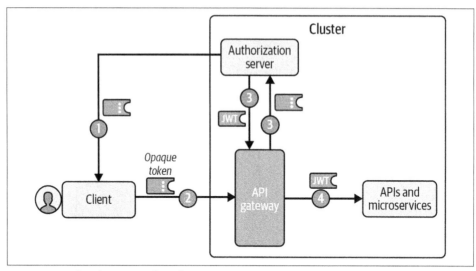

Figure 7-5. The phantom token flow

This flow solves several problems. It provides security and privacy benefits, since the token reveals no information intended for APIs to external or third-party clients. The flow also enables you to deliver a cryptographically verifiable message credential (the JWT access token) to your APIs. When required, each API can also forward the cryptographically verifiable access token to any upstream APIs. Therefore, it enables you to meet the following requirements:

- APIs accept access tokens only from a trusted token issuer.
- APIs are able to verify the integrity of access tokens.
- APIs receive access tokens containing the claims they need for business authorization.
- Clients receive opaque access tokens and are unable to read their claims.
- The authorization server uses established security standards to issue access tokens.

In addition to security, the flow provides some other useful behaviors. Since introspection is just a utility task and does not affect API security, it is best when your infrastructure performs it rather than your API code. API developers and testers can then work conveniently with JWTs and do not need to use opaque tokens at all. The gateway caching also ensures good performance and avoids calling the authorization server too often.

In Chapter 8, we show how to extend an API gateway with plug-ins. We provide an example phantom token plug-in so that you can study how to implement one and manipulate HTTP requests. We also provide a code example that you can run on a development computer to understand the deployment steps. In some cases, there could be alternative ways to meet the phantom token requirements. For example, an authorization server might provide a token exchange capability to enable swapping opaque access tokens for JWTs, instead of using token introspection.

We recommend using the phantom token in your systems to meet the requirements that we mentioned before. In most cases, there should be no obstacles to using this pattern. Although there are some specific setups in which you could use a variation of the pattern—the split token pattern.

The Split Token Pattern

The split token pattern is a variant of the phantom token pattern. It serves the same purpose: to issue opaque access tokens to external clients while delivering JWT access tokens to APIs. In this setup, the API gateway does not have to call the authorization server to introspect the token, so you can use the pattern when latency is your priority. You can also use it in a multicluster environment, when not all clusters that host your APIs also host the authorization server, to minimize cluster-to-cluster traffic.

In the split token pattern, you split the JWT into two parts: the header and payload comprise one part and the token signature the other. The token signature serves as the opaque access token that the authorization server returns to the client. Thus, you do not expose any sensitive data to the client, as the client only ever handles the opaque token. The authorization server also hashes the signature part and sends that together with the other part of the JWT—the header and payload—to the API gateway. The gateway uses the hashed signature as the cache key and the JWT header and payload as the cached value.

When a client makes an API request with the opaque access token (which is the JWT signature), an API gateway plug-in looks up the token value in the cache and glues the two parts back together: the header and payload from the cache and the signature part received in the request. The API gateway is therefore able to reconstruct the entire JWT access token and forward it to your APIs. The cache never stores complete JWTs and the gateway needs to receive the original signature in client requests. This ensures that even if an attacker manages to breach the gateway cache, they will not get hold of the tokens.

One way to implement the split token pattern is for the authorization server to run custom logic to alter the client's access token and publish event messages to the API gateway during token issuance. We illustrate this flow in Figure 7-6.

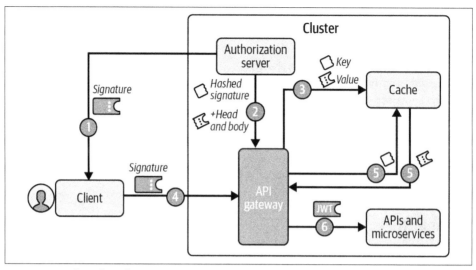

Figure 7-6. The split token pattern

To implement this pattern, you do not need to rely on your authorization server supporting advanced standards or behaviors. If you use a cloud native authorization server in Kubernetes, you are already hosting it behind an API gateway. You can then use gateway plug-ins to customize token behavior. To implement the split token pattern, you would run an API gateway plug-in to postprocess requests to the authorization server's token endpoint. This plug-in would split the token, alter the client response, and populate the cache. You would then run another gateway plug-in to preprocess API requests. This plug-in would reproduce the JWT from the incoming opaque token (signature) and forward the entire JWT to your APIs.

The split token pattern requires you to operate a dedicated token cache. Usually, you cluster your API gateway, so this cache must run out-of-process. As the API gateway relies on its cache for incoming token validation, you must plan for the rare occurrence when the API gateway does not manage to populate the cache yet but the client already posts a request with the token. These are usually not a barrier to the adoption of the pattern, but you have to take these requirements into consideration when validating your options.

Whichever pattern you use—phantom or split token—you now meet some key security requirements, to keep tokens confidential from clients, while also enabling zero trust JWT security for your APIs. With the token delivery on track for both APIs and clients, you have some essential secure access token foundations. You shouldn't stop there, though, because sometimes stronger security is possible without a great deal of effort. Your foundations should enable you to occasionally upgrade to more secure forms of access tokens. Next, let's discuss ways to harden your secure access tokens.

Hardening Access Tokens

An authorization server can provide additional options to issue stronger access tokens, but there is not a one-size-fits-all solution. Instead, there are several techniques. Which ones you choose depends upon the characteristics of your clients. In some cases, you can strengthen access tokens by using stronger cryptographic techniques, yet in others, it is more important to understand the client environment and its best practices. In this section, we explain the various ways to harden access tokens. Let's start with the cryptographic strength of JWT signatures.

Choose a JWT Signature Algorithm

In Chapter 5, we explain that authorization servers use digital signatures to sign JWTs. If a malicious party altered the JWT's header or payload, then your API's JWT validation can detect that the signature no longer matches the data and reject the access token. The algorithm that you configure in your authorization server affects the cryptographic strength of access tokens that your APIs receive.

RFC 7518, the "JSON Web Algorithms (JWA)" specification (*https://oreil.ly/Eqw3o*), contains the original list of token signing algorithms. As a general-purpose specification, it covers both symmetric and asymmetric algorithms. However, you should always use an asymmetric signing algorithm for JWT access tokens. This ensures that APIs can safely verify access tokens with only a public key. If symmetric keys were used, APIs would need the authorization server's secret key to verify access tokens. A malicious API would then be able to impersonate the authorization server by issuing access tokens using the same key and gain unauthorized access to any other API's data.

The Internet Assigned Numbers Authority (IANA) maintains an up-to-date list of algorithms for signing and encrypting JWTs (*https://oreil.ly/zK-2p*). Specialist security components use the list to ensure that they implement most of the algorithms for interoperability. The industry has also registered new algorithms since the publication of RFC 7518, for example, the Edwards-curve Digital Signature Algorithm (EdDSA). At the time of writing, the industry considers EdDSA one of the most secure options, but it is relatively new and not all JWT libraries support it.

When you configure token signing in your authorization server, choose an up-to-date asymmetric algorithm and ensure that any JWT libraries that your APIs and clients use support signature verification for that algorithm. The most mainstream and interoperable algorithm is RS256 but the industry does not consider it the most secure option. Elliptic curve algorithms use much shorter keys than RSA and create shorter signatures. What is more, they provide stronger signatures than RSA for the same key size. We use ES256 in the book's code examples, which most JWT libraries should support. When you use this algorithm, the authorization server must generate a new, unique nonce value for every JWT that it issues, as otherwise it is possible to calculate the secret key from signatures, which renders the algorithm useless. Your authorization server should manage this type of requirement correctly. If you can't use elliptic curve cryptography, use PS256. The RSA cryptography specification[3] recommends using the RSA-PSS (PS) algorithm over RSA-PKCS1 (RS). Banking-grade systems use the former and the industry considers it secure.

In any case, you should make sure that you design your environment with crypto-agility in mind. This means that you should always be ready to exchange any part of your crypto facility—private keys, certificates, or the algorithms you use. This allows you to quickly intervene in critical situations (e.g., when someone manages to intercept your private keys or when the industry finds vulnerabilities in the cryptographic algorithms that you use).

Although modern JWT algorithms can strengthen access tokens, a more compelling use case for cryptography is to prevent an attacker from using a stolen access token for impersonation. Let's explain how you can upgrade bearer tokens to sender-constrained tokens where the sender needs to provide a proof of possession of a private key together with the access token.

Use Proof of Possession

The most mainstream way to utilize access tokens is to issue them as bearer tokens. Bearer tokens are not tied to a client—whoever has the token can use it and interact with APIs. This, of course, means that if the token falls into the wrong hands, the perpetrator is able to use it to access the APIs and steal data. There are ways to ensure that only the legitimate client can use an access token. We call such tokens sender-constrained tokens. Other names for sender-constrained tokens are proof-of-possession (PoP), holder-of-key, or key-bound tokens. The idea is that the access token contains a reference to a key that only the legitimate client can control. Whenever the client uses the sender-constrained access token, it needs to provide a proof that it still controls or possesses the referenced key. One way to provide that proof is mutual TLS (mTLS).

"OAuth 2.0 Mutual-TLS Client Authentication and Certificate-Bound Access Tokens" (RFC 8705) (*https://oreil.ly/z0v2K*) describes how you can use information from an mTLS connection to bind tokens to a client. In this solution, the client owns a client certificate and a private key. The client uses an mTLS connection to the authorization server and receives an access token using one of the standard OAuth flows. The authorization server issues the token with a cnf (confirmation) claim that contains the certificate's thumbprint. In this way, the authorization server binds the

---

3 "PKCS #1: RSA Cryptography Specifications Version 2.2," RFC 8017 (*https://oreil.ly/xI2_c*).

token to the client certificate. On all API requests, the client must again use mTLS and send the same client certificate in addition to the access token. The API must verify that the current client certificate matches that in the access token's cnf claim, before validating the access token in the usual way. This enables the API to distinguish between a genuine caller, who has the private key, and a malicious caller, who has only the access token. We illustrate a flow with sender-constrained tokens in Figure 7-7.

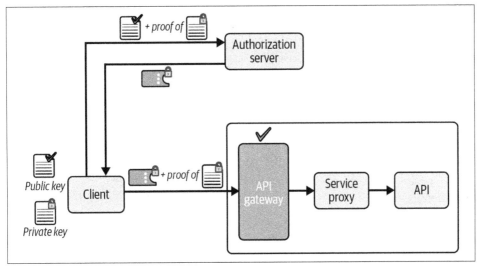

Figure 7-7. Sender-constrained access tokens reference a key, and the client must prove ownership of this key on every API request

Certificate-bound tokens are not the only option for creating sender-constrained tokens. Another solution is to use the "OAuth 2.0 Demonstrating Proof of Possession (DPoP)" specification (RFC 9449) (*https://oreil.ly/VmOkX*), which you can use when public key infrastructure (PKI) is not available. To use DPoP, the client first creates an asymmetric key pair in the JWK format. The client then issues a DPoP proof—a specialized JWT that contains information about the upcoming request—and signs it with the private key. The client then sends the DPoP proof to the authorization server when requesting tokens. The authorization server issues the access token with a cnf claim that contains a thumbprint of the public key that the client presents with the DPoP proof. In this way, the authorization server binds the token to the client's private key. On all API requests, the client must again issue a DPoP proof, sign it with the same private key, and attach it to the request. The API must verify that the current DPoP proof's public key matches that in the access token's cnf claim, before validating the access token in the usual way. Again, the API is able to distinguish between genuine and malicious callers. A malicious caller will not have access to the private key and thus will not be able to issue fresh DPoP proofs.

Using mTLS to create sender-constrained tokens is a strong-security option for APIs with confidential clients, such as B2B APIs, since these clients can easily present a client certificate. You may also be able to implement sender-constrained access tokens for mobile clients in some advanced use cases, if, for example, an organization owns the devices and can preprovision each of them with a unique key. However, sender-constrained access tokens are not practical for all types of clients. A common type of API client with environmental limitations is the browser-based application which, effectively, has nowhere secure to store cryptographic keys. Therefore, let's explore how to harden the use of access tokens in browser-based applications.

Strengthen Browser Credentials

Browser-based applications run in an environment with particular characteristics. Consider a web client that used DPoP to get sender-constrained access tokens. Although the mechanism would work, the browser would have nowhere secure to store its private key. The client could use the Web Crypto API (*https://oreil.ly/X5H4J*) and IndexedDB storage to ensure that an attacker cannot exfiltrate the private key; however, this does not guarantee that no one steals the key.[4] Therefore, you should not consider sender-constrained access tokens a safe solution for browser-based applications.

In Chapter 13, we explain how browser-based applications face particular threats from malicious JavaScript. Although it is technically simplest for browser-based applications like single-page applications (SPAs) to send access tokens to APIs, malicious JavaScript could use cross-site scripting (XSS) exploits to abuse it. Attackers might intercept access tokens (and refresh tokens) and send them to a malicious host for a more concerted and sustained attack against your APIs.

To counteract browser threats, we recommend that you use the latest and most secure HTTP-only SameSite cookies as API message credentials for browser-based applications. For that, you set up a Backend for Frontend (BFF) component that returns HTTP-only cookies to the browser that no JavaScript code can access. The cookie data can be an encrypted opaque access token. You can consider such a cookie a hardened credential for a browser-based application. Security is not perfect since XSS exploits can still make malicious requests that cause the browser to send the cookie and steal secured data. However, when you use cookies, browser attacks are less sustained and end when the user closes their browser window or navigates to a different page. Therefore, using cookies helps to reduce the impact of an XSS exploit.

---

4 "Filesystem Considerations for Browser Storage APIs" (*https://oreil.ly/VKa6m*), Section 8.6 of "OAuth 2.0 for Browser-Based Applications" (IETF draft).

Now that we have explained the special requirements of browser-based applications, let's return to general threats. First, we explain how to limit what an attacker can do with a stolen bearer token.

Use Least-Privilege Access Tokens

As we have seen, you cannot always rely on cryptography to ensure that your access tokens are fully secure against all threats. You should therefore design your access tokens so that you limit the impact of exploits. In Chapter 6, we explained how you should design least-privilege access tokens and show how to scale their usage to many APIs. We reiterate the need for least-privilege access tokens here since it is an essential part of your secure access token design.

Configure scopes in your authorization server to limit which APIs and API endpoints accept an access token. This enables you to set boundaries for your API architecture. Also configure claims in your authorization server and associate each claim to one or more scopes. Claims enable your APIs to implement their business authorization and lock down access to business data. For example, you can ensure that an access token for a customer can access only that customer's data. If an attacker intercepts a least-privilege access token they can only use it in a limited way, which reduces the business impact.

As well as reducing which resources clients can access with an access token, you also need to minimize the time window of exploits by using short-lived access tokens. Let's explain how you can keep access tokens short-lived without compromising the user experience.

Limit Access Token Lifetimes

We have seen that there are different formats for access tokens. We have also seen that you can transport them in different ways, such as over an mTLS channel or using an HTTP-only cookie. Whatever type of access token a client sends, it is ultimately just an HTTP header that represents access to your APIs. There are risks that a malicious party might somehow intercept the header and then use it to gain access to your APIs. Therefore, keep API credentials short-lived so that you minimize the time window for exploits. We recommend using expiration time as short as 15 minutes, or even 5 minutes, in high-security cases. We strongly recommend against using expiration times longer than an hour or two.

As we explain in Chapter 2, refresh tokens enable to keep an access token short-lived without impacting the users who interact with your applications. You configure the refresh token with a longer lifetime, such as a number of hours or even days. When (or just before) the short-lived access token expires, a client can silently renew it using their refresh token. Only when the refresh token expires will the user have to reauthenticate to provide the client with a fresh set of tokens.

The refresh token is a longer-lived credential that clients expose in HTTP requests less often. Whenever possible you should use confidential clients. Doing so ensures that an attacker who intercepts a refresh token cannot simply send it to the authorization server to get an access token. Any such request would require the attacker to also authenticate using the client's credential. OAuth 2.1 recommends that each token refresh should return a new *rotated* refresh token, which gives another level of protection against refresh token misuse.

In a worst-case scenario, when you know that an attacker managed to steal your tokens, you may need to inform your authorization server that it should no longer accept these tokens. Next, let's explain OAuth token revocation, and some finer points about token lifetimes.

Plan for Token Revocation

OAuth 2.0 token revocation is the act of marking a token as invalid even though the token would be deemed valid otherwise. Applications can trigger revocation for many reasons, either as part of common usage or to mark tokens as invalid if particular tokens have been compromised:

- A user may want to revoke an application's long-term access to their resources.
- An application may revoke tokens after certain events, such as user logout.
- An administrator may want to revoke tokens for a specific user and application.
- An administrator may want to revoke all tokens that the authorization server issued before a given timestamp.

The format of access tokens influences behavior when you design revocation. You cannot easily revoke by-value access tokens like JWTs, as commonly, the token validation happens only in the API. When an API validates a JWT, it usually does not query the authorization server, so it has no means of learning that someone revoked the token. To revoke a by-reference token you can send an HTTP POST request to the authorization server's revocation endpoint. However, as we have seen, API gateways may cache introspection results for opaque tokens. Therefore, clients may be able to make API calls for a short time with a revoked opaque access token. You can implement more sophisticated access token revocation, but it requires additional work. For example, your authorization server could notify the API gateway when it revokes an access token so that the gateway can remove entries from its cache.

How you approach token revocation depends on your concrete use cases and your architecture. For example, when both access tokens and refresh tokens are short-lived you may not need to implement revocation at all, since tokens expire soon anyway. In administrator use cases, you may not possess the actual tokens that you want to revoke, so you will not be able to call the OAuth revocation endpoint.

It can be useful to know how your authorization server tracks related tokens and their lifetimes. When a user authenticates and consents, very often the authorization server will create a database record. We sometimes call it a *delegation*. The authorization server uses it to manage the overall set of access and refresh tokens that the server issues as a result of a given OAuth flow. We call such a set of related tokens a *token family*. To link tokens to the delegation, the authorization server can add a delegation ID claim to tokens. Figure 7-8 illustrates a token family. When refresh token rotation is in use, then only the latest refresh token is active and the authorization server considers rotated refresh tokens revoked.

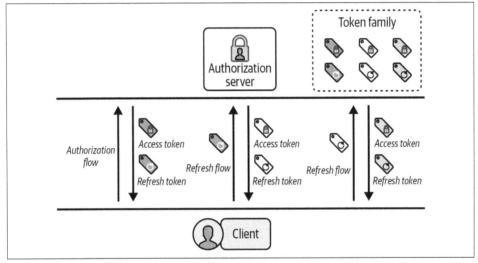

Figure 7-8. A family of access and refresh tokens

Once you understand how your authorization server manages and stores related tokens, you can implement a solution for revoking them. For example, you can design a database update to mark the current refresh token as revoked for one or more users. Revoking a refresh token should invalidate that user's entire token family, after which the user must run a fresh OAuth authorization flow.

We have completed our content on hardening access tokens to meet the remaining requirements. By separating concerns and implementing some security in your API gateway, you can avoid adding undue complexity to your APIs and clients:

- Clients transport access tokens using security best practices for their environment.

- The authorization server issues least-privilege access tokens to limit the impact of exploits.

- The authorization server issues access tokens with a short lifetime to limit the impact of exploits.
- You are able to prevent the use of compromised tokens when there is an exploit.

To complete our coverage of secure tokens, let's make a final point about secure practices, since API and client developers also play a role in protecting access tokens.

Follow Secure Development Practices

Using access tokens securely isn't solely a case of using cryptography and design patterns. You must also follow secure practices if you are an API or client developer. Your security does not end with your OAuth implementation, and you share a responsibility to keep access tokens secure. When working with access tokens, you should take particular care to limit access token sending. Only ever send access tokens to APIs that need them. Send tokens in the HTTP `Authorization` header, or the `Cookie` header if calling APIs from a browser-based application. Never log access tokens or use them in URL query strings.

Summary

We hope that in the last two chapters we managed to show the vital role that the access token plays in the overall security of your APIs. We wanted you to understand how different design choices, like the access token format, impact your APIs. APIs should receive access tokens in a cryptographically verifiable format so that they can use the tokens to implement zero trust security. JWT access tokens, however, reveal sensitive data, so you should not issue them to external clients. Instead, issue clients with opaque access tokens that keep such information confidential. Your access token delivery should enable the best options for both APIs and clients.

Once you have these token foundations, you are well placed to further harden your access tokens. There is not a one-size-fits-all solution and different types of clients have their own best practices. In addition to hardening security, you also need to assume there will be an exploit at some point and design to minimize the impact. Follow our recommendations from Chapter 6 to ensure that access tokens use the principle of least privilege. Always keep API message credentials short lived so that attackers cannot misuse a stolen access token for long.

With all these ingredients, you have a secure token-based architecture where the API gateway plays an important role. In Chapter 8, we dive much deeper into the role of HTTP proxies in API security. We talk about the specifics of how API gateways enable both TLS termination and token termination for external traffic. We also explain how service meshes and workload identities play a role in hardening your API security.

Proxies, Gateways, and Sidecars

You have now seen how to design a zero trust architecture for APIs that use token-based security. APIs commonly consist of many services that need to communicate. Microservices in a backend cluster often call each other directly, but you can also place proxy-based infrastructure between APIs. This chapter shows how you can involve this type of middleware in API security.

We start by explaining how you can use HTTP proxies during API communication for egress and ingress traffic. Next, we summarize the role of an API gateway. We outline how API gateways fit into the cloud native landscape, the problems they solve, and the details of how you expose APIs from your cluster. We illustrate how you can terminate tokens in API gateways, to translate from client-specific API message credentials to the JWT access tokens that your APIs need. We then discuss the role of a sidecar. We highlight which security tasks a sidecar can perform on behalf of the API, and which tasks the API should manage itself.

We finish up the chapter with a Kubernetes example. This example shows you how to integrate an API with an API gateway and get an external API URL. The example includes a client that you can run to call that URL with an opaque access token. The API gateway performs token termination and translates the opaque token to a JWT, which it forwards to the API. The API then performs the main security using the JWT access token.

First, though, let's explain the theory, starting with how you can use HTTP proxies for ingress and egress.

HTTP Proxies, Ingress, and Egress

An HTTP proxy is an infrastructure component that senders or receivers can use to route HTTP requests to their destination. The use of HTTP proxies predates cloud native architectures; they have been available for many years. Figure 8-1 shows an example where an API client in one organization, Organization A, sends an API request to an API in another organization, Organization B. The example shows where both forward and reverse proxies fit in this setup.

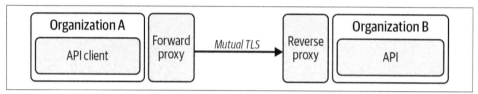

Figure 8-1. API requests routed via HTTP proxies

In Figure 8-1 there are two types of proxies, the forward proxy and the reverse proxy. The API client's HTTP request from Organization A first passes the forward proxy. A forward proxy represents exit or egress from a network area—in this case from Organization A. It can, for example, upgrade an HTTP connection to HTTPS and attach a client certificate. When the request reaches Organization B, it passes through a reverse proxy that manages incoming requests. Thus, the reverse proxy represents the entry or ingress of Organization B. It can verify the mTLS connection and might downgrade the connection to HTTP when it forwards the request to the API. Consequently, proxies contribute to API security.

Proxies terminate requests and can therefore analyze or modify the contents. An ingress proxy commonly manipulates incoming requests by replacing or adding HTTP headers. It can, for example, add a tracing header to the request or replace an incoming access token. An egress proxy, on the other hand, can control outgoing requests, preventing an API from calling arbitrary external services.

You can not only find proxies at the perimeter of a network area but also within a network. As mentioned before, APIs need to communicate internally, and as part of that, you often add a service mesh to a Kubernetes cluster that handles cross-cutting concerns in your microservice architecture such as connectivity between services including resilient connections and load balancing. For that, a service mesh can add an HTTP proxy to your microservices that provides localized forward and reverse proxy capabilities for internal requests. One way to implement the HTTP proxy is to use a sidecar container through which Kubernetes routes all incoming and outgoing requests for its corresponding microservice. We say more about the role of a service mesh and sidecar variations in "The Service Mesh Role" on page 169.

In addition to operations, HTTP proxies can also be useful during development to trace HTTP requests. A local HTTP proxy lets you intercept all HTTP traffic from your machine and thus can help you to debug messages. For example, when a security library generates OAuth messages, you may want to inspect the messages to and from the authorization server, to view the exact OAuth protocol fields. To do so without having to reconfigure the library (like adapting log levels), use a tool such as the open source mitmproxy (*https://mitmproxy.org*) and configure your application component to use it as a forward proxy for requests to the authorization server.

Generally, you should find an HTTP proxy at the perimeter of a network. We have emphasized one particular kind of proxy before in Chapter 3, the API gateway.

The API Gateway Role

When you use a cloud native platform like Kubernetes, the services, pods, and containers can talk to each other, thanks to the internal network the platform provides. Eventually, you will want to expose some APIs to the outside world. To enable this you use an API gateway, which clients call using a publicly available URL and port, such as `https://api.example.com`.

An API gateway is a specialized piece of software that lives between your public API endpoints and the internet. Think of it primarily as an advanced reverse proxy. The concept of an API gateway is not reserved for cloud native environments; it is just a common term for software that centralizes some common features that APIs require to function. The API gateway concept enables you to expose many APIs to the internet in a consistent way.

An API gateway can use multiple paths within the same internet domain to make multiple APIs feel like a single application to external clients. It also implements some common behaviors so that you do not need to implement them in every API. The main features that an API gateway provides and that you should consider when selecting a product are:

Advanced routing capabilities
Routing based on the request's method, path, or headers to pass a request to the correct service.

Request and response manipulation
Behaviors like rewriting paths, headers, or even parts of the request's or response's body.

Commercializing your APIs
For example, charging integrators or users for API usage, or rate-limiting applications with quotas.

Centralized logging and monitoring

This can help you to understand which clients use which API endpoints and how often.

Authentication and authorization

The gateway can perform part of your API security by inspecting incoming tokens and applying coarse-grained validation of requests.

Some API gateway implementations offer additional vendor-specific features. For example, some vendors have started to incorporate machine learning to help detect irregular behavior in API traffic that may indicate malicious usage. As you can see, the list is quite long. Implementing all of these responsibilities in your APIs would require a considerable amount of plumbing code. Even if you develop one library and distribute it among all your services, you have the problem of maintaining the library, updating versions, ensuring that every new service uses the library, and so on. This type of process does not scale well. Therefore, handle shared utility tasks in the API gateway. As you progress in this chapter, you will understand that such utility tasks include token termination.

There are many readily available API gateway products on the market—Kong, Nginx, Apigee, and Tyk, to name a few. Some have free or open source versions, so choosing a product does not automatically mean paying for it. You can even extend a base product to build your own API gateway. Just take your pick. When you choose an implementation for an API gateway, you should consider a cloud native product to protect your cloud native APIs with. A cloud native API gateway has an important trait—you always deploy the gateway component physically close to your APIs, in the same cluster. This helps to reduce the latency of API requests and limit the use of resources. If latency is critical in your project, then you can even leverage features like the Service Traffic Policy (*https://oreil.ly/b91Jo*) to ensure that you limit the communication between the gateway and your services to the same zone within your cluster.

We always recommend to expose your APIs with an API gateway, though Kubernetes supports other techniques as well.

Exposing APIs in Kubernetes

It is possible to expose an API from your cluster using a few different techniques. For convenience during development, you can use Kubernetes port-forwarding to get an external URL for the API. You then connect to the API using a port above 30000, such as `http://localhost:30219`. This method is suitable only when using local clusters and URLs but not when exposing APIs.

For production APIs, you need an external IP address and domain name. You could configure your production API as a Kubernetes Service that uses `ServiceType=Load Balancer`, to expose the API directly to the internet. We don't consider this approach as a good security practice because it exposes the API's container that most likely contains sensitive information. For example, if an attacker is somehow able to get a remote shell to your API's container using the external IP address, they might be able to access database connection strings and connect to your business databases via that container. Instead, you should expose only certain components from a Kubernetes cluster to the outside world.

The perimeter network that provides the entry point of your backend cluster should not include APIs or databases, but an API gateway—a specialized component that you can expose to the internet. It is therefore secure to assign the gateway the ServiceType=LoadBalancer property. If an attacker breaks through your defenses, like your firewall and intrusion detection systems, and somehow gets a remote shell to the API gateway, they have only breached the perimeter network. The attacker should not be able to get database connection strings and connect directly to databases. You should use additional infrastructure security to ensure that the gateway cannot connect to business databases.

When you deploy your APIs, you should usually assign them ServiceType= ClusterIP to give them a load-balanced internal URL that can distribute load across multiple instances. This is the default value for Kubernetes Services. Figure 8-2 illustrates the different types of services.

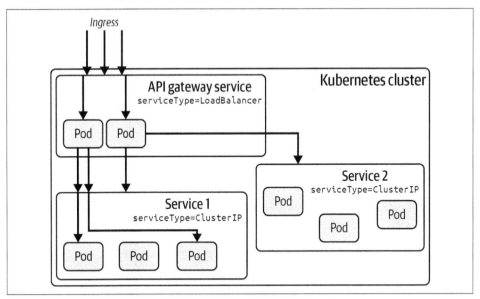

Figure 8-2. Service types in an API deployed to a Kubernetes cluster

Next, let's get started on the details of how you expose APIs using an API gateway. First, let's take a closer look at how Kubernetes uses networking to enable external connectivity.

Configure Networking

To call into a Kubernetes cluster, you must give clients an external URL for the API gateway. You must ensure the following networking behaviors so that clients can contact such a URL:

IP address
　　Use networking infrastructure to provide one or more external IP addresses for the API gateway.

DNS resolution
　　Purchase a domain name and map it to the external IP addresses.

Kubernetes itself does not assign IP addresses or DNS host names. Instead, it relies on networking infrastructure that runs outside of the cluster. For example, you might use your cloud platform to purchase domain names that you associate to one or more static IP addresses. Whenever you deploy a component with ServiceType=Load Balancer, the cloud platform can spin up load balancer infrastructure. You can control the load balancer's IP addresses using Kubernetes annotations. The load balancer can then route TCP-level traffic to the API gateway inside the cluster. You then use the API gateway's features to control routing to workloads in a vendor-neutral way.

When you work on your local computer (which we also refer to as a development computer), this type of advanced networking infrastructure is not available. By default, you cannot deploy a local Kubernetes cluster and get an external IP address or call the cluster's API gateway using a DNS name. Instead, you can use tools to ensure that local development clusters use the same logical networking steps as clusters that cloud providers manage. In the example deployment at the end of this chapter, we show how to implement the required networking tasks by following these steps:

IP address
　　Run a utility Docker container that assigns a private IP address from the local Docker bridge network.

DNS resolution
　　Use a local computer DNS solution such as adding entries to your *hosts* file.

This type of setup enables you to design, validate, and test your production deployments as early as possible, on a development computer. It also enables you to operate locally in a more real-world manner. For example, you can run entire end-to-end OAuth flows on a local computer, with web clients, mobile clients, APIs, and the authorization server. This technique can be highly useful in many use cases:

- Architects who want to design and validate future deployments
- Developers who want to troubleshoot issues in deployed systems
- Testers who want to perform end-to-end integrations

With the IP address and DNS in place, you now need the API gateway that can take on the request. Therefore, let's explain how to deploy the API gateway as a Kubernetes Service.

Deploy the API Gateway

To enable ingress to your cluster you must use a Kubernetes-compliant API gateway. The gateway is one or more Kubernetes workloads consisting of Pods, Deployments, and Services. Figure 8-2 shows an example of a deployed API gateway that routes incoming requests to services. There is usually an automated installation capability, such as a Helm chart, to facilitate the deployment of the API gateway components.

The API gateway consists of multiple services, which usually include a proxy and a controller. The proxy routes to APIs within the cluster. Most implementations default to `ServiceType=LoadBalancer` for the proxy. You can think of the controller as a bridge between the underlying proxy and Kubernetes. The controller translates Kubernetes configuration into product-specific configuration of the API gateway. In its default state, the API gateway rejects all HTTP requests until you configure ingress.

You should configure the API gateway to use HTTPS with one or more server certificates and keys for its TLS. You can get certificates in various ways. For example, you can purchase certificate files from a certificate vendor and have the API gateway load the files. You can also use cloud native tools like cert-manager to integrate with certificate issuing services like Let's Encrypt to automatically retrieve and renew certificates.

The API gateway can receive HTTPS requests for multiple host names (e.g., to distinguish between requests to your APIs and requests to your authorization server). When clients call your APIs with a particular host name, the API gateway sends requests to concrete services, which can then distribute incoming traffic across instances of the service (pods). The API gateway usually terminates TLS when it receives internet requests, though in special cases it can use TLS passthrough, to terminate TLS at an upstream gateway or API.

Host-based routing

You can potentially deploy multiple API gateways. For example, you might have a public API gateway as the entry point to your cluster and host a separate internal API gateway in front of APIs. In this case, the outer gateway sends a host header to the inner gateway. This allows the inner gateway to implement host-based routing of client requests. You might also consider this type of deployment if you use an existing public API gateway that lacks the extensibility to implement the token behaviors we explain in "Terminating Tokens" on page 165.

In some cases, an API gateway product may also allow you to do other advanced types of API routing. For example, you could do a canary deployment with version 1 and version 2 APIs side-by-side but only initially route 5% of requests to the version 2 API until you deem it stable.

The API gateway's controller can use two built-in ways in Kubernetes to configure the routing of HTTP requests to APIs, either by implementing the Kubernetes Ingress specification or the Kubernetes Gateway API specification. Either option enables you to use Kubernetes YAML resources to expose your API endpoints. Let's have a closer look at the two options. We'll start with the original Kubernetes Ingress resource.

Use Ingress Resource to Expose APIs

Ingress is a frozen feature

At the time of writing, the Kubernetes project has already frozen the Ingress resource in favor of the Kubernetes Gateway API. Nevertheless, we believe it's good to know this technique as many real-world Kubernetes clusters could still use it. In this part we also highlight the Ingress resource's limitations that led the community to work on the newer option.

To expose an API with the Ingress resource, you first assign a class name to match your particular API gateway. Most commonly, your API gateway represents an API base URL and you use paths to route to each particular service. You can expose all endpoints of an API or only a subset. Example 8-1 declares an Ingress that exposes an orders API at a URL of https://api.example.com/orders. The API gateway uses the HTTP host name, the HTTP method, and the URL's path prefix of requests to match them to that base URL.

Example 8-1. An Ingress resource to expose an API at the /orders route

```
apiVersion: networking.k8s.io/v1
kind: Ingress
metadata:
  name: orders-api
  annotations:
    konghq.com/methods: "GET"
spec:
  ingressClassName: kong
  rules:
    - host: api.example.com
      http:
        paths:
          - path: /orders
            pathType: Prefix
            backend:
              service:
                name: orders
                port:
                  number: 8080
```

You can browse the Ingress reference (*https://oreil.ly/kBkRK*) to learn more about options for configuring Ingress properties and matching requests in various ways. The Kubernetes documentation also contains a list of Ingress controllers (*https://oreil.ly/iU9Yf*) that you can use when working with the Ingress resource. As you can see, the list is quite long and you have plenty of choices. Note the configuration entry ingressClassName in Example 8-1. This discriminates which controller should process this concrete Ingress resource. This enables you to run multiple gateways and mix more than one type of Ingress controller, to meet niche requirements with a particular API gateway or to perform a phased migration to a new gateway.

One of the biggest problems with Ingress resources is that the API and API gateway usually have different owners within your organization. For example, if you are a developer interested in exposing API endpoints from your cluster, very often a separate person or team manages the API gateway. The current Ingress specification does not enable different Ingress permissions across roles.

Another limitation of the Ingress resource is its capabilities, or lack thereof: the Ingress resource has only limited support for request routing. The specification does not support advanced options such as using header values to route requests to different endpoints. However, the Ingress resource is extensible using the Kubernetes mechanism of annotations. This allows you to activate features of your chosen API gateway. These annotations are vendor-specific, though, and very often they implement the same common functionality to overcome the limitations of the Ingress resource. For example, compare the two annotations from Example 8-2. Both apply to requests with the HTTP GET method only. You will use the first one with the Kong

Ingress Controller, while the second is used with the NGINX Ingress Controller. Such differences make it difficult to keep your implementation portable.

Example 8-2. Vendor-specific Ingress annotations

```
metadata:
  annotations:
    konghq.com/methods: "GET"
    nginx.ingress.kubernetes.io/configuration-snippet: |
        if ($request_method != GET) {
          return 403;
        }
```

The preceding problems have led the community to start working on a new specification for exposing APIs in Kubernetes. Let's now look at the Gateway API resource, to understand its benefits over the Ingress resource.

Use Gateway API Resources to Expose APIs

The *Gateway API* (*https://oreil.ly/NrreC*) is a relatively new addition to the Kubernetes landscape, but CNCF has declared the project as stable and you can safely use it in production deployments. For new projects, you should evaluate the Gateway API instead of the Ingress resource since, at some point, you will need to migrate to the newer solution. The Gateway API comprises the following three resources in your Kubernetes configuration:

- GatewayClass
- Gateway
- Route

The GatewayClass resource, in simple terms, represents the underlying API gateway implementation. You use this resource to configure common, cluster-wide settings and behaviors for the gateway. If you are a developer working with APIs, then most of the time you will not work directly with this configuration object. Instead, the Gateway API documentation defines the owner of this configuration resource as the infrastructure provider.

The Gateway resource represents the more detailed configuration of the API gateway, except for HTTP routes. It is a way of telling Kubernetes which incoming traffic the gateway should handle and which GatewayClass it should use. Again, you will probably not configure this resource as an API developer when exposing APIs. The Gateway API documentation defines the owner of this configuration resource as the cluster operator.

The Route resource is of most interest here. You use this resource object to expose concrete endpoints to the traffic that the cluster operator defined in the Gateway resource. Here you define which requests Kubernetes should route to which services in your cluster. You use parameters such as the path, HTTP method, and header values to achieve that.

Example 8-3 shows an example that configures all three types of Gateway API resources for the Kong API gateway. The HTTP route exposes a simple orders API equivalently to Example 8-1.

Example 8-3. Endpoints from the orders service exposed using the Gateway API

```
apiVersion: gateway.networking.k8s.io/v1
kind: GatewayClass
metadata:
  name: kong-api-gateway
  annotations:
    konghq.com/gatewayclass-unmanaged: 'true'
spec:
  controllerName: konghq.com/kic-gateway-controller

---

apiVersion: gateway.networking.k8s.io/v1
kind: Gateway
metadata:
  name: http-kong-gateway
spec:
  gatewayClassName: kong-api-gateway
  listeners:
  - name: http-traffic
    protocol: HTTP
    port: 80
    hostname: api.example.com

---

apiVersion: gateway.networking.k8s.io/v1
kind: HTTPRoute
metadata:
  name: orders-api
spec:
  parentRefs:
    - name: http-kong-gateway
  rules:
    - matches:
      - path:
          value: "/orders"
          type: "PathPrefix"
      - method: "GET"
```

```
- backendRefs:
  - name: orders
    port: 8080
```

The Gateway API specification provides the following improvements over the Ingress specification:

- The Gateway API uses a better separation of concerns and roles, which allows you to configure more flexible and fine-grained permissions. For developers, you will only need to grant Route permissions as they will not need any access to the overall gateway.

- The Gateway API exposes in its configuration common features that API gateway products use. This reduces the usage of vendor-specific features, and it makes it easier to work with implementations. It also keeps your API gateway management portable.

- The Gateway API provides rich ways to match routes. In the Ingress resource, you could use only the hostname and path to match a request. In the Route resource, you can also match by header values, HTTP methods, or query parameters.

As the Gateway API is a fairly new product, it may still have compatibility issues but those will gradually disappear. Many vendors have already implemented the Gateway API or have plans to upgrade their current implementation to use it. You can look up the Kubernetes documentation for a list of Gateway API implementations (*https:// oreil.ly/u0f11*).

So far, we have described the process to expose an API to the internet and route requests to your target API. The Gateway API and Ingress resources both do the same job: they enable you to expose APIs from your cluster to the outside world. You do so by configuring an API gateway product using Kubernetes configuration. When dealing with secured API requests, expect that you need to run custom logic in the gateway to transform HTTP requests before routing to upstream APIs. To support this you will have to be able to extend the API gateway.

Choose an Extensible Gateway

Before you route requests to your APIs, you may want to run some utility tasks. When you choose an API gateway, a key differentiator is its extensibility. It becomes crucial once you reach a point where you have to extend the gateway functionality beyond its default behavior.

To extend an API gateway, you commonly use plug-ins. Ideally, your gateway should have an existing ecosystem of plug-ins for the most common tasks. When you can't find an existing plug-in that meets your needs, you should be able to develop a new plug-in. When you develop plug-ins, consider how you will write the plug-in code and what capabilities it needs. Is it a common programming language, a JVM-only language, JavaScript, or maybe a proprietary domain-specific language (DSL)? If you have to use complex or proprietary languages, it can make your solution more difficult to maintain, extend, or port to other gateways in the future. Plug-ins that implement security tasks may also need to perform cryptographic operations, so make sure you are able to use up-to-date security libraries.

Avoid website plug-ins for API routes

You may encounter plug-ins that you can place in front of websites to trigger a code flow. If a website client makes a backend request without a valid access token, the plug-in returns an HTTP redirect response to send the browser to the authorization server. This approach is not suitable for APIs, since most API clients, like single-page applications and mobile applications, send fetch requests and a redirect response would attempt to send the fetch client to the authorization server, resulting in application errors. Instead, APIs should not be aware of OAuth client configuration settings and should reject invalid tokens with a 401 HTTP status code. You should only initiate a code flow from clients.

Token termination is the main use case where API gateway extensibility serves your OAuth-secured APIs. To terminate tokens, you verify client-specific security and then update the HTTP request with a JWT access token before you route the request to the upstream API. This ensures that your APIs receive request credentials in a consistent manner, which simplifies API logic. Let's explain the details next.

Terminating Tokens

In Chapter 7, we outlined some security best practices that result in client-specific API message credentials. You can terminate these incoming API message credentials at the API gateway rather than sending them to your APIs. In a zero trust architecture, token termination consists of two tasks. First, it validates an incoming client-specific API credential; then it translates that credential into a JWT access token for the upstream API. When you handle client-specific security differences in your API gateway, you enable a unified security model for your API code, based on JWTs and claims. For this, token termination updates the Authorization header of upstream API requests. In this section, we explore the following token termination use cases:

- Termination of opaque tokens
- Termination of secure cookies from browser-based applications
- Termination of sender-constrained tokens

Termination of Opaque Tokens

For privacy and security reasons, the *phantom token pattern* suggests that clients handle opaque access tokens that do not reveal any API claims. The API gateway can
introspect incoming opaque tokens and get a JWT access token, which it forwards to
the upstream API to ensure the unified security model for APIs. Figure 8-3 illustrates
the flow.

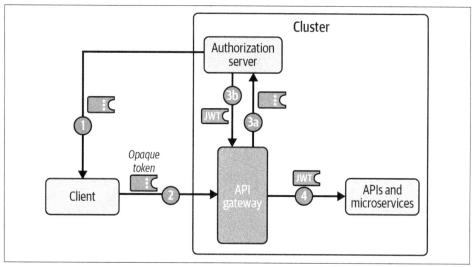

Figure 8-3. API gateway terminates opaque access tokens (phantom token flow)

When you configure your API gateway to perform the opaque token introspection,
you manage token termination and exchange in a single place. Ideally, you would
have a single plug-in for the API gateway that you activate for multiple API routes.
You then need to secure the connection between the API gateway and the authorization server's introspection endpoint. For example, you could use mTLS to allow only
the API gateway to call the introspection endpoint and deny access to all other services. Doing so would ensure that no other party could introspect the opaque token,
even if they somehow managed to intercept it.

You don't have to introspect tokens in the API gateway; however, we recommend
that you do. Otherwise, you will have to do so in all services directly, which means
that you will introduce these issues to your architecture:

- You have to keep track of entry point services and implement introspection in
  each of them.
- If your services use different technologies, you need to implement introspection
  in all API languages. You cannot easily use a single plug-in or library to perform
  introspection.

- You need to allow all of the services that perform introspection to contact the authorization server's introspection endpoint.
- You are not able to cache the results of introspection, or you can cache them only at the service level.

These considerations are also valid for many other API gateway features. In the case of the phantom token approach, the API gateway also serves as a well-placed security component. With this pattern, you always configure your APIs to require JWT access tokens. Even if an attacker manages to bypass your API gateway and call the API directly, they will have only the opaque token, which the API won't accept as a valid token.

We demonstrate an example phantom token API gateway plug-in later in this chapter. Once you understand the coding approach you will also be able to implement many other API gateway plug-in use cases, such as terminating cookies for browser-based applications.

Termination of Secure Cookies

As we noted in "Strengthen Browser Credentials" on page 148 and describe in Chapter 13, we recommend that SPAs do not handle tokens directly but use secure, HTTP-only, same-site cookies instead. The API gateway once more plays an important role because it can terminate cookies and forward JWT access tokens to APIs. For that, it can run a plug-in that acts as an *OAuth Proxy* for the browser-based applications. This plug-in retrieves tokens from the cookies. It also performs web-specific security checks, such as verifying the precise web origin. If the cookie transports an opaque token, you can combine this approach with the phantom token pattern that we have mentioned previously. In Chapter 13, we provide an SPA code example that uses cookies to transport opaque tokens. Figure 8-4 illustrates the flow, where eventually the API gateway forwards a JWT access token to APIs.

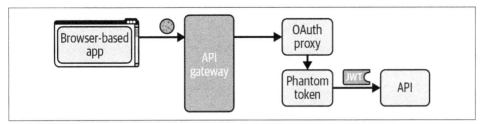

Figure 8-4. API gateway terminates cookies

So far we have explained how the API gateway can manage token-based flows for APIs and clients with the help of bearer API credentials. In some use cases, you have hardened access tokens that require the sender to provide a proof of possession of a private key in addition to the access token. Let's explain how the API gateway can terminate this type of sender-constrained token.

Termination of Sender-Constrained Tokens

Sender-constrained tokens are tokens that refer to a key pair (see also Chapter 7). When the client authenticates at the token endpoint of the authorization server to get a token, it sends a proof-of-ownership of a private key. When a client uses mTLS, the request must terminate at the authorization server, which verifies a client certificate. You use an infrastructure solution to enable this. For example, the authorization server might use one token endpoint that requires mTLS and another that does not. The API gateway could use TLS passthrough to the authorization server's mTLS token endpoint, which could listen on HTTPS using the gateway's external SSL certificate and key.

The authorization server then issues a cnf claim to the token, which represents a hash of the corresponding public key. With that reference, the authorization server effectively binds an access token to the client's key. The client must again send proof-of-ownership of the private key on every API request. Your API infrastructure can then verify that the request's public key still evaluates to the hash in the access token. An attacker cannot use an intercepted sender-constrained access token on its own but also needs to be able to generate the proof because the API will reject any request without a valid proof.

For API connections from the outside world, the API gateway usually terminates TLS and mTLS. So, we recommend that you implement key verification for sender-constrained access tokens in the API gateway and forward a JWT bearer access token to the upstream API. This technique also supports chaining of API requests, since APIs can easily forward a JWT access token to each other. If you instead verify sender-constrained access tokens in your API code, it can lead to several problems that add complexity and do not scale well:

- You may need to use TLS passthrough to call internal services.
- The internal services would need to maintain server certificates trusted by internet clients.
- APIs could not easily call each other unless they were also assigned their own PoP key.
- Routing directly to APIs may conflict with sidecar mTLS security used in service mesh deployments.

For these reasons, terminate the tokens in the API gateway. When you issue sender-constrained access tokens, continue to send opaque tokens to clients. In the API gateway, first perform introspection to get a JWT access token and then verify the cnf claim with the public key from the client. Finally, forward the JWT access token to the upstream API, which does not need to verify PoP.

The API gateway does not have to send the original JWT access token to the upstream API. An alternative option is to use token exchange to get a new JWT access token, as we explained in "Token Exchange" on page 126 in Chapter 6. The new token can even include claims to assert that it was originally a sender-constrained token and that the API gateway performed the validation.

API Gateways and Zero Trust

You should avoid perimeter security, where you implement your main API authorization in the API gateway. Instead, we consider token termination to be the primary token responsibility of the API gateway. You can optionally implement basic JWT access token validation in the API gateway, to check values like the issuer or audience. You might do so to prevent obviously invalid tokens from ever reaching APIs (e.g., access tokens from untrusted issuers) or to ensure that internal API tokens are not accepted at public API endpoints.

Despite the policies of the API gateway, in a zero trust architecture you should keep verifying requests for internal traffic. Therefore, you should implement your main API security within each API. This means that, for every incoming request, your APIs must validate the JWT access token and then use its claims to apply business authorization. This remains true even if you use mTLS connections between APIs.

You should also ensure that you avoid unwelcome deployment dependencies between APIs and the API gateway. For example, you might initially decide to validate scopes in the API gateway before forwarding requests to APIs. However, if you add a large number of scopes, and they change often, validating scopes in the API gateway might become difficult to manage. You would need to frequently update the API gateway when you deploy APIs. To prevent this type of problem, you can safely disable JWT validation in the gateway, as long as you implement all of the correct business authorization in your APIs.

We have seen that your overall API security is distributed between the API gateway, APIs, and possibly additional components such as service meshes. Let's take a closer look at the role of a service mesh.

The Service Mesh Role

A service mesh enables your APIs to use an HTTP proxy for internal requests within a Kubernetes cluster. The mesh allows you to outsource some common concerns from the API itself. Whenever you deploy a pod for your API workload, the service mesh can inject an additional sidecar container into pods. A workload could have multiple sidecar containers if required, yet the sidecar from the mesh takes care of the interservice communication. The service mesh can configure the workload's networking traffic to route via the sidecar. The sidecar then acts as a forward proxy for all HTTP requests from your API, and the sidecar acts as a reverse proxy for all HTTP requests to your API.

A sidecar has similarities to an API gateway. The main differences are that an API's sidecar is used to route internal traffic and that the sidecar shares the same lifecycle as the API itself. We use the term *sidecar* to represent the general concept of an HTTP proxy for internal traffic. Some service meshes may implement this HTTP proxy capability in alternative ways to reduce the number of sidecar containers or to provide sidecarless solutions. For example, multiple API containers could share a single sidecar, HTTP proxying could route via a Kubernetes worker node, or you could customize the networking stack itself. The important point is that there is internal middleware that can perform various tasks on behalf of the API:

- Observability tasks like logging and tracing
- Retrying HTTP requests when there are intermittent failures
- Ensuring request confidentiality using TLS
- Using workload identities to limit which workloads are allowed to call each other

A service mesh adds some essential infrastructure security to zero trust Kubernetes clusters. When you deploy APIs to a service mesh environment, you should use TLS for internal requests, to keep their data confidential. A service mesh should be able to use PKI to issue short-lived certificates and to automatically renew keys before they expire. Sidecars receive new certificates and keys and automatically update endpoints to use them. When your APIs call each other, they make plain HTTP requests that the mesh upgrades to mTLS. Figure 8-5 illustrates how a service mesh enables confidentiality for internal API requests.

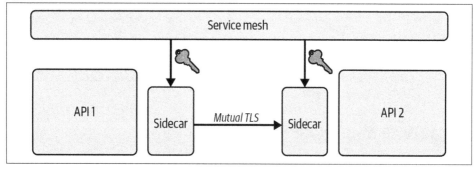

Figure 8-5. Confidential internal API traffic

The mesh assigns credentials (e.g., certificates) to sidecars. These credentials are called *workload identities*. The platform should enable your workload's main container to explicitly use their workload identities. You should be able to use workload identities as cryptography-based credentials to replace string secrets in particular. For example, your API may be able to use its workload identity as a credential when making database connections, or a backend OAuth client may be able to use a workload identity as an OAuth client credential. We discuss OAuth and workload identities in detail in Chapter 10.

An API has a close trust relationship with its sidecar(s). Your API already trusts its sidecar for some security tasks, like upgrading plain connections to TLS or presenting the API's workload identity to other parties. Thus, the API could also trust the sidecar for other security tasks, like JWT validation or some authorization checks. You remain responsible for your API's security and its end-to-end design. Your overall API workload must make all of the correct security checks and this design must scale to many APIs. In a zero trust architecture, this means APIs must always be able to actively work with their access tokens so that they can perform tasks like token exchange and calling upstream APIs.

Although you may be able to implement JWT validation and check claims in a sidecar, there can be pitfalls to this approach. There might be technical limitations, such as a lack of support for up-to-date JWT signature algorithms, or access token validation may not verify all important claims. The API may be unable to actively use its JWT access token and call other APIs. Too much reliance on a sidecar can also complicate the developer experience since service meshes and sidecars are not usually portable to API development setups. Without care, moving API authorization responsibilities from a developer's computer to sidecars can easily result in multiple future security bugs. For this reason, we recommend that you apply access token validation and claims-based authorization in your API code by default. This enables you to frequently test all the correct JWT behavior on a development computer as we demonstrate in Chapter 5.

By default, APIs treat access tokens as bearer tokens inside the Kubernetes cluster. In the future, we expect you to be able to harden internal API traffic using sender-constrained access tokens. This will satisfy several additional security use cases.[1] Workload identities are likely to provide the cryptographic keys needed to enable sender-constrained access tokens and sidecars could implement the verification.

We have explained various types of HTTP proxies and how they play a role in API security. Your overall zero trust API security is distributed between the API code, the API gateway, and a service mesh. Let's finish this chapter with a deployment example

---

[1] "Workload Identity Use Cases" (*https://oreil.ly/OntbF*), Section 3.2 of "Workload Identity in a Multi System Environment (WIMSE) Architecture" (IETF draft).

for a development computer to enable you to get up and running with the most essential proxy, the API gateway.

API Gateway Extensibility Example

The GitHub repository (*https://oreil.ly/CNDS-supp*) provides an example demo-level Kubernetes deployment in the *chapter-08-api-gateway* directory. The example shows how to perform the following tasks:

- Deploy a Kubernetes cluster.
- Run a development load balancer and use external IP addresses.
- Associate the authorization server and API host names to the external IP address.
- Deploy an API gateway that listens on HTTPS using OpenSSL development certificates.
- Deploy a cloud native authorization server and expose it at `https://login.democluster.example`.
- Deploy a minimal cloud native API and expose it at `https://api.democluster.example`.
- Run a minimal OAuth client outside of the cluster.
- Use the OAuth client to get an opaque access token from the authorization server.
- Use the OAuth client to send opaque access tokens to the API.
- Use an API gateway plug-in that performs introspection and forwards JWT access tokens to APIs.

The overall focus is on enabling an end-to-end OAuth flow against security components running in a Kubernetes cluster. Each of our example Kubernetes deployments focuses on a subset of security behaviors. The particular focus of this deployment is API gateway extensibility. We introduce security behaviors gradually and we start with simple OAuth client secrets. In Chapter 10, we show how to harden the deployment, to correctly manage secrets and use HTTPS for internal URLs.

We use YAML resources to express our desired state and the `kubectl` tool to instruct Kubernetes to deploy components and meet our desired state. You can coordinate the overall deployment by any form of simple scripting. We use bash scripts and provide the files in the following list:

- *1-create-cluster.sh*
- *2-deploy-api-gateway.sh*
- *3-deploy-authorization-server.sh*

- *4-deploy-api.sh*
- *5-run-oauth-client.sh*

We do not explain every aspect of these scripts here. We provide a list of prerequisite tools that you need in the repository's main *README* file. The repository contains additional documentation to explain technical details. The scripts contain additional comments and some useful commands that you can run if you are new to Kubernetes.

Create a Cluster

The *1-create-cluster.sh* script is specific to a development computer. It creates a developer-specific Kubernetes cluster using Kubernetes in Docker (KIND) (*https:// oreil.ly/X55VR*). Once the cluster creation is complete, you can run the kubectl command that we show at the beginning of Example 8-4, to view the list of Kubernetes nodes. Each node can be considered a virtual machine that hosts containers. The worker nodes will host instances of APIs and security components when you run the subsequent scripts.

Example 8-4. List Kubernetes nodes

```
kubectl get node -o wide

NAME
example-control-plane
example-worker
example-worker2
```

On a development computer, we run a utility called the Kubernetes Cloud Provider for KIND (*https://oreil.ly/QCwds*). This tool enables clients to connect to the KIND cluster using an external IP address in a similar way to cloud clusters. When you create a service of type LoadBalancer, this utility assigns an external IP address for the service from the host computer's Docker network and creates a local Docker container that serves as an external load balancer. Both KIND and the Kubernetes Cloud Provider are tools provided by the Kubernetes SIGs (special interest groups), which provide many cloud native components.

To create a cluster in a deployed system, you need a different cluster creation script. For example, you could use the commands in Example 8-5 to create clusters in the Amazon, Microsoft, or Google cloud environments. You could also use a technology like Terraform (*https://www.terraform.io*) to express cluster creation in a portable way.

Example 8-5. Create a cluster using different commands

```
eksctl create cluster ...
az aks create ...
gcloud container clusters create ...
```

Once you create a cluster and enable external connectivity, all remaining deployment scripts (your main deployment logic) behave identically on development computers and in deployed systems. With the cluster up and running, you are ready to move on to deploying security components. Next, let's deploy a cloud native API gateway so that we can expose components from the cluster.

Deploy the API Gateway

The *2-deploy-api-gateway.sh* script deploys and exposes an API gateway. We use the free version of the Kong API gateway and install the gateway's Docker containers to the cluster using its Helm chart. We also use the OpenSSL tool to create a wildcard certificate and key that we reference in a Kubernetes secret, to enable the API gateway to use HTTPS for the external URLs of the authorization server and example API. After running the script, execute the kubectl command we show at the start of Example 8-6 to find the external IP address.

Example 8-6. List the API gateway service

```
kubectl get svc -A

NAMESPACE  NAME            TYPE         EXTERNAL-IP
kong       kong-kong-proxy LoadBalancer 172.18.0.5
```

If you run Kubernetes on a cloud platform, you purchase real internet domain names. You then use a DNS service like AWS Route 53, Azure Traffic Manager, or Google Cloud DNS to map a domain, or its subdomains, to the external IP address. On a development computer, you must instead use a local DNS solution. The simplest option is usually to add an entry to the local computer's *hosts* file. Follow the *README* instructions to make the example URLs contactable. You are then ready to start exposing components from the cluster. Let's do this for the next component: a cloud native authorization server.

Deploy the Authorization Server

The *3-deploy-authorization-server.sh* script deploys the Curity Identity Server as the default authorization server. Once deployment has finished, run the kubectl command we show at the start of Example 8-7. You will see that an admin workload is running, which provides an admin user interface for the authorization server. You will also see that two runtime workloads are running, which provide OAuth endpoints that the API and OAuth client call.

Example 8-7. Cloud native authorization server

```
kubectl -n authorizationserver get pod

NAME
curity-idsvr-admin-7bd8ffdd94-p9gqj
curity-idsvr-runtime-59b795fd87-jtrvg
curity-idsvr-runtime-59b795fd87-nhvdn
postgres-7d9c8767db-zc24w
```

In this book, we use a PostgreSQL database to represent the authorization server's data. We use a *data-backup.sql* file to create the authorization server's schema for user accounts and other identity data. This script also restores some preshipped user accounts to enable user logins.

Data storage in Kubernetes

We do not cover data storage in depth. There are many possible ways to manage data in Kubernetes, such as persistent volumes, cloud-managed databases, or any database designed to work with Kubernetes. For a deep dive, we recommend the book *Managing Cloud Native Data on Kubernetes* by Jeff Carpenter and Patrick McFadin (O'Reilly, 2022). Whatever your preferences, you should be able to use the same type of data storage for both your business data and identity data.

At this point, if you have updated your *hosts* file according to the *README* instructions, you will be able to contact the following base URLs:

- `https://admin.democluster.example`
- `https://login.democluster.example`

You now have a Kubernetes cluster with an API gateway and an authorization server up and running. We say much more about designing the deployment of a cloud native authorization server in Chapter 11. Next, let's complete the Kubernetes deployment by exposing an API endpoint.

Deploy the Example API

The *4-deploy-api.sh* script deploys a minimal Node.js API whose only role is to provide proof that the API receives a JWT access token. After you deploy the API, you should be able to reach the following URL:

```
https://api.democluster.example/minimalapi
```

Once the deployment is complete, run the `kubectl` command we show at the start of Example 8-8 to see details of deployed workloads, where each workload consists of one or more pods. You will see the pods for both application components (the minimal API) and security components, along with the Kubernetes node that hosts each pod.

Example 8-8. Cloud native workloads

```
kubectl get pod -A -o wide

NAMESPACE            NAME                                   NODE
applications         minimalapi-6f9fd76b8d-sqxl4            example-worker
authorizationserver  curity-idsvr-admin-7bd8ffdd94-p9gqj    example-worker
authorizationserver  curity-idsvr-runtime-59b795fd87-jtrvg  example-worker2
authorizationserver  curity-idsvr-runtime-59b795fd87-nhvdn  example-worker
authorizationserver  postgres-7d9c8767db-zc24w              example-worker
kong                 kong-kong-5c9c6bdf5-m548v              example-worker2
```

Now that you have deployed the backend components, and the API gateway exposes external URLs that route to Kubernetes workloads, we can run end-to-end OAuth flows. Let's test the deployment using an OAuth client.

Run an OAuth Client

Finally, run the *5-run-oauth-client.sh* script to execute a very simple OAuth client. First, the client gets an opaque access token by running the client credentials grant request we show in Example 8-9.

Example 8-9. Simple OAuth client

```
curl -s 'https://login.democluster.example/oauth/v2/oauth-token' \
    -H 'content-type: application/x-www-form-urlencoded' \
    -H 'accept: application/json' \
    -d 'client_id=phantom-token-test' \
    -d "client_secret=$TEST_CLIENT_SECRET" \
    -d 'grant_type=client_credentials'
```

Next, the client calls the example API with an access token and receives a response to confirm that the example API received a JWT access token. This completes an end-to-end OAuth flow, albeit in a trivial server-to-server scenario. In later chapters, we run many other end-to-end flows in the same way but with more full-featured APIs, clients, and using flows that require user interaction. To finish up, let's look at how you can implement token termination in the Kong API gateway.

Use the API Gateway Plug-in

We used Lua (*https://www.lua.org*) to implement the example API gateway plug-in. Lua is a high-level scripted programming language that many cloud native API gateways use. We include the plug-in's code in the GitHub repository (*https://oreil.ly/CNDS-supp*) in case you need to customize it. Kong requires three distinct files, which we deploy using a Kubernetes ConfigMap. The main implementation is in a file called *access.lua*.

Example 8-10 shows the most essential plug-in code, which starts by reading the incoming opaque access token from the HTTP Authorization header. Next, the plug-in introspects the opaque access token at the authorization server and uses the HTTP Accept header to request a JWT response. On success, the plug-in updates the HTTP Authorization header with a JWT access token before the gateway routes the request to the upstream API. The full plug-in implementation performs some additional work including caching of introspection responses.

Example 8-10. API gateway plug-in

```
local auth_header = ngx.req.get_headers()['Authorization']
local access_token = string.sub(auth_header, 8)

local httpc = http:new()
local clientCredential =
    ngx.escape_uri(config.client_id) .. ':' .. ngx.escape_uri(config.client_secret)
local authorizationHeader = 'Basic ' .. ngx.encode_base64(clientCredential)

local result, error = httpc:request_uri(config.introspection_endpoint, {
    method = 'POST',
    body = 'token=' .. access_token,
    headers = {
        ['authorization'] = authorizationHeader,
        ['content-type'] = 'application/x-www-form-urlencoded',
        ['accept'] = 'application/jwt'
    },
    ssl_verify = config.verify_ssl
})

local jwt = result.body
ngx.req.set_header('Authorization', 'Bearer ' .. jwt)
```

We configure the plug-in in the Kong API gateway using a Kubernetes custom resource. Example 8-11 shows how you can configure this resource to an HTTP route for particular APIs or API endpoints and then apply an annotation to activate the plug-in. You can study the repository resources to understand other aspects of the deployment. These include building a custom Docker image containing the plug-in's Lua dependencies.

Example 8-11. API gateway plug-in activation

```
kind: KongPlugin
apiVersion: configuration.konghq.com/v1
metadata:
  name: phantom-token
plugin: phantom-token
config:
  introspection_endpoint: "http://curity-idsvr-runtime-svc.authorizationserver:8443\
    /oauth/v2/oauth-introspect" ❶
  client_id: api-gateway-client
  client_secret: p4os1Atrlgac3cHEQo2u
  token_cache_seconds: 900

kind: HTTPRoute
apiVersion: gateway.networking.k8s.io/v1
metadata:
  name: minimal-api-route
  annotations:
    konghq.com/plugins: phantom-token
```

❶ Kubernetes service discovery enables an internal URL for the introspection endpoint.

Once you understand the techniques, you can use them to develop and deploy any other type of API gateway plug-in. Your particular API gateway may use different plug-in technologies but the main steps should remain the same.

Summary

We first explained the main roles of HTTP proxies, where a reverse proxy manages entry (ingress) and a forward proxy manages exit (egress). When you design your Kubernetes deployments, the most important proxy is your API gateway, which acts as a reverse proxy that advertises your APIs to the outside world. The API gateway typically exposes an external base URL to represent all of your APIs. For each API that you want to publish to the internet, you configure the API gateway to use Kubernetes resources. The API gateway then routes requests to your underlying services.

The API gateway plays an important role in handling client-specific security differences since clients send different types of API message credentials depending on best practices for their environment. The API gateway needs to be extensible so that you can run utility tasks when your APIs receive requests. For example, the API gateway should perform validation checks of client-specific requests and then consistently forward a JWT access token to APIs.

Service meshes and sidecars play an important role in hardening internal API traffic. They enable TLS and introduce workload identities. This leads to an architecture that distributes API security over several components. In any case, your APIs must implement the main security and business authorization before releasing any data.

There are various techniques that APIs can use to enforce business authorization. In Chapter 5, we explained an API coding approach where APIs work with claims to enforce fine-grained access control. While we encourage you to base your authorization rules on claims, you do not necessarily have to implement them in API code. You can also manage the policies outside of the API code. This policy-based approach can enable you to share complex authorization and change your business security rules with greater agility. We explore this in Chapter 9.

Entitlements

You have seen how to design and work with access tokens so that you create a secure solution from the authorization server's token issuance to clients sending the tokens to APIs. Eventually, the access token is a credential that your APIs use to perform authorization decisions, and you should understand what authorization techniques you can apply to it.

In this chapter, we introduce you to common models for designing entitlements and access control policies. We discuss how you can evolve your access control mechanisms with an entitlement management system (EMS) that makes sure that APIs grant users the right entitlements at the right time in a consistent and scalable manner with the help of the OAuth access token. To demonstrate the theory, we look into Open Policy Agent (OPA) and the relevant features as part of an EMS. Finally, we showcase our arguments with an end-to-end example that connects all the dots.

Access Control Models

Access control (aka authorization) is a security primitive that determines who can access what, in which way, and in what context. It distinguishes between the subject, that is, the entity requesting access; the object, that is, the protected resource like the user's order history or company files; and the action, that is, what the subject is trying to do with the object (like read or write). Authentication is an important prerequisite for access controls to reliably identify the subject ("who"). In OAuth, the access token can use scopes and claims to describe some aspects of the subject and object.

Access control policies define the set of rules for access decisions. Access control policies are business specific. Things like company size, infrastructure, and regulations, among others, impact how you build and formulate policies. However, there are common strategies to structure access rules called *access control models*. In this book, we introduce you to three models that we consider most relevant in the context of securing access to data: role-based access control (RBAC), relationship-based access control (ReBAC), and attribute-based access control (ABAC). We start with the most common one, RBAC.

Role-Based Access Control

Role-based access control (RBAC) groups access permissions based on users' roles within an organization. For example, with RBAC you can define a rule such as an *employee* that is a *customer service agent* is allowed to *list all orders*. The idea is that users with the same business function share the same privileges. Consequently, in this model you assign access permissions to roles and not to individuals. Such permissions are typically static. In Example 9-1, we have predefined the role `customer_service_agent` using JSON. This role has the permission to view a list of orders. The pseudocode illustrates a role-based rule where users (described via the principal) get access only if they have a role (i.e., `customer_service_agent`) with permissions that match the request. By default, the rule denies access.

Example 9-1. Policy for role-based access control that gives users access only if at least one of their roles allows it

```
{
    "roles": [
        "customer_service_agent": [{
            "actions": ["list"],
            "resource_type": "order"
        }]
    ]
}
is_user_allowed (roles, principal, request) {

  user_role = roles[principal.role]

  IF (user_role.actions.contains(request.action) AND
      user_role.resource_type == request.resource_type) THEN
    RETURN true;
  ELSE
    RETURN false;
}
```

With RBAC, you do not need to assign users individual permissions in a system but can set up roles with predefined permissions in advance. Even if you do not have to assign individual permissions, you still need to assign users roles. Ideally, you would try to centralize and automate this task using an identity management system. In this way, RBAC helps to reduce administrative workload, to improve security by reducing human errors when assigning privileges and to meet compliance requirements by being able to prove that roles only have the permissions they need.

RBAC is not suitable for fine-grained access controls, as a group of people share permissions via their role. In addition, RBAC cannot easily support context-related decisions like authorizing a request based on the time of day or location of the user. As a result of their efforts to meet granular requirements with RBAC, organizations risk *role explosion* where the number of roles becomes hard to manage. If you find yourself using roles like these, it is a sign that you need a different approach:

- `customer_service_agent_usa`
- `customer_service_agent_europe`
- `customer_service_agent_asia`

Role explosion implies high management overhead and security risks due to role misconfiguration. The ReBAC model helps to overcome some of the limitations of RBAC.

Relationship-Based Access Control

Relationship-based access control (ReBAC) models users, resources, and relationships in a graph. Users and resources are the nodes in the graph and the relationships are the connections. Instead of looking at a user's role to derive the permissions on a resource, you look for a relationship between the user and the resource. If there is a relationship between two nodes in the graph, then the system can check the associated permissions; otherwise it denies access by default. Systems that support ReBAC models often store current active relationships as a tuple of `user:relationship:resource`.

Background on ReBAC

The ReBAC model gained attention after Google published a description of their implementation of a relationship-based access control called Zanzibar.[1] Other implementations take after and, for example, use the same structure to store relationships.

With ReBAC, you can group users, resources, and permissions similarly to RBAC. Because of the graph, you can easily handle hierarchical, nested (parent-child) and ownership models with ReBAC. For example, a rule like "*customers* are allowed to *list all their orders*" simply requires an `owner` relationship between a customer and an

---

1 Pang et al., "Zanzibar: Google's Consistent, Global Authorization System" (*https://oreil.ly/U3IZf*), 2019.

order. A relationship can, for instance, imply a set of permissions comparable to roles in RBAC. This means that the owner relationship could give a user the permissions to update, read, delete, and even transfer ownership of a document. In this way, you do not have to maintain the relationships of a user for every single permission on a resource.

Relationships can also map directly to permissions. For example, you can define edit as a relationship. A user that has the edit relationship with a document has the permission to edit it. Consequently, in contrast to RBAC, ReBAC is suitable for fine-grained access control that allows you to assign permissions at any level in a graph. What is more, it allows you to traverse the authorization question; that is, you can not only answer the question, "Is this user allowed to access this resource?" with the graph but also, "Who is allowed to access this resource?" which is very helpful for auditing policies.

Example 9-2 shows an example policy in pseudocode that implements the ReBAC model. The relationship comes from the data model as you commonly find it in relational databases. In this example, an order has an owner attribute that points to a user. The policy allows access if the graph contains a relationship between the user and the order, and if the relationship grants the appropriate permissions. For illustration, we predefined the permissions and the relationship graph in JSON.

Example 9-2. Policy for relationship-based access control

```
{
    "permissions": [
        "owner": {
            "actions": ["list"]
        }
    ],
    "graph": [{
        "source": "user:dana",
        "target": "order:123",
        "relation": "owner"
    }]
}

FOR (edge IN graph) DO {
  IF edge.source == principal.id AND edge.target == request.order_id THEN {
    relation_permission = permissions[edge.relation]

    IF relation_permission.actions.contains(request.action) THEN
        RETURN true
  }
}

RETURN false
```

You could extend the example if you have a requirement that users should be able to list not only their orders but also related payments and shipments. With ReBAC, you can set up a relationship between the order and the payment or shipment. You probably already have that kind of relationship in your data which you can reuse for the policy. Let's say your policy states that *users* can *list payments* of *orders they own*. There is no need to define any permissions on the payment or shipment itself, nor a direct relationship to the user, but you derive the permissions from the parent relationship to the order. We illustrate the hierarchy and data relations in a flow chart in Figure 9-1.

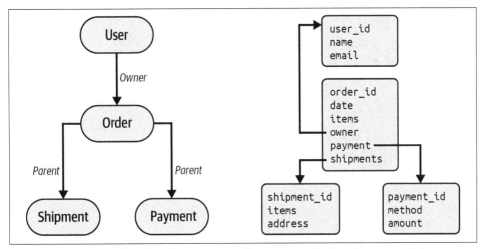

Figure 9-1. Relationship-based access control can reuse existing data to model relationships

ReBAC allows you to reuse existing data models and implement access controls that align better with the real world than RBAC does. However, the real world is more complex than the presence (or absence) of a relationship. Sometimes you need to describe the relationships, users, and resources as well as the context of a request to be able to set constraints like "*customers* can *get a particular benefit* if they *live in Europe*". This is where ABAC comes in.

Attribute-Based Access Control

In contrast to RBAC and ReBAC that consider a single attribute (role or relationship, respectively), attribute-based access control (ABAC) can take multiple attributes into account when evaluating access rules. In an ABAC model, access control policies define the allowed subject and object attributes as well as conditions under which an operation is allowed. For example, with ABAC you can easily describe a policy such as a "*customer service agent* can *list all orders for the regions they manage during office hours*". We demonstrate this example ABAC policy in Example 9-3 with pseudocode that shows claims, some policy data, and the policy enforcement logic. Attributes can describe the user (employee working with customer service, responsible for some regions, such as the USA, Europe, or Asia), the operation (list), the protected resource (all orders), or context (e.g., time). Consequently, you can apply ABAC for fine-grained and flexible policies.

Example 9-3. Policy for attribute-based access control that only allows customer service agents to list all orders of their authorized regions during office hours

```
{
    "sub": "1234567",
    "roles": {
        "customer_service_agent": {
            "regions": ["US", "EMEA"]
        }
    }
}
{
    "businessHours": {
        "from": "9:00",
        "to": "17:00",
        "zone": "GMT+2"
    }
}
IF (request.action == "list" &&
  request.resource_type = "order" &&
  request.user.roles.includes("customer_service_agent") &&
  request.user.roles.customer_service_agent.regions.includes(request.order.region)
  &&
  request.time.within(businessHourTimeSpan) ) {
    RETURN true;
  }

RETURN false;
```

With ABAC, you can consider the requested operation and contextual attributes for access decisions like the time of day, user's location, threat level, and many more. As a result, you can use ABAC to adopt a dynamic access control model like the risk adaptable access control (RAdAC) model where the risk level is a contextual attribute. As cyberattacks become more sophisticated, there is a trend to look at usage patterns. A specialist component can calculate a risk level based on the user's behavior and other data. You can then use the resulting risk level in application-level components like the API or policy engine to perform the access decision. In that way, you can take an overall risk level of a request into account when performing an access decision.

ABAC provides the best flexibility but you need a good process for managing access control as the number of users, resources, and attributes grow. You need to understand the meaning of an attribute in the current context (e.g., whether a department attribute is the user's primary department or where they are currently located). Such semantical differences can result in security bugs.

We explained in Chapter 6 how you should work with data when you consider authorization and how you should design attributes in your access tokens. We believe that this knowledge will help you manage policies in an ABAC model. One thing we want to highlight again is that you should always adhere to the principle of least privilege.

The Principle of Least Privilege

As we briefly mentioned in other chapters, the principle of least privilege is a concept in information security that aims to grant entities only the bare minimum of permissions that their function or a specific task requires for a legitimate purpose. The principle is core to preventing overprivileged access rights that malicious users might abuse to steal data. It helps to reduce the attack surface by providing boundaries without limiting users in their legitimate actions. When applying the principle of least privilege, at a bare minimum you must ensure that a user cannot elevate their own privileges.

You can implement the principle of least privilege with various models. In RBAC, for example, you can design roles with a minimum set of privileges. Whenever a user switches roles, the user gets new permissions via the new role, which ensures that the user is able to perform only the tasks that this role allows but not more. Least privilege in ReBAC works similarly but with relationships. ReBAC provides a more granular enforcement of least privileges as you can set up relationships with individual users, giving each user only certain permissions on a resource or set of resources. You can continue to share privileges for users by granting a group of users (e.g., via a membership relationship) certain permissions on a given resource.

In the ABAC model, access policies can encompass the principle of least privilege by narrowing down the essential attributes for requested operations. In other words, access policies can define strictly required attributes that users must have to perform certain actions. Policies can then deny access whenever attributes do not fulfill the requirements. In that way, policies can ensure that systems only grant permissions when applicable and required.

Access rules, however, are just one part of the equation. Designing roles and policies in a way to perfectly limit what a single user can do is not effective if users get roles or attributes they are not supposed to have. Therefore, you should also implement procedures that prevent overprivileged accounts. For example, ensure sign-off when a user requests new privileges, perform yearly reviews of entitlements, or ensure that you remove privileges when you move employees between posts or departments. Such procedures are part of identity and access management.

Once you decide on the minimal sets of attributes your users should obtain, you can leverage the functionality of an authorization server to issue access tokens that contain that limited data.

The Role of Token-Based Authorization

When applying token-based authorization, the access token serves as the source of truth of identity data for any access control in the system. APIs can use the data in an access token for processing, like identifying the user, retrieving the user's role, or looking up business-related data such as order records associated with the user. Eventually, APIs can forward tokens to upstream APIs.

When you implement a zero trust architecture in a cloud native environment, you have to enforce access control at various places. We recommend considering an EMS as part of your cloud native security architecture. We explain why this is a good solution next.

Benefits of an Entitlement Management System

An entitlement management system (EMS) is a solution for access control that allows not only for managing user entitlements centrally but also for decoupling the writing and maintaining of policies from software development. It enables you to centralize and reuse the more intricate areas of your authorization. The access token still serves as the source of truth for identity data and your APIs should send access tokens to the EMS when they ask for a decision.

With an EMS, you can benefit from the following: flexibility, auditability, security agility, and quality assurance via policy as code

We go through these benefits one by one in the following sections, starting with the flexibility an EMS can give you.

Flexibility

An EMS provides extra choices on how you can handle authorization. You can start small and focus on your most critical authorization rules, or those that need to be dynamic. Centralize more rules over time, depending on your needs. The technical details of how you implement the policy (e.g., what claims you read from the access token) are externalized from your APIs. You can implement RBAC, ReBAC, or ABAC in your policy. You probably want to combine multiple models to maximize the benefits. The API cares only about the output. You can change the policy or related claims in the access token without having to change code or redeploy APIs.

What's more, you can audit authorization decisions. In larger organizations, you can unify policies across systems and applications, even if they use different languages or technologies. You can thus lower the burden of managing them separately.

Auditability

Having central policies that you can enforce and audit consistently across multiple APIs and technology stacks can be a game-changer when it comes to compliance. It enables you to centrally monitor who has gained access to which business resources and when. Centralized policies are easy to audit, which improves the ability to demonstrate regulatory or internal compliance. As a result, it makes sense to use central policies wherever and whenever auditing is important. You can audit both changes to the policy as well as its enforcement.

A policy engine can log metadata related to decision processing. You can feed your log aggregation software with the audit data. So, when you have a compliance review, you do not have to gather information of potentially varying quality from various places but you can query the logs of the policy engine to get the full picture. When you combine the EMS with OAuth, you use the authorization server for auditing identity-related events while the EMS audits access to business resources.

Security Agility

Oauth enables a token-based architecture where you rely on claims in access tokens for access decisions. Consequently, for the decisions to be correct, access tokens need to contain sufficient data. There are likely many stakeholders for the information contained in access tokens, potentially with conflicting interests. As we mentioned in Chapter 6, some attributes are more static than others. If your policy depends on attributes that you expect to change and if it is important for your policy to operate on the latest values, you should consider fetching such attribute values in real time rather than from the access token. An EMS can—just like an API—load external data for that purpose. Decoupling access control decisions from software development helps to remove the burden (and responsibility) of handling claims from software developers. Developers can focus on features while other teams design and update the access token as well as the policies. Policies can then, for example, load external data to complement the access token with real-time data.

If you write policies in a high-level language that is natural to read, you can more easily involve nontechnical stakeholders proactively, benefit from their know-how (e.g., business domain, legislation), and ensure early in the process that you fulfill the access control requirements. In this way, you can adapt to changes in business or security requirements without depending on development cycles. This means that you can update decoupled policies faster and adapt quicker to changes than with embedded authorization. You may still depend on the development lifecycle in certain situations, though. For example, when you launch a new feature, you may also need to deploy new rules in conjunction. A decoupled approach still provides great agility because you can define, validate, and test policies using automated processes independently from the development lifecycle of APIs and applications.

Decoupling policies from applications means to treat policies as code. As a result you can build, compile, test, and deploy policies independently to make sure the policy meets quality standards.

Quality Assurance via Policy as Code

When you write policies as code, you typically use a domain-specific language to implement the rules, such as eXtensible Access Control Markup Language (XACML), ALFA, Rego, or Cedar. A policy engine then processes the machine-readable policies. Thanks to the decoupling, you can have specialized people and teams write and test policies. Typically, the policy has its own test framework that uses the same domain-specific language.

There is no need to implement the same authorization rules in various API programming languages—implementations where each may introduce security holes through human errors and discrepant behaviors. Instead, APIs make a request to the policy engine to ask it for an authorization result. During API development, API developers can mock responses from the policy engine for their tests. They do not have to account for testing the logic of a policy but only cover its possible outcomes. A policy engine therefore simplifies API development. At the same time, it improves security because it enables organizations to enforce consistent and tested rules across a diverse technology stack. What is more, an EMS can automatically distribute and enforce any policy updates. Consequently, an EMS enables a scalable authorization solution.

Scalable Authorization

Scalable authorization means a manageable solution where you can reuse the same authorization mechanisms (e.g., the OAuth access token) across many and a growing number of components in your architecture. An EMS adds additional benefits to OAuth, as we have just outlined. It is worth noting that you do not have to place all authorization decisions in policies. You can continue with defining some rules in your APIs but have central policies for complex, high-value, and/or dynamic decisions. Though a policy is central in an EMS, you can enforce it in a distributed manner, that is, across many components. To enable this behavior, a cloud native EMS needs separated responsibilities, as we illustrate in Figure 9-2.

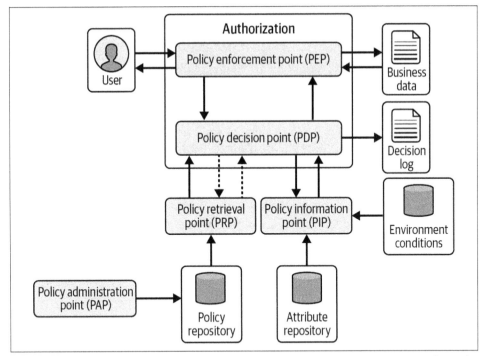

Figure 9-2. The components of a cloud native entitlement management system for scalable authorization

The framework for a cloud native EMS in Figure 9-2 is inspired by the AAA authorization framework of RFC 2904 (*https://oreil.ly/1VyjX*), the dataflow in XACML, and Axiomatic's pioneering work in the area of ABAC. In summary, the architecture includes the following roles:

- Policy administration point (PAP), which provides interfaces and tools for managing policies
- Policy enforcement point (PEP), which is responsible for enforcing policies (i.e., executing a decision from the policy decision point)
- Policy decision point (PDP), which evaluates a policy and returns a decision to the policy enforcement point
- Policy information point (PIP), which provides data relevant to the policy decision point to make a decision
- Policy retrieval point (PRP), which is responsible for distributing policies to the policy decision points

The PAP allows policy administrators to configure, maintain, and manage policies. Whenever there is a need for an authorization decision, a PEP is responsible for enforcing policies. It requests a decision from the PDP. The PDP collects data (e.g., attributes) from the PIP, evaluates the policy, and returns a decision to the PEP. The PEP then executes that decision. In the context of API security with OAuth, your API implements the PEP and it consults a PDP using the access tokens as a PIP. To avoid latency and availability issues, you can deploy the PDP with your APIs (e.g., in a side-car container or as a process). Consequently, you can have many instances of a PEP and PDP in your architecture. The distributed PDPs get the policy from a central PRP that, in turn, loads it from a policy repository.

You do not have to use particular tools to implement the framework. However, as always, the choice of your tools impacts your possibilities, and in this case, your API security. For example, policy decision points typically support a very specific policy language; for example, OPA uses Rego, and Cedar refers to both a policy language and engine. Thus, your choice of policy decision point impacts how you can manage and write policies—from a technical perspective but also from a security perspective (e.g., which access control models you can apply).

In the following sections, we discuss the various roles of an EMS in detail. The policy is technically not a role but nevertheless crucial for the function of an EMS and central for all the roles. Therefore, let's look at what constitutes a policy.

Policy

Policies have a machine-readable format so that the policy decision point can process them accordingly. The XACML (*https://oreil.ly/zDzb6*) is an example of an XML-based standard language specifically designed for ABAC policies. The Abbreviated Language for Authorization (ALFA) (*https://oreil.ly/rdKf7*) is an XACML-compatible, high-level language. Cedar (*https://oreil.ly/d6NUn*) and Rego (*https://oreil.ly/j2vXk*) are examples of domain-specific languages that allow you to write policies. OpenFGA (*https://oreil.ly/Jd9aJ*) is an example of an authorization system that allows configuring policies without a dedicated policy language.

Policies commonly stem from documents that describe an organization's procedural rules and business processes. A policy language defines the grammar, syntax, and operators that allow you to create the machine-readable abstraction of the rules in those documents. Policy engines load and run the code when evaluating policies. Despite having machines interpret policies, the process of writing and reviewing still includes humans. Therefore, you should consider a policy language that is easy to understand for the people that write and review them. What is more, you should provide them with tools that facilitate policy administration.

Policy Administration Point

The policy administration point (PAP) allows for creating, updating, and deleting policies. For text- and file-based policies, you can edit policies in a text editor and get help with syntax highlighting or validation. However, specialized software can also provide an administration layer that guides the policy author. This might enable a domain expert such as an information security officer or business analyst to use a graphical user interface to reliably write and test policy code.

If the PAP supports file-based policies, you can store the files in a version control system, keep track of the versions, and integrate with your CI/CD tools, for example. You can then use similar processes as for your APIs to write, review, and test policies. In the end, you publish and distribute policies via the policy retrieval point.

Policy Retrieval Point

The policy retrieval point (PRP) provides a trusted interface or mechanism to distribute policies. For example, a CI/CD pipeline can serve as the PRP by pushing out new policy files when they change in the policy repository. You can also just announce policies on a central server or datastore and have the policy decision points load new policies from there. Alternatively, you could have a separate tool like Open Policy Administration Layer (OPAL) (*https://www.opal.ac*) that automatically distributes policies to the policy decision points.

As policies define the authorization rules, it is important to protect their integrity. For this reason, the PRP should distribute only signed policies. When policy decision points receive a new policy, they must verify the signature. In this way, they can validate that a policy comes from a trusted authority and no one modified it. In addition, you should keep track of the versions of your policies so that you can roll out, withdraw, and enforce specific versions. The latter, for example, is useful in cases where you want to temporarily enforce certain decisions, or for an incremental deployment where you update the policy decision points one after the other. We've mentioned the policy decision point several times now, so let's examine that next.

Policy Decision Point

The policy decision point (PDP), also called a policy agent or a policy engine, is a component that parses and evaluates policies to produce a policy decision. Basically, you can use any access control model, whether it is based on RBAC, ReBAC, or ABAC (or a combination of those), to make a decision. However, your options can sometimes be limited by the technology you choose—some of them might specialize in only one type of access control model. In principle, there are two ways for an application to ask for a decision: locally, via an embedded SDK, or remotely. Remotely in this case means that the policy agent runs on its own (e.g., in a sidecar, pod, node) or even as a managed service. The policy enforcement point then requests a decision from the policy decision point.

Policy Enforcement Point

The policy enforcement point (PEP) is any point in your architecture that enforces authorization rules. For example, it can be an object in your API code or implemented in a service mesh proxy. Instead of hardcoding the rules, the PEP ideally includes some code that calls the policy decision point over a well-defined interface to evaluate a policy. For example, as mentioned before, you may embed SDKs in your APIs and use the provided classes for policy evaluation, or you could call the policy decision point over a REST API or similar endpoint.

Once the policy enforcement point gets an answer from the policy decision point, it is responsible for enforcing the policy. Very often, the policy enforcement point will get only a basic instruction to either accept or reject the request. However, the policy decision point can return additional data with detailed information about why the policy enforcement should accept or reject the request (e.g., the policy decision point can instruct the policy enforcement point to deny a request because it is after office hours). The policy enforcement point is also responsible for forming a suitable response depending on the technology it uses. For example, in the case of a REST API, the policy enforcement point will most probably create an HTTP 403 response when the policy decision point instructs it to deny the request.

A policy decision point requires some input to be able to process policies. When it comes to authorization, you commonly need to provide the policy decision point with some data about the context of a request such as who is requesting access to what. With OAuth, the access token already conveys such data. The policy enforcement point can forward the access token to the policy decision point to provide the necessary information. In other words, the access token serves as a PIP.

Policy Information Point

A policy information point (PIP) provides the attributes that the policy decision point requires to form an adequate decision based on the current policy. Examples of PIPs are data stores (e.g., Lightweight Directory Access Protocol [LDAP], Active Directory [AD], databases), REST APIs, or by-value access tokens, and it's important to note that a policy decision point can use multiple information points to reach a decision. The authorization server plays an important part since it enables secure delivery of authorization data to the policy decision point. The policy decision point can take the relevant attributes from the access token directly, without the need for additional communication.

Now that you are familiar with the different roles in an EMS, let's study a concrete example of a system that combines the benefit of OAuth with the benefit of distributed policies. For that, we use the popular CNCF project OPA.

Open Policy Agent

Open Policy Agent (OPA) is a CNCF-graduated project that helps you to enforce access rules in a cloud native environment. CNCF-graduated projects are stable open source projects that many organizations run in production and that have a living community with large groups of contributors. Consequently, those projects tend to have rather good support, something that we think is a decisive factor for successful implementations.

Being a policy engine, OPA lends itself well to the PDP that parses access control policies, evaluates queries, and returns a decision, as Figure 9-3 illustrates.

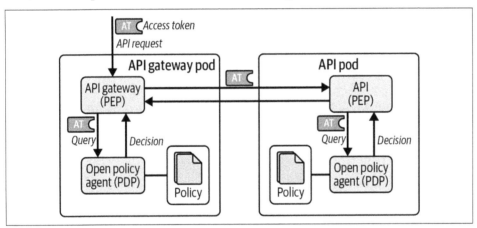

Figure 9-3. Open Policy Agent as policy decision point

In this section, we explore OPA as a component of a cloud native EMS. We examine some important features and finish the section with a code example that you can run on your local computer. Since a policy engine is nothing without a policy, let's kick off with how you write policies for OPA.

Writing Policies in OPA

OPA's policy language is Rego. Rego is an easy-to-read language with a descriptive syntax that lets you focus on the output—that is, the result—rather than the instructions on how to achieve it. Everything in Rego is structured data that's called a *document*. OPA does not assume any data model (schema) for the document. As a result, it can support a variety of use cases from admission control in Kubernetes[2] to enforcing business rules and access control for APIs. We focus on the latter.

When you define a policy in Rego, you write rules. A rule is just another document. The basic format of a rule is *rule-name := value if body* where the *body* contains one or more expressions. Example 9-4 shows a rule in Rego called `allow`. The rule returns `true` if the `user` from the input is called `dana` (that is, it implements an ABAC model).

Example 9-4. A policy in Rego

```
package policy.example

# allow rule
allow := true if {
    input.user == "dana"
}
```

Since OPA handles rules (and their results) as data, you can query a rule via OPA's *Data API*, a group of endpoints at `/v1/data` that lets you read and write documents. As we have pointed out before, you commonly have some input for your policies to make them dynamic, like in Example 9-4, where the policy validates a username. This input comes from an external source. Let's explore how to load external data in OPA to be able to feed policies with dynamic values.

Loading External Data

You can select between two approaches to get external data into OPA:

- Asynchronous
- Synchronous

In the asynchronous approach, you can push data to OPA using OPA's REST API or have OPA periodically fetch external data from an endpoint. For example, you can provide a centralized service that hosts bundles that OPA can download. Each bundle can contain both Rego policies and data. The data might express fine-grained business permissions that complement an access token. A bundle can serve multiple APIs by including multiple policies and various data.

When writing rules in Rego, you do not have to bother about the specifics; you simply assume that the external data is present. You reference the data via the global `data` variable. For example, the rule in Example 9-5 implements RBAC to check

---

2 Open Policy Agent, Kubernetes Overview & Architecture (*https://oreil.ly/zFoK-*).

whether a user can list orders. It assumes that OPA has a list of role permissions in its global data variable under data.permissions. We provide an example of how that data could look. OPA would have to receive that information independently of the policy (i.e., asynchronous to the policy evaluation).

Example 9-5. A policy in Rego using the global data variable

```
{
    "permissions" : {
        "customer": {
            "can_list_orders": true
        }
    }
}
# allow only if user can list orders
allow := true if {  ❶
    role_permission = data.permissions[input.user.role]
    role_permission.can_list_orders
    input.request.method == 'GET'
    input.request.endpoint == 'list_orders'
}
```

❶ Returns true if data.permissions contains permissions for input.user.role that allow the user to list orders.

Synchronous means that you get the data on demand during the policy evaluation. You can either fetch data using a built-in function like http.send in your policy, or you can use data from the query request. You can access data from the request via the global input variable, as we show in Example 9-5. To provide some input to the agent, send a POST request with the input in the request's body. Example 9-6 shows a request that queries the allow rule from Example 9-5 for a decision. The body of this HTTP request contains a JSON object called input that, in turn, holds all the input parameters for the policy. In this example, the input contains the parameters user (with the name and role of a user) and request (with the request's HTTP method and the endpoint name).

Example 9-6. A decision request to OPA with input data

```
POST /v1/data/policy/example/allow HTTP/1.1  ❶
Content-Type: application-json

{ "input" :
    {
        "user": {  ❷
            "name": "dana",
            "role": "customer"
```

```
    },
    "request": { ❷
        "method": "GET",
        "endpoint": "list_orders"
    }
    }
}
```

❶ The path comes from the package name of the rule (package policy.example) plus the rule name (allow).

❷ The parameters user and request match the ones in the policy (input.user and input.request).

The request in Example 9-6 contains a JSON object with the name and role of a user. As you know by now, there is a common, more secure source for user attributes—the access token. And this brings us to claims-based authorization.

Claims-Based Authorization

With OAuth, you can append the access token to the decision request instead of sending each user attribute in the query. In this way, your API does not need to care about the claims in the access token; it becomes independent of the claims principal. Instead, OPA takes over that part. It parses the access token and uses the claims it needs for its rules. Consequently, when you use this approach, you can update your policies and the related claims in the access token without having to update any API code. Thus, you can truly decouple API development from policies.

Example 9-7 illustrates a request that includes the access token in the body. It uses an input parameter called accessToken for that purpose. Since OPA does not make any assumptions on the data model, you can choose any name for the parameter or add any additional data with the access token such as the requested action and the resource type.

Example 9-7. A decision request to OPA with the access token

```
POST /v1/data/policy/example/allow HTTP/1.1
Content-Type: application-json

{ "input" :
    {
        "accessToken": "...", ❶
        "action": "list",
        "type": "order"
    }
}
```

❶ The parameter name `accessToken` contains an access token. This is the same access token that an API received from a client and that it forwards to the policy agent.

Of course, you need to adapt your policy to read and parse the access token to get to the claims. OPA has built-in functions for parsing JWTs. Example 9-8 shows how to decode the access token and get the role from the claims.

Example 9-8. You can use OPAs built-in functions to decode a JWT access token

```
package policy.example

import rego.v1

default allow := false
# allow rule
allow := true if {
    # get claims from token payload
    claims := io.jwt.decode(input.accessToken)[1] ❶
    role_permission = data.permissions[claims.role] ❷
    role_permission.can_list_orders ❸
}
```

❶ Parse the payload of the JWT access token from the input.

❷ Look up permissions based on the claim value.

❸ Check if the role from the access token has the permission to list orders.

Now, the policy agent implements claims-based authorization. It reads the relevant attributes from the access token, fetches additional data from the global data object, and returns the result according to the rule; that is, in Example 9-8 the rule returns `true` if the user has a role with the required permissions. Since both the API and the policy agent now use the access token for authorization, OPA becomes part of the token contract that we've highlighted in Chapter 6.

It is possible to validate the access token solely in OPA instead of your APIs. In that case, the API becomes completely unaware of the token details and does not need to maintain any scopes. The API also no longer has a direct trust relationship with the authorization server but only enforces the decision of the policy agent. In this case, however, you mix technical concerns (access token validation) with business concerns (authorization policies). You would need to distinguish between technical decisions and business decisions, as the former require a different behavior from APIs such as standard OAuth error codes. Therefore, you may want to separate concerns so that APIs implement JWT validation while OPA implements business authorization.

JWT validation with Rego in OPA

In case you decide to validate JWTs with Rego, you still need to follow the JWT validation best practices that we explain in Chapter 5. This includes validating the JWT digital signature, issuer, audience, and time-related claims and also enforcing required scopes. Use the built-in function `io.jwt.decode_verify` to decode and verify a JWT. This function can perform some basic validation such as checking the issuer, audience, and validity time. You still need to check the scope manually. In addition, you also need to cache token signing keys from the authorization server. Further, you need to communicate token validation failures to the APIs so that they can return appropriate error codes to their clients. As you can see, validating JWTs directly in OPA can actually complicate your setup instead of simplifying it. Thus, we recommend that you validate tokens in your APIs.

Decision Results

OPA returns the decision result of a policy evaluation in the HTTP response body. Using the example policy from Example 9-6, OPA returns only a Boolean in a JSON object but it can technically return any structured data. For example, it can return constraints for when it allows access, such as only allowing users to list orders with a given customer ID. Example 9-9 shows what such a response may look like.

Example 9-9. Decision response with constraints

```
HTTP/1.1 200 OK
Content-Type: application/json

{
    "result": true,
    "constraint": {
        "customer_id": "2099"
    },
    "decision_id": "3548ef94-0509-431b-b91c-3d136a4dbcde"
}
```

After parsing and checking the response from OPA, the API needs to enforce the decision and can then continue with its logic, and eventually return a response to the client. The response in Example 9-9 also contains a decision ID. OPA returns the decision ID if you enable decision logging. This ID can be useful for auditing purposes.

Auditing Authorization Decisions

OPA enables auditing with the help of decision logs that contain detailed and customizable information about authorization events. Since decision logs contain detailed information about a query, you can locate the entry which matches the `decision_id` of a response and analyze the logs to gain an understanding of the decision logic. You can also use decision logs to debug policy decisions.

OPA either sends decision logs periodically to external services, the local console output, or both. In Kubernetes, console output is collected as logs on Kubernetes nodes and a log shipping agent can deliver those logs to your log aggregation system instead. Alternatively, OPA can send HTTP `POST` requests directly to a log aggregator service and in this case expects the service to expose a suitable endpoint. To enable remote decision logs, configure OPA to use a service, as we show in Example 9-10.

Example 9-10. Enable remote decision logs

```
service:
  some-external-log-aggregator:
    url: https://logs.example.com/v1

decision_logs:
  service: some-external-log-aggregator
```

Now that you have some insights into writing Repo policies and audit policy decisions, let's explain how OPA can retrieve policies and receive updates.

Policy Retrieval in OPA

For OPA to make any decision, it needs to load the policy files. You should keep those policy files in a version control system to be able to audit changes. Set up a process to roll out updates to all or a set of OPA instances. The details depend on your preferences on how to retrieve policies and policy updates in OPA. You can choose between the following mechanisms:

- Update an embedded policy in code and redeploy the application. In this case, you lose some of the decoupling effect because you depend on the development lifecycle to roll out new policies.

- Update the policy files on OPA's file system. Let OPA watch (local) files and pick up changes automatically (the `opa run` command supports a `--watch` mode). If your distributed policy agents watch a shared file system, then you will have to update the policy at only one place for all instances.

- Use the REST API to push policies into OPA. You have to push the new policy to every instance of OPA. This means you also need to know which instances you have and how to call them.

- Package and publish the policy files (called *bundles* in OPA) via a REST API or an Open Container Image (OCI) registry. Configure OPA to periodically download bundles. In this way, all agents automatically receive updates when available.

Automate your workflow to distribute your policies. If you do not want to bother with the technical details, you may consider a tool like OPAL that automates the workflow for you. OPAL can monitor a policy repository for changes and automatically distribute new policies to various instances of OPA in real time. However, you can also utilize a CI/CD pipeline to automatically build your bundles with OPA's CLI and update your bundle-service, for example.

Authorization policies are a sensitive part of the overall security of your system. Make sure you have governance in place so that you allow only certain people to modify and deploy them to a production system. Always implement procedures that will allow you to audit who makes changes to policies and when.

So far, you've learned about the basics of authorization, how to work with an EMS, and OPA in particular. It's time to look at a concrete example to join the dots together.

Example Deployment

We provide a code example with this chapter that uses a policy engine for entitlements. You can find it in the folder *chapter-09-entitlements* of the GitHub repository of this book (*https://oreil.ly/CNDS-supp*). We illustrate the example deployment in Figure 9-4.

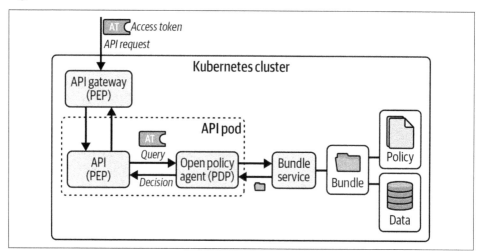

Figure 9-4. Setup of the example deployment with an API that uses OPA for fine-grained authorization

The example deployment consists of an API gateway, an API, and an OPA. When you deploy the example, OPA runs as a sidecar container next to the application container that runs the API code. We set up OPA to fetch policies from a bundle-service. To enable an end-to-end flow, we include a bundle-service in the example as well. The bundle-service is an HTTP server that hosts the policy bundle, which is effectively just a TAR archive.

The API is the code example from Chapter 5 and its deployment configures policy-based authorization using OPA. The API is an order service that includes operations to access orders. Example 9-11 shows the Kubernetes YAML file to deploy an API and OPA container in the same pod.

Example 9-11. Deploy OPA as a sidecar

```
kind: Deployment
apiVersion: apps/v1
metadata:
  name: zerotrustapi
  labels:
    app: zerotrustapi
spec:
  replicas: 1
  selector:
    matchLabels:
      app: zerotrustapi
  template:
    metadata:
      labels:
        app: zerotrustapi
    spec:
      serviceAccountName: zerotrustapi
      containers:
      - name: zerotrustapi
        image: zerotrustapi:1.0.0
        env:
          - name: NODE_ENV
            value: "production"
          - name: PORT
            value: "8000"
          - name: JWKS_URI
            value: "http://curity-idsvr-runtime-svc.authorizationserver:8443\
              /oauth/v2/oauth-anonymous/jwks"
          - name: AUTHORIZATION_STRATEGY
            value: "policy"
          - name: POLICY_ENDPOINT
            value: "http://127.0.0.1:8181/v1/data/orders/allow" ❶
      initContainers: ❷
      - name: policyengine
        image: openpolicyagent/opa:latest
        restartPolicy: Always ❷
```

```
args:
  - "run"
  - "--ignore=.*"
  - "--server"
  - "--addr"
  - "127.0.0.1:8181" ❸
  - "--set"
  - "decision_logs.console=true" ❹
  - "--set"
  - "services.policyRetrievalPoint.url=\
    http://policy-retrieval-point-svc" ❺
  - "--set"
  - "bundles.policyRetrievalPoint.resource=bundle.tar.gz" ❻
  - "--set"
  - "bundles.policyRetrievalPoint.persist=false"
  - "--v1-compatible"
readinessProbe: ❼
  httpGet:
    path: /health?bundle=true
    scheme: HTTP
    port: 8181
  initialDelaySeconds: 5
  periodSeconds: 5
```

❶ The containers in a pod share the same network namespace. The API can therefore communicate with OPA over the loopback interface.

❷ We start the OPA container as a sidecar to the application container.

❸ Listening address of the policy engine.

❹ Enable decision logs.

❺ Base URL of the PRP (with line break for display purposes).

❻ Path to the bundle.

❼ Sidecar containers support probes in Kubernetes.

The API uses an object called PolicyAuthorizer that has the PEP responsibility. This object makes an HTTP request to the OPA sidecar, which serves as the policy decision point. Example 9-12 shows how the API makes a request to OPA and provides input data. The API then receives a response containing a policy decision from OPA. All of the authorization logic takes place in OPA. The API must enforce only the OPA response.

Example 9-12. Querying OPA from the API for a policy decision

```
const options = {
    url: `${this.configuration.policyEndpoint}`,
    method: 'POST',
    headers: {
        'Content-Type': 'application/json'
    },
    data: {
        input: { ❶
            accessToken,
            action,
            type,
        }
    }
} as AxiosRequestConfig;

const axiosResponse = await axios(options); ❷
return new AuthorizationResult(axiosResponse.data.result.allowed,
axiosResponse.data.result.condition); ❸
```

❶ The API sends attributes as input that includes the access token. Note that we're using JavaScript's shorthand notation for fields that share the same name as the variable (accessToken instead of accessToken: accessToken).

❷ We use the Axios HTTP client to make HTTP calls to the policy agent.

❸ The API receives a policy result that indicates whether the policy allowed access and under which conditions.

We protect the example API using OAuth. This means that any requests to the API need to include a valid JWT access token that the API forwards to OPA. The API validates the JWT access token and requests a decision from OPA. The OPA policy decodes the JWT access token, reads the claims, and uses their values to apply a Rego policy similar to that from Example 9-8. OPA then writes a decision log entry that contains data related to the authorization event.

The GitHub repository (*https://oreil.ly/CNDS-supp*) provides some scripts that you can follow to deploy the overall system to a Kubernetes cluster. The deployment builds upon the Kubernetes cluster we explain in Chapter 8. Newly deployed components are the example API, its OPA sidecar, and a PRP containing OPA bundles. The *README* instructions explain how to run an end-to-end flow to get an access token and call the API using one of our client examples.

You can update the API code and redeploy that component, or you can update the Rego policy code and redeploy the PRP with a new OPA bundle. If you update the policy bundle with new rules, they come into effect when the API's OPA sidecar downloads the updated policy, without needing to redeploy the API. You should understand that the API developer role is usually separate from that of the person or team that implements policies. We show the API and Rego code together only so that you can see how they interact in deployed systems.

Summary

In this chapter, you have learned about the various strategies to express authorization rules. We discussed role-based (RBAC), relationship-based (ReBAC), and attribute-based access control (ABAC) models. ABAC can take into account any arbitrary attribute of the user, the protected resource, or context. Consequently, ABAC enables fine-grained yet flexible authorization policies. You can combine it with RBAC or ReBAC. As the access token contains authorization-related attributes, it is a suitable source for attributes in an ABAC model.

We have outlined that a policy engine assists in reducing the complexity of authorization in APIs by externalizing decisions. Instead of having APIs implement authorization rules in code, APIs can integrate with a policy engine to retrieve an authorization decision. OPA is an example of a policy engine that supports cloud native paradigms to enable scalable authorization. We have demonstrated that you can easily implement claims-based authorization by forwarding an access token to the policy engine.

This concludes the second part of the book. We hope you got a better understanding of access tokens and their role in authorization and API security. We wanted to show you many aspects of working with access tokens—from efficient API development, through design, secure usage of tokens, and how proxies work with tokens, to advanced authorization techniques. In the next part, we focus more on the cloud native environment and how its elements complement OAuth. We start with explaining how you can utilize cloud native infrastructure to further harden the security of your microservices, when multiple API calls inside a cluster process a single request from a client.

PART III

Operating Cloud Native OAuth

CHAPTER 10

Workload Identities

Once you complete your API authorization and deploy your APIs to Kubernetes, you are likely to have some further API security requirements, since OAuth alone does not solve all API security problems. Some security best practices, like hardening of containers and authorizing access to Kubernetes cluster resources, are outside the scope of this book. Instead, we want to highlight some characteristics of cloud native environments that can help to meet the following OAuth-related requirements:

- Malicious parties must be unable to read confidential internal API traffic.
- Only trusted clients must be able to reach the target APIs.
- Malicious parties must be unable to impersonate your APIs by using its secrets.
- Malicious parties must be unable to gain API access with a stolen token.

Cloud native infrastructure security provides additional building blocks that allow you to harden your API's security by leveraging workload identities. A workload is a piece of software such as a microservice running in Kubernetes. A workload identity is a set of attributes including a workload identifier that describe a workload. Workloads can prove their identity via a cryptographically verifiable credential.

In Kubernetes, you commonly deploy workloads as a Deployment containing a ReplicaSet with one or more pods. Each pod contains the application container and zero or more sidecar containers. Platform components can provide each workload a cryptographically verifiable assertion of its workload identity that the workload can send as a message credential and which recipient workloads can verify. We refer to this assertion as the *workload credential*. The difference between a workload credential and a workload identity is subtle, and literature tends to use the terms interchangeably because workload credentials provide the necessary security properties for workload identities to make them verifiable. In this chapter, we use the term *workload identity* to cover both the set of attributes of a workload and the related assertion. We call out the workload credential when we explicitly want to refer to the assertion and when we think a distinction is important.

Workload identities are an important building stone for your zero trust architecture because they enable workloads to authenticate to other workloads. With policies, you can further control access between workloads. In addition, the introduction of workload identities typically comes hand in hand with encrypted service-to-service communication. Such features reduce the attack surface in a cluster significantly. One of the important characteristics of workload identities is automation. This means that the platform takes care of automatically issuing and renewing workload credentials, which further improves the security of an API architecture.

In this chapter, we first explain how platform components can issue workload identities, to enable infrastructure credentials. We show how to use workload credentials to solve various security problems. We start by explaining how to enable TLS for internal requests. We then summarize how to restrict callers by their workload identities. We then explain how to use workload credentials as strong client credentials for OAuth-related flows, to prevent impersonation. Finally, we describe how you might use workload credentials to upgrade OAuth bearer tokens to sender-constrained tokens, which are constrained to particular senders of each such token. We complete the theory by pointing out some limitations of workload identities. We then finish the chapter with some practical content, to provide a Kubernetes workload identities deployment example that you can run locally on a computer.

First, let's explain how platform components can issue credentials to your application workloads.

Workload Identity Issuance

There are multiple platforms that can issue workload credentials to control how workloads interact. For example, managed cloud platforms, such as those from Microsoft, Amazon, and Google, enable you to use their workload credentials to authenticate applications. The platform assigns each workload a unique identifier. As an administrator, you may also be able to use workload identities to configure policies. For example, you may grant your API permissions to write to a managed logging service. When required, a workload can also get a credential with which to assert its identity in remote requests. Interoperability features may enable workloads from different managed platforms to call each other. You may also be able to assign workload identities to workloads in nonplatform environments (such as on-premise servers) so that they can interact with workloads that use other technologies.

Kubernetes provides a built-in mechanism to assign identities to workloads—the service account. If you do not specify a service account for a pod in your deployment, Kubernetes will use the `default` service account of the namespace. We recommend to explicitly assign each workload a unique service account name, to provide it with a workload identity. You can also use Kubernetes roles and role bindings to limit the access that a service account has to other workloads or the Kubernetes API server. Starting with Kubernetes v1.22, a workload can request a service account token for its service account in a JWT format, with which the workload can assert its identity to other workloads.

Ideally, when running in Kubernetes, you should choose a standards-based solution for workload identity issuance that enables you to solve a range of security problems. Standard-based solutions are likely to provide you with the best future interoperability. Interoperable workload identities across clusters is the goal of the Secure Production Identity Framework for Everyone (SPIFFE) (*https://spiffe.io*), which is a set of standards for establishing trust between workloads. SPIFFE enables you to deploy your workload identities anywhere, in the same manner as with Kubernetes itself. We therefore use SPIFFE to explain workload identity design patterns.

When using SPIFFE, you assign workloads a URI-based identifier, called a SPIFFE ID. The SPIFFE ID for a workload can be a value like `spiffe://example.com/ns/applications/sa/myapi`, deriving from the service account name and the namespace where you deploy the workload. Each workload can request a workload credential, a SPIFFE Verifiable Identity Document (SVID), with which it communicates its workload identity to other workloads. One type is an X.509 SVID, which can serve as a client credential for internal requests that use TLS. Another type is a JSON Web Token (JWT) SVID, where the JWT can serve as a client credential for internal requests that use application-level security. SPIFFE gives these credentials, and the public signing keys, a short default lifetime, such as 24 hours, which you can override if needed. In any case, the platform automatically renews the keys and related credentials.

The SPIFFE Runtime Environment (SPIRE) (*https://oreil.ly/PUbfU*) provides an implementation of the SPIFFE specifications. In a multicluster deployment, you typically need to establish trust across different trust domains. To achieve that, you may, for example, set up a federation between different SPIRE servers or use independent SPIRE deployments within each cluster and share certificate authorities to enable them to interoperate. We show one possible deployment in Figure 10-1, where two clusters use the same upstream root certificate authority and issue workload credentials using distinct intermediate certificate authorities.

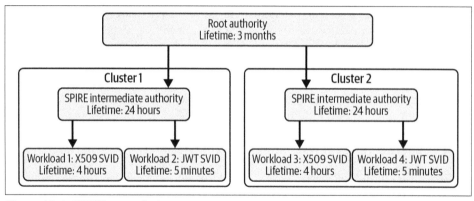

Figure 10-1. SPIRE trust chain

A pod that needs to use SPIFFE workload identities interacts with a SPIRE agent on the same Kubernetes node. Instances of the SPIRE agent contact the main SPIRE server to get SVIDs to issue to workloads. The SPIRE agent makes environment-specific validation checks to attest each workload before issuing it with a workload credential. For example, the agent might interrogate the operating system kernel of the Kubernetes node to verify expected properties of the running workload instance. The agent might also verify Kubernetes details configured against the workload's service account name. If all attestation checks pass, the agent issues the workload with an SVID. In Figure 10-2 we illustrate the issuance of distinct workload identities to two workloads. SVIDs are short lived and the SPIRE agent pushes an update to each workload before its SVID expires.

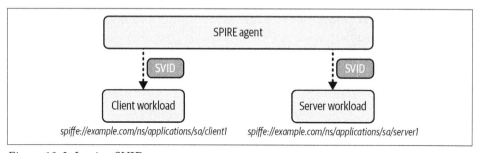

Figure 10-2. Issuing SVIDs

Once a pod has its SVID, it can prove its workload identity when communicating with a target workload. The recipient can validate the certificate or JWT credential, after which it considers the request authenticated and can trust the received SPIFFE ID. The target workload could allow or deny the source workload access based on the SPIFFE ID received.

The infrastructure required for workload identities is practically transparent to APIs. Often, APIs are not even aware of it. Workload identities are a highly useful addition to your security toolbox and can solve several problems. Next, let's look at a common use for workload identities, to enable request confidentiality inside the cluster.

Implementing Request Confidentiality

For endpoints exposed outside the Kubernetes cluster, it is usually straightforward to provide TLS, to ensure the confidentiality of API requests sent over the internet. The API gateway can use server certificates from a trusted root authority, which all internet clients trust. The certificate and its external domain name details are published as public information.

In a Kubernetes deployment, requests inside a cluster do not automatically use TLS. Instead, it is common for API requests, OAuth requests, and database requests to use plain protocols without TLS. In Figure 10-3 we show a flow from a client to an API to another API and then to a database, where the connection uses TLS only up to the cluster perimeter.

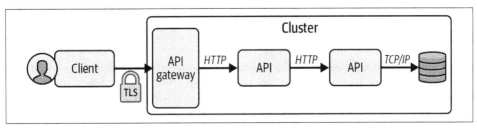

Figure 10-3. Nonconfidential connections inside the cluster

In a zero trust cluster, you should use a TLS solution to ensure the confidentiality of internal requests. Multiple solutions are possible. For example, the implementation of the Kubernetes networking stack uses the Container Networking Interface (CNI). It is possible to replace the default implementation with one that supports network-level encryption. Some specialist CNI implementations enable transparent encryption with a communication protocol such as WireGuard (*https://www.wireguard.com*) as an alternative or complement to TLS.

An option with greater application-level capabilities is to use an internal public key infrastructure (PKI). We have seen how SPIRE provides an internal PKI, though other PKI solutions are possible. For example, you could use the cert-manager cloud native component (*https://cert-manager.io*) to automate the issuance of certificates and keys to each workload. In Figure 10-4 we show an upgraded flow from a client to an API, to another API, and then to a database, using TLS.

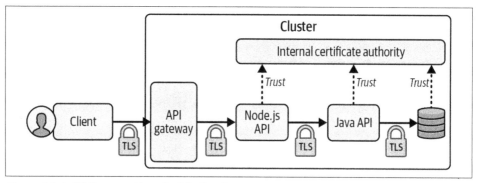

Figure 10-4. TLS connections inside the cluster

This type of implementation is difficult or impractical to manage. Firstly, you may need to deploy new certificate authorities to trust stores for the Java API, Node.js APIs, and database server. These business-focused applications must also deal reliably with certificate expiry and renewal. In addition, they must support revocation in case someone steals a long-lived certificate key. Ideally, you should ensure that API developers do not have to manage the complexity of SSL trust.

Service meshes help to overcome the difficulties because they manage lower-level certificate details for you. A service mesh can ensure that workloads cannot call HTTP endpoints of other workloads directly. Instead, each workload request passes a proxy, which could be a sidecar container, an agent running on its Kubernetes node, or its networking stack. APIs can call each other using plain HTTP and the middleware upgrades the connection to use TLS. The service mesh can provide an API gateway implementation that uses the same proxy technology to call upstream workloads using mTLS. Again, the API is not aware of this infrastructure and API developers only need to use the correct URLs for upstream calls. In Figure 10-5 we show an example that illustrates the use of sidecars in an end-to-end flow between APIs.

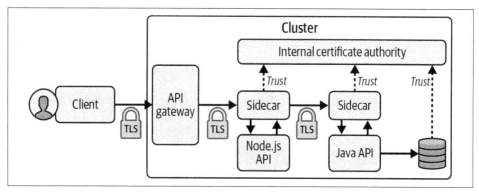

Figure 10-5. Managed TLS connections inside the cluster

You should aim to implement request confidentiality for all workloads that make API and OAuth requests, including requests from the gateway to APIs and requests from backend clients to the authorization server. These workloads do not usually need to know details about their sidecar's certificates and keys or deal with certificate trust, expiry, or revocation. The PKI can use short lifetimes for certificates and keys, including those for the intermediate certificate authority. Service mesh components (like sidecars) receive new certificates and keys from the PKI before existing ones expire.

Operating an internal PKI remains nontrivial. There is a learning curve and you are likely to need to scale the deployment across multiple clusters. The cloud native building blocks should do most of the work for you. Once you have deployed the PKI infrastructure to enable request confidentiality, you can use the same infrastructure for other workload identity use cases. The simplest of these is to restrict which workloads can call each other.

Restricting Workload Access

When a server uses TLS, the server presents an X.509 certificate to clients. A service mesh also provides mTLS. This means the client also presents an X.509 certificate to the server. The server therefore knows which workload is calling it and can decide whether or not to allow the request.

A target workload's proxy can use mTLS to restrict access based on the source workload's identity. To restrict which workloads can reach an API, you just express your desired state using Kubernetes CustomResourceDefinitions (CRDs) that the service mesh provides. For example, you may be able to express an array of SPIFFE IDs. Restricting access by workload identity is useful for many simple workload-to-workload security use cases. For example, if only APIs should be able to call a log aggregation workload, you can deny access to non-API workloads. Doing so can reduce the impact of an incident as the infrastructure-level security limits the possible traffic of compromised workloads.

Some target workloads, such as authorization servers and database servers, must receive a workload identity and map it to a different client identity. This requires the client workload to explicitly send a workload credential to the server workload, instead of relying on the proxy to implicitly add the workload credential. By doing so, the client presents hardened credentials.

Hardening Credentials

We recommend that you review your end-to-end usage of client credentials and understand where you can strengthen them. We show an initial deployment in Figure 10-6, where a browser-based application uses a backend client to get tokens from the authorization server and encrypt them into HTTP-only cookies. Inside the cluster, the API gateway can decrypt a cookie and forward a JWT access token to APIs, which ultimately returns authorized data to the browser-based application.

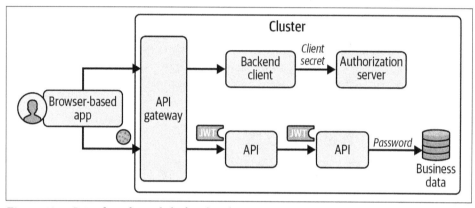

Figure 10-6. Initial credentials before hardening

Notice that different clients use different types of credentials:

- The backend client uses a client secret.
- The API's database connection uses a password.
- The browser-based application sends an HTTP-only cookie containing an encrypted access token.
- APIs call each other inside the cluster using the cookie's underlying signed access token.

A malicious party could steal and misuse any of these, so you need to protect all of them. In the example flow, the client secret and database password are not time restricted. Ideally, you should rotate them frequently, but doing so can be difficult to manage since you must coordinate rollouts to both a client and a server. This some-times leads to string-based credentials that you never renew. If a malicious party steals such a value, it could exploit the credential for a long time.

Clients like browser-based applications run in a constrained environment and cannot assert their own workload identity. Instead, the best they can do is follow environ-mental best practices. For a browser-based application, this includes calling APIs using a server-issued HTTP-only cookie. We provide detailed security recommendations for browser-based applications in Chapter 13.

In the example flow, the cookie and token are cryptographically strong but they are bearer credentials. A malicious party that somehow intercepts such a credential can use it to gain unauthorized access. An alternative to bearer tokens is sender-constrained tokens, where clients need to provide a proof that they are the legitimate sender.

Workload identities and cloud native infrastructure should enable you to harden the security of all credentials inside your cluster. To do so, follow cloud native security recommendations. In particular, check out the IETF working group for Workload Identity in Multi System Environments (WIMSE) (*https://oreil.ly/cBGno*) that works on recommendations that combine cloud native and OAuth security. In the following sections, we explain some techniques you can use, starting with a way to harden OAuth client credentials.

Using Platform-Issued JWTs as Credentials

You can harden OAuth client credentials of your workloads with platform-issued JWTs. The IETF draft on "Workload Identity Practices" (*https://oreil.ly/9VWJY*) lists common patterns on how workloads can authenticate at the authorization server's token endpoint using the platform-issued JWT. The JWT serves as a client assertion in accordance with the "JSON Web Token (JWT) Profile for OAuth 2.0 Client Authentication and Authorization Grants" specification (RFC 7523) (*https://oreil.ly/i16Mx*). According to the draft, the JWT must meet certain preconditions.

- The iss claim is the identifier for the platform component that issues the JWT.
- The sub claim must contain the workload's identity.
- The aud claim must contain a value that identifies the authorization server.

Your workload could use either a Kubernetes service account token, or a JWT SVID that SPIRE issues. In both cases, the workload can receive a client assertion file on disk and the platform keeps this file up-to-date. In the authorization server, you configure the client to require client assertion JWTs for authentication and provide a link to the verification keys of the platform. When the authorization server receives a client assertion JWT, it validates the JSON Web Signature (JWS) of the client assertion, along with standard protocol claims including the issuer and audience. In Figure 10-7 we illustrate a flow where an OAuth client authenticates at the authorization server using a service account token.

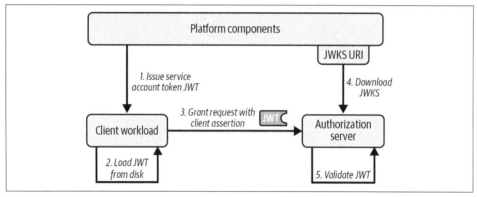

Figure 10-7. OAuth client assertion grant with platform-issued JWT

We provide an example payload for a platform-issued service account token (JWT) in Example 10-1. The client workload only needs to load this JWT from disk and send it to the authorization server. Note that the sub field uses a Kubernetes-specific identity, whereas the authorization server requires its own client identity (the client ID). Therefore, your authorization server should enable you to map between the two client identities.

Example 10-1. Payload of platform-issued client assertion

```
{
    "aud": [
        "https://login.democluster.example/oauth/v2/oauth-token"
    ],
    "exp": 1701463685,
    "iat": 1701456485,
    "iss": "https://kubernetes.default.svc.cluster.local",
    "kubernetes.io": {
        "namespace": "applications",
        "pod": {
            "name": "oauthclient-69466d7678-qc2cv",
            "uid": "7ff9e2e4-addc-4f98-8769-93d8cd5b79fe"
        },
        "serviceaccount": {
            "name": "oauthclient",
            "uid": "ed4e6cf1-5cbf-452a-91c4-4c985299f6bc"
        }
    },
    "nbf": 1701456485,
    "sub": "system:serviceaccount:applications:oauthclient"
}
```

If your authorization server supports using client assertions with the client credential grant, we recommend that you use it in your backend clients to get tokens from the authorization server. You no longer need to use client secrets or deal with rotation. Instead, the platform keeps the service account token short lived and automatically renews it. Next, let's look at a use case that requires a different technique, where you use X.509 SVIDs as workload credentials.

Using X.509 SVIDs as Credentials

Some types of workloads support authentication using trusted client certificates. For example, a database server might be able to accept X.509 client certificates that map to database users. In such cases, clients can use X.509 SVIDs. The client workload (or its sidecar) must get an X.509 SVID that maps to the client identity that the server workload requires. Rather than using proxies and the features that a service mesh provides, the client workload can use a specialist helper utility that retrieves X.509 SVIDs such as the SPIFFE Helper (*https://oreil.ly/VS3V-*). The client workload can then explicitly send a client certificate when applicable.

In the case of SPIFFE Helper, you deploy the utility as a sidecar, which uses the SPIFFE workload API to download SVIDs to a volume that it shares with the main container. The SPIFFE Helper sidecar receives SVID updates, to keep keys, workload certificates, and certificate chains up-to-date. When the source workload needs to make a remote connection, it loads from the shared volume the certificate files that the SPIFFE Helper downloaded and uses them to make an mTLS connection. We illustrate the approach in Figure 10-8, where a client workload uses mTLS to connect to a server workload, without the use of HTTP proxies.

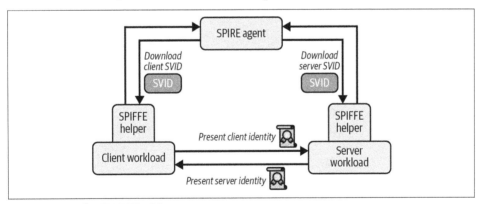

Figure 10-8. The SPIFFE Helper pattern

You can also override the certificate's subject name. For example, an API that calls a database server might need to present an X.509 certificate with a common name that matches a database user. In Example 10-2, we show some example certificate details for an API workload that represents a database user. Note that the full SPIFFE ID remains in the SVID's subject alternative names (SANs) so that other recipients of the workload's X.509 SVID can continue to use that identifier in the certificate to verify the caller.

Example 10-2. X.509 SVID with multiple identities

```
Common Name : apidatabaseuser
Alternative Names : apidatabaseuser,
                    URI:spiffe://democluster.internal/ns/applications/sa/demoapi
Organization : SPIRE
Country : US
Valid From : March 1, 2025
Valid To : March 1, 2025
Issuer : SPIFFE
```

The SPIFFE Helper pattern provides an alternative way for clients to authenticate at the authorization server. When a client needs to authenticate, it can present an X.509 client certificate credential. Instead of using a proxy, the authorization server containers can terminate mTLS connections using the SPIFFE Helper pattern. Each container receives the server certificate and key that it uses to present at HTTPS endpoints, and the certificate authorities and intermediate certificate authorities that the platform uses to issue client certificates. To authenticate a request, the authorization server first verifies the received client certificate's trust chain and then reads the SPIFFE ID from the client certificate. Authentication succeeds when the authorization server locates an OAuth client whose configuration includes the SPIFFE ID.

Since X.509 SVIDs are key-based credentials, you can also potentially use them to upgrade a bearer token to a sender-constrained token once the bearer token enters your cluster. Let's explore how that might work next.

Hardening Bearer Tokens

Typically, you issue access tokens for web and mobile clients as bearer tokens. Even if you use sender-constrained tokens with your external clients, you most probably terminate them in the API gateway and forward bearer tokens, as we've shown in "Terminating Tokens" on page 165. When bearer tokens reach the backend cluster, they could leak and introduce the potential for exploits. For example, a token might leak if a developer unintentionally outputs a JWT to API logs. Alternatively, a malicious API might use an access token in unexpected ways, sending it to other APIs.

One partial resolution might be to use service mesh features where the API's sidecar validates the access token and then forwards claims as JSON to the target API. With Istio (*https://oreil.ly/5Nd6y*), for example, you can define authorization policies based on the access token in the header. In this case, Istio rejects a request before it gets to the API if an access token does not meet its authorization policy. For simple use cases, if the sidecar follows the JWT validation practices we explain in Chapter 5, this is fine, since the API trusts its sidecar. In more complex use cases, though, receiving claims in a form of a JSON from the sidecar will prevent an API from interacting with upstream APIs using the token sharing techniques that we explain in Chapter 6.

Instead, you might combine workload identities with OAuth token exchange to enable a more complete solution. This would enable you to upgrade bearer tokens to sender-constrained tokens once they enter your cluster. Such a sender-constrained token is bound to a workload identity.

Service-to-service communication using workload identities

At the time of writing, the WIMSE working group is working on future best practices on how to use workload identities for service-to-service authentication. You can track their progress in the "WIMSE Service to Service Authentication" draft specification (*https://oreil.ly/sRd_K*).

In Figure 10-9 we illustrate one possible flow that you could use to strengthen access tokens inside your cluster. The flow starts with the client initiating calls through an API gateway to two upstream APIs. The API gateway calls the authorization server to exchange the incoming token for a sender-constrained token, which it forwards to the first API. The first API completes its work and then calls the authorization server to exchange its sender-constrained token for a new sender-constrained token, then forwards it to the second API. All access tokens that APIs receive are therefore hardened.

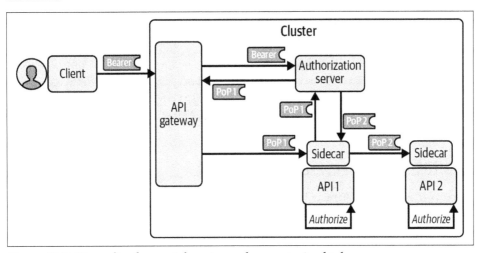

Figure 10-9. Upgrading bearer tokens to sender-constrained tokens

When using OAuth token exchange (RFC 8693) (*https://oreil.ly/zVKgB*), an API acts as an OAuth client. The API can initiate a token exchange request to the authorization server's token endpoint to get a sender-constrained token. The authorization server uses the API's X.509 SVID for the `cnf` claim as we illustrate in Example 10-3. You can read up on sender-constrained tokens in Chapter 7.

Example 10-3. Sender-constrained access token

```
{
    "iss": "https://login.example.com",
    "aud": "api1",
    "scope": "openid retail/orders",
    "sub": "c2adfb75-d73e-4012-9ff1-0dd0a5aa9c03",
    "iat": 1690564981657,
    "exp": 1690565941657,
    "customer_id": "7791",
    "roles": ["customer"],
    "cnf":{
        "x5t#S256": "FjeHcvJwiHXlr8dgnP7UvLQ7dLLMTe_3SgMYMuEpekc"
    }
}
```

On every API request with a sender-constrained token, the target API's sidecar could verify that the X.509 client credential in the current request matches that in the access token's `cnf` claim. For valid requests, the API's main security responsibility remains authorization, to enforce business rules using claims received in access tokens. If an access token leaks and a malicious party replays it, the API's sidecar would reject the request, since the malicious party would be unable to supply the correct private key. Similarly, if another workload tries to send an intercepted access token using a different workload credential, the hash over its credential does not match the `cnf` claim, so the target API rejects the request.

We have seen that OAuth and SPIFFE identities can work together to improve security. We expect further use cases, design patterns, and best practices to emerge, which you can use once you have this type of infrastructure setup. As for any security building block, workload identities do not solve all problems. Let's briefly reiterate some limitations of workload identities.

Limitations of Workload Identities

Workload credentials primarily enable authentication-only solutions. The platform issues, and automatically renews, hardened credentials to enable backend workloads to prove their identity to each other with strong security. We have seen that it potentially enables you to meet the requirements listed at the start of this chapter:

- Malicious parties must be unable to read confidential internal API traffic.

- Only trusted clients must be able to reach the target APIs.

- Malicious parties must be unable to impersonate your APIs by using their secrets.

- Malicious parties must be unable to gain API access with a stolen token.

Workload identities and workload credentials are not meant to provide a complete security solution for your APIs, though. They are an internal tool to authenticate workloads. You should not use workload identities to implement business authorization or to replace access tokens. Workload identities cannot help you to solve the following types of requirements:

- Each API must receive runtime claims about users and deny access to unauthorized business resources.

- Clients must receive a least-privilege message credential designed in terms of business permissions.

- Users must authenticate to enable a frontend client to get an access token.

- Users who own API resources must consent to the client's level of API access.

You still need OAuth flows and access tokens to fulfill these requirements. You need the OAuth code flow to authenticate and interact with users. You still need access tokens to authorize requests and enforce business rules. Workload identities complement OAuth with secure, managed client credentials.

Now that you understand how to use workload identities, let's finish with some practical content so that you can see workload identities in action on your local computer.

Workload Identities Code Example

We provide a demo-level Kubernetes code example for a development computer to enable you to run some application use cases. You can find the example in the folder *chapter-10-workload-identities* of the GitHub repository of this book (*https://oreil.ly/ CNDS-supp*). The example is the most complex of the book's Kubernetes deployments, since it uses more infrastructure than the other examples. We illustrate the components in Figure 10-10.

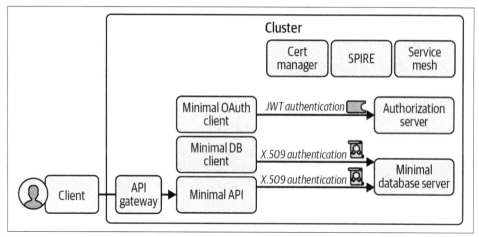

Figure 10-10. Components that the example deploys

The code example has multiple *README* files that you can browse, with links to further information, to enable you to understand prerequisites, technical settings, and behaviors. Since the objective is solely to get connections working, the application workloads are minimal. Our main motivation is to show you how to implement the following use cases:

- Enable transparent mTLS connections.
- Use JWT client assertions to authenticate at the authorization server.
- Demonstrate how workloads can use X.509 SVIDs.

Base Setup

We provide several scripts, similar to the example Kubernetes deployment from Chapter 8. You run the following four scripts, to first create the Kubernetes cluster with an external load balancer. Next, we deploy cert-manager and use it to create a root certificate for SPIRE and deploy SPIRE as the issuer of workload identities. We then deploy a service mesh to enable application workloads to use transparent mTLS. Finally, we deploy an API gateway that receives external requests and routes them to internal workloads within the mesh.

- *1-create-cluster.sh*
- *2-deploy-pki.sh*
- *3-deploy-service-mesh.sh*
- *4-deploy-api-gateway.sh*

Base infrastructure

We use Istio as the service mesh, with SPIRE configured as its issuer of its workload identities and credential. We deploy both of these subsystems using the official Helm charts, though we mostly use default settings. Our example deployment aims only to get you up and running in a basic way, to demonstrate some workload identity use cases. For your real environments, you would need to do further work to harden the deployments and refine your PKI settings. Check out Istio's recommended best practices (*https://oreil.ly/QsKEq*) for setting up and managing an Istio service mesh.

The example deployment enables you to apply a custom Kubernetes label to your workloads, such as `spire-managed-identity`. When you configure this label against a workload and the platform deploys pods, the SPIRE controller manager registers a SPIRE entry for each pod in the workload. In Example 10-4, we show a Kubernetes CRD called a `ClusterSPIFFEID` that enables this behavior.

Example 10-4. A custom resource that enables SPIFFE ID registration

```
apiVersion: spire.spiffe.io/v1alpha1
kind: ClusterSPIFFEID
metadata:
  name: default-spiffe-id
spec:
  spiffeIDTemplate: "spiffe://{{ .TrustDomain }}/ns/{{ .PodMeta.Namespace }}/sa/\
  {{ .PodSpec.ServiceAccountName }}"
  podSelector:
    matchLabels:
      spire-managed-identity: "true"
```

This setup enables your workloads to use both the service mesh's transparent mTLS and also to actively use SVIDs when required. Since this example deployment uses certificate infrastructure, we also use an OpenSSL script to create an external TLS certificate and key and configure it against the gateway. We use a wildcard certificate that supports multiple host names. We show the gateway configuration in Example 10-5.

Example 10-5. A Gateway resource for HTTPS requests to `*.democluster.example` and `*.webapp.example`

```
apiVersion: gateway.networking.k8s.io/v1
kind: Gateway
metadata:
  name: kong-gateway
spec:
  gatewayClassName: kong
```

```
listeners:
- name: https-democluster
  port: 443
  protocol: HTTPS
  hostname: "*.democluster.example"
  allowedRoutes:
    namespaces:
      from: 'All'
  tls:
    mode: Terminate
    certificateRefs:
      - kind: Secret
        name: external-tls
- name: https-webapp
  port: 443
  protocol: HTTPS
  hostname: "*.webapp.example"
  allowedRoutes:
    namespaces:
      from: 'All'
  tls:
    mode: Terminate
    certificateRefs:
      - kind: Secret
        name: external-tls
```

Once you deploy the base infrastructure, the API gateway pods use a service mesh sidecar to initiate calls to upstream workloads using mTLS. In this type of deployment, you can configure some or all of your application workloads to require mTLS. We show how to do so in our first practical use case, to use a workload credential as an OAuth client credential.

Using Workload Identities Transparently

The next two scripts deploy an authorization server and a simple client. The connection from the client to the authorization server uses mTLS transparently. The authorization server deployment is also hardened, to protect its secrets. We explain authorization server secret protection in Chapter 11. Once deployed, the client calls the authorization server's token endpoint to get access tokens.

- *5-deploy-authorization-server.sh*
- *6-deploy-oauth-client.sh*

You can use labels and annotations to enable transparent mTLS between pods with SPIRE-issued workload identities. Using `sidecar.istio.io/inject: 'true'` means that an Istio proxy sidecar should be spun up, to intercept all inbound and outbound traffic to the main container. The `spire-managed-identity: 'true'` label instructs the SPIRE controller manager to register a workload identity for the pod. The `inject.istio.io/templates: 'sidecar,spire'` annotation template is responsible for mounting the SPIFFE workload endpoint into the workload's sidecar container so that it can receive SVIDs from SPIRE. We illustrate a partial Deployment resource for the client in Example 10-6.

Example 10-6. Transparent mTLS using a SPIRE identity

```
apiVersion: apps/v1
kind: Deployment
metadata:
  name: oauthclient
spec:
  replicas: 1
  selector:
    matchLabels:
      app: oauthclient
  template:
    metadata:
      labels:
        app: oauthclient
        sidecar.istio.io/inject: 'true'
        spire-managed-identity: 'true'
      annotations:
        inject.istio.io/templates: 'sidecar,spire'
```

The client is not aware of the service mesh and the infrastructure security it provides. As far as the client is concerned, it calls HTTP endpoints. However, when requesting tokens, the client must authenticate. For that it utilizes a service account token.

Using JWT Workload Identities

The client receives a client assertion JWT from Kubernetes with which it can authenticate at the authorization server. We show the relevant configuration in Example 10-7, where the client requests a service account token whose audience includes the identifier of the authorization server.

Example 10-7. Requesting a service account token

```
spec:
  serviceAccountName: oauthclient
  containers:
  - name: oauthclient
    image: oauthclient:v1
    volumeMounts:
    - mountPath: /var/run/secrets/kubernetes.io/serviceaccount
      name: client-assertion-location
  volumes:
  - name: client-assertion-location
```

```
    projected:
      sources:
      - serviceAccountToken:
          path: token
          expirationSeconds: 3600
          audience: 'https://login.democluster.example'
```

Once deployed, you can get a shell to the client pod and make an HTTP request using the curl command line tool. Note that the identifier of the authorization server (aud) is not necessarily the same as the token endpoint. The token endpoint that a client calls may be a URL that differs from the audience value. Workloads, for example, use internal URLs to connect to the authorization server. We show an internal request from the client to the authorization server's token endpoint in Example 10-8.

Example 10-8. Token request with a client assertion credential

```
SERVICE_ACCOUNT_TOKEN="$(cat /var/run/secrets/kubernetes.io/serviceaccount/token)"
curl -X POST \
    http://curity-idsvr-runtime-svc.authorizationserver:8443/oauth/v2/oauth-token \
 -H 'Content-Type: application/x-www-form-urlencoded' \
 -d 'grant_type=client_credentials' \
 -d 'client_id=oauthclient' \
 -d "client_assertion=$SERVICE_ACCOUNT_TOKEN" \
 -d 'client_assertion_type=urn:ietf:params:oauth:client-assertion-type:jwt-bearer' \
 -d 'scope=products'
```

In this example, the client uses a plain HTTP URL and the service mesh upgrades the connection between the client's sidecar and the authorization server's sidecar to use mTLS. The client also sends its service account token as a JWT client assertion and successfully receives a token response. To upgrade a workload from client secrets to workload identities you only need to load the token from disk and alter a couple of parameters. For other types of connections, you may need to use a different type of credentials. Therefore, in the next section, we show how to work with X.509 SVIDs.

Using X.509 Workload Identities

The final scripts enable you to use X.509 SVIDs. As an example, we use an mTLS connection between a REST API, developed in Kotlin, and a PostgreSQL database server. First, you deploy a database server with a minimal database. Next, you deploy a shell-based database client, which enables you to test sending SVIDs manually. Finally, you deploy a REST API, which also acts as a database client.

- *7-deploy-dbserver.sh*
- *8-deploy-dbclient.sh*
- *9-deploy-api.sh*

To receive SVIDs, all three workloads must mount the SPIFFE workload API. They do so using a utility called the SPIFFE CSI Driver (*https://oreil.ly/VMR-v*), which binds the Unix domain socket to a Kubernetes Volume. We show a partial deployment configuration for the API workload in Example 10-9.

Example 10-9. Mounting the SPIFFE workload API

```
spec:
  serviceAccountName: demoapi
  containers:
  - name: demoapi
    image: demoapi:v1
    env:
      - name: API_PORT
        value: '8000'
      - name: API_DB_CONNECTION
        value: "jdbc:postgresql://dbserver-svc/products?sslmode=verify-full&\
        sslfactory=io.spiffe.provider.SpiffeSslSocketFactory"
      - name: SPIFFE_ENDPOINT_SOCKET
        value: 'unix:///spiffe-workload-api/socket'
    volumeMounts:
      - name: spiffe-workload-api
        mountPath: /spiffe-workload-api
        readOnly: true
  volumes:
    - name: spiffe-workload-api
      csi:
        driver: "csi.spiffe.io"
        readOnly: true
```

Once you have run the deployment scripts, you can remote to the database server and shell-based database client containers and view the SVID files downloaded to disk. In Example 10-10, we show how you can use the command line to establish a secure database connection using X.509 SVID files that the SPIFFE Helper downloaded to a volume.

Example 10-10. Database connection with X.509 SVIDs

```
export PGSSLKEY='/svids/svid_key.pem'
export PGSSLCERT='/svids/svid.pem'
export PGSSLROOTCERT='/svids/svid_bundle.pem'
psql postgresql://dbclient@dbserver-svc/products?sslmode=verify-full
```

The API uses a slightly different technique, where a helper library listens on the SPIFFE workload API to receive X.509 SVIDs and then stores them in memory. The library uses a custom socket factory object to connect to the database server using mTLS, and present the client certificate. The technique of forming an X.509 client credential from SVID documents could be used for other types of connections. For example, an API could use it in an OAuth token exchange request to the authorization server, to swap a bearer token for a sender-constrained token.

If you successfully deploy the cluster and work through the *READMEs*, you will understand how to use workload identities in multiple ways. With this knowledge, you could apply the same building blocks to other security use cases.

Summary

When you use OAuth correctly, you enable an architecture to deal with business authorization and user identities in your APIs. You can then use workload identities to further harden your backend cluster to securely retrieve and transport access tokens. There are various ways to implement workload identities, and we discussed service meshes as well as SPIFFE. Workload identities enable encrypted channels and workload-to-workload authentication solutions. Each workload communicates its identity using a short-lived credential. SPIFFE supports different identity documents, to send credentials using either transport (X.509) or message-level (JWT) security.

Platform components provide the low-level components to enable an internal PKI with good manageability. These building blocks enable you to use workload identities reliably, and to externalize the complexity from your APIs. You gain access to cryptographically strong, short-lived, and automatically renewed client credentials. These enable various solutions for internal traffic, including request confidentiality, restricting access, credential hardening, and sender-constrained access tokens.

Workload identities are an authentication solution that you can and should combine with OAuth. For that, an authorization server should support JWT assertions for client authentication. In addition, it needs to be able to map workload identities to OAuth client configurations for you to be able to utilize workload identities in an OAuth context. Since the authorization server is such a central component of your API security architecture, we believe you should have full control over its deployment. Therefore, we discuss the requirements and what you should think about when managing a cloud native authorization server in the next chapter.

CHAPTER 11

Managing a Cloud Native Authorization Server

An authorization server is a critical security component that you must manage over time. When getting started, you may have a number of concerns:

- How do I ensure zero-downtime upgrades?
- How do I manage changes to security settings across multiple teams?
- How do I ensure that my authorization server is highly available?
- How do I troubleshoot failures during OAuth flows?
- How do I monitor API security and receive early warning of threats?

You might prefer to use a managed identity-as-a-service (IDaaS) solution for your authorization server. You then get some deployment conveniences and can point your applications and APIs to internet OAuth endpoints. You do not need to deploy any containers and upgrades occur automatically. You also trust the provider to ensure high availability. You still need to manage identity data like user accounts and configuration settings for all stages of your deployment pipeline. In some cases, an IDaaS service may meet all of your main requirements.

Your requirements may evolve over time. With a cloud native authorization server, you get more control over how to adapt to your specific needs and future requirements. We think that control is important because the authorization server is, after all, a critical component to your business. We believe that if you can manage APIs using cloud native patterns, you can manage a cloud native authorization server as well. You then get a solution that allows you to maximize the capabilities that OAuth provides. To keep your options open and ensure that it is possible to migrate from an

IDaaS to a cloud native authorization server, we recommend that you use portable OAuth code in your APIs and clients.

In this chapter, we demystify the management of a cloud native authorization server. You will learn about the requirements for managing a cloud native authorization server that further enables you to ask informed questions to vendors no matter their business model. We explain how to address the primary concerns using cloud native patterns so that you can operate your authorization server efficiently. Much of what we describe is standard deployment and operational architecture. Even if you already follow these practices for other components, the overall knowledge is often split between roles like developers, platform engineers, and DevOps. We therefore provide an overview so that you get familiar with the patterns no matter your role. We keep the content fairly high level and explain how you should reason about an authorization server if you haven't deployed one before.

Out of scope

Full details of cloud native patterns or database administration are outside the scope of this book. You can read much more about them online, starting in the Kubernetes Concepts articles (*https://oreil.ly/tAwZH*). For a deep dive into best practices, we recommend the book *Production Kubernetes* by Josh Russo, et al. (O'Reilly, 2021), which provides many operational insights.

We first explain hosting, which components to deploy, how they share data, how to cluster them, and how you assign them URLs. We then show how deployment, configuration, and zero-downtime upgrades work. Next, we explain how various teams can operate on the authorization server's data to manage users and OAuth configuration. We then explain reliability, where you use cloud native techniques to ensure high availability and resolve OAuth errors promptly. To finish, we explain security auditing, where you report on both your authorization server's logs and your API's authorization after the event, to centrally govern your security.

Let's get started on the details, to explain how you host a cloud native authorization server.

Hosting

A cloud native authorization server is a specialist API that you usually do not develop yourself. You should choose from either an open source or a commercial implementation and then need to deploy it. To design the hosting of your authorization server, start by understanding the components. Let's explain what components you need and how they interact.

Components

A cloud native authorization server typically consists of three main types of workloads:

- A workload to provide OAuth endpoints for your applications
- A workload for administration
- A workload that provides data storage

You should separate the concerns of operation and administration. Thus, you should have separate workloads for the OAuth and administrative tasks of your authorization server. We call the main workload that implements the OAuth protocol interfaces the runtime workload. The workload that offers administration capabilities for the authorization server is the admin workload. These workloads can share the same code base; that is, they can be part of the same product but they have different responsibilities. You also need a dedicated workload for data storage. You may be able to pick your preferred choice for the data storage workload(s) depending on the support of the authorization server. Figure 11-1 shows the workloads you typically need to deploy.

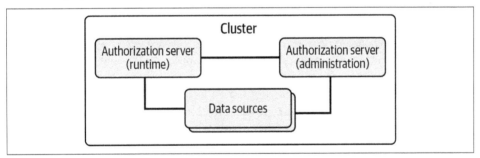

Figure 11-1. Authorization server workloads

You should be able to logically structure runtime workloads. OAuth deployments require some design thought since there can be different requirements depending on the characteristics and nature of OAuth clients. For example, you typically have different requirements for internal clients and external clients (e.g., supporting workload identities for internal clients, as discussed in Chapter 10). Consequently, you may decide to deploy runtime workloads as multiple services. You might assign each runtime workload a logical service role, where each role provides only a subset of OAuth behaviors that you need to fulfill the requirements of certain clients.

A service role matches what Kubernetes calls a Service. Service roles enable you to design deployments in interesting ways. For example, you can define an internal service role that includes only features relevant for internal clients, with JSON Web

Key Set (JWKS) and token exchange endpoints and the use of workload identities. You can then scale those workloads with the `internal` service role independently from workloads that serve external clients. Similarly, you can have workloads with distinct service roles for each tenant in a multitenant deployment, to provide a service tailored to each tenant. Ideally, you should manage all service roles with the same admin role; that is, they should be part of the same authorization server and share the same key material. You should not need to duplicate a whole authorization server.

Use the admin workload to manage the configuration of your authorization server including, but not limited to, any OAuth configuration. Depending on how often you need to update the configuration, you may only spin up the admin workload when you need it and thus minimize risks (a system that does not exist cannot be misused). The admin workload can offer user interfaces for manual configuration. While an intuitive user interface can help you to integrate, the admin workload should also offer programmable interfaces like APIs or CLIs that allow for tool-based integrations. In a highly dynamic environment that cloud native commonly implies, it is important to be able to automate tasks and quickly update configuration on demand. The admin workload then distributes the configuration to the runtime workloads.

The runtime workload is the main component of your authorization server; thus, many of the requirements and techniques discussed further are mostly relevant for the runtime workload. As the techniques that we describe are general enough, you can apply them to the admin workload as well, if applicable. One of the concerns we listed at the beginning was availability. To address availability concerns, you can use Kubernetes ReplicaSets when deploying the authorization server. ReplicaSets create multiple instances of a pod (e.g., a runtime workload). Let's therefore discuss how multiple runtime workloads share state, both within a cluster and across multiple clusters.

Clustering

We recommend running at minimum two runtime pods so that you avoid a solitary pod that is a single point of failure. Though there are several instances of a pod, they still form the same logical application that you route traffic to. In Kubernetes, you use Kubernetes Service resources for that purpose. You would have services for your runtime instances and, if applicable, admin instances. With the default Kubernetes `ServiceType` of `ClusterIP` the platform load balances requests between the pods of a service. For best scalability, the workloads of your authorization server should not require server affinity so that multiple pods can process the set of messages in an OAuth flow. To enable this, the pods must share state.

In Chapter 4, we explain the three types of state an authorization server uses: for configuration, user data, and operational data. The instances of your cloud native authorization server interact with your data sources to manage state. A shared database is usually the default option. If a database becomes a performance bottleneck, you may consider the addition of a distributed cache. The workloads of an authorization server may also send messages to each other to manage state. For example, the admin workload can notify the runtime workloads of configuration updates.

You can scale the use of your cloud native authorization server across multiple clusters. For example, if you host APIs in three global locations, you should also host your authorization server in these locations. We think this is important because in such deployments, the runtime instances of the authorization server communicate within a local cluster so that request latency remains low and performance becomes predictable. You can use database replication to share state across clusters when required. Figure 11-2 illustrates an example deployment where each region uses clustered runtime workloads and a single admin workload, with shared state stored in a SQL database.

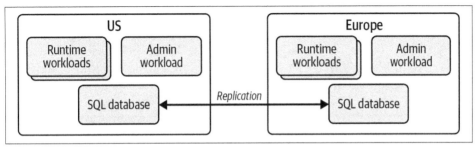

Figure 11-2. Authorization server multicluster deployment

Once you understand how to deploy the instances of the authorization server, whether it is in a single Kubernetes cluster or multiple, you need to ensure addressability for your OAuth endpoints. Let's explain how to design your OAuth base URLs.

Addressability

The first URLs you should consider are the publicly available OAuth endpoints for internet clients, such as web and mobile applications. If you host in multiple regions, you have two main options: you can use distinct internet URLs per region or a single global internet URL. In the first case, users need to identify the correct URL for their region. When you go for the latter, you can reduce the risk of users and applications using incorrect URLs. Therefore, prefer a single global internet URL over regional URLs. When there is only a single URL for all locations, you need to make sure you can dynamically route traffic to the right cluster. We illustrate a common global deployment for an authorization server in Figure 11-3.

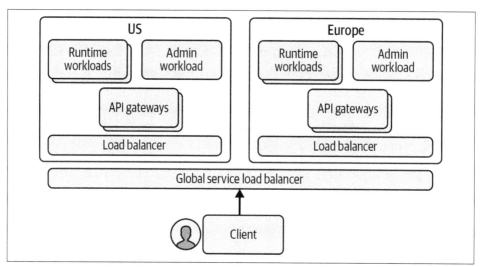

Figure 11-3. Authorization server with global load balancing

As we outline in Chapter 8, you should expose both your APIs and authorization server from the cluster using an API gateway. A URL's domain name then resolves to one or more external IP addresses, each of which represents load-balancing network infrastructure for an API gateway. In multicluster deployments with a single global URL, you can also use global service load balancer (GSLB) features to route users to the nearest IP address. Ultimately, instances of the API gateway for each region route OAuth requests to instances of your runtime workloads within that region.

Besides deciding on the strategy for addressability, you also need to design base URLs for the API gateway. This means you should design the base URLs for your APIs and your authorization server. Table 11-1 shows the base URLs we use in this book's example Kubernetes clusters.

Table 11-1. Example base URLs for APIs and the authorization server

Component	Base URL
APIs	`https://api.democluster.example`
Authorization Server	`https://login.democluster.example`

It is common to choose URLs that represent your organization name, or a subdivision of it. Public API URLs are typically visible only to client developers while your users see the public URL of your authorization server when they interact with authentication screens. Therefore, the authorization server's base URL often has a prefix such as `login`, `sso`, or `accounts`. Be cautious not to leak any technology choices in the URL; for example, avoid product or vendor names like `keycloak` or `curity` as part of a URL. The internet domain names you can purchase from a cloud provider, who may also be able to provide managed and autorenewed SSL certificates that you reference in your API gateway.

You typically have not only a production environment but multiple environments where you deploy your APIs, such as one for each stage of your deployment pipeline. Your cloud native authorization server should be part of such a CI/CD approach. Therefore, you should design URLs for all of your environments. Let's discuss some approaches for doing that next.

Runtime workload URLs

When you have various deployments for your APIs, design URLs that account for all of those environments. You might do this in various ways, if you have test, staging, and production environments. In Table 11-2, we use a separate URL for each environment (deployment stage) so that URLs are easy to understand. You can use your environments to test your solutions end-to-end before you release to production. You may need to purchase multiple internet domain names to enable the URLs. Your URL design should also enable future unknown environments, such as one you might spin up occasionally for load testing.

Table 11-2. Authorization server base URLs for a deployment pipeline

Stage	URL
Local Computer	`https://login.democluster-dev.example`
Test	`https://login.democluster-test.example`
Staging	`https://login.democluster-staging.example`
Production	`https://login.democluster.example`

You configure your cloud native authorization server with an external base URL to ensure that internet clients receive resolvable URLs. For example, the authorization server returns redirect responses to web and mobile clients during user authentication. The URLs in redirect responses need to begin with the runtime workload's external base URL. If you design service roles, you may be able to use different external base URLs for each of them, such as one per tenant.

Note that Table 11-2 includes a URL for local development, that is, from a developer's local computer. Such a URL is important since it enables early validation and rehearsal of your deployments. All of the example deployments we provide use domain-based URLs. Once you know your runtime URLs, you can design equivalent admin URLs. Let's explain some details of administration endpoints next.

Admin workload URLs

Typically, you use the admin workload to manage the authorization server's settings and data. Your authorization server should provide a frontend administration user interface. You might use the admin UI to register an OAuth client or a cryptographic key or to create a user account. You can expose the admin UI outside of the cluster. When doing so, you usually choose a descriptive URL that contains the word admin or similar. We provide a list of example URLs in Table 11-3.

Table 11-3. Admin base URLs for a deployment pipeline

Stage	URL
Local Computer	`https://admin.democluster-dev.example`
Test	`https://admin.democluster-test.example`
Staging	`https://admin.democluster-staging.example`
Production	`https://admin.democluster.example`

The admin workload can also provide API endpoints that you use to manage the authorization server's resources. You do not call these APIs from your frontend clients or APIs. Instead, you use them only for management operations. For example, you might use admin APIs to automate the creation and renewal of token signing keys for each stage of your deployment pipeline. If you have to expose administration endpoints to the internet, make sure that both admin UI access and admin API access use strong security that includes proper user authentication and authorization by employing the techniques that we describe in this book. To mitigate risks, consider administration URLs internal and avoid exposing them to the internet.

When operating OAuth, you not only have external clients, like web and mobile applications, that connect to OAuth endpoints using the internet URLs but also internal ones. Internal clients, like your APIs or administration tools, should connect to URLs that resolve only within a cluster or network. Keeping internal requests within the cluster performs better and enables you to reduce the endpoints exposed to the internet. Let's explain how internal URLs for OAuth work next.

Internal URLs

Within a cluster, workloads call the authorization server using a different address to the internet URL your API gateway provides. Those workloads act as internal OAuth clients. Kubernetes' service discovery provides internal URLs that it automatically generates based on the scheme, workload name, port, and namespace that you configure in the authorization server's YAML resources. The authorization server's containers typically run on a port above 1024 so that they can listen for HTTP requests while running as a low-privilege system account. In Table 11-4, we provide some example internal URLs within an `authorizationserver` namespace. It is possible to use identical internal URLs for all stages of your deployment pipeline.

Table 11-4. OAuth internal endpoints

Endpoint	URL
Token Endpoint	`http://runtime-svc.authorizationserver:8000/oauth/v2/token`
JSON Web Key Set Endpoint	`http://runtime-svc.authorizationserver:8000/jwks`
SCIM Endpoint	`http://runtime-svc.authorizationserver:8000/scim`
Administration API	`http://admin-svc.authorizationserver:8000/api/admin`

HTTP internal URLs

Internal URLs often use HTTP since HTTPS URLs require cloud native components to manage their own TLS keys and certificates and deal with renewal. An elegant way to use TLS for your authorization server's internal URLs is to use a service mesh. Clients call endpoints of your authorization server using a plain HTTP URL while middleware, such as sidecars, transparently upgrades connections to use HTTPS. We explain how to enable this in Chapter 10. If you cannot use service meshes that transparently encrypt HTTP messages, you should consider HTTPS even for internal URLs to mitigate potential threats inside the cluster.

Now that you have an idea of what components to deploy and how to design URLs, let's look at some deployment patterns that we recommend to promote an authorization server down a deployment pipeline.

Deployment

In this section, we explain how you can configure and deploy a cloud native authorization server. Despite the data source being an important part of the authorization server, we do not cover details of particular Kubernetes database technologies. Typically though, you need to choose one or more data sources for the authorization server to use for its configuration, user accounts, user credentials, and token data. Ideally, you are able to use the same database technologies that you use for your APIs, which enables you to reuse acquired knowledge and tools for its deployment.

With the data source in place, you then deploy the authorization server workloads. You can reuse patterns from your API development lifecycle to trigger a deployment of your authorization server. For example, you can base your containers on a container image that includes customized resources such as branded login screens. You should be able to use various Kubernetes resources or environment variables for environment-specific values when deploying the containers. Let's discuss a deployment process for your authorization server that builds container images that you promote down a pipeline.

Build Process

Some authorization servers follow an open source model and may require you to download and build their complete source code. You then need to build the code, manage library dependencies, and create your own Docker image. Even though you build the code yourself, you will not have the same understanding of the authorization server's code base as for your APIs. We believe that you should avoid building the authorization server from scratch if possible. Instead, use a tested Docker image that your authorization server provider supplies.

Over time, the base image alone is likely to be insufficient. You eventually need to deploy additional files. These files might include customizations to login branding, or code extensions like libraries that customize the logic of authentication or token issuance (see also Chapters 6 and 14). It should be possible to deliver customizations without rebuilding all of the authorization server's code.

One way to deploy additional files is to use Kubernetes ConfigMap and Volume resources. Another way, which we prefer, is to take the authorization server's base image and build a custom image that copies in your customization files. To upgrade, you take a new image of the authorization server, copy over customization files, and publish a new version of your custom image. Your build pipeline takes care of the process.

We illustrate an example build process for your authorization server in Figure 11-4. You typically use a repository such as source control to store customizations. You assign a version tag to produce a new Docker image. Over time, you push multiple versions of the custom Docker image to a Docker registry.

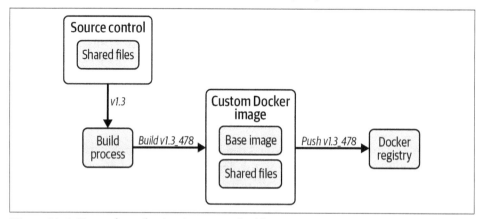

Figure 11-4. Example authorization server build process

You can then promote the same binary Docker image to all stages of your deployment pipeline. This image should not contain any sensitive data like secrets and keys. You must provide those at runtime. Further, to get a working system you must include environment-specific configuration settings. Configuration and data are the most intricate areas to manage in any type of authorization server. Let's explain some techniques that you might use to manage your OAuth configuration.

Environment Configuration

In Chapter 4, we describe various types of configuration data. Over time, you manage many security settings for authentication, external identity providers, clients, API permissions, and cryptographic keys for signing, verification, and encryption. We think that you should first create configuration in the admin UI. For example, you might set up authentication methods or register a new client. You can then run the client and test the integration (e.g., user authentication). When satisfied, you need to migrate the configuration to other deployments (i.e., stages in your development pipeline).

From a manageability viewpoint, it can be difficult to keep your OAuth configuration synchronized between all of your deployed environments even though the vast majority of settings are likely to be the same for all stages of your pipeline. If you fail to keep them consistent, there is the potential for application errors. To help prevent this, your authorization server should allow you to manage your configuration in a way that reduces duplication and human error. You then ensure that your production configuration is updated reliably.

One such approach is text-based configuration, which you manage in source control. The configuration becomes a shared resource that is the same for all stages of your deployment pipeline. You may be able to split the configuration into multiple files to enable both a shared core configuration and environment-specific differences. Alternatively or in addition, you may be able to use parameters for environment-specific values (e.g., passwords or URLs). In Example 11-1, we show a partial pseudo-configuration in JSON. The values that begin with a $ character are parameters that we assume can be substituted with environment-specific values.

Example 11-1. Text-based configuration

```
{
    "token-signing-keys": [{
        "id": "default",
        "algorithm": "ES256",
        "curve-name": "P-256",
        "data": "$TOKEN_SIGNING_KEY"
    }],
    "authentication-methods": [{
```

```
        "id": "usernamepassword1",
        "type": "username-password",
        "allow-account-recovery": true,
        "allow-registration": true
    }],
    "clients": [{
        "client_id": "web-client",
        "client_secret": "$WEB_CLIENT_SECRET",
        "redirect_uri": "$WEB_CLIENT_REDIRECT_URI",
        "scope": "openid retail/orders",
        "authentication_methods": ["usernamepassword1"]
    }],
    "scopes": [{
        "name": "retail/orders",
        "claims": {}
    }]
}
```

When you use text-based configuration, you dynamically assign the real values for parameters at deployment time. For example, redirect URIs are usually different for each stage of your deployment pipeline and you need to specify which values a particular deployment uses. You might be able to use a tool like the Linux envsubst utility to produce a final configuration file from a template file, then deploy it as a Kubernetes ConfigMap.

You must protect sensitive values (e.g., client secrets and token signing private keys) in a text-based configuration to avoid disclosing their values to unauthorized parties. To do so, you can store any underlying secret values in a secure area, such as a vault that your cloud platform provides. Your deployment process can download secrets from the vault and use cryptography to protect them. For example, the deployment pipeline could produce hashes of your client secrets and encrypt your token signing keys, or the whole configuration.

You can then deploy protected values as Kubernetes Secrets. The authorization server's deployment might translate values from Kubernetes Secrets to protected environment variables. At deployment time, you can give the authorization server a decryption key that it uses to read any encrypted values.

Cryptographic keys and Hardware Security Modules

You may be able to manage crypto keys in hardened ways. For example, your cloud native authorization server might read token signing keys that reside within a Hardware Security Module (HSM). When the authorization server needs to perform cryptographic operations such as signing tokens, it requests a token signature from the HSM. It does not need direct access to the key.

If you use database storage for configuration data, you should instead use your admin workload's configuration APIs to promote new settings down your deployment pipeline. You should manage the authorization server's configuration via its APIs and avoid operating on the configuration data directly, as the latter requires a profound knowledge of the authorization server's internal data structure. These API updates are not strictly part of your deployments. Instead, we classify them as postdeployment data update operations. We explain that concept in "Data Operation" on page 247. Once you know how you will manage your environment-specific configuration, you can deploy your authorization server. Let's look at an example deployment process next.

Deployment Process

To deploy a cloud native authorization server, you follow an infrastructure-as-code (IaC) approach. In Kubernetes, you create YAML resources that describe the authorization server's desired state such as a Service, ServiceAccount, or Deployment. You then apply the resources to your cluster. A Deployment resource enables you to express a ReplicaSet with your desired number of pods. In addition, you also need to deploy a resource that enables ingress into the cluster so that you can expose the authorization server's OAuth endpoints to the outside world. The platform itself then maintains your desired state; that is, it updates the cluster to match your declarative resources and replaces unhealthy pods.

Which resources you need to define and how to combine them depends on the specifics of the authorization server. The provider may give you a Helm chart, or similar, that creates all of the Kubernetes YAML resources for you so that you start with a working deployment and override only particular values. For example, such a chart might enable you to use a custom Docker image, with environment-specific settings in Kubernetes ConfigMaps and Kubernetes Secrets.

The deployment process itself should be relatively straightforward, since it only needs to create Kubernetes resources that ultimately spin up containers. If you use text-based configuration, you get synchronization benefits but you also need to supply configuration values at deployment time. We show an example deployment that includes text-based configuration in Figure 11-5.

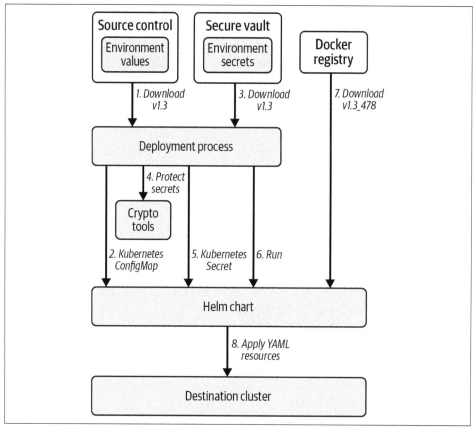

Figure 11-5. Example authorization server deployment process

We summarize the main steps of the deployment process from Figure 11-5 in the following list:

1. Download environment-specific values from source control.
2. Save these nonsecret values to a Kubernetes ConfigMap.
3. Download secrets from a secure vault.
4. Use crypto utilities to protect secure values.
5. Save protected values to a Kubernetes Secret.
6. Run the Helm chart to apply the desired state to the target cluster.
7. Pull the specified Docker image from the Docker registry.
8. Create YAML resources and apply them to the cluster.

Ultimately, Kubernetes makes any shared configuration and environment-specific values available to the authorization server containers. A Helm chart could, for example, transform environment-specific values from ConfigMaps and Secrets to environment variables in the deployed containers. You can provide a decryption key to the authorization server pods to enable it to access underlying secure values.

Example deployment with protected secrets

We provide a script called *protect-secrets.sh* in the deployment example for Chapter 10. You can study the script as an example on how to generate, and cryptographically protect, secure values like token signing keys.

The deployment process we explain is similar to that for many cloud native components. You build binary container images only once and then deploy the same binary multiple times with different configurations. If you treat the local computer as the first stage in your deployment pipeline, you should be able to implement the main work there. Typically, this results in a script with the deployment logic. When you want to deploy to a different stage of your pipeline, you can run the same script. You can also spin up a completely new stage of the pipeline. To do so, just add a new configuration and run the same script.

The exact details of your authorization server's deployment may vary depending on the provider you choose. One of the key goals should be a reliable deployment that the platform can run many times to maintain your desired state. To complete the coverage of deployment, let's explain how you upgrade your authorization server when you want to roll out a new release.

Upgrades

Your authorization server typically provides you with at least a couple of new releases per year. These may include support for new security standards, new authentication methods, or improvements to operational behaviors. To upgrade to the new version, you rebuild your custom Docker image from a new base image. Your deployment process should enable you to use different Docker image versions per stage of your deployment pipeline. To perform an upgrade, you move version tags forward for a stage of your pipeline and trigger a deployment. This enables you to use the existing version in production environments while you test the new version in earlier stages of the pipeline. In Figure 11-6 we illustrate one possible phased upgrade of an authorization server, from version 1.3 to version 2.0.

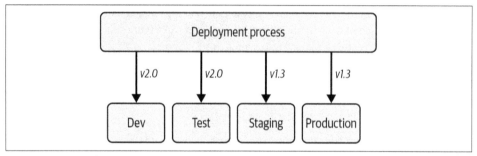

Figure 11-6. Authorization server phased upgrade

During minor upgrades, you use the features of the cloud native platform to ensure zero downtime for users. The default Kubernetes upgrade behavior is to deploy new pods in a phased manner and run them alongside old pods. When a new pod passes readiness probes it starts processing OAuth requests. During an example upgrade, version 1.3 pods handle some in-flight requests and version 1.4 pods handle the others. As new pods become available, the platform terminates old pods after a grace period so that they can complete the processing of in-flight requests. Eventually, only version 1.4 pods remain.

You can also use advanced cloud native deployment patterns, such as canary deployments where you run a full set of old pods and a full set of new pods side by side, and define a percentage of OAuth requests to be initially processed by the new version. This percentage is gradually increased to 100% of requests. Eventually, only pods on the new version process OAuth requests.

Whatever upgrade mechanics you use, it is possible that you could experience unexpected errors a short time after an upgrade. In a worst-case scenario, you may need to roll back the authorization server with a downgrade. In Kubernetes, a downgrade works almost exactly the same as an upgrade. You follow the same mechanics as an upgrade, to move version tags backward for a stage of your pipeline and then trigger a deployment. Leave any database schema upgrades in place to avoid data loss.

Major upgrades are likely to introduce breaking changes. Breaking changes might include updates to the database like a new table or column, or updated screens for an authentication method. You should not need to change the code in your clients and APIs even when there is a new major release of the authorization server. Ideally, you are able to identify and fix broken integrations in a test environment. Make use of observability to check which applications still integrate with the old version and help them migrate.

If you have concerns about the upgrade or downgrade reliability of a cloud native authorization server, you can rehearse the process quite easily in a Kubernetes cluster on a local computer. For example, you can practice upgrades and downgrades using the Docker image tags in the Helm charts we use in this book's example deployments.

After you roll out your cloud native authorization server, there are several ways in which you update its data. We explain these operational events next.

Data Operation

After the deployment of your authorization server, you operate it, which can affect various people in your organization. For example, developers and testers may need to register an OAuth client for a new application, or DevOps teams might need to add a new authentication method to integrate a business partner's identity provider with an existing frontend application. In this section, we describe some techniques that you can use to automate changes to data. Let's start with API-based updates to user accounts.

User Account Updates

In Chapter 4, we explain a common way to populate your customer user accounts using APIs after you first deploy an authorization server. You can potentially run this type of extract, transform, and load (ETL) postdeployment operation to import various types of data into the authorization server using its APIs. First, identify the data to update. Then, run a program to migrate the data from existing data sources (extract and transform) to the authorization server (load). This program calls the appropriate API of your authorization server to apply updates.

You may need to update user accounts multiple times. For example, you may need to add extra users from a new business partner or you might need to add a new product-specific user identifier to existing users when a new area of your business onboards to your authorization server. It is common to run this type of update as a dependency, before updating a particular application. You typically initiate this type of process using continuous delivery tools that run automatically or on demand.

You should test automated API updates for reliability. For example, if you lose connectivity halfway through an ETL process you should be able to rerun the update without creating duplicates. This type of rehearsal derisks updates to your production system. You should also be able to manage updates to your OAuth configuration data, which you can do in a couple of ways. Let's explain configuration updates next.

Configuration Updates

After you deploy your runtime and admin workloads, deployed containers read the latest configuration data. The source of the data can be either a database or text-based configuration. You then evolve the configuration over time. For example, you register scopes and claims to secure your APIs and authentication methods that your clients use. When you get started you are likely to use the admin UI to apply these settings, where their meaning is visually clearest. Your admin workloads make the configuration available to runtime workloads. This mechanism could work in various ways: via a shared database, a pull mechanism where runtime workloads poll the admin workload for changes, or a push mechanism where the admin workload publishes event messages to runtime workloads.

We do not recommend manually entering configuration changes into an admin UI for all stages of your deployment pipeline, since doing so can lead to human error. Instead, make sure to persist manual configuration updates and then automate the rollout to other environments. Whether using text-based configuration or data-based configuration, you are likely to check automation resources into source control. We illustrate an abstract configuration update process in Figure 11-7.

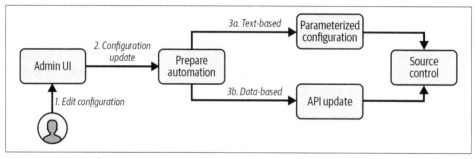

Figure 11-7. Configuration updates

If you use text-based configuration, your authorization server may enable you to subscribe to an event like `ConfigurationUpdated` and run custom logic. For example, you might save the new configuration to a source control branch and create a pull request. In simple cases, your pipeline may automatically approve such a pull request, update version tags, and merge the changes. In other cases, you may need to request a peer review to approve the change. After committing the change, you might trigger so-called GitOps rollouts of new runtime workloads with the latest text-based configuration. These deployments could update all stages of your pipeline, or all regions within a global deployment. In the event that you need to rollback a change, you follow a similar process.

Data-based updates may be a better choice for some types of configuration data. For example, if you have hundreds of OAuth clients, managing them as data is likely to be easier than managing them as text. To use data-based storage, call the admin workload's configuration APIs to automate changes to data. In your CI/CD system, you configure tasks to update data. You can run configuration update tasks without redeploying workloads. You might prefer to use an API-based approach for all of your configuration updates.

Authorization server configuration updates can affect multiple teams. Although the ultimate owner is often an identity team, you typically want to avoid such a team from being a bottleneck. Aim to design a process where teams have some control over their application settings, yet you can avoid granting everyone full access to the admin interfaces (APIs as well as UIs) of the authorization server. Ideally, your authorization server should enable you to grant people different levels of administrative access depending on their role. When they apply configuration changes in one stage of your pipeline, you must ensure that you can make equivalent updates to all other environments. Self-service portals and automation are two ingredients that help to manage the configuration efficiently.

One part of managing an authorization server is the data and configuration; another is daily operations. Stakeholders may be concerned about the authorization server's endpoints becoming unavailable, or the potential for OAuth-related errors that block users. Therefore, let's explain some cloud native techniques to ensure reliability.

Reliability

Like any API, an authorization server can adversely impact any application that depends on it. If the authorization server endpoints are not available, or if the authorization server returns an unexpected error response to an OAuth request, users can experience downtime. Therefore, you must have ways to avoid these points of failure. Let's start with what you need from the authorization server to ensure high availability in a cloud native environment.

High Availability

In this section, we discuss some requirements for the authorization server and deployments in general that enable you to use common cloud native patterns for high availability. We address the following well-known availability problems:

- Unhealthy containers
- Performance degradation
- Spikes in load
- Dependency failures
- Data center outages

To identify and eventually eliminate unhealthy containers, you need monitoring. Each runtime workload of your authorization server should provide a health end-point that the cloud native platform calls to monitor the pod's availability. In Kubernetes, configure liveness and readiness probes (*https://oreil.ly/VHIpB*) to call that endpoint, at a configurable frequency, such as 30 seconds. Also, configure an `initial delay` so that the platform allows time for the authorization server's process to start. If a container becomes unhealthy, and *N* consecutive probes fail to get a healthy response, where *N* is the failure threshold, the cloud native platform can ensure auto-healing. The platform marks down the unhealthy pod and tries to recover by spinning up a new pod to maintain your desired replica count.

Even with all runtime workloads running, you may experience performance issues due to overloaded workloads. A high load of OAuth requests from applications could result in requests queueing up and then timing out, leading to OAuth responses such as HTTP 503 `Service Unavailable`. To avoid the problem in the first place, use automation in test environments to put your authorization server under a realistic load so that you know your base setup can handle common loads. Such an exercise can also help you to identify the limits of your deployment. If you suspect that data queries are going to be a bottleneck, you may be able to integrate a cache to decrease the load on the authorization server's main data stores. In any case, use metrics to monitor applications so that you can detect, identify, and act upon performance issues and high loads.

Kubernetes provides generic metrics about containers and pods such as their CPU and memory usage. While this kind of metric gives you an indication of the health state of a workload, it is not very specific. A more targeted metric, like the 95th percentile of the OAuth request time, can be a better measure of the need to scale. To enable monitoring OAuth-related metrics, the authorization server needs to expose its specific metrics in a way that can integrate with your cloud native infrastructure. For example, the authorization server can provide a metrics endpoint that a monitoring system such as Prometheus (*https://oreil.ly/DiOM_*) can poll to fetch metrics. Prometheus can then store and visualize the metrics. Configure thresholds for the metrics and automate as much as possible (e.g., by enabling autoscaling). You can use the Kubernetes HorizontalPodAutoscaler (HPA) (*https://oreil.ly/Lo3Ce*) to trigger autoscaling. The HPA instructs the control plane to increase the replica count when the current average value of a metric fails to reach its target, or to decrease the replica count when the metric comfortably reaches its target for some time. Check out Kubernetes' documentation on autoscaling (*https://oreil.ly/9RX32*) for more options like vertical scaling to automatically adjust the resources of a workload such as CPU or memory.

While autohealing and autoscaling help to recover from certain erroneous states, they are no help when dependencies fail. For example, a runtime workload could lose connectivity with data sources, leading to multiple failures, or it may fail to connect with an external system, such as a cloud service that the authorization server uses for a particular authentication method. In such cases, restarting or spinning up new instances of runtime pods does not solve the problem. Instead, you should treat this type of event as an alarm condition. Your authorization server should provide you with the necessary data to identify such conditions and allow for automatic processes like alarms and notifications. For example, the authorization server might publish an internal error rate from its metrics endpoint so that you can configure your monitoring system to send emails to one or more administrators.

In some cases, an entire data center could become unavailable. For example, an electrical failure or a natural event might take down a particular data center. Of course, such an event affects not only the authorization server but also your whole business in the affected area. To ensure availability of your services you must deploy to multiple clusters in physically independent locations. For example, you might run clusters in Eastern US and Western US zones. As part of such a setup, you must replicate data from one cluster to the other on a regular basis (see also "Clustering" on page 234). You can use a GSLB that fails over when a particular regional load balancer becomes unavailable. In the event of a failure in one region, the load balancer would route users to the alternate zone.

Data replication and load balancing failover are the main disaster recovery ingredients for an authorization server and you should be able to follow the same approaches that you already use for your APIs. You also need to ensure that you have regular (offline) backups of the authorization server's other resources, including installation files, Docker images, plug-ins, custom forms, styles, cryptographic keys, and configuration. When you practice your disaster recovery strategy, you should include your authorization server in the process. Any failover process should be seamless for your users.

In addition to availability, you should also prepare for the possibility of technical incidents during OAuth flows and ensure that you follow an approach that enables fast problem resolution.

Fast Problem Resolution

When you use OAuth 2.0, you operate a distributed architecture. Technical problems such as connectivity issues or misconfigurations are likely to happen. Most issues of this kind occur during integration testing and should not occur in your production systems. You should invest some time to prepare for failures that could impact users and ensure that you can resolve OAuth problems promptly. Ensure that your chosen security components, including the authorization server, provide useful error responses and logs. Any client or API developer should have good tools to identify and (hopefully) resolve OAuth issues without depending on the provider of the authorization server. Given those foundations, you can implement an incident resolution process. To understand how, let's start with the data contained in OAuth error responses.

When a client or API calls the authorization server, an OAuth request could result in an error response. Each error response contains a code in an error field, to indicate the type of error. The error_description field optionally provides further details. Either front-channel or back-channel responses can return these errors. RFC 6749—the "OAuth 2.0 Authorization Framework" specification (*https://oreil.ly/8wZDS*)—includes a list of standard error codes that the authorization server may return. Example 11-2 shows an example of an OAuth error response. When it comes to OAuth-related error codes that you want to return from APIs (resource servers in OAuth terms), you should refer to RFC 6750, the OAuth specification on bearer token usage (*https://oreil.ly/W7Vv0*).

Example 11-2. An OAuth error response

```
HTTP/1.1 400 Bad Request
Content-Type: application/json
Cache-Control: no-store
Pragma: no-cache
{
    "error": "invalid_request",
    "error_description": "grant_type is missing"
}
```

Some OAuth error codes allow clients to recover without impacting the user. For example, if the access token expires, the client can silently request a new one using the refresh token. In other cases, the client cannot recover and must present an error display to the user. The problem may persist if the user retries the operation. In many applications, it is important for a technical support team to resolve such problems quickly. Error displays should therefore contain details that help to enable problem resolution without revealing any sensitive data or overwhelming the user; design error displays with care. For example, an application might first present an error summary view with a basic message. The user might be able to click a "Details" button that presents an error details view containing further information. The error details should provide sufficient data, such as identifiers, to enable you to quickly look up the error cause in backend systems. For example, an application might display an error code, error time, and a correlation identifier, along with an option to send this information to your technical support team.

The failure could occur in any backend component, such as an API, the authorization server, the API gateway, or an entitlement management system. In a cloud native environment, the OpenTelemetry observability framework (*https://oreil.ly/rug7N*) provides a built-in correlation identifier for traces. When a client sends an outgoing request, it can generate a Trace ID. This ID propagates to all backend subrequests that process the client's request. If a request does not contain any trace ID yet, because, for example, the client did not send one, the backend component can create one and eventually return it to the client. Each backend component that supports OpenTelemetry provides trace records to an OpenTelemetry collector. The OpenTelemetry project lists many libraries and SDKs that take care of the details. In Figure 11-8 we visualize how the trace ID propagates from the client to your cluster.

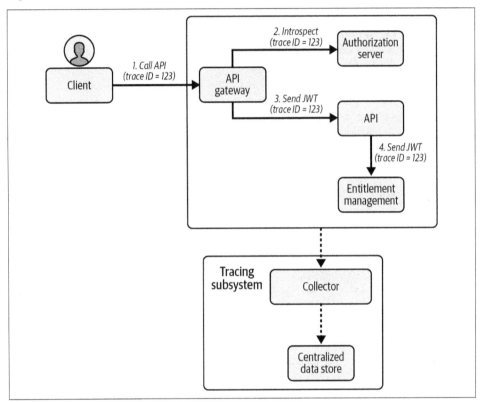

Figure 11-8. Tracing of requests

Given such a trace ID, you should be able to feed it into a standard user interface tool that queries a data store to get summary information for all requests in the overall trace. The user interface visualizes the data to highlight the failing workload and might also provide basic error information. In simple cases, this may be sufficient to understand the cause. Otherwise, you need to look at the workload's system to understand the technical cause of the failure. Therefore, you should be able to filter logs by the trace ID to get the matching log entries. Your authorization server needs to implement good quality technical support logs so that those log entries contain a detailed description and the failing code location (the stack trace).

Your authorization server is a specialist API and can output various types of logs. When doing so, it might follow the design principles of a logging framework. A logging framework uses concepts such as loggers (a category of data), logging events (the data for a particular log entry), and output locations (like a file, a database, or the standard output, stdout). Workloads typically write technical system logs to stdout, in which case the Kubernetes platform automatically captures the log data and writes it to a file on the Kubernetes node that hosts the pod.

You can use a cloud native log shipper to send log file data from Kubernetes nodes to a log aggregation service. The log aggregation system should provide a frontend that you use to view and filter logs. This enables you to diagnose logs and resolve errors even when the system is under a heavy load and there are many log entries. There is nothing unique about the way in which you resolve authorization server problems. If you operate cloud native APIs, it is likely that you already follow this type of process.

Both your APIs and your authorization server should write system logs that enable you to resolve technical problems. We think that your APIs and the authorization server should also audit security events so that you can govern API security at scale. Let's briefly summarize how security auditing works.

Security Auditing

Auditing is the process of analyzing completed security events. The authorization server should provide an audit logger that enables you to track activity such as login attempts and tokens issued. We recommend that APIs also produce audit logs containing their authorization decisions and permissions checked. In Chapter 9 we explain how an entitlement management system can distribute centralized policies that APIs use for their authorization. Once authorization completes, the policy decision point writes authorization decision logs, which can serve as your API's audit logs.

You provide audit results to stakeholders who govern security, like a security architect or a compliance officer. There may be a large volume of audit results, so you typically run a frontend tool to filter and analyze the data. Such a process might help to identify insecure APIs or clients that operate with too much privilege, or provide early warning of security threats. As a default option, you might ship audit logs to your log aggregation system and grant only authorized users access to audit logs.

A cloud native API or authorization server can write audit logs to a file on the pod's container and use a logging framework to restrict the file's maximum size. By default though, log files on containers are not written to the Kubernetes node. To do so, you can run a sidecar container that uses the Linux tail command to write logs to stdout. The platform then captures the output and writes log data to a file on the

Kubernetes node. You can then use the same log shipping techniques that you use for system logs to ship audit log data.

You should also be able to use cloud native patterns to subscribe to particular security events. For example, you may want to raise alerts to a particular group of employees if there is a large number of recent failed authentication attempts. To do so, you might provide a metrics endpoint that your monitoring system calls frequently. The authorization server might provide a built-in metric or you may be able to subscribe to authorization server logging events and produce your own metrics endpoint. Your monitoring system should be able to store custom metrics as a time series and take occasional actions without sending floods of alerts. For example, it might display a value such as `authentication_failure_rate` on a dashboard or send an hourly email when the value exceeds a safe threshold that you configure.

Summary

A cloud native authorization server is a specialist API that you do not develop yourself. You manage it like your other APIs and perform various operational tasks. You begin with hosting to operate a deployment pipeline. In any authorization server, the most challenging management area is data and configuration management. When you use OAuth, you outsource sensitive user data and intricate security settings so that your applications no longer need to manage them. Nevertheless, you still need to securely manage these values for your deployment pipeline.

The cloud native ecosystem provides well-known design patterns and supporting components to ensure high availability. We recommend that you also invest in good tracing and logging so that you can troubleshoot the distributed architecture and quickly resolve reliability issues. With the right separation of security concerns, you should also be able to plug in tools to enable the people who care most about security to govern it. They can use audit logs to monitor security after the event, or configure cloud native monitoring to react to specific security threats.

We have now completed our content on securing APIs and operating OAuth. You should understand how to run a cloud native authorization server with the correct data setup to serve your APIs. Next, we move on to the final part of the book, where we explain client flows and say more about user authentication. First, in Chapter 12, we explain OAuth for native applications.

PART IV

Securing API Clients

OAuth for Native Applications

Native applications are platform-specific executable programs that you build for and run on a dedicated operating system. The main types are desktop applications and mobile applications. In most cases, users operate those applications and they interact with APIs to present secured data to the user. To call APIs, platform-specific applications run a code flow with Proof Key for Code Exchange (PKCE) (RFC 7636) (*https://oreil.ly/0YSzr*) as we explain in Chapter 2, to retrieve an access token that identifies the user. The client sends the access token to APIs, which use the token's claims to implement business authorization. The client continues to call APIs until the user closes the application or the user's authenticated session expires.

This chapter explains the options you have when you use OAuth to secure platform-specific applications. We first provide a refresher on the code flow, where the client sends an authorization request using the system browser. We then explain how to implement OAuth for platform-specific applications in the standard ways, which requires special types of redirect URIs that use features of the operating system. Next, we describe methods with which you can harden the security of the OAuth implementation and mitigate threats that exist in the various environments. To complete the theory, we explain how OAuth could use browserless flows to authenticate users with device features that the browser cannot access. To finish up, we provide practical content with code examples so that you learn how to write code that runs a code flow in a few different technology stacks.

The basic steps to run a code flow require you to handle some straightforward HTTP messages, so let's reiterate them next. We also explain some behaviors specific to desktop and mobile applications.

The Code Flow

Platform-specific applications should follow the best practices from the "OAuth 2.0 for Native Apps" specification (RFC 8252) (*https://oreil.ly/ILDqD*) when implementing OAuth. Consequently, OAuth clients for platform-specific applications should use the code flow with PKCE to authenticate users. As part of the flow, clients must use an external user agent. When using an external user agent, users do not reveal any credentials to the application but present them to the authorization server directly using its login forms. Example 12-1 shows the start of the code flow, where the browser sends an authorization request to the authorization endpoint of the authorization server.

Example 12-1. An authorization request for OAuth clients (URL-encoding omitted for readability)

```
GET https://login.example.com/oauth/v2/authorize
    ?client_id=native-client
    &redirect_uri=[redirect_uri]
    &response_type=code
    &scope=openid profile retail/orders
    &state=BOOcOhiqk1LmaLq0eQC1nQjWWnnhfkAhTYAz_fxbV9A
    &code_challenge=EXQbCzv3TQlTUI8cwCrvn7Rjt38G37bCwrJAe4JU-Nc
    &code_challenge_method=S256 HTTP/1.1
```

Typically, the authorization server requests the user to authenticate upon an authorization request. Once complete, the client receives an authorization response on its redirect URI and validates that the response state matches the request state. We show an example authorization response in Example 12-2.

Example 12-2. Authorization response returned to the OAuth client's redirect URI

```
GET [redirect_uri]
    ?code=DY9jAYHPuHSiW2OpWUaNRW4otei
    &state=CVZU3iBS7guJi9j8TgkIujj2nfBAjtRQ6jJUrYhLbeNZvnkCCnvPLPK5jErAQEs HTTP/1.1
```

Once the client receives the authorization code, it sends a token request to swap the code for tokens. RFC 8252 mandates the use of PKCE for clients to protect against authorization code interception attacks. A compliant authorization server must enforce PKCE for OAuth clients of platform-specific applications.

Recall from Chapter 6 that an authorization server can return opaque access and refresh tokens to clients. Consequently, the client of a platform-specific application receives a token response similar to the one in Example 12-3.

Example 12-3. Token response to the platform-specific application

```
{
    "access_token": "79ed4e85-954d-4044-9362-99ac9695d7e0",
    "refresh_token": "ff8cfad8-9888-44c7-afb2-8c597cf96037",
    "id_token": "eyJraWQiOiItMzgwNzQ4MTIiLCJ4NXQiOi ...",
    "scope": "openid profile retail/orders",
    "token_type": "bearer",
    "expires_in": 900
}
```

We recommend issuing opaque tokens as a security best practice so that the client cannot read token data that only APIs should be able to access. In addition, you should configure short-lived access tokens for clients, along with refresh tokens, so that clients can silently renew access tokens without frequently requiring user re-authentication, to ensure a good user experience. Make sure to protect refresh tokens as they allow for long-lived, silent access.

Platform-specific applications such as mobile and browser-based applications imply risks because you must make assumptions about the security of the platform. Therefore, you need to be extra careful when handling any sort of sensitive information in platform-specific applications. Consider sender-constrained refresh tokens as well as short-lived client credentials. We give you some inspiration in "Hardening Security" on page 267. First, we focus on the specifics of platform-specific applications concerning OAuth integrations.

One of the differentiating behaviors for clients of platform-specific applications is the redirect URI to where the user agent forwards the authorization code. Unlike web applications, platform-specific applications do not automatically have an address where they can listen for the authorization response. As of RFC 8252, clients should use one of the following three options for their redirect URI:

- A loopback address like `http://127.0.0.1:3000/callback`
- A private-use URI scheme like `com.example.app:/callback`
- A claimed HTTPS scheme like `https://mobile.example.com/callback`

Private-use URI schemes

When you use a private-use URI scheme, there is no naming authority for the scheme and only a single slash (/) appears after the colon character. You can read more about this in Section 7.1 of the RFC 8252 document.

The exact type of redirect URI that you choose depends on the operating system that the application runs on, since the corresponding OAuth client uses the platform's specific features to receive the authorization response. Let's take a closer look at redirect URIs and other behaviors when you implement OAuth clients for platform-specific applications.

Implementing OAuth Clients

When you develop any type of OAuth client, the main work is to send outgoing OAuth requests and process incoming OAuth responses. You also need to learn about the specifics of redirect URIs, which work a little differently for desktop and mobile applications. Let's first explain how to use OAuth in desktop applications.

OAuth for Desktop Applications

A desktop application runs on a desktop operating system, most commonly Windows, macOS, or Linux. There are various types of desktop applications. We differentiate between a console application (e.g., a CLI tool for technical users) and a desktop application with custom screens. From an OAuth viewpoint, there is no technical difference between console and desktop applications, so we refer to both as *desktop clients* here.

Device code flow for CLIs

Some CLIs may use the device flow to implement OAuth which is a suitable choice for cases where the CLI runs on remote machines. Often, the CLI or a terminal is the only user interface on such machines. Consequently, such platforms are constrained devices where the user cannot authenticate. The device flow accommodates for such constraints. With the device flow, the CLI prints a link that the user has to open on a separate device, such as their local machine, in order to log in. See also "The Device Flow" on page 28 for the details on the device flow. For cases where the user can authenticate using the same device, the code flow works fine even for CLIs.

The most common way to implement a desktop OAuth client is to use a loopback address for the redirect URI. The client can use features of the desktop operating system to start an HTTP listener on a port using the built-in loopback network interface, at an address such as http://127.0.0.1:3000. The client uses a redirect URI such as http://127.0.0.1:3000/callback. Since you only use this URL to receive an authorization response on the same system where the application runs, the redirect URI does not require HTTPS, since the request does not leave the device. We show the relevant parts of a desktop code flow in Figure 12-1.

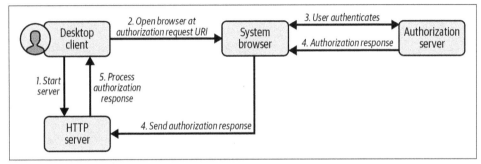

Figure 12-1. Desktop flow using a loopback HTTP server and the system browser

We summarize the main steps from Figure 12-1 in the following list. Ultimately, the desktop client gets an authorization code via the local HTTP server.

1. The desktop client runs an HTTP server within its process.

2. The desktop client forms an authorization request URI and opens the system browser at that address.

3. The system browser presents the authorization server's login screens and the user authenticates.

4. The authorization server uses the system browser to send an authorization response to the redirect URI of the client's HTTP server.

5. The desktop client processes the authorization response to get the authorization code, then stops the HTTP server.

The HTTP server requires some special management to ensure the correct security and so that users do not experience technical prompts from the operating system. By default, an HTTP server may use a general network address like `0.0.0.0` that would allow external connections to the user's computer, which could be a security concern. Therefore, the HTTP server should only use a loopback IP address (`127.0.0.1` for IPv4 or `[::1]` for IPv6). The HTTP server must also listen on a port above 1024 so that the user does not need administrator privileges. As the application cannot assume that a given port is always available, it is usual to dynamically find an available port at runtime. To facilitate random ports, you should register the loopback redirect URI without the port, using a value like `http://127.0.0.1/callback` for IPv4, or `http://[::1]/callback` for IPv6. The authorization server must, in accordance with Section 7.3 of RFC 8252, accept any runtime port when the client sends its redirect URI.

Instead of starting an HTTP server to listen on the loopback address, desktop clients can use private-use URI scheme redirect URIs, which use the desktop operating system's support for deep links, which can reference a specific page in an application. To make use of such a feature, you first need to decide on a redirect URI with a private-use scheme such as `com.example.app:/callback`. In this example, the scheme is the value `com.example.app`. Choose a value that does not conflict with other installed applications. You then need to register the scheme with the operating system to associate it to the application's binary location. Common desktop operating systems provide a mechanism to enable this, such as protocol handlers in Windows or URL scheme handlers in macOS. Unix-based operating systems have similar functions.

Despite the name, private-use URIs are not exclusive or private to applications and malicious actors could potentially also use them. Similarly, another desktop application could spin up an HTTP server listening on the loopback address to impersonate your OAuth client. The best mitigation is for users to not run desktop applications from untrusted sources. To help users, you should sign your desktop applications with a code signing certificate so that users can verify and trust your executable files. In corporate environments, an administrator can restrict the allowed desktop applications to those from trusted publishers.

OAuth in desktop applications has side effects concerning user experience, due to the external user agent. After completing authentication via the system browser and redirecting back to the desktop application, there is a leftover browser window. By default this presents a blank page, though you can improve the user experience a little by redirecting the browser to a custom location, such as a page on your organization's website. If you also use a private-use URI scheme for your redirect URI, the browser may present a prompt where the user must explicitly allow the browser to invoke the desktop application before it can receive the authorization response. Mobile applications can mitigate the UX challenges related to the disconnected browser. Let's explore OAuth for mobile applications next.

OAuth for Mobile Applications

Mobile applications most commonly run on the Android and iOS operating systems. We therefore explain OAuth in terms of these platforms. Any other mobile environment should provide equivalent behaviors. A mobile code flow again invokes the system browser, and the authorization response is returned to the client using the features of the mobile operating system.

Rather than using a disconnected browser, you can use an integrated form of the system browser that overlays the mobile client application. Such a browser window may share cookies and saved credentials with the system browser. The mobile application closes the browser window automatically once login completes. Therefore, mobile applications can provide better user experience than desktop applications. To use an integrated system browser you use *Custom Tabs* on Android (*https://oreil.ly/uNSFV*) or an `ASWebAuthenticationSession` on iOS (*https://oreil.ly/S_O1k*).

Private-use URI schemes are a convenient way to manage OAuth redirects in mobile applications. In this case, you typically name the scheme after your organization and application and provide a value like `com.example.myapp:/callback`. As with desktop applications, you must register the scheme with the operating system using platform-specific configuration settings. At installation time, the mobile operating system associates the private-use URI scheme with your particular mobile application. When a user authenticates, the operating system invokes a deep link to return the authorization response to your mobile client. We show the relevant parts of a mobile code flow in Figure 12-2.

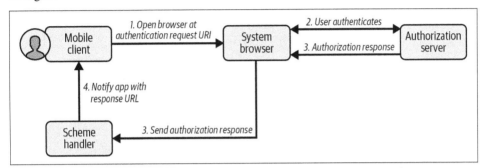

Figure 12-2. Mobile flow using a private-use URI scheme and the system browser

We summarize the main steps from Figure 12-2 in the following list. Ultimately, the mobile client gets an authorization code via the scheme handler of the operating system.

1. The mobile client forms an authorization request URI and opens the system browser there.

2. The system browser presents the authorization server's login forms and the user authenticates.

3. The authorization server uses the system browser to send an authorization response to the redirect URI using a private-use scheme.

4. The mobile operating system's scheme handler invokes a deep link to deliver the authorization response to the mobile client.

Private-use redirect URIs have the same security issues for mobile clients as they do for desktop clients. A malicious mobile application can register and use the same scheme to impersonate a client. However, for mobile clients, you can defend against this threat using a claimed HTTPS scheme redirect URI such as `https://mobile.example.com/myapp/callback`. Your mobile client then uses a more secure form of deep link where the operating system performs certain verification checks before it allows an application to receive deep links using the HTTPS domain. To use secure deep links, you use *App Links* on Android (*https://oreil.ly/ TnF2f*) or *Universal Links* on iOS (*https://oreil.ly/Jjf9n*).

To enable your application to use an HTTPS domain for deep linking, you must prove that you own the HTTPS domain and authorize your application to use it. To bind your application to your domain, you provide a mobile assets document at an HTTPS endpoint on the domain. This document references the package name and certificate details of your mobile application. When a user installs your mobile application, their mobile operating system initiates a verification process and on success registers the deep link against your application.

If a malicious application configures itself to use the HTTPS domain, the verification process fails, since the operating system cannot verify the signature of the malicious application with the key material that your domain's assets document references. A malicious application could still use your mobile client ID and trick the user into authenticating. However, the mobile operating system will not return the authorization response to the malicious client. Therefore, the malicious client cannot complete the flow and get an authorization code.

For any form of deep link, the system browser may not reliably invoke an application after a login or logout operation that consists solely of automatic redirects. Instead, for security reasons, the browser may require a user gesture like a button click before it invokes the mobile application. You can enforce a user gesture if you require a login during the code flow using the OpenID Connect `prompt=login` parameter. Another option, which you may need to use with a claimed HTTPS scheme redirect URI, is to set your mobile client's redirect URI to that of a custom web page that you host on an internet URL. The web page can then force a user gesture, such as the click of a continue button, then use JavaScript to invoke a deep link URL that forwards the authorization response query parameters to the mobile client.

In some cases, you may want to prevent an application from closing the integrated browser window automatically (e.g., to enable users to save their passwords in the browser). To do so, you should be able to configure your authorization server to present an additional screen once login completes, such as an acknowledgement screen that presents a Continue button and some informational text.

Desktop and mobile applications can both incorporate the secure storage features of the operating system into their OAuth flows. Let's briefly summarize how you can use secure storage.

Device Secure Storage

OAuth clients need to store sensitive data, like tokens, which all clients should handle with great care. What is more, confidential clients need to securely store the credentials they use to authenticate at the authorization server. Both desktop and mobile operating systems provide secure storage features. A desktop application can ask the operating system to create and store a cryptographic key that is private to the application and current operating system user. For example, you can use the Data Protection API (DPAPI) on Windows or Keychain Access on macOS. A desktop application might use the operating system API to encrypt sensitive data, after which the application stores the protected data in user-specific storage. For example, you might store OAuth tokens in this way so that the user does not have to reauthenticate every time they restart the application.

Do not use device secure storage for shared secrets

You should never embed a fixed secret into a native application that is shared by all users, like a client_secret or cryptographic key. An attacker may be able to decompile or reverse engineer a native application to gain access to such secrets.

Mobile operating systems also provide application-specific secure storage. For example, you can use the Android DataStore or the iOS Keychain to store secure values like tokens. When you store OAuth tokens in mobile secure storage, you must also consider the threat of lost devices. You should take measures to ensure that a malicious party who steals a device after a genuine user authenticates cannot gain access to your API data by simply running your mobile application. For example, your mobile application might make a startup check that a device meets security prerequisites, such as a strong lock screen authentication method, before allowing the user to interact with screens that use API data.

Secure storage also plays a part when hardening the security of OAuth clients in platform-specific applications. Let's see how that works next.

Hardening Security

When you implement the RFC 8252 standard you start with OAuth 2.0 and PKCE, to implement baseline security, but some threats remain. Your application is a public client that cannot provide client credentials. Consequently, there are impersonation threats from phishing applications and the client can only use bearer tokens. Therefore, APIs cannot know whether the genuine client sends the access tokens they receive.

You can harden the security of the OAuth implementation for a desktop or mobile application if you can upgrade the public client to a confidential client without hardcoding any secrets. One technique that you can use is a unique client credential on each device that runs your application. One way to do that, without any user prerequisites, is to use the Dynamic Client Registration protocol.

Dynamic Client Registration

The "OAuth 2.0 Dynamic Client Registration Protocol" standard (RFC 7591) (*https://oreil.ly/yPQRL*) provides a way to create OAuth clients at the authorization server without preregistration. For platform-specific applications, you can use DCR to register a unique OAuth client per device. Each client receives a distinct `client_id` and can use a unique client credential. Since each client has a unique credential, you get improved refresh token protection and the ability to revoke access per device. It is then more difficult for an attacker (e.g., a phishing application) to mount a large-scale attack against your mobile application.

To use DCR the authorization server can require an initial access token with a particular scope that you use only to enable DCR. You could deliver such an access token to your platform-specific application in various ways. One option is for the user to run two code flows when they onboard to your mobile application. You could prompt the user to register their application instance and run the first code flow to request an access token with the client's main client ID and the registration scope. We show such a request in Example 12-4.

Example 12-4. Initial code flow to get an initial access token (URL-encoding omitted for readability)

```
GET https://login.example.com/oauth/v2/authorize
    ?client_id=native-client
    &redirect_uri=com.example.app:/callback
    &response_type=code
    &scope=dcr
    &state=kONzMIjrkFpFKWHrFzdTOeFGFxqmx4-WvccdxNnx5f0
    &code_challenge=J_sP1tFjO8tYAq2lbRqVVj7NQPcWIUEZ60RE6dCQYCI
    &code_challenge_method=S256 HTTP/1.1
```

The application can then send a registration request with the initial access token to create a dynamic client at the authorization server. Typically, the authorization server creates a database record to store each dynamic client's configuration settings. The response to the registration request returns a dynamically generated client ID that is unique to the instance of the application that runs on the device. The dynamic client gets a distinct client credential using one of the following methods:

- The authorization server can return a client secret in the DCR response, which the application saves to secure storage. The application then sends the client secret to authenticate in subsequent requests to the token endpoint.

- The application can generate a JSON Web Key and save it to secure storage. It then sends the public key to the authorization server in the `jwks` parameter of the DCR request to register the key. The application then uses its asymmetric key to authenticate at the authorization server. Any DCR-related secrets are private to the user and other users cannot access them.

The initial login continues with a second code flow for the dynamic client, which is a single sign-on event, the first time the user runs it. In Example 12-5, we show how all future user logins for the client on that device use the dynamic client ID along with the application's real scopes.

Example 12-5. Subsequent code flows with a distinct client ID per device (URL-encoding omitted for readability)

```
GET https://login.example.com/oauth/v2/authorize
    ?client_id=c0059d1a-ba4f-46d3-be0c-641decab74a6
    &redirect_uri=com.example.app:/callback
    &response_type=code
    &scope=openid profile retail/orders
    &state=AlAE2RfG-9j6q8eGOmQPeprejHK-3WKOj640VxyJZ6c
    &code_challenge=fTRSlthIgWLYBym-Eerh-uD76BvTZtCdkZ81_ogm92I
    &code_challenge_method=S256 HTTP/1.1
```

DCR improves on the security of RFC 8252. However, DCR also has a management overhead. When making any changes to the general OAuth client settings of the application, like adding a new scope, it must reflect all dynamic client instances stored in your authorization server. To help alleviate management concerns you can use the "Dynamic Client Registration Management" standard (RFC 7592) (*https://oreil.ly/283yI*), which provides a self-service API for clients to read and update their registered client data at the authorization server. In this way, clients can, for example, update and rotate their credentials programmatically or remove their dynamically registered client configuration from the authorization server.

A popular application may result in many dynamic client configurations in your authorization server that become hard to manage. In such a case, consider application attestation as an alternative. Use DCR if you expect to be able to manage the number of dynamically registered clients. If you can control the device, a more complete way to provision device-specific credentials is to use mobile device management (MDM). Let's explore how such a deployment works next.

Unique Keys Per Device

In some use cases, you may be able to deliver both devices and applications together to your user base. For example, you may be able to dictate that financial employees have to use their work mobile device to run the organization's financial mobile applications. In such cases, you could use an MDM solution that deploys one or more distinct keys and certificates to each device, to enable mutual TLS connections.

When a platform-specific application can make mutual TLS connections and each instance of the application can authenticate with a distinct client certificate at the authorization server, you can upgrade your public OAuth client to a confidential client. The client certificate serves as an OAuth client credential that protects token requests. If the authorization server supports certificate-bound access token as defined in RFC 8705 (*https://oreil.ly/z0v2K*), it can then issue the client with sender-constrained access tokens that it binds to the client's certificate. In Figure 12-3 we show a hardened code flow where the client presents a client certificate credential to the authorization server's token endpoint.

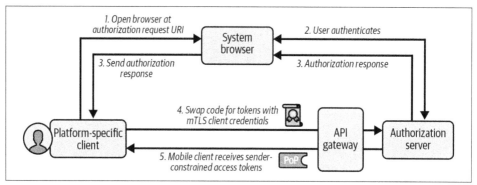

Figure 12-3. OAuth client with mutual TLS and sender-constrained access tokens

If an attacker steals a particular device, you can revoke a certificate to deny access. If a malicious application attempts to impersonate your client, it should be unable to gain access to the required cryptographic key. Therefore, client authentication at the token endpoint fails. You can read more about sender-constrained tokens in Chapter 7. You can read more about how to manage external mTLS connections in Chapter 8.

Using mutual TLS and sender-constrained tokens solves the main security problems with OAuth clients of platform-specific applications since it prevents client impersonation and protects refresh tokens. Being able to provision devices with an initial key and certificate allows you to bootstrap verifiable trust. However, in many use cases, you instead provide internet mobile applications and you cannot control devices. In this case, you should consider the use of application attestation to establish trust.

Application Attestation

Operating systems can provide attestation features to prove the identity of a particular application to server components. For example, modern Android and iOS devices use a hardware element that contains a private and public key pair from the platform provider (i.e., Google or Apple). The manufacturer adds those keys when it creates the device. On such a device, a mobile application can call the operating system's attestation system to request a digital signature that asserts its application identity.

A mobile application can provide input data to the attestation system and receive attestation data consisting of a digital signature and the corresponding public key. The signed attestation data contains the input data and information about the state of the device, such as the device integrity (whether the device has been rooted or tampered with) and whether the device stores its keys in a hardware-backed element.

The mobile application can send the attestation data to an attestation service that verifies the signature and the public key's trust chain to ensure that its root authority is the expected provider. The attestation service issues information from the attestation data to an attestation JSON Web Token (JWT). Other server components, such as the authorization server, can receive the attestation JWT in a secure request, verify the JWT, and decide whether to authorize the request based on the claims in the JWT payload.

Standard SDKs and attestation services exist to simplify the end-to-end process, such as Google Play Integrity (*https://oreil.ly/BoH-j*) and Apple's App Attest (*https://oreil.ly/nc4h6*). We show an example end-to-end flow that uses such an attestation service in Figure 12-4.

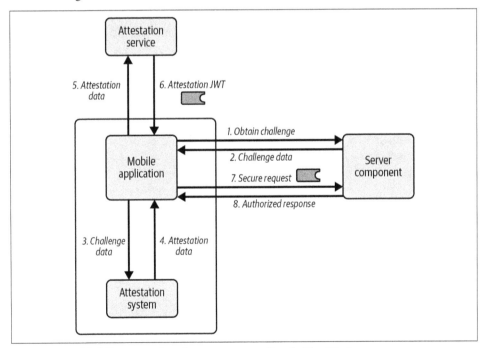

Figure 12-4. Mobile attestation flow to prove a client's identity to a server

We summarize the main steps from Figure 12-4 in the following list:

1. The mobile application asks a server component to provide some challenge data.

2. The server component returns challenge data, such as a randomly generated string, and also caches it for a short time.

3. The mobile application sends the challenge data to the attestation system to request attestation data.

4. The attestation system verifies the application and device state and then returns attestation data.

5. The mobile application sends the attestation data to the attestation service.

6. The attestation service issues an attestation JWT and returns it to the mobile application.

7. The mobile application sends the attestation JWT in a secure request to the server component.

8. The server component validates the JWT, verifies that the challenge data exists in its cache, and authorizes the request.

From an OAuth perspective, attestation JWTs can serve as cryptographic proof of the client's identity and you could use them to harden OAuth flows, to make the mobile client operate similarly to a confidential client. For mobile clients, you could implement custom logic in requests to the authorization server to implement the role of the server component in Figure 12-4. You might implement such logic as an extension to your authorization server.

At the time of writing, some older mobile devices use hardware that does not support attestation, so you must deal with that limitation. Attestation can increase the trust in the client's authenticity. For security reasons, you should combine attestation with a proof-of-control mechanism like Demonstrating Proof of Possession (DPoP)[1] or mTLS. In the future, we expect the use of attestation to become mainstream for platform-specific OAuth clients.[2] It has the potential to enable strong mobile security without the management overhead of MDM or DCR.

Another area of particular interest for OAuth in platform-specific applications is browserless user authentication. Let's explain how that would work next.

---

1 "Hypermedia Authentication API Security in Detail" (*https://oreil.ly/-XZr8*), whitepaper, *Curity*.

2 See "OAuth 2.0 Attestation-Based Client Authentication" (*https://oreil.ly/hMEDD*) (IETF draft).

Browserless User Authentication

The original OAuth specification mandates that a client should not gain access to user credentials. That is why, normally, you run an OAuth flow by opening a browser and redirecting the user to the authorization server. The user provides any credentials directly to the authorization server, not to the client. This is especially important when the user provides a third-party credential, like a social login password, that might enable access to many of the user's digital services. However, user authentication can work in many possible ways and is not limited to entering passwords or using social providers, as we explain in Chapter 14.

In a first-party relationship where one and the same party maintains the authorization server, the API, and the client, this party already has access to the user's data and credentials. Consequently, the requirement to use the browser remains essential only for particular authentication methods. This opens new possibilities. For example, you may have particular authentication requirements that a browser cannot meet, or the browser may not provide any security value for your use case. The following list provides some examples where the built-in features of a device could prove useful during authentication flows:

- Improve the login user experience for desktop applications.
- Enable users to authenticate in a mobile app using a browserless passkeys experience.
- Enable users to use App2App authentication with a specialist login app that you install on the same device.
- Enable an application to use the device camera to scan a user's passport.
- Enable a shop's kiosk application to use the device camera to scan a QR code from a user's membership application.

If you have these types of user authentication requirements, you should not need to abandon OAuth and resort to writing user authentication code directly in your front-end applications. Instead, your authorization server could provide authentication capabilities that integrate with the operating system so that you implement the responsibilities in the correct places and avoid incurring any technical debt. This means, for example, that if the authorization server mandates passkey logins for an OAuth flow, the application can rely on the capabilities of the platform (e.g., mobile operating system) to fulfill that requirement. You then continue to ensure that your authorization server audits authentication events and that your platform-specific application receives correctly issued access tokens.

The "OAuth 2.0 for First-Party Applications" draft specification (*https://oreil.ly/ LGTXu*) explains how authentication with browserless features of the operating system could work within the context of an OAuth flow. The authorization server provides a new *Authorization Challenge Endpoint* that a client can call multiple times with different proofs of the user's identity. After each request, the authorization server can return an error response with context when it requires further authentication details. In this way, you can implement multifactor authentication (MFA) and complex authentication flows that include core features of the platform. For some user credential types, the flow could include an instruction to open the system browser. Eventually, user authentication completes and the authorization server returns an authorization code to the client, which the client uses to get access tokens in the usual way.

We illustrate the basic multifactor flow from "OAuth 2.0 for First-Party Applications" in Figure 12-5. The OAuth client of the platform-specific application starts the flow with an HTTP POST to the challenge endpoint with standard authorization request parameters, like `client_id` and `scope`, along with a proof of the user's identity. The client may then receive an error response indicating that authentication is incomplete and to express what the client does next. The client then sends a second proof of the user's identity to complete the flow and receive an authorization code.

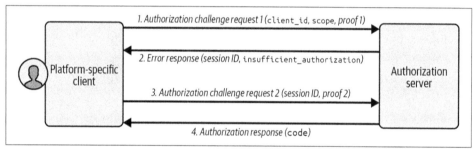

Figure 12-5. OAuth first-party authentication flow

The specification leaves some behaviors to the authorization server implementation. Therefore, an authorization server that implements the specification could provide convenience features, like client-side SDKs, to enable you to keep the complexities of client-side security external to your application code.

In a code flow, the authorization server typically returns Hypertext Markup Language (HTML) forms to your browser. You provide input and post it back to the authorization server, which redirects the browser to the next screen until authentication completes. For a browserless flow, the authorization server could use a Hypermedia REST API implementation, where responses direct clients in similar ways to how HTML responses direct the browser. A client-side SDK could render forms dynamically from API responses, perform the security work, and then call the authorization challenge endpoint.

Now that we've completed the theory on OAuth clients for platform-specific applications, we show you some practical content to get you connected. The main focus of the code examples is to show you how to implement a reliable code flow in a few different technologies.

Code Examples

We provide some code examples in the folder *chapter-12-platform-specific-apps* in the GitHub repository of this book (*https://oreil.ly/CNDS-supp*). You can run any of the following OAuth clients:

- A console client that uses Node.js
- A desktop client that uses Node.js and Electron
- Mobile clients that use Kotlin and Swift

Each client calls a cloud native authorization server and the example zero trust API from Chapter 5. You can deploy these backend components to a Kubernetes cluster that runs on your local computer, in a similar manner to the example in Chapter 8. To do so, run the scripts that we summarize in Table 12-1.

Table 12-1. Deployment scripts

Script	Responsibilities
1-create-cluster.sh	Creates a Kubernetes cluster and runs a local load balancer that enables connectivity from the local computer.
2-deploy-api-gateway.sh	Deploys an API gateway that introspects opaque access tokens and forwards JWT access tokens to APIs.
3-deploy-authorization-server.sh	Deploys an authorization server that issues opaque tokens to clients.
4-deploy-api.sh	Deploys the API from Chapter 5, which clients call after the user authenticates.

Each code example implements the main best practices from RFC 8252 to implement a code flow with PKCE, using the following steps:

- Run an HTTP server or register a private-use URI scheme.
- Create an authorization request URL that includes a PKCE code challenge.
- Open the system browser at the authorization request URL to start a user login.
- Notify the client with the authorization response URL.
- Swap the authorization code for tokens using a PKCE code verifier.
- Use a security library to cryptographically verify the ID token.

The console application runs a code flow to get an access token, calls the demo API, and then exits immediately. The desktop and mobile clients also present a basic user interface and run an OAuth lifecycle that deals with expiry conditions, including token refresh and a basic logout. All code examples also show how to handle OAuth errors. To reduce complexity and infrastructure, we do not implement any of the security hardening techniques from this chapter.

All examples implement their code flow using a plain HTTP library to produce the OAuth request messages and read the OAuth response messages. We use a security library to validate ID tokens. We believe this is the best way to teach the code flow so that you understand its steps. In the following sections, we explain some particular details. You can gain a more complete understanding of how to run each example by studying its *README* documents. Let's start with the simplest example, a console application.

Console Application

We use a minimal Node.js console application for the first code flow implementation. The application starts, runs a loopback HTTP server, and then invokes the system browser to authenticate the user. Once user authentication completes, the console client gets an access token, calls the demo API, renders some response data, and then exits. The only tricky code is that used to open the system browser at the authorization request URL and receive back the authorization response using an HTTP server. We show the main code to enable that in Example 12-6.

Example 12-6. Node.js code to run a code flow using loopback address

```
public async login(authorizationRequestUrl: string): Promise<URL> {

    this.httpServer = http.createServer(this.handleLoopbackHttpRequest);
    this.httpServer.listen(this.port, Configuration.loopbackHostname);

    await open(authorizationRequestUrl);

    return new Promise<URL>((resolve, reject) => {
        this.eventEmitter.once('LOGIN_COMPLETE', (authorizationResponseUrl: string)
        => {
            this.stop();
            resolve(new URL(authorizationResponseUrl));
        });
    });
}

private async handleLoopbackHttpRequest(
    request: http.IncomingMessage,
    response: http.ServerResponse): Promise<void> {
```

```
const requestUrl = new URL(request.url || '', `http://${request.headers.host}`);
if (requestUrl.pathname !== '/callback') {
    response.end();
    return;
}

response.write('Login completed successfully');
response.end();

this.eventEmitter.emit('LOGIN_COMPLETE', requestUrl);
}
```

The desktop code example uses similar technology for its logins but runs a more complete lifecycle. Let's provide an overview of the desktop application and some particular behaviors next.

Desktop Application

The desktop application uses the cross-platform Electron technology stack and presents its frontend views in a renderer process that uses the Chromium browser. Views have no access to the desktop environment and must call the main process to start the HTTP server and open the system browser. Initially, the desktop client presents an unauthenticated view with a login button that invokes the system browser. Once the user authenticates, the desktop client presents an authenticated view that renders ID token claims and enables you to call APIs and the OpenID Connect userinfo endpoint. You can also perform a basic logout, to discard tokens and return the application to its unauthenticated view.

In Example 12-7, we show the code that the desktop application uses to build its authorization request URL. Note that we use PKCE and the OpenID Connect prompt=login parameter to force the user to authenticate. This can be a useful technique for platform-specific applications if you have problems implementing logout in your preferred way and you want to run the application for multiple test users.

Example 12-7. Node.js code to force a new login using the OpenID Connect prompt=login parameter

```
function buildAuthorizationRequestUrl(
    state: string,
    codeChallenge: string,
    redirectUri: string): string {

    let requestUrl = Configuration.authorizationEndpoint;
    requestUrl += `?client_id=${encodeURIComponent(Configuration.clientId)}`;
    requestUrl += `&redirect_uri=${encodeURIComponent(redirectUri)}`;
    requestUrl += '&response_type=code';
    requestUrl += `&scope=${encodeURIComponent(Configuration.scope)}`;
    requestUrl += `&state=${state}`;
```

```
requestUrl += `&code_challenge=${codeChallenge}`;
requestUrl += '&code_challenge_method=S256';
requestUrl += '&prompt=login';

    return requestUrl;
}
```

The other interesting area of the desktop application's code is the token refresh logic. We recommend that you always implement token refresh from frontend views, which runs in the renderer process for an Electron application. If your application presents multiple views that call APIs concurrently, views can then synchronize token refresh to ensure that the actual refresh token request only occurs once. Doing so prevents possible race conditions where you use single-use refresh tokens and one view sends an outdated refresh token that is no longer valid.

In Example 12-8, we show a simplified version of the desktop client's code to manage API requests and handle error and expiry events. When the client receives an API error with an HTTP 401 status code, the client does a token refresh and retries the API request. When the refresh token eventually expires, token refresh fails with an `invalid_grant` error code. The client then moves back to its unauthenticated view and prompts the user to reauthenticate. If required, you could update this frontend code to implement refresh token synchronization.

Example 12-8. Node.js code to call APIs reliably

```
export async function makeApiRequest(options: ApiOptions): Promise<any> {

    try {

        return await callApi(options);

    } catch (e1: any) {

        const error1 = e1 as ApplicationError;
        if (error1?.statusCode !== 401) {
            throw e1;
        }

        try {

            await refreshAccessToken()

        } catch (e2: any) {

            const error2 = e2 as ApplicationError;
            if (error2?.errorCode !== 'invalid_grant') {
                throw e2;
            }
```

```
        throw new ApplicationError(
            'login_required', 'User must reauthenticate'
        );
    }

    return await callApi(options);
  }
}
```

The mobile code example uses the same behaviors as the desktop client, with authenticated and unauthenticated views. The login mechanism uses private-use URI schemes as the simplest technical way to get integrated. Let's look at a few details next.

Mobile Applications

We implement the mobile code examples in Kotlin on Android, and in Swift on iOS, since they are productive languages that give you control over platform-specific behaviors. The code separation is largely identical to that for the desktop application, although the technology is different. To connect the mobile clients to the local Kubernetes cluster, you run the mobile code examples on an Android emulator or an iOS simulator. The mobile *README* files provide further details on local connectivity. Once you understand how to implement a mobile code flow, you can connect applications on real devices to your deployed Kubernetes clusters.

The first main difference for mobile examples is that they register a private-use URI scheme redirect URI. On Android you use the *AndroidManifest.xml* file to register an activity that uses the scheme to receive the login response. On iOS you instead declare a URL scheme in the *info.plist* file. In both cases, when you install the mobile application, the operating system associates the application with the scheme. When a user authenticates, the operating system notifies the mobile client with the authorization response URL. When the mobile client runs, it interacts with the integrated form of the system browser to send the authorization request and get the authorization response.

On Android you use an Intent to invoke the custom tab and receive responses from it. In Example 12-9, we show how the application's main activity sends an authorization request URL to a LoginRequestResponseActivity that manages the custom tab communication. When user authentication completes, the LoginRequestResponse Activity receives an authorization response and forwards the response URL back to the main activity. The mobile client extracts the authorization code and then uses an HTTP library to get access tokens and call APIs.

Example 12-9. Kotlin code for starting and finishing a code flow

```kotlin
class MainActivity : ComponentActivity() {

    private val loginLauncher = registerForActivityResult(
        ActivityResultContracts.StartActivityForResult()
    ) { result ->
        this.onFinishLogin(result.data)
    }

    private fun onStartLogin() {

        val authorizationRequestUrl = this.model.startLogin()
        val requestIntent = Intent(this, LoginRequestResponseActivity::class.java)
        requestIntent.putExtra("AUTHORIZATION_REQUEST_URL", authorizationRequestUrl)
        this.loginLauncher.launch(requestIntent)
    }

    private fun onFinishLogin(intent: Intent?) {

        val responseIntent = intent?.extras?.getString("AUTHORIZATION_RESPONSE_URL")
        ...
    }
}
```

For iOS, the code is similar. You use an instance of the ASWebAuthenticationSession system service to send the authorization request URL and receive the authorization response. The remainder of the code requires only Swift HTTP handling.

Example 12-10. Swift code to run a code flow

```swift
func startLogin(authorizationRequestUrl: String,
    onComplete: @escaping (_: URL?, _: Error?) -> Void) throws {

    authSession = ASWebAuthenticationSession(
        url: URL(string: authorizationRequestUrl)!,
        callbackURLScheme: "com.example.demoapp",
        completionHandler: { (callbackUrl: URL?, error: Error?) in

            defer {
                self.authSession?.cancel()
                self.authSession = nil
            }

            onComplete(callbackUrl, error)
        }
    )

    authSession?.presentationContextProvider = self
    authSession?.start()
}
```

You could upgrade the mobile code examples from a private-use URI scheme redirect URI to a more secure claimed HTTPS scheme redirect URI. To do so you would first need to provide additional infrastructure, in particular to host a mobile assets document. The code would remain essentially the same, to resume the flow when the mobile application receives an App Link or Universal Link that contains the authorization response.

Summary

The current mainstream OAuth solution for platform-specific applications follows the best practices defined by RFC 8252. You should implement the best practices from the standard to ensure the correct basic level of security. Use Proof Key for Code Exchange (PKCE) and authentication via the system browser. The end-user and type of browser varies depending on the platform. The redirect URI on which the application receives the authorization response is either a loopback URI, a private-use URI scheme, or a claimed HTTPS scheme. For mobile apps, claimed HTTPS schemes are the most secure option.

You can go beyond RFC 8252 to improve the security capabilities of your mobile clients. If you own all devices on which your platform-specific application runs, you might be able to preprovision each device with a unique key to enable mutual TLS. For general internet applications, consider using attestation or DCR to improve security. Some authorization servers may also enable you to remain within the OAuth framework but use a browserless user experience and device features to authenticate users.

Now that you understand the code flow, you are well placed to implement the remaining type of OAuth client that users interact with. In Chapter 13 we dive deep into OAuth for browser-based applications. Browser-based clients are more complex than they may appear at first sight since they require you to understand and mitigate the threats of the browser environment. We show that if you cleanly separate web and API concerns, you can implement the right protections and also run a modern web architecture.

OAuth for Browser-Based Applications

Browser-based applications are dynamic web applications that can run entirely in the browser. They make use of client-side scripts like JavaScript to retrieve data from business APIs and update screens. Because of their tight integration with the browser, you must be aware of browser behavior when running browser-based applications. The browser behaviors are guided by web standard technologies and related threats impact any application running in browsers.

This chapter explains best practices for browser-based applications. We start with a definition of browser-based applications. We then outline important threats as well as the main security measures that you should be aware of. We continue with a discussion of OAuth implementations. We go from a JavaScript-only implementation to explaining how a Backend for Frontend (BFF) approach for OAuth provides security benefits. Next, we explain how an API-driven solution can help to avoid almost all adverse effects on your web architecture. We provide a considerable amount of content but end the chapter with a code example that you can run to see a working browser-based application that demonstrates the theory.

Web Application Basics

Being a global space that reaches more than 60% of the population on earth and almost everybody in high-income countries,[1] the web is a powerful place for organizations to present their business. In general, there are two approaches for an online presence: a website or a web application. They are not mutually exclusive and you may combine web applications with websites.

---

[1] "Global Offline Population Steadily Declines to 2.6 Billion People in 2023" (*https://oreil.ly/JKuD7*), Facts and Figures 2023, International Telecommunication Union (ITU).

Website Versus Web Application

Websites are a composition of web pages that users access via the browser. Technologies involved commonly include HTML, CSS, and some JavaScript. The main purpose of a website is to inform visitors. Consequently, their content is primarily static. This conveys that websites do not allow users to shape their content. Thus, websites provide one-way communication channels where visitors navigate through the pages to consume the information. Users cannot engage with the website to dynamically update, create, or delete any content. Often, websites are public and do not require any user authentication.

Web applications, on the other hand, are programs that use web technologies to provide an interface for users to interact with. The technical stack for web applications commonly includes HTML, CSS, and JavaScript but also programming languages such as Java, Python, Ruby, or Node.js for server-side logic. As with websites, users load web applications via the browser. Web applications provide a customized user experience. While users simply visit websites, they engage with web applications by loading, changing, filtering, or updating content. Consequently authentication is often an obligatory aspect of web applications. You can think of GitHub as a representative of a web application, where you can log in, create pull requests, and leave comments. Browser-based applications are a specific form of web applications that imply a certain architecture.

Web Application Architecture

Simply put, web applications consist of three logical layers—a frontend with a user interface (presentation layer), a backend with the business logic (business layer), and a data store (persistence layer). Users interact with the frontend via the browser while the frontend in turn communicates with the backend. The backend loads and stores data in the data storage (e.g., a database or data warehouse). This is, of course, a very simplified view of a web application. Often, a web application involves other components, such as message queues. A web application architecture describes the relationship of the components and how they interact.

The most basic architecture is a monolithic architecture where the frontend (presentation) and the backend (business logic) are one unit that is tightly coupled to the persistent storage. Such a standalone server application connects directly with the database (if any). It commonly implements its own authentication method that uses cookies for maintaining user sessions (see Figure 13-1). Cookies provide a user-friendly and relatively secure solution to represent the authenticated state of a user.

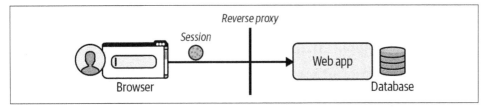

Figure 13-1. Web application architecture for standalone web application

A three-layer architecture separates the business and data storage logic from the presentation logic to improve user experience, scalability, and availability. The result may be a service-oriented architecture that divides a web application into services that each implement a business function. When you break down the services even further and make each responsible for a specific, definitive task (compared to a service that implements several tasks), you have a microservice architecture. In a microservice architecture, the business layer encompasses the microservices, and the presentation layer encompasses the frontend applications. The frontend calls the endpoints of the microservices to aggregate the desired user experience.

The three-layer approach enables organizations to develop different frontend applications, such as mobile- or browser-based applications using the same backend. Instead of having a web server call upstream services and render the frontend, frontend applications can call APIs directly to fetch data and update the user interface accordingly. This is often where OAuth comes into play.

When using OAuth, the web application frontend (and any other frontend application) needs an access token to call APIs. The user no longer authenticates in the frontend application but as part of the OAuth flow to the authorization server. The frontend application can still use cookies to identify a user's session. Figure 13-2 illustrates a web application architecture with microservices.

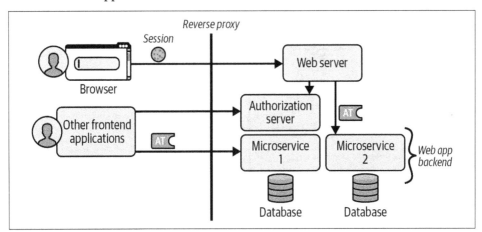

Figure 13-2. Web application architecture with microservices

Let's study the characteristics of browser-based applications in more detail.

Browser-Based Applications

A browser-based application is a web application where all web application logic runs entirely in the browser. When the browser hits the URL of the web application, it downloads the client-side code, typically some JavaScript files, from the web server. The browser then executes the program. Single-page applications (SPAs) are browser-based applications that offer a single page that the user interacts with. The browser loads the page once and dynamically updates content after user actions without having to fully reload the page or load other pages. A well-known example of an SPA is Gmail.

Progressive web applications are an evolution of SPAs that take after platform-specific applications. You can install a progressive web application and work with it offline, and it can send you messages using push notifications. The main distinction between progressive web applications and platform-specific applications is that the former runs its logic in a browser engine, whereas platform-specific applications do not. We consider both SPAs and progressive web applications to be browser-based applications.

Browser-based applications communicate via the browser engine with the backend APIs (see Figure 13-3). As with other frontend applications, a browser-based application needs access tokens to be able to call the backend APIs. For this, it needs to integrate with the authorization server to get access tokens. Since browser-based applications run in the browser, they can benefit from web technologies, such as cookies, in their communications. The authorization server typically uses cookies to store the user's login status, which enables an SSO experience in (but not limited to) browser-based applications.

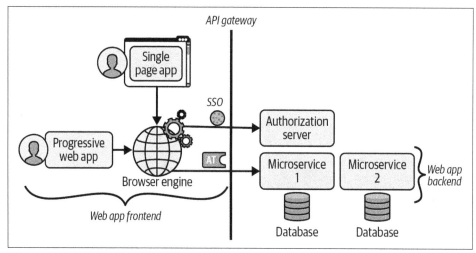

Figure 13-3. Browser-based applications depend on the browser engine to communicate with backend APIs

The main challenge of this architecture is to securely obtain and store access tokens in browser-based applications. We therefore highlight some browser security threats next.

Browser Security Threats

In simple terms, the browser follows various web standards that allow a user to browse and interact with web applications. It is a universal user interface to resources on the internet. As such it becomes an attractive target for attackers. Attackers can misuse browser vulnerabilities, web standards, and the behavior they define to circumvent security measures.

Most browser security exploits result in an attacker gaining unauthorized access to data. One way to do so is to steal a user credential in an account takeover attack. Some other threats try to exploit your browser-based application's access tokens or cookies. Each threat may target a particular security weakness. Let's explore some details of the most common threats targeting user impersonation, starting with clickjacking.

Clickjacking

Clickjacking is an attack that tricks users into performing unintended actions by clicking on a hidden button or link. Attackers create a seemingly innocuous page on their website, which they overlay with a transparent iframe to carefully align hidden buttons or links, as we show in Figure 13-4. When users click on a button, they actually activate the hidden button and trigger unsolicited requests to a target site like the authorization server. In this way, attackers can, for example, get users to grant access to resources or reveal their authentication credentials without their knowledge. The user is unaware that they are interacting with a malicious website.

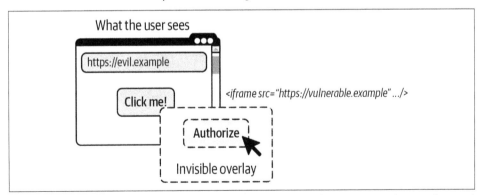

Figure 13-4. Invisible overlay in browser window to trick the user to send an authorized request

Clickjacking requires user interaction that bad actors can exploit. With OAuth, you can mitigate some risks because the authorization server manages user authentication. You are still responsible for ensuring that your browser-based application does not have other vulnerabilities. In particular, you must protect against cross-site request forgery.

Cross-Site Request Forgery

Cross-site request forgery (CSRF) attacks are similar to clickjacking attacks in the sense that a malicious website tricks users into performing an authenticated but unsolicited request to your browser-based application. Attackers may include crafted image tags or hidden forms on a site that trigger a request from their website to your server. The browser may automatically send a request with a cookie from your browser-based application when a user loads a page in the malicious website.

Most commonly, CSRF attacks try to exploit cookies. Cookies are small pieces of data that a server sends to the browser for storage.[2] They are simply name-value pairs with some attributes that the browser stores for a predetermined period of time. Consequently, cookies lend themselves very well to session management, to represent the user's authenticated state. Browsers automatically add server-issued cookies in requests back to the HTTP server. If attackers can use your cookies, they can silently perform requests on behalf of the user. Therefore, CSRF attacks are also known as "session riding." Attackers often cannot read responses, though, and therefore commonly aim for state-changing requests such as transferring money or updating passwords. We illustrate a CSRF exploit in Figure 13-5, where a hidden form on a malicious site results in the browser automatically sending a POST request to a vulnerable site.

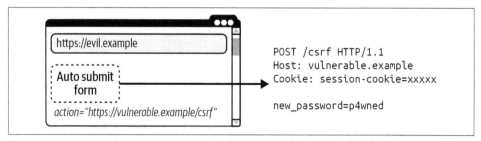

Figure 13-5. Cross-site request forgery with embedded and invisible form

From an HTTP server perspective, it is impossible to determine whether requests with cookies are solicited or unsolicited. Therefore, OAuth clients, including browser-based applications, must protect their redirect URIs against CSRF attacks.

---

2 See "Using HTTP Cookies" (*https://oreil.ly/VFBNS*), *MDN Web Docs.*

Some website frameworks like ASP.NET Core (*https://oreil.ly/x9bIP*), Spring Boot Spring Security (*https://oreil.ly/lIhVn*), or Angular2 (*https://oreil.ly/knjms*) provide built-in CSRF protection using antiforgery tokens. An antiforgery token is a cryptographically strong string from the HTTP server that only the legitimate frontend can read and send. You can also use the browser's built-in defenses to ensure that the browser only sends cookies from your browser-based application's precise web origin. We explain these techniques in "Secure Cookie Settings" on page 293 and "Cross-Origin Resource Sharing" on page 295.

Implementing CSRF protections against malicious websites has mature solutions and is relatively straightforward. The biggest threat for browser-based applications by far remains cross-site scripting, where you must protect against attacks from inside your browser-based application.

Cross-Site Scripting

Cross-site scripting (XSS) is a powerful type of attack because it allows a bad actor to run client-side code in the context of an otherwise trusted web application, as we illustrate in Figure 13-6. This means that malicious code can do whatever the legitimate application can do. In particular, it can circumvent any application-level defenses. In other words, it can make use of any (dynamic) key material, access APIs, load secrets, or even override functions including built-in functions (prototype pollution) which can completely change the behavior of an application.

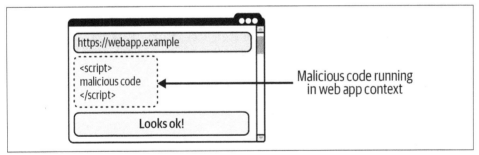

Figure 13-6. XSS runs malicious code in the context of a web application

Attackers can compromise whole applications and impersonate their users with XSS. In worst-case scenarios, they can take over the application, at least temporarily. They can, among other things, steal access and refresh tokens using browser APIs (such as the Web Storage API to access LocalStorage or SessionStorage), obtain new tokens utilizing SSO features (silent authentication), send tokens and data to remote hosts (persistent token theft), circumvent CSRF mitigation, and carry out session riding to perform authenticated requests. Simply put, XSS attacks can cause great damage. Because of the high risk, you must protect your browser-based application and its OAuth implementation against XSS.

XSS attacks originate from vulnerabilities in your own applications or dependencies that your application uses. The best protection against XSS is to avoid vulnerabilities in the first place. Therefore, take some basic measures as a first line of defense. Only use respected libraries, minimize the number of libraries that you use, and frequently use vulnerability scanning tools to identify and fix security issues. In your code, carefully sanitize any user input. You should also apply sanitization at places where the output is generated from user input. Some frameworks like Angular2 provide some built-in protection.

For your second or third line of defense, use security mechanisms from both the HTTP and the OAuth protocols to limit the likelihood or impact of XSS attacks. In the next section, we discuss some web security mechanisms that you should consider for the in-depth strategy for defense of your browser-based applications.

Web Security Mechanisms

Backends like the authorization server, APIs or web hosts should implement security mechanisms to mitigate some of the threats that we have identified, including XSS. These mechanisms depend on the browser to enforce policies. One well-established mechanism that the browser already enforces by default is the same-origin policy.

Same-Origin Policy

To understand the same-origin policy, you first need to be familiar with the origin of a web application. The origin of a web application is defined as the combination of the scheme, the host, and the port of its URL. Two URLs share the same origin if their scheme, host, and port match. To illustrate the concept, Table 13-1 compares some origins against `https://www.webapp.example`.

Table 13-1. Origin comparison for `https://www.webapp.example`

URL	Is same origin?	Explanation
`https://www.webapp.example/path`	Yes	Same scheme, host, and port
`https://www.webapp.example:443`	Yes	Same scheme, host, and port because default port for `https://` is 443
`https://www.webapp.example:8443`	No	Same scheme and host but different port (8443)
`http://www.webapp.example`	No	Same host but different scheme (`http`)
`https://api.webapp.example`	No	Same scheme and port but different host (`api.webapp.example`)

For security reasons, browsers prevent JavaScript code from one origin to read resources from another origin. This policy is called the same-origin policy. The same-origin policy protects against attacks where a script from one origin reuses an authentication state to read (possibly) sensitive information from another origin. The browser applies the policy only to scripts and not to HTML tags. Consequently, the same-origin policy does not protect against CSRF. It does not prevent XSS attacks either because malicious code can run on the same origin as the web application.

There are techniques that you can actively apply at a backend like the authorization server, APIs, or web hosts, to secure a browser-based application without having to change the application itself. Among others, there are various standardized security headers that allow an HTTP server to control browser behavior. The most important one with regard to XSS mitigation is the Content Security Policy header.

Content Security Policy

With the help of the `Content-Security-Policy` HTTP response header, an HTTP server can control some browser behaviors for a web application. You can see Content Security Policies as a form of access control where the value of this header provides one or more directives that tell the browser what the server allows.[3] Consequently, Content Security Policies are not part of the browser-based application itself but the responsibility of the web host that serves the application. Further, it is the responsibility of the browser to enforce the policies.

Content Security Policies support many directives, including `frame-src`, which lists the approved sources that the browser may load iframes from, or `frame-ancestors`, which lets a website specify in which context the browser may embed it. The latter mitigates clickjacking. The authorization server should use a Content Security Policy that prevents unauthorized web applications from rendering its login screens—visible or not.

The web host of a browser-based application should use Content Security Policies to specify that the browser must load JavaScript files only from a trusted source, or with a given hash. This prevents the browser from loading arbitrary, potentially malicious scripts from unauthorized sources which mitigates certain XSS attacks. You should disallow unsafe-inline scripts in browser-based applications because they are an easy target for XSS exploits. We highly recommend also specifying a `connect-src` directive to limit the URLs the browser-based application and any code running in its context are allowed to call. In this way, you can prevent attackers from sending data like stolen access tokens to a remote host that they control (e.g., via a `fetch()` command).

---

3 See "Content Security Policy Cheat Sheet" (*https://oreil.ly/0ALAg*), *OWASP Cheat Sheet Series.*

Content Security Policies and cross-origin requests

With Content Security Policies, you can, for example, define which APIs a browser-based application may send requests to. However, you cannot override the same-origin policy. To allow cross-origin requests, the remote server like the API also needs to notify the browser to relax the same-origin policy for the browser-based application (more on that under "Cross-Origin Resource Sharing" on page 295).

We illustrate a strict Content Security Policy in Example 13-1, where line breaks and indentation are only for readability. The example policy instructs the browser to run scripts only from the server's origin (`script-src 'self'`), which prevents an XSS attack from running scripts from other origins. The `connect-src` directive in the policy allows any loaded script to send a request only to the server's origin (`'self'`) or `https://api.example.com`, making sure a script cannot call any untrusted source.

Example 13-1. Example Content Security Policy header

```
Content-Security-Policy:
    default-src 'none';
    script-src 'self';
    connect-src 'self' https://api.example.com;
    child-src 'self';
    img-src 'self';
    style-src 'self' https://cdn.jsdelivr.net;
    font-src 'self';
    base-uri 'self';
    form-action 'self';
```

Some potential exploits may be subtle. For instance, the `src` attribute of an `<img>` tag can initiate a request to a remote host that sends data out of the browser (the `connect-src` directive of a Content Security Policy does not prevent such a call as it only applies to JavaScript APIs and not HTML attributes). Therefore, follow the principle of least privilege and deny access to any remote hosts by default (`default-src 'none'`). Then, add any exceptions that you need, as for the `img-src` and `style-src` directives in Example 13-1. The MDN web docs (*https://oreil.ly/uqJvK*) have great resources to look up and learn more about Content Security Policies.

Content Security Policies are an important part of XSS protection. A strict Content Security Policy can mitigate the risk of XSS attacks because it can make it harder for attackers to exploit vulnerabilities in your browser-based application. Be aware that users may sometimes run insecure browser settings that disable Content Security Policy evaluation. Therefore, your major defenses against XSS remain thorough input and output sanitization, combined with careful dependency management.

Despite XSS being the biggest threat for browser-based applications, other threats like CSRF still remain a risk and could result in user impersonation. CSRF commonly misuses standard browser behavior related to cookies. Consequently, to protect against CSRF start by hardening cookies.

Secure Cookie Settings

When HTTP servers send cookies, they add a Set-Cookie HTTP response header for each cookie that they want the browser to store. The header value contains the name and value of the cookie as well as some attributes that allow the server to define the security properties of the cookie. This section describes the most important attributes that can improve the security of cookies and their data.

Expires *and* Max-Age
> These attributes specify, in two different ways, a time when the cookie expires and should be removed. Expires defines an absolute time relative to the browser's clock while Max-Age specifies the relative lifetime in seconds. Cookies with an expiration date are persistent cookies that the browser keeps even between sessions. When the server does not set any expiration, the cookies are considered session cookies that are deleted when the session ends (e.g., when the user closes the browser). It is at the discretion of the browser to decide when a session is actually over. There is no guarantee that session cookies are actually deleted when the browser shuts down because browsers may keep them to support restore session features. A Max-Age attribute with a value less than or equal to zero invalidates a cookie immediately.

Domain
> The server can specify the host to which a browser can send the cookie. Note that it is more restrictive to omit this attribute than to set it. When this attribute is set, the browser includes the cookie in requests to the domain and any of its subdomains. This means that a cookie with the attribute Domain=webapp.example is also available to its subdomains such as www.webapp.example and api.webapp.example. When the attribute is not set, the browser will include cookies in requests to only the same host that originally set the cookie and will not include it in requests to subdomains. Do not set the domain attribute unless subdomains really need to send cookies.

Path
> The Path attribute is another attribute that allows for restricting access to cookies. This attribute instructs the browser to only send the cookie in requests that contain the given path in their URL. For instance, cookies with Path=/api are sent with any requests that target /api, /api/, or subpaths like /api/v1/.

Secure

> With this attribute, the browser sends the cookie only over a secure channel (i.e., HTTPS). This prevents attacker-in-the-middle attacks where a bad actor could read or modify the cookie in transit.

HttpOnly

> The HttpOnly attribute of a cookie instructs the browser to use the cookie only in HTTP requests and not make it available to JavaScript code. This means such a cookie is inaccessible via the document.cookie property. This attribute helps to mitigate the impact of XSS attacks, as malicious scripts cannot read HTTP-only cookies.

SameSite

> This attribute controls whether the browser sends the cookie in cross-site requests. The value Lax indicates a relaxed rule where the browser sends the cookie in top-level navigations from a site (e.g., when clicking on a link). When the value is Strict, the browser sends the cookie in requests that originate only from the same site that initially set the cookie. This flag can help to protect from CSRF attacks.

A site is the name of a web application, identified by the scheme (e.g., https) and the registrable domain. The two sites https://www.webapp.example and https://api.webapp.example are the same site if webapp.example is considered a registrable domain. The registrable domain is often the same as the domain name.

Formally, a registrable domain is the effective top-level domain (eTLD) plus the element to the left (eTLD+1). The eTLD can be the same as the top-level domain (com, org, example, etc.) but does not have to be. Some registrars allow different organizations to share the same domain name. Then, the eTLD is not the top-level domain but a domain name or subdomain like gov.uk; in that case, two websites under the eTLD are two different sites and must not share the same-site cookies despite their common domain name. By way of illustration, Table 13-2 includes the results of some same-site evaluations.

Table 13-2. Same-site evaluations

Site	eTLD	Registrable domain (eTLD+1)	Are same site?	Explanation
https://www.webapp.example	.example	webapp.example	Yes	Same scheme and eTLD+1
https://api.webapp.example	.example	webapp.example		
http://www.webapp.example	.example	webapp.example	No	Same eTLD+1 but different scheme (http versus https)
https://api.webapp.example	.example	webapp.example		

Site	eTLD	Registrable domain (eTLD+1)	Are same site?	Explanation
https://www.one.example	.example	one.example	No	Different eTLD+1
https://www.two.example	.example	two.example		
https://www.gov.uk	.gov.uk	www.gov.uk	No	Different eTLD, thus different eTLD+1
https://www.api.gov.uk	.api.gov.uk	www.api.gov.uk		

There is no algorithm to determine whether a domain is a registrable domain. The public suffix list (*https://publicsuffix.org*) mitigates this challenge by listing common eTLD.

The concept of a *site* is relevant when dealing with cookies because the browser will not include same-site cookies in cross-site requests. The challenge with CSRF attacks is that servers cannot determine whether an authenticated request comes from a trusted or malicious source. Same-site cookies ensure that the browser includes only the authenticated state (i.e., the cookies) in requests where the origin and target share the same site (registrable domain). Consequently, same-site cookies eliminate authenticated cross-site requests and thus mitigate some CSRF attacks. In addition, Cross-Origin Resource Sharing can further protect against CSRF attacks in browser-based applications. Let's examine the details.

Cross-Origin Resource Sharing

Cross-Origin Resource Sharing (CORS) is a protocol that allows for relaxing the same-origin policy. A server's CORS policy can enable a browser-based application to interact with resources hosted in another origin. For that, the server must be able to determine whether it trusts the source of a request. For instance, servers can check the Origin and Referer headers, if available, and deny the request if the headers contain untrusted values. To instruct the browser whether it should share the results with the scripts of the browser-based application, the server returns a response with HTTP headers that begin with Access-Control-Allow.

A request from a script may trigger the browser to send a preflight request prior to the actual request using the HTTP OPTIONS method. The preflight request is an extra request with which the browser can check with the server whether it would allow a particular request from a script. For that, the browser sends HTTP headers that begin with Access-Control-Request to describe the intended request from the script. We show some preflight request and response headers in Example 13-2.

Example 13-2. CORS preflight request and response headers

```
OPTIONS https://api.webapp.example/data HTTP/1.1
HOST: api.webapp.example
Access-Control-Request-Method: GET
Access-Control-Request-Headers: api-version

HTTP/1.1 204 No Content
Access-Control-Allow-Origin: https://www.webapp.example
Access-Control-Allow-Credentials: true
Access-Control-Allow-Headers: api-version
Access-Control-Allow-Methods: GET,POST,PUT,DELETE
Access-Control-Max-Age: 86400
Vary: Origin,Access-Control-Request-Headers
```

When the server does not authorize a request, or if you configure CORS incorrectly, the browser abruptly terminates the request and throws an error. You should understand the meaning of CORS response header so that you apply the best security and so that you are able to troubleshoot CORS errors. We explain the meaning of some CORS response headers in Table 13-3.

Table 13-3. CORS response headers

Response header	Description
Access-Control-Allow-Origin	The server instructs the browser to allow requests from the origin returned in the header value.
Access-Control-Allow-Credentials	The server returns a value of true to inform the browser that it can send cookies to the remote origin.
Access-Control-Allow-Headers	The server authorizes a browser in the remote origin to send the HTTP headers listed in the response.
Access-Control-Allow-Methods	The server authorizes a browser in the remote origin to make requests using the HTTP methods listed in the response.
Access-Control-Max-Age	The server instructs the browser that it may cache the response from this endpoint for a number of seconds to prevent subsequent preflight requests.
Vary	The server can instruct the browser to ignore cached results and trigger a new preflight if particular headers change.

As a developer, you do not need to write extra code in a browser-based application to work with cross-origin requests, as the browser takes care of the details. However, to include cookie credentials in cross-origin requests, you need to explicitly instruct the browser to do so. Use the mode credentials: 'include' to ensure that the browser sends credentials. Study Example 13-3 for how the code may look like.

Example 13-3. Include cookie credentials in API request from JavaScript

```
const init = {
    credentials: 'include',
    headers: {
        'api-version': '1'
    },
    method: 'GET',
} as RequestInit
const response = await fetch('https://api.webapp.example/data', init);
```

CORS alone does not guarantee that the browser actually sends cookies to the server. Whether or not a browser sends a cookie depends, as we've discussed before, on the cookie's attributes. In addition, browsers can implement third-party cookie restrictions to protect user privacy and prevent unwelcome user tracking. Typically, browsers send cookies in cross-origin requests only where the browser-based application's web origin and the server's domain are in the same site (eTLD+1).

Some HTTP requests, like certain GET requests, are so-called CORS-safelisted requests (*https://oreil.ly/2Zrs3*) that do not cause the browser to trigger a preflight. To prevent attackers using such requests to bypass preflight requests, IETF best practices (*https://oreil.ly/PF9rv*) recommend that the server enforces a static custom header like api-version: 1. Requests with custom headers always trigger the browser to send a preflight request the first time the browser calls a particular server endpoint. Adding a custom header in requests is a straightforward and robust option for browser-based applications.

If a preflight grants the requested access, the browser-based application sends its main request to the API, such as an HTTP GET or HTTP POST request. The server processes the request and again returns the Access-Control-Allow-Origin response header and, for cookie requests, the Access-Control-Allow-Credentials response header. If you omit these headers, the browser will deny a browser-based application access to the response (despite a successful preflight request).

By enforcing preflight requests, you can utilize CORS for CSRF protection because preflight requests ensure that the browser sends requests only from trusted origins. It is the browser's responsibility to apply CORS. Note that insecure browser settings can result in the browser not respecting CORS headers. Therefore, OWASP's "Cross-Site Request Forgery Prevention Cheat Sheet" (*https://oreil.ly/8UHhc*) recommends that you combine CORS with using same-site cookies and/or validating the Origin header sent from the browser.

Content Security Policy, secure cookie settings, and CORS are all examples of browser defenses that you should consider to secure web applications. If aligned correctly, they enable you to secure your browser-based application and defend against common threats. The Content Security Policy is always the responsibility of the web host that serves static content for the browser-based application. You apply CORS and secure cookie logic at your backend entry point to APIs, after which APIs implement their main authorization using the access token. When it comes to OAuth in browser-based applications, you should also minimize risks when you obtain or store tokens. Therefore, you also need to consider browser threats when you implement OAuth.

Implementing OAuth Using JavaScript

The threats that we have listed so far apply to any web application and are not specific to OAuth. There are, however, some OAuth-specific concerns that you should be aware of. In this section, we therefore highlight some characteristics of both OAuth and browser technologies that you should consider when implementing a client that runs in the browser. First of all, make sure you obtain the token in a secure way.

Obtaining Tokens

Historically, the same-origin policy prevented browser-based applications from running the code flow because it does not allow JavaScript to exchange the code for an access token. As an alternative, such applications were forced to use the implicit grant. There are many security concerns related to the implicit grant that we do not want to iterate over here (refer to Chapter 2). The main concern is that the implicit grant uses a front-channel request which implies an insecure channel that is not suitable for transporting any tokens.

CORS opens up new possibilities that facilitate the replacement of the implicit flow. It allows for relaxation of the same-origin restrictions, to enable browser-based applications to retrieve access tokens from authorization servers via cross-origin requests in JavaScript. Therefore, best current practices recommend that browser-based applications use the code flow together with PKCE to obtain tokens (see "OAuth 2.0 for Browser-based Applications" (*https://oreil.ly/Wu_oK*)).

In the code flow, the client retrieves the access token on the back channel. A back-channel request implies a direct connection between the client and server, which has security benefits. Since the code flow is more secure, it enables browser-based applications to retrieve refresh tokens together with access tokens. Despite the code flow, the browser-based application is a public OAuth client; that is, it does not authenticate as part of the token request.

Public Clients

OAuth in browser-based applications remains a challenge, because browser-based applications run in the browser and consequently their (assembled) code is public. This means that anyone can inspect and reverse engineer browser-based applications, and read any provisioned secret. As a result, browser-based applications are considered public clients that cannot store any secret.

The authorization server cannot verify the identity of a public client because such clients cannot authenticate reliably. As a consequence, any malicious client with a given client ID can exchange an authorization code for an access token. The authorization code in the code flow passes the front channel and is therefore more exposed (compared to the tokens in the back-channel request). PKCE mitigates risks related to the authorization codes because it binds the authorization code to the session that the client started. Always use the code flow with PKCE when obtaining tokens with the code flow, as we have mentioned before.

The traditional JavaScript flow for browser-based applications does not use refresh tokens. Instead it typically performs a silent authentication to get new access tokens. Let's summarize how that works next.

Silent Authentication

As a way to bootstrap the browser-based application and allow an SSO experience over multiple applications, an application can try to silently obtain a set of tokens. It can do it by using OpenID Connect and adding the prompt=none query parameter to the authorization request. This parameter tells the authorization server to not render any user prompt if the user is already authenticated, as proven by the existence of a valid authorization server cookie. When such a cookie is not present and the authorization server cannot fulfill the request without user interaction, the client receives a response that includes a login_required error code. This request commonly runs in the background and the technique is called silent authentication. Silent authentication also provides a way to refresh access tokens without user interaction.

Silent authentication usually happens in a hidden iframe that communicates the responses from the authorization server to the client while avoiding a main window redirect. The authorization server cookie is usually from a different site than the browser-based application. As a consequence, cookies need to be third-party cookies; that is, cookies need to have the SameSite=None attribute for the browser to send silent authentication requests. Due to tracking policies, browsers may send third-party cookies only in top-level requests (treating them as SameSite=Lax by default), such as during main window redirects, where the user can interact with forms that show the authorization server's domain name. If you aim to send a third-party cookie from an iframe, browsers may refuse to add the cookie and break silent authentication.

Malicious JavaScript can potentially misuse silent authentication and run its own silent flow. Therefore we recommend that you avoid using it. Instead of using iframes to renew access tokens, use refresh tokens.

Refreshing Tokens

Applications should use the refresh token flow for refreshing tokens. The refresh token flow is a simple back-channel request where the application exchanges the refresh tokens for new access tokens. Refresh tokens are long-lived tokens enabling applications to retrieve new access tokens over a period of time without having to interrupt the user experience with authentication. As a result, the refresh token flow is a convenient way to get new access tokens without the need for iframes.

Since applications can extend their authorization with the help of the refresh token, the refresh token needs special protection. The refresh token should be bound to the client, which is the case when the authorization server can reliably authenticate the client. The authorization server cannot authenticate browser-based applications, which are public clients. For public clients, the refresh token is effectively a bearer token. An attacker who manages to intercept a refresh token will easily be able to obtain new access tokens. Consequently, using refresh tokens in the browser significantly increases XSS risks.

You can attempt to mitigate the security impact of refresh tokens in the browser. Something you should do in that context is to limit the lifetime of refresh tokens and revoke them upon user logout. Alternatively or in addition, your authorization server may implement an idle timeout, where it automatically revokes unused refresh tokens after a configurable time period. There are a couple of particular refresh token strategies to limit the impact of stolen refresh tokens. One of the best current practices is refresh token rotation.

Refresh token rotation

When applying refresh token rotation, the authorization server issues a new refresh token with every new access token. Applications need to discard their existing refresh token and replace it with the new one. This implies that applications can use refresh tokens only once. The authorization server can detect if a client uses a refresh token multiple times and, in such a case, revoke all related access and refresh tokens.

With refresh token rotation, attackers cannot simply retrieve and store a refresh token for later use. If the authorization server records that a refresh token is used more than once, it will suspect a malicious activity and revoke any related tokens. Consequently, with this strategy the authorization server has a chance to detect malicious activities and limit the impact of an attack. Refresh token rotation is therefore a best practice for any client that uses refresh tokens.

Refresh token rotation is still not a bullet-proof mechanism. If an attacker can intercept and possibly exfiltrate refresh tokens, they can decide to wait until the user becomes inactive before they consume the latest intercepted refresh token. Ideally, the browser-based application should be able to bind its refresh tokens to a dynamically created private key to enable sender-constrained tokens. Let's see how that might work.

Sender-constrained refresh tokens

An authorization server can issue sender-constrained refresh tokens to mitigate the risks of stolen bearer tokens. Commonly, sender-constrained tokens are key-binding tokens that contain a reference or copy of a public key. As part of using such a key-binding token, the sender needs to prove that it controls the private key that satisfies the key-binding. This means that in order to refresh access tokens with a sender-constrained refresh token, the client needs to create a key-binding proof with the help of the correct private key.

A browser-based application can create a private key on demand. Consequently, a browser-based application could use the "OAuth 2.0 Demonstrating Proof of Possession (DPoP)" standard (RFC 9449) (*https://oreil.ly/VmOkX*) to get a sender-constrained refresh token. This makes attacks more difficult, since any bad actor needs to get hold of the private key to use a stolen refresh token. However, an attacker could generate their own private key and use silent authentication on an iframe (which at the time of writing still works in some browsers), to get their own sender-constrained tokens.

When a browser-based application uses secure values like private keys and refresh tokens, they must remain available for the lifetime of the user's authenticated session. This brings us to the topic of token storage.

Token Storage

To ensure good usability, you usually need access tokens (or other secure values like private keys) to remain available if the user reloads the page, or if the user runs the browser-based application across multiple browser tabs. You can then use the refresh token whenever you need to get a new access token. In any case, you need a token storage strategy. Browser-based applications rely on the browser engine to store tokens. If the browser-based application handles tokens directly, it can choose between the following options:

- Web Storage API (`LocalStorage`, `SessionStorage`, `IndexedDB`)
- In-memory storage (web worker, service worker)
- JavaScript cookies

Web Storage API

The Web Storage API is a JavaScript API that allows browser-based applications to persist data. The variants `LocalStorage` and `SessionStorage` impact the exposure of the data in terms of both accessibility and time. They define whether or not the browser shares the data between multiple tabs, and if the browser wipes the storage when the user session ends (e.g., when the user closes the tab).

You may use `LocalStorage` to store your tokens across all browser tabs and to survive page reloads or browser restarts, thereby achieving good usability, but doing so would open up many XSS threats. Malicious code could easily read access tokens or refresh tokens from local storage and attempt to exfiltrate them from the browser. The browser-based application could use the Web Crypto API to encrypt tokens, as we explain in "Strengthen Browser Credentials" on page 148. For that the browser-based application would need to create an encryption key and use it to protect secure values in browser storage. Regardless of the storage, malicious JavaScript can still use browser APIs to read stored tokens and decrypt them if required. As an alternative, you might therefore consider keeping secrets in memory.

In-memory storage

Browser-based applications can isolate tokens and prevent direct access to them with techniques such as closure variables, web workers, or service workers. The browser-based application could call APIs using tokens stored in closure variables but an XSS attack could use prototype pollution to override the browser's fetch API and intercept tokens. Alternatively, the browser-based application could proxy all calls to the back-end API through a service worker. This prevents an XSS attack from intercepting tokens but an attacker may still be able to obtain a fresh set of tokens from the authorization server by impersonating the public OAuth client of the browser-based application.

In-memory storage has a great number of usability issues, since you have little or no control over the storage lifetime. For example, the browser automatically discards any in-memory tokens or private keys if the user reloads the page. Typically, this results in usability problems such as users needing to reauthenticate. With both Web Storage API and memory ruled out, you may think of storing access tokens in cookies.

JavaScript cookies

Cookies, as mentioned earlier, can store data, and you can store tokens in cookies. However, JavaScript cookies lack the `HttpOnly` property, so an XSS attack can easily read the cookies and use the underlying values. Browsers also add cookies (and any tokens they contain) automatically in HTTP requests. As a result, the browser may end up disclosing tokens via the cookie to endpoints that are not supposed to handle tokens like public endpoints or content delivery networks (CDNs) that serve scripts. This means, in comparison to the other storage mechanisms, there are additional risks to unintentionally expose access tokens when using JavaScript cookies. Therefore, do not use JavaScript to store tokens in cookies. Instead use a secure alternative.

Secure token storage

When you store secure values in the browser using JavaScript APIs, you either make them immediately available to any XSS attack (Web Storage API), or you lose control of the storage lifetime (in-memory storage). All storage mechanisms have particular characteristics and come with risks. Whatever storage solution you choose ultimately depends on the data that the browser-based application handles and on the confidence that you have in it to be free from any vulnerabilities that may allow attackers to run XSS. For the best mitigation against XSS threats, choose a solution such as a BFF for OAuth that avoids handling tokens in JavaScript in the first place and instead builds upon HTTP cookies.

HTTP cookies have the `HttpOnly` attribute. This means that they hide the token from any JavaScript, which other storage mechanisms fail to do. Therefore, HTTP cookies can limit the impact of XSS exploits. HTTP cookies also provide good usability, since they survive page reloads and the cookies are available across all browser tabs. You cannot set HTTP cookies from the browser-based application (JavaScript). Consequently, a solution that builds upon HTTP cookies to transport tokens requires a mediating backend component (a BFF) between the browser-based application and the authorization server, that can obtain tokens and put them in cookies.

Implementing OAuth Using a Backend for Frontend

The BFF pattern minimizes the risks related to XSS attacks by taking all the burden of token handling from browser-based applications and returning cookies to the browser. For that, the pattern introduces two roles with different responsibilities:

OAuth client
    Responsible for the OAuth flow

API router
    Routes all requests to the backend API

The pattern utilizes established web technologies, namely cookies, for authenticated sessions that browsers have supported for decades. The BFF OAuth client follows the OAuth protocol to obtain the tokens for the browser-based application. It then issues hardened cookies with encrypted tokens to the browser. When the browser-based application calls the backend API, the browser automatically adds cookies. The BFF API router decrypts cookies and fetches the corresponding access tokens. It then updates the request's HTTP `Authorization` header and forwards an access token to the API. Due to the dependency on cookies, the BFF components must implement CSRF protections. In Figure 13-7 we illustrate the BFF-for-OAuth pattern with a browser-based application, its static web server, and the two BFF components.

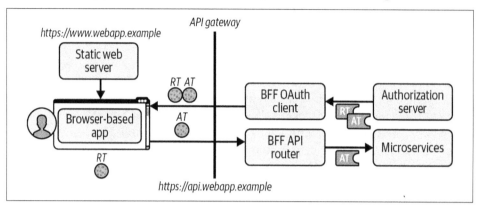

Figure 13-7. Browser-based application with BFF for OAuth

You can implement the BFF pattern in multiple ways. Some implementations use backend databases to store tokens, yet a simpler option is to issue tokens to HTTP cookies. Doing so provides a stateless solution that is easier to manage.

Terminology

The BFF for OAuth is sometimes also referred to as the *Token Handler*.

The BFF-for-OAuth pattern should be your first choice when implementing OAuth for browser-based applications. It keeps tokens out of the browser, which reduces the security risks significantly. Next, let's examine the BFF-for-OAuth pattern in more detail and look at some particular behaviors that we recommend for the BFF OAuth client.

The BFF OAuth Client

The BFF OAuth client is a confidential client that can securely obtain the access and refresh tokens on behalf of the browser-based application, as we illustrate in Figure 13-8. It issues separate cookies representing the short-lived access token and a long-lived refresh token. The BFF-for-OAuth pattern mitigates public client risks, like an attacker being able to obtain new tokens either through a code flow or refresh token flow. With a confidential client an attacker needs to get hold of the client's credentials to be able to get any new tokens. Such credentials live outside the browser-based application in the BFF OAuth client.

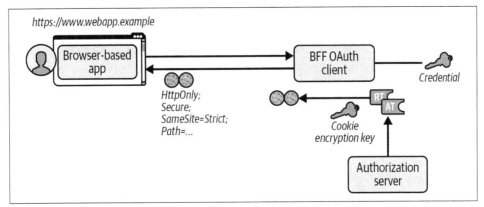

https://www.webapp.example

Browser-based app

HttpOnly;
Secure;
SameSite=Strict;
Path=...

BFF OAuth client

Credential

RT
AT

Cookie
encryption key

Authorization
server

Figure 13-8. OAuth client as part of the backend for frontend for browser-based applications

The BFF OAuth client ensures that the cookies meet the security requirements. For that, it should follow OWASP's best practices for session management (*https://oreil.ly/Xwkt_*). Best practices include setting the Secure, HttpOnly, and SameSite= Strict attributes for the cookies to mitigate browser-related threats like XSS and CSRF, as discussed earlier in this chapter. What is more, the BFF's OAuth client should also encrypt any cookie data so that no party can get the underlying tokens and use them directly, bypassing CSRF protections.

Cookies without an expiration date are called session cookies. Browsers commonly delete session cookies when the user closes the browser. A BFF-for-OAuth architecture can take advantage of this behavior by storing tokens in session cookies. While the user interacts with the browser-based application, the effective cookie lifetimes are those of the underlying tokens. When the user closes the browser, the session ends. The user must reauthenticate the next time they use the browser-based application.

Session lifetime

Whether and when a session ends is at the discretion of the browser. Some browsers may offer features to restore sessions upon restart, resulting in everlasting session cookies. When using OAuth, tokens in cookies expire eventually even if the browser considers a session to be alive. The browser-based application then triggers a new OAuth flow and the BFF OAuth client replaces any previous cookies.

In a BFF-for-OAuth approach, the BFF OAuth client can restrict the exposure of cookies with the help of the Path attribute. The refresh token cookie, for example, is required only when refreshing an access token and the browser must not send this cookie in every API request. Similarly, access tokens are required only for API calls. The BFF OAuth client can set the `Path` attribute to different values for the access token cookie and the refresh token cookie, to control where the browser sends them. When the browser-based application calls APIs, the browser sends the cookie with the access token in the request that passes the BFF API router.

The BFF API Router

The BFF API router is an intermediate component between the browser-based application and the API. This component decrypts the cookie containing the access token and adds the access token to the request to the target API. As part of the setup, the BFF API router must share a key (public or symmetric) with the BFF OAuth client. The BFF OAuth client must encrypt the cookies with the right key so that the BFF API router—and only the BFF API router—can decrypt cookie values and retrieve the access tokens. We illustrate this in Figure 13-9.

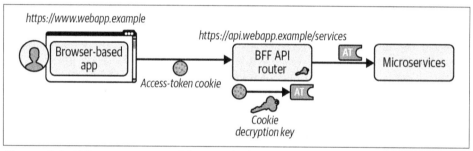

Figure 13-9. API router as part of the BFF for browser-based applications

We have seen that the BFF-for-OAuth pattern hides tokens from JavaScript code, which does not prevent XSS attacks as such but can reduce their impact. Malicious code cannot exfiltrate tokens and thus cannot run out-of-band requests against your APIs. If there is an XSS exploit, however, your application is vulnerable to session riding, where malicious code can call your APIs, have the browser attach cookies, and gain access to data. Such requests look just like ordinary requests. The API or BFF components cannot distinguish them.

Secure token storage

You should see the BFF-for-OAuth pattern as a hardened way to deliver access tokens from the browser to your APIs. It is not a complete security solution. You still need to protect browser-based applications against XSS vulnerabilities; you still need to secure your APIs against unauthorized access and use access tokens to implement claims-based authorization.

Now that you understand the various components of the BFF-for-OAuth pattern, let's see how an API-driven BFF implementation can give your browser-based application best control over usability.

API-Driven Implementations

A BFF OAuth client can use a server implementation that issues HTTP redirects to the browser. In its simplest setup, the browser-based application is more or less unaware of the BFF OAuth client. In that case, the OAuth client initiates an OAuth flow with a redirect to load the authorization request. The browser-based application leaves all control to the browser. When finished, the BFF OAuth client redirects the browser back to the browser-based application and the server processes the authorization response. However, when a server and the browser dictate behavior, the browser-based application may lose some usability control.

In an API-driven approach, the BFF OAuth client gives the browser-based application the control to load the authorization request and initiate the OAuth flow itself. Instead of redirecting the browser automatically when starting a session, the BFF OAuth client returns the redirect URL (i.e., the authorization request) to the browser-based application. The application can then store any state and guide the user before it sends the authorization request to trigger the OAuth flow.

The authorization server authenticates the user, collects any consent if required, and returns the authorization code to the browser-based application via a redirect. Now, the browser-based application can notify the BFF OAuth client to end the login, retrieve the tokens for the given authorization code, and return the cookies. After that the browser-based application can restore any state, if necessary, and start calling APIs via the BFF API router. We illustrate an API-driven approach in Figure 13-10.

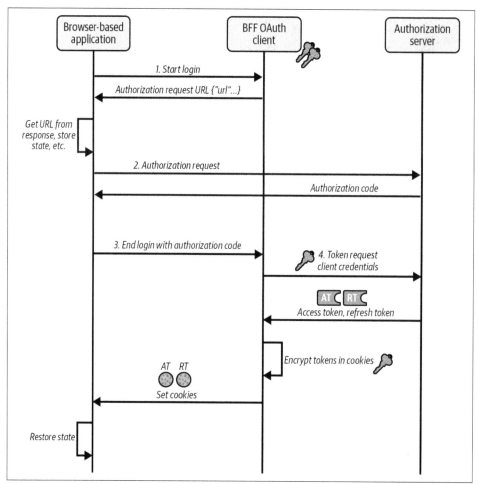

Figure 13-10. API-driven approach for the BFF OAuth client

To enable an API-driven flow, the BFF OAuth client presents an API interface to the browser-based application. Let's summarize the operations the BFF OAuth client might provide in its API interface.

The BFF API Interface

A BFF API interface provides various endpoints that reflect the common use cases of session management. These include starting and ending a login, getting the authentication status, using ID token claims, refreshing tokens, and logging out. You can design such an interface in multiple ways. In Table 13-4 we outline the REST API of a BFF OAuth client that Curity provides.

Table 13-4. BFF OAuth client REST endpoints

Endpoint	HTTP method	Parameters	Description
/login/start	POST	`scope`, `ui_locales`, ...	Create a session and start a login to get the URL to trigger an OAuth flow.
/login/end	POST	`iss`, `code`, `state`	End login to retrieve HTTP-only, encrypted cookies, and session status including ID token claims.
/session	GET	-	Get the login status of the session and, if available, return ID token claims.
/refresh	POST	-	Refresh the tokens and cookies.
/logout	POST	-	Clear cookies and, if available, get logout URL to allow user to log out from authorization server.

A browser-based application cannot read its HTTP-only cookies, but it can ask the BFF OAuth client for its authentication status. For this, the browser-based application can call the session endpoint upon page load. The response contains the login status and, optionally, the claims of the ID token that the browser-based application can use to customize its UI.

If the user does not yet have an active session with the browser-based application or more specifically with its BFF, the application can render a login button or similar to ask the user to log in and authenticate. When the user clicks the button, the browser-based application sends a start-login POST request to the BFF OAuth client for the browser-based application and, as such, crafts an authorization request according to best practices; that is, it uses `response_type=code` and creates the `code_challenge` as the PKCE specification requires to protect the code flow.

The browser-based application uses the authorization request to redirect the user to the authorization server, which in turn authenticates the user according to its policies. In the code flow, a front-channel response returns the authorization code to the browser-based application. In some BFF implementations, this triggers a server request that processes the response and redirects the browser-based application. In an API-driven approach, the browser-based application triggers the processing of the response. To do so it makes an end-login POST request to the BFF OAuth client, instructing it to process the response, get tokens, and issue cookies. The browser-based application then manages its post-login redirect, with the best usability control.

The browser-based application can receive ID token claims in the end-login response, or it can request that data from the session endpoint. Alternatively, the browser-based application can also send an API request through the BFF API router to the authorization server's userinfo endpoint, to get up-to-date user information. Besides login and session data, the BFF OAuth client should support other operations as well such as refreshing tokens and rewriting cookies, or requesting an end-session URL with which the browser-based application can perform a logout.

The API-driven approach gives the browser-based application best usability control. Since the approach defines how a browser-based application obtains tokens, it impacts the development lifecycle and the daily work of web developers writing and testing such applications.

Web Developer Experience

Using an API-driven BFF can provide a productive setup for you as a web developer, since you can externalize the cookie and CSRF security to deployed APIs. In this way, you can focus on the frontend and its customer experience. You can run a secure development setup with exactly the same security as your production systems. The browser automatically takes care of sending and receiving cookie credentials. As a result, API calls with cookies become straightforward. As for other APIs, you can mock BFF responses when implementing unit tests. This allows you to bypass the infrastructure when required. You can also write tests to verify that your frontend correctly handles error and expiry events from BFF components.

There are two options to run the BFF during development: either you spin up a BFF on your local machine, or you deploy BFF for development purposes that browser-based applications can communicate with. For the latter you could deploy the BFF components to a domain such as `https://api.webapp-dev.example` so that a local setup only needs a static web server that hosts the browser-based application. Developers can alias localhost to a domain in the same site as the remote BFF, using a DNS solution such as adding `www.webapp-dev.example` to their *hosts* file.

A BFF can provide strong browser security, combined with good usability and a productive developer experience. In addition, it also allows you to apply advanced OAuth features for an even stronger implementation of the protocol.

Hardening OAuth Security

The plain introduction of a confidential client in the BFF-for-OAuth pattern improves the security of the OAuth code flow significantly. It means that the client can authenticate at the authorization server whenever it gets tokens—a fundamental problem in browser-based applications otherwise. Since authentication is such an important part of security, you can harden the deployment by choosing robust authentication methods for the BFF OAuth client. Instead of using a client secret, which is technically just a password that the client sends to the authorization server, you should consider key-based authentication. The following client authentication methods all use either symmetric or asymmetric keys:

- Mutual-TLS Client Authentication (RCC 8705)
- JWTs for Client Authentication (RFC 8723, OIDC)

With a key-based client authentication, the client does not send its secret directly to the authorization server but generates its credential from a key, to prove ownership of the key without disclosing it. In this way, it minimizes the exposure of its sensitive authentication data.

When hardening an OAuth implementation, consider also the integrity of browser requests. If, for whatever reason, some attacker-in-the-middle manages to modify an authorization request (e.g., via XSS in the browser-based application), you could risk security incidents where a client receives more privileges than it intended to request. To avoid this kind of attack, implement "OAuth 2.0 Pushed Authorization Requests" (RFC 9126) (*https://oreil.ly/bzV2V*). Pushed authorization requests (PARs) are back-channel requests, and as such, the parameters of the authorization request never pass the browser. There is no chance for an XSS attack to manipulate the values. What is more, the authorization server authenticates confidential clients as part of the back-channel request and thus gets higher confidence in the source and values of the authorization request.

While it is not possible for XSS attacks to manipulate the authorization request parameters of a PAR, it can still manipulate the authorization responses from the authorization server. PKCE already protects the authorization code and prevents many attacks that target the authorization response. If you nevertheless need to protect the response, consider implementing the JWT Secured Authorization Response Mode (JARM) (*https://oreil.ly/_B7-D*). With this response mode, the authorization server packages its authorization responses in JWTs that allows it to protect the integrity, and optionally the confidentiality, of the messages.

As you can see, the BFF for OAuth has many potential security benefits. Check whether your authorization server supports the necessary standards to harden the OAuth integration. When adding a BFF for OAuth, a browser-based application should be able to continue to call APIs with largely the same code that it would use if handling access tokens directly. Let's drill a bit deeper into the impact of cookies in API requests.

Using Cookies in API Requests

When your browser-based application calls APIs using a BFF for OAuth, it uses cookies as a transport mechanism. Other than that, behaviors should be the same as for other user-facing OAuth clients, like mobile applications, meaning the browser-based applications should be able to reuse and renew their access token for API calls. This is a core requirement because browser-based applications commonly present multiple views to users that render secured data. You can also run multiple browser windows for the same application at once. All views of a browser-based application across all browser windows share the same API message credential (aka cookie) that they send to APIs.

We prefer to encrypt the actual tokens into cookies since doing so is the simplest way to store tokens and helps to maintain the core behavior of the API message credential. When encrypting tokens into cookies, you must ensure that you do not exceed the maximum size of a cookie attribute expected by browsers (4KB at the time of writing), or the maximum HTTP header size in HTTP servers to which you send the cookie (this is typically either 4KB or 8KB). Many authorization servers use the RS256 token signing algorithm when issuing JWTs. With small access token payloads, these JWTs should produce cookies of around 1.5KB, which is comfortably under the browser's 4KB cookie limit. You do not exceed the browser limit unless your JWTs have unusually large payloads. To best reduce cookie sizes, use opaque tokens, or an efficient JWT token signing algorithm (e.g., based on elliptic curve cryptography).

Some BFF implementations may provide alternative solutions using session IDs. This ID references an entry with session-relevant data in a backend store (not necessarily tokens). When your authorization server issues opaque tokens, you get an out-of-the-box token storage solution, so we recommend considering opaque access tokens over web session IDs. Cookies containing opaque access tokens are short lived so that any stolen cookie exploit will last just for the lifetime of the access token. Web sessions do have the benefit that you can easily revoke access during its validity time. The backend can immediately reject a cookie header when the backend session data for the session ID no longer exists, such as when the user signs out. In OAuth clients, including browser-based applications with cookies, access tokens may be usable for a short time after logout.

The time window for replaying an access token after logout depends on the token format. If the cookies contain JWT access tokens, APIs will continue to accept them until the tokens expire. If the underlying access tokens are opaque tokens, you can immediately deny all access by revoking both access and refresh tokens. You may need to notify the API gateway to clear its introspection result cache upon token revocation. In this way, you force the API gateway to send a new introspection request to the authorization server if a request includes a cookie with a revoked access token. The authorization server can notify the API gateway that the token is not active (anymore). The API gateway can then deny access. Such a solution works equivalently for all OAuth clients.

As we've mentioned, the access token should be short lived. This means that the browser-based application needs to refresh access tokens when, or before, they expire. For this, it sends a request to the BFF OAuth client with a separate cookie, to transport the refresh token. After a token refresh, the BFF OAuth client rewrites the access token cookie. For best security, you should also use single-use refresh tokens, in which case the BFF OAuth client also rewrites the refresh token cookie.

When required, multiple views can synchronize token refresh and prevent race conditions that could otherwise result in usability problems. The browser-based application sends the refresh token only once, after which all views use the same new access token cookie to resume their API requests. When the user's authenticated session ends, or if the user explicitly signs out, token refresh fails eventually. In both cases, the BFF OAuth client ends up deleting the cookies and the browser no longer sends them.

The design of cookie-based security for a browser-based application is closely related to the design of its deployment (i.e., the sites, origins, and URLs that you use). Therefore let us explore some deployment choices.

Deployment Choices

As we explain in previous chapters, the API gateway plays an important role in OAuth deployments. The BFF-for-OAuth pattern is no exception. In this pattern, the API gateway lends itself very well to the BFF API router that decrypts the cookies from the BFF OAuth client to get the access token and forward it to the API. The BFF OAuth client can be a utility API or an add-on to the authorization server. Many gateways including AWS (*https://oreil.ly/xr3Fe*), Azure APIM (*https://oreil.ly/yp3sm*), Cloudflare (*https://oreil.ly/fd4xx*), and Nginx-based variants like Kong (*https://oreil.ly/b4-f3*) allow you to run custom code like plug-ins, which is what we use in our code example. We illustrate this in Figure 13-11.

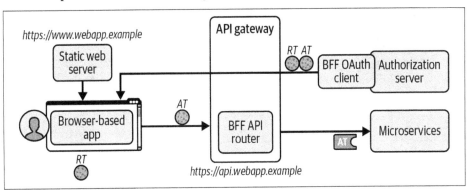

Figure 13-11. Deploying the browser-based application and BFF for OAuth as separated services

The BFF OAuth client sets HTTP cookies that contain encrypted access, ID, and refresh tokens. For security reasons, those cookies have certain attributes. Namely, they have the Secure, HttpOnly, Path, and SameSite=Strict attributes. The SameSite attribute impacts the deployment and your choice of domain names. The browser will send cookies in API requests only when the browser-based application and BFF API router have the same eTLD+1 (which is usually the domain) and scheme (e.g., https).

The easiest deployment to reason about is a same-origin deployment, which any BFF implementation should enable. Your components might then use base URLs such as these:

- Static web server: `https://www.webapp.example`
- BFF OAuth client: `https://www.webapp.example/oauthclient`
- BFF API router: `https://www.webapp.example/api`

A BFF implementation should enable you to deploy the BFF components on the API side of your deployments, independently to the static web server. This gives you additional deployment choices. For instance, you might prefer to deploy BFF components to Kubernetes, and use a content delivery network as the static web server. As Figure 13-12 illustrates, the browser-based application and its BFF for OAuth have to be in the same site to make the token cookies flow. However, the authorization server and microservices can be hosted in any domain.

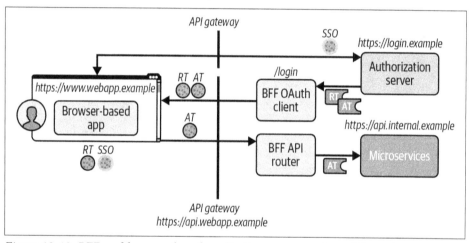

Figure 13-12. BFF and browser-based application are same site, while authorization server and microservices can be hosted anywhere

In most real-world organizations, you are likely to have multiple browser-based applications. You therefore need to understand options to scale your deployments.

Scaling Deployments

In Chapter 6 we have outlined that access tokens have a scope that defines what actions an OAuth client may perform. With the BFF for OAuth, the cookie embodies that scope. Multiple browser-based applications often represent different business areas and thus have distinct scopes. When implementing the BFF for OAuth for multiple browser-based applications, it is important to separate the interests of those applications and to not mix security concerns. In other words, you need to isolate the cookies of multiple browser-based applications.

The best way to achieve that isolation is to have one BFF per browser-based application and further have one browser-based application per site. Doing so keeps both cookies and XSS threats isolated between browser-based applications. This means you configure one domain per frontend. In Figure 13-13 we illustrate cookie isolation, since app 2 runs at `https://brand2.example` and calls a BFF at `https://api.brand2.example`. No other application can send cookies to this BFF.

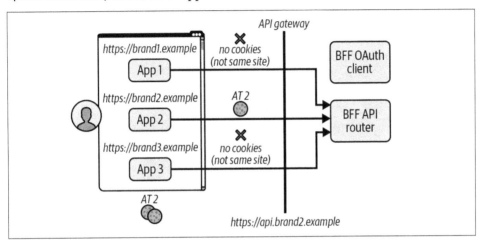

Figure 13-13. Separation of duties with one browser-based application per site

With one BFF per browser-based application and site, you get the help of the browser to separate cookies. You can further adapt the OAuth flow to the security requirements of each browser-based application. In particular, you can harden the flow of a certain browser-based application with PAR, JARM, and key-based client authentication. Each BFF implements the needs of a particular browser-based application.

A browser-based application may consist of multiple, independent, mini applications, so-called microfrontends, where each implements a part of a bigger frontend application. Those microfrontends form one logical application. They can, for example, run on the same site using different paths. In this case, the browser adds the appropriate cookies to an API request no matter which frontend triggered the request on the site. This means that multiple frontend applications share the same cookies and can use them to call APIs (see Figure 13-14).

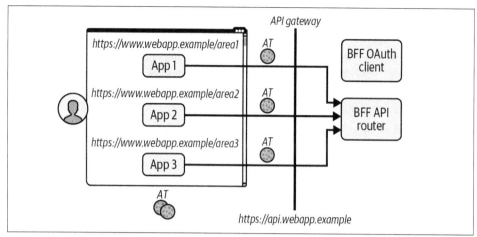

Figure 13-14. Browser-based applications on same site share cookies

Our theory to explain an end-to-end flow for a browser-based application is now complete. We separated concerns to deal with cookies on the API side of the architecture, since their role is to transport access tokens to APIs. We also considered the developer experience, usability control, and how you deploy your static web content. Next, you will want to choose your own BFF implementation.

Choosing a BFF Implementation

The BFF for OAuth pattern that we explain is relatively new but various implementations exist, which may be open source or paid offerings. For example, you might use the Spring Cloud Gateway (*https://oreil.ly/jerr1*), the Duende BFF Security Framework (*https://oreil.ly/q7l8q*), or the Curity Token Handler (*https://oreil.ly/7OoGs*). Ideally, choose an implementation that provides tested Docker containers that you only need to configure and deploy, after which your browser-based application calls HTTPS endpoints.

If you do not find a pluggable implementation that meets your requirements, you may implement the BFF-for-OAuth design pattern yourself, in any API technology stack. To do so you must implement the BFF OAuth client logic and the BFF API router logic. Use mature libraries to manage lower-level aspects, like cookie issuing, cookie encryption, and CORS. Then configure and deploy the BFF components. To demonstrate how to integrate with a BFF, we provide a code example that you can run on a development computer, where a browser-based application uses an API-driven BFF running in Kubernetes.

Browser-Based Application Code Example

The code example of this chapter includes a browser-based application that calls an OAuth-secured API using `SameSite=Strict` cookies. You can find the example in the folder *chapter-13-browser-based-apps* of the GitHub repository of this book (*https://oreil.ly/CNDS-supp*). The frontend is a basic SPA developed with the React framework. The backend is a Kubernetes cluster whose deployment is very similar to the one in Chapter 8. In Table 13-5 we summarize the scripts that set up the backend infrastructure of the end-to-end solution.

Table 13-5. Deployment scripts

Script	Responsibilities
1-create-cluster.sh	Creates a Kubernetes cluster and runs a local load balancer that enables connectivity from the local computer.
2-deploy-api-gateway.sh	Deploys an API gateway that runs plug-ins to provide the BFF API router role.
3-deploy-authorization-server.sh	Deploys an authorization server that issues tokens to the browser-based application so that it can call APIs.
4-deploy-api.sh	Deploys the API code example from Chapter 5, which the SPA calls.
5-deploy-bff.sh	Deploys BFF components that implement OpenID Connect security and cookie handling for the SPA.

You can then use run `npm start` to run the browser-based application (SPA) outside of the cluster in development mode. Although the solution is highly separated, the code in the browser-based application and API is straightforward. Let's take a closer look at the behavior of the BFF components that support the browser-based application, starting with the BFF OAuth client, aka the OAuth Agent.

OAuth Agent

At Curity we use the term OAuth Agent to represent the role of the BFF OAuth client. The OAuth Agent configuration settings are shown in Example 13-4. The example implementation uses Node.js and Express. It is a utility API that you can study and adapt the code for, if required. The OAuth Agent is deployed as a stateless Docker container. It presents a BFF API interface to the browser-based application. The OAuth Agent deployment includes several environment variables. We list a subset of them in Table 13-5.

Example 13-4. OAuth Agent configuration settings

```
env:
  - name: TRUSTED_WEB_ORIGIN
    value: https://www.webapp.example:3000
  - name: AUTHORIZE_ENDPOINT
    value: https://login.democluster.example/oauth/v2/oauth-authorize
  - name: TOKEN_ENDPOINT
    value: "http://curity-idsvr-runtime-svc.authorizationserver:8443\
      /oauth/v2/oauth-token"
  - name: CLIENT_ID
    value: bff-oauth-client
  - name: REDIRECT_URI
    value: https://www.webapp.example:3000/
  - name: POST_LOGOUT_REDIRECT_URI
    value: https://www.webapp.example:3000/
  - name: SCOPE
    value: "retail/orders openid profile"
  - name: COOKIE_NAME_PREFIX
    value: example
  - name: COOKIE_ENCRYPTION_KEY
    value: $COOKIE_ENCRYPTION_KEY
```

Next, let's explain how the API gateway works, to enable the browser-based application to call directly to APIs using cross-origin requests.

API Gateway Routes

The browser-based application runs at a URL of `https://www.webapp.example:3000` and calls a BFF at `https://api.webapp.example`. We configure two HTTP routes in the API gateway so that the BFF runs in the same parent site as the browser-based application. In Example 13-5 we show the route that the SPA uses to call APIs.

Example 13-5. BFF API gateway routes

```
apiVersion: gateway.networking.k8s.io/v1
kind: HTTPRoute
metadata:
  name: orders-api-web-route
  annotations:
    konghq.com/plugins: cors,oauth-proxy,phantom-token
spec:
  parentRefs:
  - name: kong-gateway
    namespace: kong
  hostnames:
  - api.webapp.example
  rules:
  - matches:
    - path:
```

```
    value: /orders
backendRefs:
- name: zerotrustapi-svc
  kind: Service
  port: 8000
```

Notice that the API route runs gateway plug-ins. At Curity we use the term *OAuth Proxy* to represent a plug-in that implements the BFF API router; that is, the OAuth Proxy decrypts the access token cookie and sets it in the HTTP authorization header. The phantom token plug-in replaces the opaque access token in the HTTP authorization header with a JWT access token. The gateway then routes the request to the target API. The API gateway and plug-ins together form the BFF API router. Let's take a closer look at how the OAuth Proxy plug-in works.

OAuth Proxy

We deploy the OAuth Proxy plug-in in the API gateway's Docker container. You can apply it to zero or more API gateway routes. In Example 13-6 we show the OAuth Proxy configuration settings for the browser-based application's API gateway route. These settings enable the plug-in to decrypt the access token cookie. You can also study the Lua code for the plug-in to understand its logic and adapt it if required.

Example 13-6. OAuth Proxy configuration settings

```
kind: KongPlugin
apiVersion: configuration.konghq.com/v1
metadata:
  name: oauth-proxy
plugin: oauth-proxy
config:
  cookie_name_prefix: example
  encryption_key: $COOKIE_ENCRYPTION_KEY
```

Finally, let's summarize some characteristics of the browser-based application. In the example deployment, the browser-based application runs outside the Kubernetes cluster in development mode using a lightweight static web server.

Browser-Based Application

We make use of a static web server to serve the static content for the browser-based application. This enables a pure JavaScript developer experience with secure cookies. You can study the `OAuthClient` and `ApiClient` classes in the browser-based application to understand how it interacts with its BFF. The code snippet in Example 13-7 shows how the browser-based application makes a same-site and cross-origin request to APIs and consents to sending its cookie credential to the API gateway.

Example 13-7. SPA calling an API

```
private async fetchImpl(method: string, url: string): Promise<any> {

    const options = {
        url,
        method: method as Method,
        headers: {
            accept: 'application/json',
            'content-type': 'application/json',
            'token-handler-version': '1',
        },
        withCredentials: true,
    } as AxiosRequestConfig;

    const response = await axios.request(options);
    return response.data;
}
```

You can also run the npm run build command to build the SPA's release static content to a *dist* folder. You can deploy the contents of this folder to any web host, according to your preferences. If all of your users run the browser-based application close to your API hosting locations, you could deploy the static content as Kubernetes containers. Alternatively, you could copy static content to a content delivery network that distributes it to many locations so that the latency of web requests is roughly equal for all global users.

Summary

We began the chapter with a brief introduction to web technologies, concepts, and terms. We then discussed common threats that web applications should protect against. Without care, these can compromise the overall security of an OAuth implementation. You can protect against some threats, like clickjacking and cross-site request forgery (CSRF), using mature techniques.

There are particular environment-specific threats for browser-based applications. The biggest threat for browser-based applications is cross-site scripting (XSS). XSS vulnerabilities can enable powerful attacks since malicious code can do anything that the real application can do. Vulnerabilities include weaknesses in your code, especially when dealing with input and output data. They can also come from dependencies. It is therefore difficult to be entirely confident that your browser-based application will always be free of XSS vulnerabilities. Consequently, aim for limiting the impact of XSS exploits.

For the strongest security, keep all tokens out of the browser to prevent the possibility of token exfiltration. Use HTTP-only cookies with the `Secure` and `SameSite=Strict` attributes to deny cookie access to other sites, and use CORS to restrict access to your SPA's precise web origin. Use the BFF-for-OAuth pattern to issue those cookies and to harden the OAuth flow. When adding a cookie layer to a browser-based application, consider an API-driven BFF-for-OAuth pattern that separates web and API concerns so that you avoid introducing any adverse effects on the web architecture.

Now that you understand how to securely implement OAuth in all types of clients, we can move on to the final topic of this book. In the next chapter, we will talk about the different aspects of user authentication.

CHAPTER 14

User Authentication

You might be surprised that you're reading a book about OAuth, yet you find user authentication in the last chapter. This is our deliberate decision. We believe that too many OAuth tutorials focus on logins, but this is not the specification's foundation. We want you to understand API authorization before we dive in into user authentication so that your clients receive correctly issued access tokens. That is, the ultimate goal of user authentication is to identify a user to your APIs. When doing so, you want a level of assurance that a malicious party does not impersonate the real user.

The OAuth specification leaves the topic of user authentication open—all it says is that the authorization server has to authenticate the user during an OAuth flow. The authorization server can choose what user authentication methods it implements. Of course, this does not mean that authentication is simple or irrelevant. On the contrary, authentication is an essential prerequisite of authorization so that the authorization server can collect information about the subject and the authentication event to issue to access tokens.

In this chapter, we want you to understand the business possibilities when you utilize user authentication in an OAuth architecture. We first show how a modern user authentication flow works, to externalize complexity from clients and issue them with correct access tokens. We then describe the types of user authentication methods you can use. We then explain some user authentication techniques that you can use in your authorization server, to control behavior and to enable security agility. We finish the theory with a full lifecycle walkthrough, to suggest how you might implement user authentication and manage user accounts, including user experience aspects like low-friction user onboarding to your digital services. We end the chapter with a deployment example, where you run a script to upgrade the code examples from Chapters 12 and 13 to use a modern and secure authentication method.

In addition to users, you can also authenticate OAuth clients and workloads, yet those are relatively straightforward topics. User authentication is a deeper topic. There are greater threats since user authentication runs in internet environments like browsers and mobile devices. You also need to get the right blend of security and user experience. This means there is no one-size-fits-all solution. Instead, you need security building blocks that enable you to provide user authentication solutions that meet your business requirements. Let's get started by explaining modern authentication flows.

Modern Authentication Flows

It is common to associate user authentication with the entry of a username and a password. However, there are many authentication methods that you can potentially use. New methods appear frequently, and you can adjust the flow in countless ways, which is why it is increasingly important to separate user authentication concerns from clients. When using OAuth correctly, clients only ever run a code flow to initiate user authentication. The client sends an authorization request to the authorization endpoint of the authorization server and the server guides the user through the authentication flow. The authorization server can orchestrate user authentication methods and run additional actions to compose complex flows.

You should think of authentication as a journey the user has to follow, which can consist of multiple forms and user authentication methods. The user presents credentials to these forms. Some authentication methods may require the user to have an existing active account in the authorization server. Others may only require the user to provide a simple proof, such as ownership of an email or phone. Once the flow completes, the authorization server stores authentication attributes and returns an authorization code to the client. We illustrate a generalized user authentication flow in Figure 14-1.

The most critical authentication attribute is the authenticated subject, which links to the user's account data. The authenticated subject is a string value. It might be a readable string like an email, or an opaque value like a UUID. The authorization server uses the authenticated subject to issue the subject claim (sub) to access tokens. Often, the authenticated subject and subject claim are the same value, though it is possible to transform the authenticated subject to a different value and issue that as the subject claim. For example, the authorization server might use pairwise pseudonymous identifiers (PPID) to issue subject claims as opaque values, as we explain in "API User Identities" on page 66.

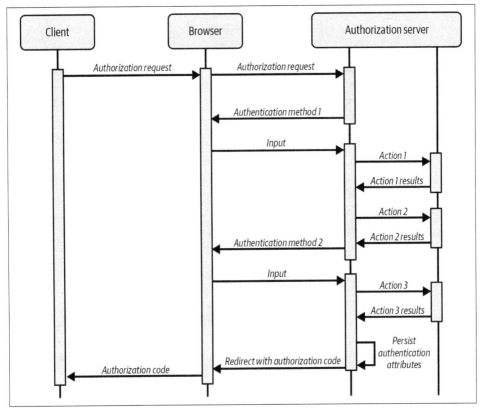

Figure 14-1. Code flow initiates a user authentication journey

When you use multiple authentication methods, the primary one sets the authenticated subject. Secondary authentication methods strengthen the security of the process or capture further proof of the user identity. They can also produce new authentication attributes. You can also produce custom user attributes, like a level_of_ assurance that represents your confidence that the right user is present.

When the flow completes, the client swaps the code for tokens. At this point, the authentication attributes flow into token issuance and enable you to issue access tokens with the correct claim values. Regardless of how the user authenticates, token issuance produces a consistent subject claim in access tokens and can include any additional claims from the user's account, like a customer ID and a role. This means that you can change the authentication flow, for example, to upgrade authentication to a newer authentication method, and your APIs continue to receive an access token with the same contract.

> ### It's All About the Attributes
>
> Regardless of the user authentication method, the most important technical consideration is the resulting user attributes. Your authorization server works with attributes to eventually create access tokens with claims that have to satisfy the needs of your APIs. Ensure that your APIs receive consistent claim values so that they can effectively handle authorization, no matter how your authentication flow evolves.

Although the main access token claims remain the same regardless of the user authentication method, it is also possible to vary claims issued depending on how the user authenticates. Doing so enables your APIs to grant partial access, to enable behaviors like fast user onboarding. APIs can then return error codes to enable clients to prompt the user to use a more complete form of user authentication to gain further access. We say more about the possibilities in "User Authentication Techniques" on page 335.

When you separate concerns between clients and the authorization server, your clients never have to manage security details like credential management, complex authentication protocols, or integration with third-party identity systems. Instead, developers externalize all of the authentication work to the authorization server. You also get business agility, where you can change authentication behavior and it comes into effect immediately, without needing to change code in your clients or redeploy them.

To ensure the right business outcomes, you need to create a list of authentication-related requirements and then implement them. For that you need an authorization server that provides you with building blocks that satisfy your requirements. Let's explain the first of these, where you choose your user authentication methods.

User Authentication Methods

These days, there are countless user authentication methods that you can use to prove a user's identity. Long gone are the days when all you had to do was to collect a user's password and save it hashed in a database. Even though there are plenty of concrete user authentication methods, most of them fall into one of the following categories:

- Passwords
- Social logins
- External identity providers
- One-time passwords

- Passwordless authentication
- Identity proofing
- Custom authentication

We use the term *authenticator* to represent a user authentication method. When required, your authorization server should allow you to configure multiple instances of each authenticator, with different configurations. When you choose authentication methods there is often a trade-off between usability and security, which may influence the options that you choose and when you use them. Let's summarize the main behaviors of the various types of authenticators, starting with passwords.

Passwords

Providing a username and password to a server is still the most common user authentication method. Its simplicity is both an advantage and disadvantage. It gives users the most freedom—they can choose any password they want (within the server's limits) and store it however they like. But this freedom, unfortunately, means that users tend to utilize passwords in a way that lowers security—they use short, simple, and guessable passwords; reuse them; or do not properly store them (think of the infamous Post-It on a monitor).

When you operate an authorization server and allow your users to log in with passwords it is partly your responsibility to help users utilize passwords in the best manner. Do not allow easy-to-guess passwords, but also don't require passwords that users will never remember. Not all users are technically savvy enough to use password managers. When you require complicated passwords it might deter users from onboarding to your system. Similarly, user satisfaction is low when users get frequently locked out and have to run an account recovery flow. Instead, encourage users to follow best practices when they work with passwords:

- Get a balance between complexity, length, and usability. A long passphrase that the user can remember is usually harder to crack than a 10-letter password containing a mix of uppercase letters, lowercase letters, digits, and special characters. Discourage the use of easily guessable passwords like names of family members.

- Dissuade the reuse of passwords across different systems. Password managers can help to adhere to this practice. When users do not feel comfortable with password managers they should store passwords in a safe place like a home notebook. It's safer to use different passwords and have them written down than to reuse the same password everywhere.

Passwords are a burden on users, who have to manage many passwords for all of the internet sites they visit. Passwords also pose a security risk that you can't avoid even if your users follow password best practices—they are susceptible to phishing and social hacking. An attacker may be able to trick your users to reveal their passwords. When that happens, the password strength doesn't matter. A password alone is insufficient when you need to implement strong customer authentication (SCA). Instead, you should consider the more secure techniques like passwordless authentication and MFA that we describe in "Passwordless Authentication" on page 332 and "Multifactor Authentication" on page 336, respectively.

A common way to externalize the use of passwords is to delegate the authentication to an external authentication system, which we call an identity provider (IDP). There are multiple use cases where you can use IDPs. Let's explain them next.

External Identity Providers

In some use cases, you might decide to allow users to authenticate with their existing credentials from a popular provider that operates a social network, like Facebook, Discord, or LinkedIn. This type of system acts as a type of external IDP. Your authorization server redirects the user to the IDP, which authenticates the user with its own authenticators. Once the provider authenticates the user, your authorization server receives back a verifiable proof of the user's identity. Your server can now use this information to start its own session with the user and issue an access token that allows the user to call your APIs.

Figure 14-2 illustrates the flow when an external IDP uses the OpenID Connect protocol. In this case, your authorization server becomes a client and runs a second authorization code flow, to redirect the user to the external IDP.

The integration most commonly uses OpenID Connect, as this is the intended use case for the standard. However, some providers might implement a slight variation of the standard, meaning that your authorization server's standard OpenID Connect authentication method may not work. You then need to use custom authentication.

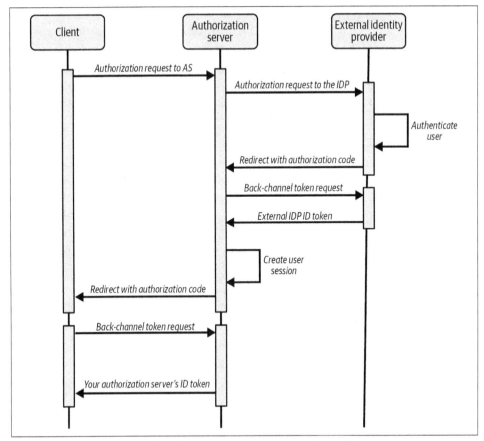

Figure 14-2. An overview of authentication using a social provider

Regardless of how you integrate, the integration serves a single purpose: to confirm the user's identity to the authorization server. This means that your authorization server gets a confirmation from the provider, usually in the form of an ID token. You should ensure that the identity in the ID token maps to a user account in your authorization server. We say more about this in "Account Linking" on page 340. Once user authentication completes, the authorization server creates a session for the user whose lifetime you control. Your client no longer depends on the user's session with the social provider.

User Sessions Are Decoupled

The authenticated user has a session with both the identity provider and the authorization server. These sessions are decoupled, and the user might sign out of the identity provider while remaining signed into the authorization server. This means your applications depend on external IDPs only for logins and not afterward.

Enabling your users to sign in with a social provider reduces the number of passwords they have to maintain and improves the user experience. Using social providers to authenticate users has its drawbacks though. If social logins are the only option you support, you couple your login availability and user experience to that of the social provider. You also share data about your users, since the provider knows whenever a user signs into your system. You are responsible for maintaining the integration with the external provider over time, and its behaviors may change. Therefore, consider offering your users additional authentication methods in addition to social logins.

Social networks are not the only type of external IDP that your authorization server can integrate with. External IDPs often manage access for employee users in a single place. For example, your software engineers might have user accounts in a cloud system from Microsoft, Amazon, or Google. Similarly, your organization's sales and marketing users might have user accounts in a customer relationship management (CRM) system. These external systems often have a built-in IDP that an authorization server can integrate with.

You might have a process where an administrator creates an account in such an IDP when an employee joins an organization and deletes or deactivates the account when an employee leaves the organization. Therefore, an IDP can be part of an organizational security policy. In some use cases, you may provide applications to business partners who require you to use their IDP when their users sign in to your applications.

Usually, when integrating with an IDP you leverage a standard protocol, like OpenID Connect (OIDC), Security Assertion Markup Language (SAML), or Lightweight Directory Access Protocol (LDAP). In some cases, the IDP may depart from these standards and use bespoke logic that requires custom integrations. In other cases, the external IDP may be the authorization server for another organization. The IDP is always separate from your authorization server, which governs the authentication flow for your OAuth clients and issues access tokens that your APIs trust.

Another potential reason to use an external IDP is when your client needs to use data from a third-party API. In some cases, you may only be able to operate on this data with a user-level access token from the third party. To get such a token, your authorization server can run a code flow to an external IDP and use an embedded token approach, to issue the external IDP's access token as a custom claim within the client's access token. We describe the approach in "Embedding Tokens in Tokens" on page 127. Your APIs can then call the third-party API on behalf of the user while continuing to correctly secure your organization's resources.

Using any external IDP (from the authorization server's point of view) poses the same issues as social logins—you now rely on the provider's availability, and you have to maintain the integration. Next, let's look at another common user authentication method, using one-time passwords.

One-Time Passwords

The principle of one-time password (OTP) authenticators is the same as for password authenticators. The user has to provide a string secret that allows the server to authenticate them. The difference is that the value works only once and can be time restricted, and the user needs to get a new one for every authentication attempt. This means that every time the user authenticates they need to get hold of the OTP in an out-of-band manner. There are many ways in which the user can get an OTP:

- The authorization server can send a one-time code in an email.
- The authorization server can send a text message to the user's phone.
- The user might receive an OTP by phone from a customer service automation.
- The user can operate a specialized application, like Google Authenticator or Microsoft's Authenticator, or a physical device (sometimes called a token). These applications and devices use time- and cryptography-based algorithms to generate passwords. The server can use a corresponding algorithm to verify generated codes.
- The user can have a list (for example, a scratch card) of predefined OTPs. In this case, the authorization server keeps a copy of the password list and removes used passwords every time the user authenticates with one.

Each type of OTP authenticator has different prerequisites and offers varying levels of security, but OTPs can be vulnerable to social engineering attacks. Sending an OTP to a user's email or phone is straightforward but may be susceptible to interception attacks where attackers gain access to the messages. OTP applications and hardware tokens are typically more secure, but add to user prerequisites and an attacker may still be able to get an OTP if they steal a user's device.

As an alternative to password-based user authentication, it is possible to avoid passwords completely. Modern passwordless solutions have the potential to improve both security and user experience. Let's look at how that works next.

Passwordless Authentication

For some years now there have been groups in the industry that work on specifications and APIs that allow you to move away from passwords. The World Wide Web Consortium (W3C) and a group of vendors under the name FIDO Alliance (*https://fidoalliance.org*) created the Web Authentication (WebAuthn) specification that enables browsers and platform-specific applications to use passkeys (*https://passkey.org*). Passkeys are a modern replacement for passwords. You can use either platform passkeys built into operating systems from Google, Apple, and Microsoft, or external security keys like key fobs.

When a user does not have a passkey yet, a server prompts the user to run a registration ceremony on their first login to a website or application. The registration process creates an asymmetric key pair and stores the corresponding private key on the local device. When you use platform passkeys, a service like Google Password Manager, Apple iCloud, or Windows Hello may synchronize the private key across multiple browsers and devices. Meanwhile, the server saves the public key against the user's account. To ensure that the server updates the correct user account, the user must authenticate somehow to register a passkey (e.g., using an email OTP).

Every subsequent login uses an authentication process that creates a digital signature using the local private key and sends the signature to the server. The digital signature provides proof-of-possession of the private key without disclosing the private key. The server uses the public key to verify the digital signature and authenticate the user. To use passkeys the user also has to prove their presence and unlock secure storage using device authentication, like a biometric or a PIN.

Passkeys have some important security traits. They are resistant to phishing and social hacking. A passkey is bound to a single server domain. Subsequently, the system only allows the use of the passkey at that domain. Therefore, a phishing domain cannot use a passkey from a legitimate domain. Also, since users never come into direct contact with cryptographic keys, it is not possible for a user to reveal the private key to a malign actor. From an organizational perspective, the server maintains only public keys, so events like server breaches cannot reveal user credentials.

Passkeys provide a more secure solution than passwords and OTPs. The user also no longer has the burden of remembering or typing password values. Instead, the platform, or an external security device, does the work to remember the private key by persisting it to secure storage. Passkeys first became widely available in late 2022 and security patches added support to many older devices. Therefore, you should be able to add passkeys to your login options without any difficult user prerequisites.

An authorization server should implement passkeys as a modern authentication method and take care of the details for you, like storing public keys against user accounts and providing account recovery features. The authorization server should also use passkeys login forms that follow FIDO user experience guidelines to help users understand the switch from passwords to passkeys. Ultimately, passkeys provide strong proof that the user is the same as previously but you do not really know who the user is. For that, you use identity proofing.

Identity Proofing

User authentication proves that the user is the same person that registered with your digital service earlier. It does not necessarily provide proof of the user's identity claims—and very often this is not a critical requirement either. However, in some industries, like financial applications, medical systems, tax systems, or some government websites, you may need strong proof of the user's authenticity. This is when you need to use an identity-proofing authenticator.

An identity-proofing authenticator aims to prove the user's identity, typically with the help of physical documents and biometrics. For example, a website may require a user to scan their passport and then take a live photo and send both files to the server. The server then integrates with a third-party service that specializes in passport image verification. Once complete, the server has assurance that the passport's owner operates the client.

Identity proofing is often a complex operation for users, in which case it is better suited to an onboarding process than to everyday user authentication. You might therefore allow the user to use a more convenient authentication method once identity proofing is complete. Ideally though, there should be standardized ways for users to seamlessly provide proof of their identity. We expect digital credentials to become the standard solution to that problem.

Digital Credentials Protocols (DCP) is an emerging technology that will enable identity proofing in the near future. We provide a simplified overview of how digital credentials work from the viewpoint of users, clients, and the authorization server.

A user first gets a wallet from a trusted authority (e.g., in the form of a mobile application). The user's wallet retrieves credentials from credential issuers and saves them to secure storage. Credential issuers are most commonly trusted parties like government agencies. The credential issuer can issue digital credentials that include attributes about the user (e.g., name, nationality, or age). The user can then use their wallet to present digital credentials to applications.

You can combine OAuth with DCP where the user presents digital credentials to authenticate at the authorization server. In this case, a client just runs a code flow, where the authorization server uses a digital credentials authenticator to authenticate the user. To invoke the wallet, the authorization server can present a login form to ask the user whether the wallet runs on the same device or a different device. When the user runs the wallet and client on the same device, such as on their mobile device, the authorization server can invoke the wallet with a mobile deep link. When the user runs the client in a desktop browser, the authorization server can present a QR code that the user scans with the wallet application.

Either the deep link or QR code provides input to the wallet with the client's digital credential requirements. The wallet then prompts the user to unlock secure storage and choose a credential to present to the authorization server. In some cases, the user may be able to reveal only a subset of claims within that credential, to preserve their privacy. To authenticate a user, the authorization server retrieves the issuer's public key from a trusted registry and uses the public key to cryptographically verify the authenticity of the credential. The authorization server can then trust the claims in the digital credential and consider the user authenticated. It can save the data from the digital credential to the user's account data and/or issue it as claims in access tokens.

The European Union's eIDAS Regulation (*https://oreil.ly/kXi-c*) will require member countries to implement electronic IDs in a standardized way. This will make identity proofing simpler in the future. For example, it will allow applications and social networks to easily verify whether accounts belong to certain people. There are many possible security solutions that organizations could design with digital credentials. The OpenID Foundation provides a group of draft specifications (*https://oreil.ly/ULRxT*) that will allow entities to securely issue and verify credentials in a decentralized manner.

We have seen that an authorization server might provide many possible built-in authentication methods. Your authorization server should stay up-to-date with standards so that your users can authenticate with the most convenient options. However, you also need to ensure that you are never blocked from meeting your authentication requirements. For that you need the ability to implement custom user authentication.

Custom User Authentication

Although modern forms of user authentication offer some compelling benefits, business continuity is often the single most important factor for organizations when they modernize security. For example, you may have many existing applications that authenticate users with existing user and credential stores or use a bespoke authentication system. Changing some of these existing solutions may be outside of your control. To manage this type of requirement, a well-designed authorization server can support an *integrate with anything* approach. This enables you to continue to use existing infrastructure while phasing in newer security capabilities.

In other cases, you may prefer to reimplement the functionality of legacy systems using the building blocks that your authorization server provides. Consider an existing non-OAuth flow where the user first enters a username and password, then confirms personal details stored against their account, and then enters an email OTP. When you upgrade to OAuth, you should be able to maintain the existing flow. In such a use case, you may be able to use the authorization server's built-in authenticators for username and password authentication and for email OTPs. However, there is unlikely to be a built-in authenticator that compares user input to the user's account data. In some cases, that could be a blocking issue.

The authorization server can provide an SDK to enable extensibility in the key places so that you can meet your custom authentication requirements. Such an SDK can enable any possible authentication method:

- You should be able to develop your own bespoke authenticators, like a date-of-birth authenticator. This should include client-side forms where the user inputs proof of identity and server-side logic to verify proofs. When required, an authenticator can present multiple forms to the user and manage navigation.
- You may also need to implement custom authentication when you integrate with certain IDPs, in which case you may need to perform actions like writing a cookie that stores state, redirecting to the IDP with parameters, then resuming the flow with the IDP response and the state from the cookie.

When you implement custom user authentication in your authorization server, you develop scripts and code libraries and deploy them as we explain in Chapter 11. Although this requires development work, you implement the responsibilities in the correct places so that you get the right security behaviors. These behaviors include auditing of login attempts and correct issuance of access tokens to clients once user authentication completes.

More generally, you use composition to implement an authentication flow. Let's look at some of the main user authentication techniques you can use.

User Authentication Techniques

To implement a complete authentication flow, you can use a number of techniques. In this section, we first explain how to compose authenticators together to implement MFA. We then show how you can inform APIs of the level of assurance of a user's identity and enable APIs to drive the login user experience. We also explain how SSO works, to reduce the frequency of logins.

When you build authentication solutions, you run into use cases where you need to apply custom logic, partly to control the user experience, but, more importantly, to ensure the correctness of user attributes so that you reliably identify users to your APIs. We use the term *authentication actions* to describe the units of custom logic, though some systems may use other terms like *authentication steps*. Your authorization server may provide an SDK to enable you to implement advanced custom logic.

Let's first see how to compose authentication methods together to enable MFA. Doing so can strengthen the authentication process. However, there are some caveats, which we explain next.

Multifactor Authentication

Authentication factors are categories of information that a user has to provide to confirm their identity. There are three different types of authentication factors:

- Something the user knows, like a password or their Social Security number
- Something the user owns, like a mobile phone, a desktop computer, or a security key fob
- Something the user is, meaning their physical traits, like a fingerprint, retina pattern, or facial shape

Each authentication method represents one or more of these factors. You implement MFA when the user must use more than one authentication method. However, sometimes this is insufficient, since you should usually combine different types of authentication factors. For example, if you use a username and password as the first factor and a security key fob as the second factor, an attacker cannot impersonate a user with just a password that they capture in a phishing exploit. Conversely, if you configure two different OTPs, where one uses email delivery and another uses a text message, an attacker can exploit both if they gain access to the user's smartphone.

Cryptography-backed user authentication

Modern authenticators, like passkeys or digital credentials, provide a built-in MFA solution. The main factor uses strong asymmetric cryptography and is something the user owns. The second factor is something the user knows (like a PIN) or something the user is (like a biometric) and serves to unlock secure storage and prove user presence. Therefore, in some cases, a single authenticator can meet your MFA requirements.

More generally, MFA helps to improve the security of authentication but might negatively impact the user experience. Therefore, your authorization server may allow you to give the user some control, such as applying a first factor on every login and the second factor less frequently. Your authorization server might also provide a user portal where your users can control some or all of their authentication factors.

Next, let's look at a dynamic technique called step-up authentication, and how your APIs can use the resulting claims in access tokens to instruct clients when the user must increase their authentication strength.

Step-Up Authentication

Step-up authentication, described in RFC 9470 (*https://oreil.ly/4Bygp*), is a technique that enables you to require strong authentication only occasionally, to improve the user experience. You configure your authorization server to issue different claims to access tokens depending on the factors with which the user authenticates. If the user enters a high-security area of the application, an API request returns an unauthorized response with an error code to inform the client that the user must provide a higher privilege access token. The client then runs a new code flow to get a higher privilege access token.

For example, a user might use MFA but, by default, provide only their first factor. When required, the user also enters the second factor, without needing to reprovide the first factor. Recall from Chapter 2 that a client that runs a code flow can send the OpenID Connect `acr_values` parameter to provide authentication context to the authorization server to ask it to use particular authentication methods.

Clients can also trigger user reauthentication at any time, to confirm a high privilege operation. For example, when the user enters a high privilege screen, the API can return a forbidden error to the client with an `insufficient_scope` error code and the scope that the API needs. The client can then request a high privilege scope, such as for a payment, that the client uses rarely. You should be able to configure your authorization server to require strong authentication before it issues high privilege scopes. Again, the client steps up authentication to gain additional API access. Step-up authentication requires careful authorization code in your APIs. When you use it you should follow the API-first approach that we recommend and write security tests to ensure that you avoid unauthorized access to high privileges.

Over time you are likely to provide multiple clients. Once a user authenticates with one client in a particular user agent, the authorization server can automatically authenticate the user in other clients, to improve the user experience. This is called single sign-on.

Single Sign-On

Single sign-on means that the user authenticates once on a particular user agent to gain access to a client and can then reuse the authentication session to gain access to one or more additional clients. When you use OAuth, the authenticated session is the session the user established with the authorization server. The authorization server uses session data to track user authentication across multiple clients, and even potentially across multiple users. The authorization server also issues an encrypted HTTP-only cookie to the user agent, with data like a session ID, that points to the session data.

The user may also have a session with an external IDP represented by another SSO cookie. In some cases, though, you may want to disable the use of SSO for a particular client, to force reauthentication. To do so, a client sends the OpenID Connect `prompt=login` parameter when it runs a code flow. The authorization server then forwards this parameter to external IDPs to force a login there. The OpenID Connect `max_age` parameter works similarly except that it forces reauthentication only if the time since user authentication exceeds the supplied value.

In the authorization server, you configure a global SSO expiration time to indicate how long a user can use SSO until they must reauthenticate. The authorization server may enable sliding expiry, where the SSO lifetime autoextends when the user is active or autoexpires when the user is inactive. You may also be able to set an SSO time per authenticator. Aim to ensure the following behaviors when you configure SSO:

- Use an SSO session time with a balance between security and usability.
- Whenever a user changes authentication methods, the authorization server should force a new login.
- Allow users to invalidate their own SSO sessions and force a new login, for example, to renew a compromised password.

Clients can end the SSO session for the user in the current user agent if they run an RP-Initiated Logout. When you use OAuth to connect to an external IDP, you end the SSO session at your authorization server only and not with upstream IDPs, to avoid impacting other applications that you do not control.

The RP-Initiated Logout specification (*https://oreil.ly/XIeVu*) links to a number of other Single Log Out (SLO) specifications, which can be more complex to implement. Some solutions may rely on sending the SSO cookie from an iframe within a web application to the authorization server. Since your authorization server runs in a different domain to your web applications, the browser considers the SSO cookie to be third-party. Browsers implement third-party cookie restrictions and are unlikely to send the authorization server's cookies reliably. Therefore, avoid using OAuth logout flows that send third-party cookies from iframes.

Although you should understand SSO behaviors, they are secondary sessions from the viewpoint of your OAuth clients and APIs. Each client's main session is with its APIs. Whether or not you use SSO, each client gets issued distinct access tokens, with its own scopes, claims, and token lifetimes. The client's refresh token's time-to-live represents its session time with APIs.

With so many authenticators and MFA options, at some point you are likely to change the methods with which users authenticate. Let's explain how to manage that next.

Changing Authentication Methods

It is usual that users change authenticators over time. There are multiple reasons why a user's current authentication method may change, some of which we list here:

- You need to meet compliance requirements to use MFA for all users.
- You enable a more secure authentication method and want to allow security-aware users to switch to the new method.
- You want to encourage users to switch to a new authentication method with an improved user experience.
- You want to give users choices so that they can use their preferred authentication factors.
- Your customer service users must sign in to your production application with your organization's security policy.
- Users from a business partner need to sign in to your production applications with their security policy.

If you offer your users multiple authentication methods, consider giving users choices unless you have particular business requirements that dictate otherwise. Be aware that changing an authenticator is a sensitive operation. Always authenticate the user with a previous authentication method, or a temporary one, as part of onboarding to a new authentication method. You then have strong assurance that no malicious actor gains access to the user's account. For example, when the user wants to register a new OTP device because they lost their previous one, authenticate them with a second factor even if they did not use one previously. For example, you might send the user an OTP by email or phone.

Once the user switches to a new authentication method, you should decide what to do with the previous method. If the user updates their password or registers a new OTP device you should ensure the removal of previous credentials for safety reasons. In other situations, the user might still want to have access to the previous method. For example, if a user switches to passkeys they might still want a backup option to log in with their password and OTP. Similarly, if a user signs up with a new social provider they may still want to be able to log in with their previous social provider.

Changing an authenticator can influence the authentication attributes of the authentication flow. These attributes are an important source of claims in the resulting access tokens that your APIs receive. In particular, the primary authentication method determines the user's authenticated subject, which determines the subject claim (sub) in access tokens. It is usually critical that this value remains the same regardless of how user authentication changes so that your APIs identify users consistently. We illustrate this in Figure 14-3.

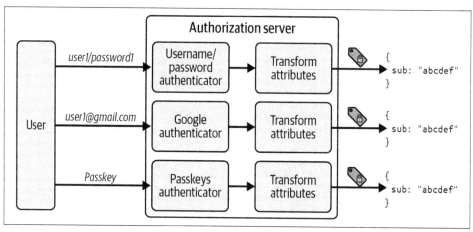

Figure 14-3. The sub claim value remains the same regardless of the authenticator used

Once APIs receive the same subject claim, they also continue to receive other claims from the user's account. This might include other user identifiers, like a customer ID. Your APIs then continue to show users their correct historical data. You avoid outcomes such as duplicate user accounts in the authorization server or your API's data. However, to ensure the right outcomes, you sometimes need to manipulate user attributes in the authorization server to set the user's authenticated subject correctly. When you apply logic to set the correct subject, you use account linking.

Account Linking

You usually store a user account in your authorization server, as we explain in Chapter 4, then issue some of the user account's attributes as claims in access tokens that your APIs receive. You create a user's account when the user onboards, as we explain in "User Authentication Lifecycle" on page 343. When a user authenticates, you ensure that the authenticated subject points to this user account. When you change the primary authentication method in certain ways, such as when a user signs in with a new external IDP, you must apply logic so that the authenticated subject continues to point to the correct user account.

When a user authenticates at an external IDP, your authorization server eventually gets confirmation of the user's identity. For example, when using OpenID Connect, your authorization server receives an ID token. This ID token contains the external IDP's subject claim and may contain other user attributes. You must then instruct your authorization server on how to set your own authenticated subject from the external ID token.

On the first login with an external IDP, a robust way to manage user identification is to force the user to authenticate with their old method to onboard to the new method. However, you will want to prevent that for every subsequent login. Therefore, the authorization server can store a linked account that maps an identifier for the external IDP, and the user's subject claim in that IDP, to the user's main account record. Figure 14-4 shows an overview of the account linking process.

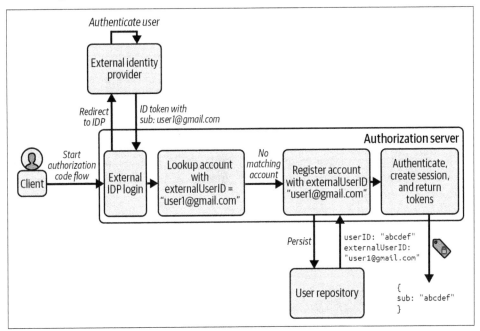

Figure 14-4. An overview of the account linking process

Your account linking can also apply custom logic to help the user to avoid confusion. Consider a situation where a user wants to sign in with their Google account, but they use multiple accounts on one device. The user might not remember which account they chose previously to log in to your system, and consequently provide you with a different identity. You should ensure that your account linking process takes this into consideration. For example, confirm with the user if they want to create a new identity in your system and allow them to switch to another account if they made a mistake. This can help you to avoid a situation where one user ends up with multiple accounts in your system.

To implement account linking, you use authentication actions to apply custom logic. There are a number of categories of authentication actions that you may need to use. Let's briefly summarize some examples next.

Authentication Actions

You can potentially run many types of custom logic during an authentication flow. These actions perform additional tasks to manipulate or collect data. For example, the authorization server may provide actions to manage user sign-up and account creation. It may also provide actions that enable you to create a linked account when a user first uses an external IDP and to resolve the link on all subsequent logins with that IDP. You most commonly configure actions to run after an authentication method and you can compose actions together when required. The output of actions produces authentication attributes that flow into token issuance.

Actions often manipulate data and can present custom screens. For example, your authorization server may enable you to implement utility tasks in a central place, like prompting a user to accept your organization's legal terms. To do so, it could run logic to read the user account to see if the terms have already been accepted, and to present a custom screen if not. Then, once the user accepts the terms, you could store the date when the user accepted the terms against the user's account. More generally, you can use actions to implement a lookup-prompt-set technique to collect new data from the user during authentication flows.

Actions commonly run a script or some code that manipulates user attributes. For example, your organization might use a cloud IDP that classifies employees into groups, like `managers`, `customer service`, or `engineers`. When you sign in to an application using the cloud IDP you might get an ID token containing a `groups` claim. An authentication action could run some simple logic to apply claims transformation, where some or all group values populate a `roles` authentication attribute. This value can then flow into token issuance and be delivered to your APIs as access token claims.

Another main use case for custom scripts or code is the ability to control authentication dynamically per user. To understand how that works, let's explain authentication selection.

Authentication Selection

In the general case, the user base for your applications may consist of subsets of users with distinct authentication requirements. This is especially the case when those users originate from different organizations. For example, business partners, your customer service employees, and customer users may all have access to a particular application. When you use a code flow, all of these authentication methods can work at once for the same client.

In the simplest case, you may present every user with a list of all authenticators that you enabled for the client in your authorization server. However, some choices may not work for some user types. When this is the case, you should be able to use

---

authentication actions to customize the options presented to each user, to avoid user confusion. For example, you could compose actions in your authorization server to provide the following flow:

- Present the user a form to capture their identity, such as an email.
- Look up user attributes for the account, such as a tenant ID.
- Calculate the authentication methods for the tenant.
- Present the user with a tailored list of authenticators.
- If a user has only one authenticator, avoid showing a list of authenticators.

You can further fine-tune authentication flows using actions. For example, the user might manage their authentication preferences in a user interface that your authorization server provides. An action can consult this data to route the user directly to their preferred authentication method or to select the user's preferred second factor in an MFA flow, or to bypass a second factor based on dynamic conditions. Actions might even integrate with external systems like risk engines to make authentication decisions.

Now that you understand authentication methods and authentication techniques, let's apply some finishing touches to explain some ways to manage an entire user authentication lifecycle.

User Authentication Lifecycle

When you use OAuth, you manage user accounts and user logins in your authorization server. When doing so you need to consider multiple aspects, like compliance, manageability, and user experience. You use the building blocks of the authorization server to enable user authentication for many use cases. There are a number of places in total where you might authenticate users:

- Account creation, to onboard users to your digital services with proof of their identity
- User authentication, so that you are confident that the user is the same as the one previously authenticated
- Step-up authentication, to reauthenticate the user and get a higher privilege access token for your APIs
- External authentication, to get an external user-level access token with which to call external APIs
- Changing authentication methods, like adding a passkey to the user's account
- Account recovery, where a user presents proof of their identity and overwrites their previous credential

Often, a very early concern when you implement user authentication in an authorization server is the appearance of forms presented to users. Let's briefly look at ways to manage that next.

Customization of User Forms

The authorization server can present a number of forms to users. In older standalone systems, you may have had full control over all aspects of form behaviors. When you use an authorization server, you no longer build login forms yourself, but you are likely to want to override the default look and feel. Most authorization servers enable you to use branding, such as changing colors to match your organization and adding a custom logo image.

In some cases though, you may need finer control than this. Therefore, some authorization servers enable you to use themes that match your product lines. Each theme can be owned by a particular product team, who can apply its theme to one or more clients. Login screens for those clients then use themes that look like the screens of the client itself. You may also be able to customize details such as text displayed, localization, and client-side logic.

The authorization server forms provide a default implementation. You may get various drag-and-drop behaviors, like the ability to choose the fields in a self-sign-up form. To gain complete control over behavior, you might be able to use the authorization server's SDK to replace the form layer while using SDK objects that implement the lower-level security.

Once you are satisfied with the basics of the user experience, you need to deal with user onboarding. Attracting new users is usually a critical business area, so let's explain some ways to manage it.

User Onboarding

In some cases, an administrator may need to create the user's account and configure settings to determine the user's level of access. You might use administrator approval for employee users but it is often an inefficient process that prevents users from gaining access in a timely manner. For your customer users, you are likely to prefer a self-sign-up experience so that users can gain immediate access. However, your user onboarding design requires care, since it is usually the user's very first experience with your digital services. A complicated experience can be a barrier to adoption.

One technique is a frictionless initial login that delays account creation. Your authorization server could be able to authenticate users and issue access tokens without storing a user account. For example, a user's initial login could require only email verification. After an initial login, the access token received by APIs can have only minimal claims and a low level of assurance, so the API can restrict access accordingly.

The new user quickly gains access to your application and navigates across screens but, at some point, needs to use a higher privilege area. API responses to the client could use error responses with particular error codes to drive the frontend behavior. At some point, the frontend can prompt the user to create an account, to trigger a new code flow where the user signs up. Once complete, the client gets an access token with higher privileges, to allow the user to perform additional operations.

Each authenticator can use multiple forms, the most visible of which are forms where the user provides credentials. These login forms can contain a link to a sign-up form. Self sign-up runs during a code flow. The authorization server should allow you to customize the forms and screens for sign-up so that you can implement your particular *know your customer* requirements. You usually need assurance that the data the user provides is meaningful, so you should implement input validation. You also want assurance to associate the data with the correct user, so you should use some form of user authentication, which we call the registration authenticator.

You can think of self sign-up as a set of reusable authentication tasks, like the following examples:

- Data collection and backend data validation via custom forms
- Creation of the account data in a deactivated state
- Proving the user's identity with the help of the registration authenticator
- Activation of the user's account

The registration authenticator can use basic security like an OTP that the user receives by email to validate the email address. More advanced options include identity proofing or digital credentials. The claims in the digital credential might already contain all of the sign-up data that you need and the user does not have to enter any data manually. With the registration authenticator you can set the authenticated subject and complete the code flow.

The flow for users who authenticate with an external IDP might work a little differently. After the user authenticates, you could use actions to determine whether an account exists. You can then either create the account automatically or present a sign-up form that collects additional attributes. In this type of flow, you may not need to use a registration authenticator, since sign-up runs after the user authenticates.

When the authorization server issues access tokens directly after self sign-up, the access token should contain all of the claims that APIs need. In some cases, as we explain in Chapter 4, you may need to notify external systems. For example, if the access token contract includes a customer ID, you may need to also create a customer record in your APIs. In Figure 14-5 we show a series of authentication actions to onboard a new user. First, the user fills in a custom sign-up form. Next, an action calls an API to create a customer record. Finally, the authorization server creates a user account containing the customer ID.

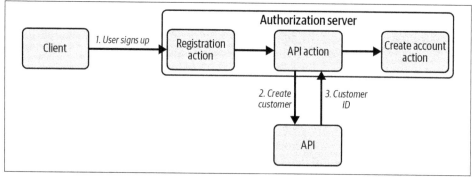

Figure 14-5. User registration actions

Your authorization server governs all of the registration logic and actions and guides the user through the flow. From a client's perspective, registration does not differ from an authentication flow. The client simply runs a code flow and receives an access token with the same claims, regardless of whether the user registered or only authenticated. The authorization server should manage user onboarding without adding any complexity to either your clients or your APIs.

A user who signs up to your digital services may sometimes struggle to re-authenticate. For example, they may return to your application and forget their password, or might unintentionally delete their passkey. Often, this type of event occurs if a user loses or replaces their computer or device. Therefore, when you design user authentication solutions, also provide an account recovery solution where users can unlock themselves.

Account Recovery

Account recovery is another area that should require a form of user authentication so that a malicious party cannot update the genuine user's account. You use the concept of authentication factors so that the user can recover using a different type of factor. The login forms for an authenticator can link to an account recovery form in the same way as they can link to a self-sign-up form.

Many authorization servers enable you to use username and password authentication with email-based OTPs for recovery. Higher-security options could include identity proofing. For example, you might allow users to onboard to a medical system using a government-issued digital credential, then use the same digital credential to recover their account.

Login forms for passkeys have a built-in method of account recovery, where a user repeats the registration ceremony to recover. There could be multiple reasons why a user needs to rerun this flow, such as accidental deletion of a passkey or technical limitations in platform passkey synchronization. The user creates a new passkey and registers its public key at the authorization server, which adds it to the user's account data. Therefore, the authorization server can store multiple public keys against the user's account. The user must reauthenticate somehow to ensure that the public key gets stored against the correct account. For example, you might use email-based OTPs to enable passkeys account recovery.

Account recovery is only as secure as the backup authentication method. When you use email-based OTPs during account recovery, your recovery process is reliable and convenient but there is an email interception risk. When possible, encourage your users to register a more secure backup method like key fob or a digital credential. Next, let's look at how you might respond to security threats and restrict user authentication.

Denying Access

At times, for instance if you suspect that your systems are under threat, you may need to change how security works. One such action is to require MFA for every user login, but you can also use dynamic logic to restrict user access. You could apply logic that implements time-based authorization so that you allow user authentication only at certain times of day, such as during business hours. Similarly, the authorization server can provide geolocation features to allow logins only from the user's expected locations. You can implement this type of dynamic authentication logic with authentication actions and it comes into effect immediately.

Some authenticators read the user's account data when they authenticate a user. The account data should include a setting to control whether the account is active. Authenticators can then deny access when you deactivate an account. The same mechanism can be used in an external IDP to deactivate an account there and deny access on all subsequent authentication operations. Be aware though that some authentication methods may enable you to configure them to not read a user's account data, in which case they continue to work for deactivated accounts.

When you deactivate a user account, APIs do not immediately reject access tokens related to that account. Therefore, you should keep access tokens short lived so that the user's access ends within a few minutes. You can go further and remove all login-related data like consents (approved delegations), access tokens, authorization codes, and SSO sessions. Similarly, to deny access to APIs you can remove all token data and follow the techniques we explain in "Plan for Token Revocation" on page 150.

With OAuth, you manage authentication in a central place, your authorization server, so you can also use it to ramp up security on demand. However, in some cases you may want to go beyond denying access and permanently remove user data. Let's see how that works next.

User Decommissioning

At times you may need to permanently decommission users, such as when an employee leaves your organization or a customer user chooses to close their account. In Chapter 4 we explain how you can store personally identifiable information in the authorization server and deliver it to your applications in tokens. This design enables you to remove sensitive data in a central place.

You most likely have other user-specific information, like business transactions, managed in your APIs. In some cases, you may not be able to remove all of it straight away, due to regulations. For example, you might be legally bound to keep some information about your employees for a number of years, or when you run an ecommerce business you might need to keep a transaction history for users in case an authority asks you for this information. There are also local regulations like the General Data Protection Regulation (GDPR) or California Consumer Privacy Act (CCPA) that can add further requirements to how you handle the user's data. You should always ensure that you remove user data with due diligence.

You can permanently remove any user credentials from your authorization server to deny access to users. To regain access in future, the user would need to onboard again and would no longer have access to previous business resources. You must remember that the user's devices could contain existing credentials like saved passwords, OTP private keys, or passkeys. You can instruct users how to safely remove these credentials. Most importantly, you should also ensure that they no longer enable the user to authenticate.

Now that we have covered user authentication methods and techniques, and all of the theory of the user authentication lifecycle, let's finish the chapter with some practical content on zero trust for user authentication.

Zero Trust User Authentication Example

In Chapter 1 we summarize how zero trust security should work for APIs, clients, and users. Throughout this book we explain how to achieve that, using environment-specific best practices and cryptographic proofs where possible. We provide API and client code examples that you can run on a development computer:

- In Chapter 5 we provide a zero trust API code example.
- In Chapter 12 we provide baseline desktop and mobile code examples that could be further hardened.
- In Chapter 13 we provide a zero trust browser-based client.

In previous chapters, you entered plain passwords for test users as the one and only authentication factor. Since the overall security is only as good as its weakest point, let's make some changes to run the examples with strong user authentication. To do so, locate the folder *chapter-14-user-authentication* of the GitHub repository of this book (*https://oreil.ly/CNDS-supp*) and follow the *README* instructions.

The instructions show how to upgrade the authorization server from passwords with email-based account recovery to passkeys with email-based account recovery. You can continue to sign in with the test user accounts. However, on the initial login you must run the passkeys registration ceremony and create a passkey. To prove that you own the account, you use an email-based OTP. You then use a passkey for all subsequent logins as a strong MFA authentication method. We show an example passkeys login screen in Figure 14-6.

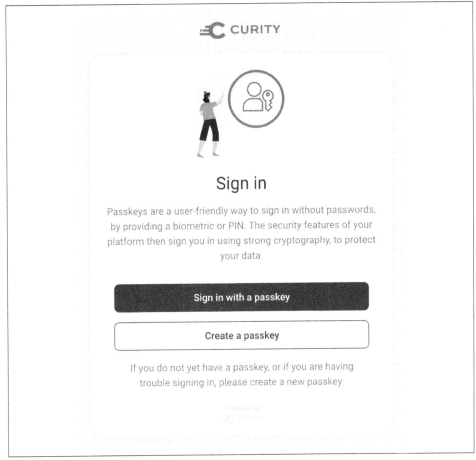

Figure 14-6. Passkey registration

Summary

In this chapter we explain many intrinsics of modern authentication so that you understand your options and can apply them to your business use cases. You should understand that authentication is a journey, where you leverage different authentication methods in a flow that allows you to verify the user's identity with as much certainty as your system requires. There are many authentication methods that you can choose from and you should try to convince your users to utilize the most secure options. If possible, use more than one factor for authentication, where each factor has a different type.

Authentication gives you a level of assurance of the user's identity, but this should go hand in hand with user experience. Some security choices can harm the user experience and deter users from using your digital services. Modern authentication methods are more secure than passwords and can also provide an improved user experience. When you design authentication journeys, make your APIs aware of the level of assurance of the user's identity. You can then onboard users gradually while your APIs correctly enforce access to resources. Also invest in planning or rehearsing the entire lifecycle for your users.

Now that you understand user authentication, you have a complete picture of securing APIs with OAuth in a cloud native environment. The authentication process serves as a source of identity data that your authorization server uses to gather information that it can issue to access tokens as claims. Your APIs can securely use these claims to make informed authorization decisions. Together with strong infrastructure security, entitlements systems, and client security, you have the building blocks to secure cloud native data, and the parties who access it, at scale.

Index

Symbols

access control models, 181-188
entitlement management, 43
entitlement management systems (EMS),
    188-191
Open Policy Agent (OPA), 195-206
role of token-based authorization, 188
scalable authorization, 190-195
environment configuration, 241
error responses, 252
ES256 algorithm, 85
expiration times (for access tokens), 149
explicit trust, 6, 8
extensible gateways, 164
external identity providers, 328-331

F

failure conditions, 96
Financial-grade API Security Profile (FAPI), 38
fine-grained authorization, 92-95
first-party clients, 23
fixed secrets, 267
flexibility, 188
flows
    abstract flow, 18
    access token flow, 82
    client credentials flow, 29
    code flow, 21-27
    device flow, 28-29
    Dynamic Client Registration (DCR), 268
    first-party authentication flow, 274
    hybrid flow, 35
    implicit flow, 33-34, 298
    microservices and introspection, 141
    modern authentication flows, 324-326
    OAuth 2.0 Authorization Code flow, 260
    outdated flows, 32-34
    password flow, 32
    phantom token pattern, 142, 166
    refresh token flow, 31, 300-301
    removing deprecated, 38
    revoke flow, 39
    roles defined in flows, 17
    split token pattern, 144
    token exchange for asynchronous commu-
        nication, 130
forward proxies, 154
front-channel requests, 23
future-proof setup, xv, xviii, 59

G

Gateway API, 162-164 (see also API gateways)
General Data Protection Regulation (GDPR),
    xv, 64
global service load balancer (GSLB), 71, 236

H

Health Relationship Trust Profile (HEART), 38
high availability, 249-251
high privilege scopes, 109
holder-of-key tokens, 146 (see also sender-
    constrained tokens)
host-based routing, 160
HS256 algorithm, 86
HTTP messages, 24-26
HTTP proxies, 154
HTTPS (Hypertext Transfer Protocol Secure),
    23, 84
hybrid flow, 35

I

IaC (infrastructure-as-code) approach, 243
IANA (Internet Assigned Numbers Authority),
    145
IANA registry for JSON Object Signing and
    Encryption (JOSE), 85
ID tokens, 26, 34-37
identity management, 42
identity operations, 68
identity proofing, 333
identity providers, 328-331
impersonation
    due to CSRF, 293
    extending OAuth, 56
    mitigating, 264
    phishing applications, 267
    preventing with mTLS, 270
    preventing with zero trust approach, 10
    security requirements preventing, 134
    use case for, 117
implicit flow, 33-34, 298
implicit trust, 6
infrastructure security, 7, 9
infrastructure-as-code (IaC) approach, 243
ingress, 154
ingress proxies, 154
Ingress resource, 160
integrate with anything approach, 334

N

native applications
  browserless user authentication, 273-275
  code examples, 275-281
  the code flow, 260
  hardening security, 267-272
  implementing OAuth clients, 262-267
  securing with OAuth, 259

O

OAuth 2.0
  abstract flow, 18
  access tokens, 19
  API supporting components, 12-13
  approach to learning, xvii, xx
  basics of, 3
  benefits of, 4
  challenges of, xvi
  client capabilities, 20-34
  cloud native platforms, 13, 209
  configuration settings, 61-63
  evolution of, 38
  extending, 56
  high-level overview of, 4-6
  interaction between clients, authorization
      server, and APIs, 5
  OpenID Connect (OIDC), 34-38
  optimal implementation of, 15
  versus other security frameworks, 5
  prerequisites to learning, xviii
  roles defined in flows, 17
  sessions and lifecycle, 39
  terminology surrounding, xx, 18, 23, 209
OAuth 2.0 Device Authorization Grant, 28
OAuth Agent, 317
OAuth Proxy plug-in, 319
OIDC (OpenID Connect), 34-38, 108
onboarding, 344
one-time password (OTP), 331
opaque access tokens, 19, 136, 166, 261
Open Policy Agent (OPA)
  auditing authorization decisions, 200
  basics of, 195
  claims-based authorization, 198-199
  decision results, 200
  example deployment, 202-206
  loading external data, 196-198
  policy retrieval in, 201
  writing policies in, 195

open standards, 46, 54
OpenAPI Specification, 105
OpenID Connect (OIDC), 34-38, 108
OpenID Foundation, 38
OpenID Provider, 35
OpenTelemetry project, 253
operational data, 59, 72, 234
origin comparison, 290
OTP (one-time password), 331
outdated flows, 32-34

P

pairwise pseudonymous identifiers (PPIDs), 67
PAP (policy administration point), 193
passkeys, 332, 336, 349
passwordless authentication, 332
passwords
  account recovery, 346
  best practices, 327
  CSRF exploits, 288
  field-level rules for, 69
  forgot password process, 63
  good practices for, 86
  hardening credentials, 216, 310
  in mobile applications, 266
  multifactor authentication (MFA), 336
  one-time password (OTP), 331
  versus passkeys, 332, 349
  password flow, 32
  renewing compromised, 338
  versus short-lived access tokens, 111
  third-party credentials as, 273, 330
  user decommissioning, 348
  using parameters for, 241
  weaknesses of, 11
PDP (policy decision point), 51, 193, 200
PEP (policy enforcement point), 51, 194
perimeter security, 6
personal data
  data design for user accounts, 63-65, 247
  multiregion deployment and, 72
  sharing, 64, 112, 118
  user migration code example, 74-77
phantom token pattern, 141, 166
phishing applications, 11, 267, 328, 332, 336
PIP (policy information point), 194
PKCE (see Proof Key for Code Exchange)
platform-specific applications
  browserless user authentication, 273-275

About the Authors

Gary Archer has worked as a lead developer and architect for 20 years, providing investment banking solutions. This work includes leading the design for many OAuth-based migrations and gaining an understanding of the code simplicity it can enable, as well as the learning curve faced by engineering teams in a distributed security architecture. His experience also includes extensive on-site support of complex business systems. Gary has worked at Curity for the last few years in a role focused on teaching many end-to-end security flows, including web, mobile, and API components and how to integrate them with security components.

Judith Kahrer's interest in security and identity started in high school. She believed that security is a critical element of the future of IT, a belief she still holds today. She has worked in different technical roles throughout her career and gained experience in various levels of security, from high-tech protocols to low-tech policies. Thanks to this diverse background, she excels in translating and explaining technical details related to, but not limited to, OAuth and OpenID Connect in blogs, articles, tutorials, webinars, and so on.

Michał Trojanowski's current role at Curity is a mix of engineering work, technical writing, and tutoring—a role he naturally gravitated to during his previous years working as a developer with several languages and frameworks. The usual work of a developer was always complemented by public speaking, teaching courses to interns and new employees, lecturing at universities, mentoring at hackathons, or helping the Stack Overflow community with his expertise. His recent focus on technologies revolving around APIs and their security has led to his strong interest in OAuth, OpenID Connect, JWTs, and some of the newer authentication solutions, like passkeys and decentralized identities.

Colophon

The animal on the cover of *Cloud Native Data Security with OAuth* is the Chilean Blue eagle, more commonly known as the black-chested buzzard eagle (*Geranoaetus melanoleucus*).

These birds of prey are found primarily in Chile but are also native to some other parts of South America. While they primarily feed on mammals, they aren't too picky in their choice of prey, letting opportunity dictate their next meal based on availability and surroundings.

Both male and female care for the eggs (one to three in a clutch). About 50 days after the eggs have hatched, the young venture out on their own, within a somewhat close radius of their parents at first. In general, however, these birds are relatively solitary in nature and can be seen contentedly flying by themselves or with one other companion.

Many of the animals on O'Reilly covers are endangered; all of them are important to the world.

The cover illustration is by Karen Montgomery, based on an antique line engraving from *Zoological Gardens Birds*. The series design is by Edie Freedman, Ellie Volckhausen, and Karen Montgomery. The cover fonts are Gilroy Semibold and Guardian Sans. The text font is Adobe Minion Pro; the heading font is Adobe Myriad Condensed; and the code font is Dalton Maag's Ubuntu Mono.

O'REILLY®

Learn from experts.
Become one yourself.

60,000+ titles | Live events with experts | Role-based courses
Interactive learning | Certification preparation

**Try the O'Reilly learning platform
free for 10 days.**

www.ingramcontent.com/pod-product-compliance
Lightning Source LLC
Jackson TN
JSHW061939090425
82325JS00016B/616